AS IF GOD EXISTED

AS IF GOD EXISTED

RELIGION AND LIBERTY
IN THE HISTORY OF ITALY

Maurizio Viroli

Translated by Alberto Nones

PRINCETON UNIVERSITY PRESS

PRINCETON AND OXFORD

Copyright © 2012 by Princeton University Press
Published by Princeton University Press, 41 William Street,
Princeton, New Jersey 08540
In the United Kingdom: Princeton University Press, 6 Oxford Street,
Woodstock, Oxfordshire OX20 1TW

press.princeton.edu

Jacket Art: *Allegory of Good Government*, 1338–40 (fresco),
Ambrogio Lorenzetti (1285–c. 1348). Location: Palazzo Pubblico,
Siena, Italy. Courtesy of Bridgeman Art Library.

Library of Congress Cataloging-in-Publication Data
Viroli, Maurizio.
[Come se Dio ci fosse. English]
As if God existed : religion and liberty in the history of Italy / Maurizio Viroli;
translated by Alberto Nones.
p. cm.
Includes bibliographical references (p.   ) and index.
ISBN 978-0-691-14235-7 (hardcover : alk. paper)
1. Liberty—History. 2. Religion and politics—Italy—History. 3. Religion
and state—Italy—History. I. Title.
JC599.I8V5713 2012
320.94501'1—dc23
2012015124

British Library Cataloging-in-Publication Data is available

This book has been composed in Sabon LT std.

Printed on acid-free paper. ∞

Printed in the United States of America

1 3 5 7 9 10 8 6 4 2

To Gabriella, Giulia, Simona, and Tino

After all, the man who does not believe in God also feels, in the end, that his morality is like a religion, although he does not like to abuse this term. He feels it is some sort of religion, for it is something he is ready to discuss, but with the certainty that no one will convert him. He has grown old with that faith; he has spoken with many people; he has put his ideas to all tests and comparisons. He knows well that his force of persuasion is meager, that his arguments should always be renewed, and that he has something to learn from each and every interlocutor. But all this no longer affects the firmness of his faith. In this sense, he belongs to a church, which admits of no betrayal on the part of its clerics. To work for this church, to promote the increment of its believers—this is the most proper job for a man. In this job lay the worth and value of his whole existence.
 —Guido Calogero, *La scuola dell'uomo*, 1939

CONTENTS

PREFACE TO THE ENGLISH EDITION

THIS EXPLORATION OF Italian history offers English-speaking readers a general, valuable lesson on the relationship between liberty and religion. My study focuses on three experiences of social and political emancipation in Italy: the free republics of the thirteenth to sixteenth centuries, the Risorgimento, and the antifascist Resistenza (also called the Second Risorgimento). Grand and noble as they were, none of these experiences resulted in long-lasting liberty: early modern city republics were all (with the exception of Venice) consumed and destroyed by open or veiled forms of tyranny, and by the mid-sixteenth century Italy fell under foreign domination; the liberal state created by the Risorgimento collapsed sixty years later under the yoke of the fascist regime; and the Italian Republic that was born in 1946 and was to a considerable degree the expression of the antifascist struggle has degenerated into Silvio Berlusconi's court system.[1] Italy, to aptly describe its political identity, is a country marked by fragile liberty.

In each case, religious sentiments and language played a fundamental role. City-republics were sustained by a civic religion that combined in a rather innovative way classical and biblical themes. The Risorgimento was preceded and accompanied by a religious renaissance made possible by the rediscovery and reinterpretation of Christianity, as well as the elaboration of various forms of "religion of duty" or "religion of humanity." The antifascist movement found inspiration in the "religion of liberty" framed by Benedetto Croce and other political writers.

The corruption and decline of political liberty, too, has been related to religious conceptions and practices. City-republics were first enervated by the degeneration of Christianity into a religion that fiercely opposed civic virtue, and then inundated by the religion of the Counter-Reformation with its fervor for appearances and exteriority along with its moral teaching founded on docility, submission, and simulation. Fascism triumphed over the liberal state, proclaiming a new religion of the nation. To a considerable degree, the decline of the democratic republic is a consequence of the neglect and destruction of what was left of the civil religion of the Risorgimento and Resistenza. Italian history, then, seems to teach us that good religion produces political liberty, whereas irreligiosity, or bad religion, produces tyranny and domination. The words "good" and "bad" here refer only to the moral and political content of religions.

This book challenges the well-established view that Italian political thought of the Renaissance drew its language from classical Greek and Roman texts, and only to a negligible extent from biblical and religious sources.[2] The truth is that as early as the thirteenth century, one of the most important sources of humanist political thought can be found in prehumanist tracts on civil government—a wealth of biblical references and religious arguments invoked to elucidate the nature of republican government.[3] All these texts make abundant use of biblical quotations to stress the sacred dimension of the republican regime as well as to argue for peace and concord. They speak with the selfsame voice to emphasize that republics need God's help, and that to obtain it, rulers must sincerely fear God and protect the Catholic faith. To urge the *podestà* (the highest magistrate of the city) to wholeheartedly respect human and divine laws, the author of one of the oldest tracts on republican government cites Matt. 5:14–16: "You are the light of the world. A city set on a hill cannot be hid. Nor do men light a lamp and put it under a bushel, but on a stand, and it gives light to all in the house. Let your light so shine before men, that they may see your good works and give glory to your Father who is in heaven." The ruler who oppresses his subjects from an excessive desire for power, on the contrary, spreads darkness on the earth and extinguishes the love for God in the hearts of the citizens.

Italian political theorists and jurists relied on both classical and biblical sources. Brunetto Latini's highly influential *Livres dou Tresor* (ca. 1260), for instance, begins its section on politics by citing Aristotle's view that the government of the city "is the noblest and highest science, and the noblest occupation on earth," and then turns to Cicero's definition: "the city is an association of men who live in the same place and in accordance with a single law."[4] But then he rapidly refers to the Old Testament to emphasize that "all dominions and dignities are conferred on us by our sovereign Father, who, in the sacred order of earthly things, wanted the cities' government to be founded on three pillars, that is, justice, reverence, and love." Reverence for God, he enjoins, quoting the apostle, is "the only thing in the world that augments the faith's merits and overcomes every sacrifice."[5]

Prehumanist and early humanist political writers contended that rulers must devoutly practice the political virtues of justice, fortitude, prudence, and temperance, as well as the theological virtues of faith, hope, and charity. They contributed to creating a republican religion founded on the beliefs that the commune is under the protection of God, Christ, and the patron saints, and that divine help is the true bulwark against sedition, discord, tyranny, and war—the mortal enemies of republican liberty. The man who undertakes the task of governing acquires a dignity that increases his likeness to God, and impels him always to follow both the political and the theological virtues. Prominent among these virtues are charity—love for God and men—and justice, understood as God's command. The principles of republican government, therefore, were not only moral and political maxims dictated by reason and prudence but also religious principles.

Rather than expelling God and Christian religion from acceptable political discourse, Italian republican theorists and republican governments put them at the center of public spaces. The most spectacular evidence is the iconography in the public buildings of Italian city-republics like the Palazzo Publico in Siena, the Palazzo Vecchio in Florence, and the Palazzo Ducale in Venice. Ambrogio Lorenzetti's *Buongoverno* (1339–41) openly instructs Siena's rulers and citizens that the "holy" virtue of justice draws inspiration from divine wisdom—indeed from the Book of Wisdom—and that the supreme magistrate must follow the theological virtues of faith, hope, and charity. Siena's republican elite was so far from secular that it gave money to see its city described and exalted as "the city of the Virgin." In the Anticappella, again in the Palazzo Publico, Taddeo di Bartolo's *Cycle of Famous Men* (1413–14) features Aristotle as the proper guide for learning the principles of good government. But Aristotle and the great Roman republican heroes are accompanied by the image of "Religion," who issues an unequivocal Christian injunction: "Omne quodcumque facitis in verbo aut in opera / In nomine domini Iesu Christi facite" (Whatever you do in words or deeds / Do it in the name of Jesus Christ).

Florentine republican iconography, too, was for the most part inspired by religious and biblical sources. One of the symbols of Florentine republican ideology was in fact David, the biblical hero who, alone and armed only with a sling, decides to confront the gigantic Goliath and overcomes him. Another was Judith, the woman who killed Holofernes, chief of the Assyrians, oppressors of the Jews. David's and Judith's bronze statues, carved by Donatello, were prominently displayed in the Palazzo Vecchio. To leave no doubt about the religious character of their popular government, Florentine leaders decided in 1494 to inscribe in the Palazzo Vecchio Girolamo Savonarola's motto proclaiming that the Great Council was "given by God, and anyone who tried to undo it, would come to no good."[6] They also agreed, again following Savonarola, to declare Christ "King of Florence."

The Venetians went even further. In the late sixteenth century, in the Palazzo Ducale, they installed nothing less than a gigantic representation of paradise executed by Tintoretto so as to bring the "kingdom of heaven in the Great Council Hall." As has been aptly remarked, the civic message of the painting was clear: "In a supreme statement of the grandeur, power and piety of one of the longest lasting republics in history, all the important decisions of state would be made under the auspices of Christ and the Virgin and with the inspiration of the heavenly hosts."[7] Can this be interpreted as a radical expulsion of God from the public sphere?

Religious themes are also visible in the works of humanist political thinkers. It is true that, as has been noticed by scholars, there are few biblical references in Petrarch's *Qualis esse debeat qui rempublicam regit*.[8] Yet his political poems abound in religious references. In one of them, in which he exalts Cola di Rienzo's ephemeral republican experiment in Rome, he copiously resorted to the Bible: "When you send your Spirit, / they are created, / and you renew the face of the earth" (Ps. 104:30). "Then I saw a new heaven and a new earth, for the first heaven and the first earth had passed away, and there was no longer any sea.... And he who was seated on the throne said, 'I am making everything new!'" (Rev. 21:1–5).[9] In his famous canzone "Italia mia, benché il parlar sia indarno," Petrarch appeals to faith in the ruler of the universe as the last remedy and only hope for Italy's afflictions. When the case required it, as in his political attack against Friar Iacopo Bussolini, who seized power in Pavia, Petrarch did not hesitate to infuse his text with an impressive succession of biblical citations.[10]

Leonardo Bruni does not use biblical citations in his *Laudatio Florentinae Urbis*, but he invokes God's protection (and that of the Virgin and Saint John the Baptist) over the city and its popular government in two fundamental parts of his oration: the exordium and the peroration. In another equally meaningful text, the *Oratio in funere Johannis Strozzi* (1427), Bruni expresses yet another tenet of republican political theology when he assures us that the soul does not die, and that the reward for virtuous deeds goes beyond the brief span of life on earth. On the basis of this argument, he then confidently proceeds to explain that the valiant citizens who sacrifice their lives for their homeland and liberty obtain their fellow citizens' love on earth as well as eternal beatitude in heaven.[11]

Coluccio Salutati, chancellor of the Florentine Republic from 1375 until his death in 1406, and the most towering representative of Italian civic humanism, often invoked God in official and semiofficial letters, and attributed the wise deliberations of the Florentine people in the most dramatic moments of the city's turbulent life to God's benevolent intervention.[12] When he praises the excellence of civil laws, he promptly stresses that the purpose of man is not to know God but rather to obtain eternal beatitude through good deeds performed on earth.[13] In his powerful defense of Florentine liberty, the *Invectiva contra Antonium Luschum* (1403), Salutati relies heavily on theological-political considerations, beginning with his affirmation that all Florentines are resolved to defend, "with God's help," their most sweet liberty, a "celestial good" more precious than all the world's treasures. We have inherited our liberty, Salutati remarks, from our fathers, but we regard it as "God's highest gift" and trust that God loves free peoples. Therefore, even if the human mind cannot grasp divine justice's decrees, it is absurd to think that God will strike down those people who protect liberty on earth and reward the tyrants who offend against it.

Niccolò Machiavelli, too, the alleged champion of the pagan and secular trend of republican political thought, illustrated a number of fundamental political arguments in religious terms. To reassure princes who deploy cruelty effectively, he writes that they "can remedy their standing both with God and with men." To enhance the persuasive power of the "Exhortation" that ends *The Prince*, Machiavelli rephrases the biblical Book of Exodus. When he tries in 1521 to lure Cardinal Giulio de' Medici to commit himself to the grand task of gradually restoring republican institutions in Florence, he confidently uses the conventional trope of God's love for the founders and reformers of republics.

Appeals to God and political arguments based on the scriptures flourished during the last Florentine Republic of 1527–30. God was constantly invoked as the city's protector, the vindicator of the rights of free peoples against the ambitions of kings, emperors, and popes, and the supreme guarantor that the merits of good citizens serving the common good will be properly recognized. Florentine republicans never failed to stress that God was the founder and foundation of their precious liberty—the founder because he gave Florence liberty, and the foundation because only his grace conferred on the city could grant Florentine people the moral strength and wisdom to prevail against the most powerful enemies of liberty.

Italian republican language of the thirteenth to sixteenth centuries was probably less "biblical" than that of the seventeenth to eighteenth centuries, but it was deeply religious—that is, inspired by a particular type of religiosity that I describe in this book as "civic Christianity." The main principles of the religious sentiment that flourished in Italian republics were that God is charity and charity is God, and that God has created human beings in his image and likeness. From these beliefs followed the moral as well as political command that it is a Christian duty to defend republican liberty and diligently serve the common good.

Also in the late eighteenth and nineteenth centuries republican political writers were hoping to resurrect a religion that taught citizens to love liberty and discharge their civic duties. Some of them searched within the Christian tradition for a God who was a friend of political liberty; others, for a brief interlude, tried to implant a new civic religion in Italy modeled after Jean-Jacques Rousseau's "religion civile"; still others framed a religion of duty or liberty compatible with, though not identical to, Christian religion. They worried above all about the damaging effects of bad religion as well as the absence of religious sentiment, because they believed that without religion or with a bad religion, republics would be short-lived.[14]

This study also claims that the Italian Risorgimento was anticlerical yet religious. Its most representative political and intellectual leaders, along with the militants who committed themselves to the cause of Italian unity and independence, were all fiercely opposed to the temporal power of the church as well as to the enervating religious and moral education that the Italian clergy had spread over the peninsula. They were also guided and sustained, though, by a religious conception of life that took different forms—reformed Catholicism, Protestantism, New Christianism, "religion of humanity," "religion of duty," and "religion of progress"—but taught one and the same principle: namely, devotion to liberty as a sacred duty.

Just as it is plainly untrue that the Italian Risorgimento was totally secular and even irreligious, it is equally wrong to contend that it was indeed religious in the sense that it produced a nationalist or political religion. Focusing on the "locus of profound tropes" (*spazio delle figure profonde*), proponents of a cultural approach have identified in the discursive practices of the Risorgimento the conception of the nation understood as a community of combatants united in a sacred commitment to uphold the quasi-metaphysical entity of the *patria/nazione* (fatherland/nation), whose distinctive features are kinship (*parentela*), love/honor/virtue (*amore/onore/virtù*), and sacrifice (*sacrificio*), with its grim complements of pain, death, and mourning. The trope of kinship, it should be noted, reveals that the nation was imagined as a "community of progeny" (*comunità di discendenza*) that reaches back to great figures of the past who belong "by nature" to the community they have illuminated with their deeds. It also indicates that the biological nexus between generations and individuals, summarized in the word "blood," was regarded as a fundamental feature of the nation. In addition, the religious connotation of the Risorgimento's nationalism clearly emerges from the relentless use of religious words like "regeneration," "apostolate," "faith," "resurrection," "holy war," and "crusade."[15]

This approach is both praiseworthy and limited. It is praiseworthy insofar as it reminds us that the Risorgimento was not just a political process; it also was sustained by stories, myths, and images that motivated strong passions. The profound tropes of lineage, honor, love, virtue, and sacrifice are particularly powerful in this regard because they connect to primary facts of human experience, such as birth/death, love/hatred, and sexuality/reproduction, and are related to centuries-old discursive practices. It is limited because it obscures a number of specific traits of the political language of the Italian Risorgimento in general and its religious dimension in particular. The profound tropes do not allow us to see, to begin with, the fundamental distinction between patriotism and nationalism.[16] Giuseppe Mazzini and other prominent moral and political leaders of the Risorgimento extolled the ideal of *patria*, or nation, understood as an association of free and equal citizens that must recognize, respect, and defend its civil, political, and social rights as well as the liberty and dignity of all nations and peoples. They also forcefully rejected the commitment to a nation interpreted as an organic cultural and ethnic community that must protect and affirm itself through purification, the elimination of alien elements, both within the nation and through conflict with other nations.

It is one thing to preach love, devotion, faith, and sacrifice in relation to the universalistic ideal of the patria, and quite another to speak of love, devotion, faith, and sacrifice as regards the particularistic ideal of the nation. In the first case, we have a civil religion centered on the political and moral value of liberty, which sustains liberal and republican institutions; in the second instance, we find a political religion centered on the principles of cultural or ethnic homogeneity and uniqueness, designed to uphold domestic political and social discrimination or aggressive foreign policy. The political language of the Risorgimento, needless to say, presents nationalist features as well, but it is historically incorrect to assert that it was a nationalist political religion.[17]

For a proper understanding of the religious dimension of the Italian Risorgimento, I maintain in this study, the most reliable intellectual mentors are still the great historians of the twentieth century, particularly Adolfo Omodeo and Croce. Both stressed that the Risorgimento proclaimed a universalistic conception of the nation that had nothing in common with the nationalist ideology of fascism, and indeed was unequivocally opposed to it. Because they got the distinction between patriotism and nationalism right, Omodeo and Croce also correctly understood the difference between the fascist political religion and the religious sentiment of the Risorgimento. In the *Manifesto of the Antifascist Intellectuals* that he composed in 1925 against Giovanni Gentile's *Manifesto of the Fascist Intellectuals*, Croce wrote:

> We oppose abandoning our old faith for this chaotic and obscure "religion": for two centuries and a half, our faith has been the soul of the Italy that was rising again, modern Italy. That faith was composed of love of truth, aspiration for justice, generous human and civil sense, zeal for an intellectual and moral education, solicitude about liberty, the force behind and guarantee of every advancement. We look at the men of Risorgimento, those who acted, suffered, and died for Italy, and it seems to us that they are offended and concerned by the words and deeds of our adversaries, and admonish us to keep their flag flying. Our faith is not an artificial and abstract contrivance or excitement of the mind provoked by uncertain and badly understood theories, but is the possession of a tradition that has become a disposition of the emotional, mental, and moral habits.[18]

If we misunderstand the specific features of the patriotism that largely pervaded the Risorgimento, as the most recent scholarship does, we also miss the moral and political connection between the Risorgimento and the religion of liberty of the antifascists of the 1920s and 1930s.[19] Colleagues and friends have remarked that the religion of liberty concept must be viewed as an analogy. If they mean by this that the "real" thing is revealed religion, and that the religion of liberty is similar but not quite the real thing, the argument strikes me as rather weak. For the antifascist militants who lived by it, the religion of liberty was as sincere and thus real as the religion of the believers in revealed religions. One could certainly make the opposite case—namely, that the religiosity of the majority of the Italians who followed the Catholic religion then was a mere facade, whereas the religion of liberty was deep and authentic. The truth of religions does not consist in the alleged or pretended authority of their founders, nor in the magnificence of their rituals, and even less in the number of believers or the religions' longevity. It consists only in their power to inspire deeds that are consistent with the principles they proclaim. On this score the religion of liberty stands the test quite well.

That being said, it is surely correct to assert that the religion of liberty notion is a metaphor or analogy. But political thought is full of metaphors and analogies. The "great Leviathan," the "mortal God," "laws are but chains," and the idea that the prince must be able "to imitate both the lion and the fox" are but a few examples. Metaphors and analogies elegantly describe political reality, give persuasive power to arguments, and effectively convey the meaning of concepts. The metaphor or analogy of the religion of liberty is, in my opinion, especially felicitous. It expresses the idea of a devotion to liberty that motivates a serious commitment and even self-sacrifice, if necessary. It also uncovers the inner dimension of liberty that lives, when it does live, in the minds of human beings independently of political and legal institutions.

But if we are talking about a moral commitment to the principle of liberty, why, as a number of my colleagues have asked, do I use the word "religion" at all? My reply is that as a historian, I have a duty to be faithful to the language used by the political writers I have been studying. To redescribe as moral what they have called religious would simply amount to producing bad historical narration. I am not prepared to perpetrate such an intellectual sin. Nor do I see a powerful theoretical reason for the redescription. It is perfectly legitimate to assert that to have moral principles means to have an inward persuasion of their truth or value, and to live by them even at the cost of self-sacrifice. Yet what would be the net intellectual gain?

The religion of liberty originated as a recognized as well as recognizable moral and political language in the context of fascist Italy. It would be incorrect, however, to regard it as just a mirrorlike image of the fascist political religion. Rather, it was a response and alternative to it. Or better still, it was a completely different picture painted with the same colors. Proponents and advocates of the religion of liberty, like fascist ideologues, used the words "devotion," "faith," "resurrection," and "martyrdom." But what they meant to do was destroy the totalitarian regime and its religion, and replace them with a free political regime and a new civil religion. The documents I found indicate that the religion of liberty was particularly effective in its struggle against fascism precisely because it used the same words with different meanings.

The presence of religious interpretations of liberty in all the experiences of political liberation I examine here suggest that these kind of movements tend to assume a religious content and produce a religious language. One reason for this is that without a religious dimension, movements of social and political emancipation lack the necessary resources to persist in struggles that may easily go on for years, face dangers, and overcome tragic and devastating defeats, moments of despair and hopelessness, and the sense of futility about one's own and everybody else's efforts. "Des peuples religieux ont pu être esclaves; aucun people irréligieux n'est demeuré libre," Benjamin Constant (1767–1830) wrote in *De la Religion*.[20]

I find his words convincing. The achievement and defense of political liberty require a disinterested sentiment at the heart of the willingness to sacrifice oneself. Any morality that is alien to the religious sentiment cannot motivate the sacrifice of one's life. The religious dimension affects the nature of the movement itself, the very content of the liberation. What kind of emancipation can movements attain when they are guided by leaders and militants who are not religiously devoted to liberty—that is, who have not chosen liberty as the highest principle of their life?

The religion of liberty is especially necessary under extraordinary circumstances, when one must resist totalitarian regimes, oppose massive violations of human rights, defend one's country against an external invasion, and struggle against organized crime and widespread political corruption. In these cases, self-interest and moral convictions based on rational evaluations (whatever they might be) are insufficient to generate the energies needed for any chance of prevailing. On examination, though, a religion of liberty is also necessary under the ordinary conditions of a free polity to help citizens discharge their civic duties. No democratic republic, no matter how strong, can impose a respect for civic duties through the mere threat of legal sanctions or by appealing to citizens' self-interest. In addition to both, one needs some kind of inward persuasion, usually described as an obligation to one's own conscience. Experience shows that a sense of duty is more solid when connected to a religious sentiment, be it in the form of a revealed religion (if it teaches the right civic message) or a religion of liberty not based on revealed religion.[21]

If this is the case, political wisdom suggests that it is crucial to dedicate serious efforts and resources to keep alive (where it exists), resuscitate (where it is languishing), or generate (where it has never existed) a religion of liberty. It also advises us not to wait for exceptional circumstances. Citizens who love liberty with all their soul, and possess a civic spirit and moral courage, do not appear on command. They must already be there with their moral resources intact, like a well-trained army. One must cultivate in ordinary times the civic resources that are needed in the extraordinary ones. It is indeed hard to believe that citizens unable or unwilling to discharge their normal civic duties (paying their taxes, participating in elections and public life, remaining loyal to the constitution, caring for public spaces, and properly remembering the efforts and sacrifices of previous generations) will rise to the occasion when they are asked to make hard sacrifices and even put their lives at risk. This is, in my view, the political wisdom to be drawn from the Italian political and intellectual history I have reconstructed in this book.

AS IF GOD EXISTED

INTRODUCTION

In the republics of the late Middle Ages, in the Risorgimento, and in the struggle against fascism, Italian liberty was the work of religious men and women. Many of them possessed a sincere Christian faith, often quite distant from or in stark contrast with the teaching of the Catholic Church; others did not believe in any revealed religion but instead were believers and apostles—sometimes martyrs—of a religion they called a "religion of duty" or "religion of liberty." Both the former and the latter people, regardless of the theological content of their convictions, were religious because they lived their lives as a mission—that is, with devotion to the ideal of liberty.

A cleric will object that true religion is only that which affirms, on the basis of a revelation, the existence of a transcendental God; some secular people will protest that there is no need to see religion as devotion to a moral ideal. To the cleric's critique, one can simply answer that his argument is arrogant and irrelevant: arrogant, for he dares to say to those who lived for the religion of duty or the religion of liberty that theirs was not a true religion; irrelevant, for his critique does not change the historical fact that there were people in Italy who lived according to those religions he considers false. A similar answer holds for the narrow-minded secular person: it is a historical fact that there were people who considered themselves religious because they lived with absolute devotion to the moral ideal of liberty; the layman is free to identify as morality what they lived as if it were a religion, but his position, just like that of the cleric, is intellectually weak.

Shedding light on the multiple bonds that tied religion and liberty allows us to better understand Italy's history. First, it helps us understand that Italy's city-republics were supported by a particular kind of civic Christianity that cultivated charity, and hence the principle that only a good citizen, who loves and serves the common good, can be a good Christian. That kind of civil Christianity also preached that Christian virtue is strength—not the strength to endure oppression while resigning oneself to corruption, but the strength to resist those men who want to impose their dominion, as well as the bad custom of placing particular and personal interests above the public good. It also affirmed that of all forms of government, the republican one is the most pleasing to God, for God created us in his own image, and thus wants us to be free. It advocated a sacred respect for the laws. It taught that the citizen who governs well and serves the common good with all his strength renders himself godlike and deserving of perennial glory. Indeed, the conflicts that opposed Italian republics and the Church of Rome against one another were not only political ones but also conflicts between two interpretations of Christianity. When the Florentine magistrates of the fourteenth century challenged the papal interdict by saying that they loved their fatherland more than their souls, they were not, nor did they feel they were, pagan or atheist; they were true Christians fighting against the corrupt Christianity of the papacy. At the root of the first experiment in Italy's history in political and civil liberty, there was therefore a civic interpretation of Christianity.

And yet notwithstanding the intensity and spread of such a civic understanding of Christianity, even the best scholars of republicanism have failed to see it, or have noted only a few aspects of it. The great works on Italian republicanism—one could dare to say—seem to echo the observation of Alexis de Tocqueville regarding Europe as a whole at the beginning of the nineteenth century: those who are interested in republicanism are not interested in religion, and those who are interested in religion are not interested in republicanism. The religious dimension of Italian republicanism is thus almost completely absent from the comprehensive narrations of Italian political thought. The history of the birth, development, and decline of the first form of the religion of liberty in the postclassical world is still to be written.

In the chapters of *Die Kultur der Renaissance in Italien* dedicated to the Italian republics, Jacob Burckhardt, for instance, confines himself to noting that the legend of Venice's sacred founding was obviously mythical, and that in Venice, the state—although it had absorbed the church more than any other state—really had some sort of ecclesiastical element to it, and its living symbol, the *doge*, walked with quasi-priestly character and pomp in the twelve solemn processions (the so-called *andate*) in which he participated. In the chapters on religion, Burckhardt underlines the well-known Italian unbelief, and emphasizes that at the height of the Renaissance, the attitude of the upper classes toward the exceedingly corrupt church was a deep, mocking discontent mixed with resigned submissiveness. Of Girolamo Savonarola, he writes that he was the most unsuitable candidate for the role of republican prophet, for his true ideal was a theocracy. All of Savonarola's thinking can be epitomized in the motto "Jesus Christus Rex populi Florentini S.P.Q. decreto creatus," which was renewed by his partisans in 1527; his connection to the world was dogmatic, and he had a tyrannical temperament. The most solid religious beliefs remained those of pagan origin. Generally speaking, just as in politics and culture, Italians display a marked subjectivism as far as religious matters are concerned. The only hint of the relationship between republican ideals and the Christian religion is negative. Burckhardt mentions the case of Pietropagolo Boscoli, who was sentenced to death because he plotted against the Medici, lords of Florence, and on the eve of his execution implored his confessor to get Brutus out of his head and help him die "as a Christian."[1]

In *The Crisis of the Early Italian Renaissance*, another fundamental study, published for the first time in 1955, Hans Baron observes that according to the humanists, the ancient poets (Virgil *in primis*) anticipated the Christian religion, and much of pagan polytheism survived in Christianity, especially in regard to the worship of the saints. Above all, Baron emphasizes the threat that classicism posed to Christianity, the church, and even republican values. He insists on the importance of the secularization of politics for the birth of the city-state, but makes no mention of the existence of a republican religion.[2] To a great extent, the same gap features in John Greville Agard Pocock's monumental reconstruction *The Machiavellian Moment: Florentine Political Thought and the Atlantic Republican Tradition*, published in 1975, and still a landmark study for documenting the links between Florentine and Anglo-Saxon republicanism. Pocock maintains that the Aristotelian ideal of the citizen that was reborn in Florence in the early modern age sets itself "in a paradoxical though not a directly challenging relation with the Christian assertion that man was *homo religiosus*, formed to live in a transcendent and eternal communion, known, however, by the ominously political name of *civitas Dei*."[3]

The ancient ideal of *homo politicus*, Pocock explains, "is one in which man asserts his nature and his virtue through political action. The human type that is closest to it is the *homo rhetor*, whereas the most antithetical type is the *homo credens*." On the basis of these assumptions, Pocock argues that for Machiavelli, "the civic ends—including the virtue of citizenship—are divorced from the ends of redemption." Furthermore, he holds that Machiavelli believed "Christian virtues and civic could never coincide," and, consequently, the "implications of the *vivere civile* are becoming pagan, secular, and time-bound; it [civic life] is most itself in a world where there is no religion but augury and no values that transcend those of this life."[4]

Three years later, in *The Foundations of Modern Political Thought*, Quentin Skinner proposed a timely reconsideration of the religious problem in Italian republicanism. He emphasizes that Dante, in his polemics against the temporal claims of the papacy, already affirms that liberty is God's greatest gift to human beings. Skinner also rightly reminds us that Marsilius of Padua (1275–1342), in his *Defensor Pacis*, clearly explains that the papacy's temporal power is at loggerheads with the teachings of Christ and the apostles, elaborating a coherent defense of the communes' right of full independence from the church.[5] In the chapter dedicated to the relationship between rhetoric and republican liberty, Skinner cites a number of examples drawn from the thirteenth-century chroniclers to demonstrate how attacks from the enemies of republican government went "against intellect and against God's will." And when he comments on the advice books for the podestà, he notes that one of the most frequent prescriptions was to "fear God and honour the Church." The most eminent figures among Florentine civic humanists, Coluccio Salutati and Leonardo Bruni, not only qualify republican liberty as "holy" but also affirm that free peoples are under divine majesty's protection.[6]

Contrary to Burckhardt's interpretation, Skinner shows that the humanists reject Saint Augustine's idea that men cannot raise themselves to virtue. He writes that beyond any doubt, Petrarch is a fervently Christian writer, who transmitted to the early Quattrocento humanists an essentially Christian view of how to analyze the fundamental concept of *virtus*. Following Petrarch, Skinner asserts, Leon Battista Alberti integrates the Aristotelian theory of virtues with two principles that reflect unmistakably Christian values: first, "that we must never congratulate ourselves on acquiring any of these 'great and excellent virtues', since we must recognise that this ability has been 'instilled in our souls' by God"; second, "no one can in consequence be said to be following a truly virtuous life unless his 'excellent deeds' are performed not merely with 'manly firmness', but also with 'a love of righteousness' and a constant desire to commend himself to his Maker." Christianity also represents the conception of virtue and glory that the humanists disseminated in the fourteenth century: "they continue to insist," Skinner writes, "on the fundamental Christian doctrine that the vices are to be avoided simply because they are evil, and the virtues pursued for no other reason than that they are good in themselves." At the same time, in contrast to Augustine, the humanists contend that a virtuous man must pursue honor and glory, conscious that honor is a wonderful thing, fame is lovely" and glory divine.[7]

Republican political writers were neither pagans nor atheists but rather maintained an interpretation of Christianity that opposed both the doctrine and the practice of the church, and, in many respects, that advanced by Augustine. Machiavelli himself, who charges the church with having extinguished a love of liberty among the men of his times (and especially among Italians), acknowledges that Christianity—if rightly understood—teaches that one must love one's fatherland and have the strength to defend it. His argument is directed against a Christianity that exalts humble and contemplative men, and not against the Christianity that kept alive the love of liberty typical of the pagan religion. Even Italian historian Francesco Guicciardini—who, if only a particular interest had not prevented him from doing so, would have loved Luther, and would have enjoyed seeing the wicked priests' power finally reduced—resolutely denied any intention "to derogate from the Christian faith and divine worship."[8]

The interpretative perspective that Skinner reopened must be enriched, which entails better outlining the specific character of republican Christianity. First, we must study the central role of charity as the foundation of patriotism and of devotion to the common good, and better examine the way in which the Florentine political writers understood the relation between republican liberty and Christianity. When Machiavelli extols liberty and the security of the republic as supreme political values—and remarks that when the security of the country is at stake, "there ought not to enter any consideration of either just or unjust, merciful or cruel, praiseworthy or ignominious; indeed every other concern put aside, one ought to follow entirely the policy that preserves its existence and maintains its liberty"—he is not expressing anti-Christian values.[9] That liberty comes before any other consideration was a well-rooted principle of Florentine republican Christianity. Late fourteenth-century republican magistrates, who decisively administered the war against the pope and yet felt they were true Christians, were the first to disseminate the phrase "to love one's fatherland more than one's soul." Whether or not Machiavelli was a Christian within his heart is another matter, but the principle that the fatherland must be preserved by any means can hardly have sounded anti-Christian to the ears of both the elite and the people of Florence.

Starting in the sixteenth century, this civic or republican Christianity almost entirely disappeared from Italian culture and customs. In this book, I do not examine why and how that interpretation of Christianity was set aside or repressed. I simply note that another religion—the religion of the Counter-Reformation—took its place: it was a religion that no longer taught people to love liberty, fight with all their strength against tyranny and corruption, and live religion as an inner faith that translates into a concrete reality in the world. On the contrary, it preached respect for the authority of the pope and secular princes, resignation to oppression and corruption, and the belief that the external practices of worship are sufficient for saving one's soul. Whereas republican Christianity was a faithful companion to liberty, the religion of the Counter-Reformation was the key ally of the powers and powerful people holding Italy hostage for centuries. A good religion makes people free; a bad one or the absence of religiosity makes people into slaves. This was the warning Machiavelli issued in the *Discorsi sopra la prima deca di Tito Livio* when republican liberty and Italian independence were on the wane. All the free peoples of antiquity and those few of Machiavelli's times, like the Germans of the free cities, were religious; all irreligious peoples, or those with a corrupt religion like the Italians, were subjects of kings or tyrants.

In the nineteenth century a further proof, and a powerful one, of the bond between religion and political liberty came from the United States. One of the aspects of the New World that impressed Tocqueville during his journey in 1831 was indeed the alliance between religion and political liberty that had originated, and continuously supported, US liberty:

> Religion regards civil liberty as a noble exercise of men's faculties, the world of politics being a sphere intended by the Creator for the free play of intelligence. Religion, being free and powerful within its own sphere and content with the position reserved for it, realizes that its sway is all the better established because it relies only on its own powers and rules men's hearts without external support. Freedom sees religion as the companion of its struggles and triumphs, the cradle of its infancy, and the divine source of its rights. Religion is considered as the guardian of mores, and mores are regarded as the guarantee of the laws and pledge for the maintenance of freedom itself.[10]

Tocqueville emphasizes that such a strong alliance in the New World was a radical novelty with respect to the Europe of his times, where Christian religion and liberty were sworn enemies. He was right, but had he looked back a few centuries, he would have noticed that in Europe, too, a republican religion had existed. Born around the thirteenth century in the context of the Italian republics, this religion was founded on a body of interconnected principles—although it never became a theological or theoretical system—that inspired the political and social action of both magistrates and citizens. It molded the public sphere and prescribed the contents of civic education. It transformed neither men into gods nor the republic into a divinity, yet it taught that men, through virtue and charity, can become godlike, and republics can count on divine blessing and protection, if they respect justice. This republican religion, in sum, was a moral force that aided the birth of the Italian republics, inspired the civic statutes and laws, and triggered the organization of civic rituals—rituals of diverse magnitude and splendor in the different cities, but always capable of actively involving the people.

When Tocqueville published *De la Démocratie en Amérique* in 1835, the best minds of the Italian Risorgimento had understood that one does not achieve liberty without a religious spirit. They were equally convinced that the religion that might have helped Italians could not be the Jacobin republican religion that had been imported from France during the revolutionary years of 1796–99, and that it was necessary to try to rediscover and revive in the soul of the Italians, or at least the best of them, a new religion of liberty. All the moral and political leaders of the Risorgimento contributed to this work, if in quite different ways. Their efforts were not vain, as the struggle for national unity was supported by a renewed and regained religious sentiment that had its own hymns, poetry, and literature, and sustained the commitment as well as the sacrifice of the Italian patriots. The Risorgimento was anticlerical (how could it not be?) but religious. Evidence of this can be found in the fact that once Italy was united, a number of political thinkers complained that the Risorgimento had not succeeded in realizing a religious and moral reform that could turn the Italians into a free people.

The failed religious and moral reform projected a disquieting shadow on the future of those liberal institutions that had been established and supported especially by men of strong religiosity. Fifty years had passed since the achievement of national unity, when the liberal state collapsed under fascism. From the outset, the fascist movement presented itself as a new religion, with its *Il Duce* divinized as a new prophet, and the fatherland—deformed by the grim strains of nationalism—as a new god with new rites and martyrs, hostile to the Christian message of charity and peace, but close instead to the Christianity of the Counter-Reformation. How could an openly anti-Christian movement, and then an openly anti-Christian regime, emerge and triumph in a Christian country, which for centuries had been the seat of Christ's vicar? The most convincing explanation is that few Italians had a truly Christian faith, and those few were deserted by the Vatican, which hastened to bow before the new god (and make good business with the regime) instead of fighting it to the point of martyrdom, if necessary.

It was up to those few true Christians and those few other non-Christian but profoundly religious people to try once more, as had happened during the Risorgimento, to revive a religious conscience among Italians so as to supply the strength needed to face the suffering imposed by the fight for liberty. From Piero Gobetti's first reflections on the religion of liberty, to the religion of duty of Carlo and Nello Rosselli, to the religion of liberty of Benedetto Croce, and all the other contributions that I have tried to bring to light in this book—all, in different ways, attempted to teach by word and example, sometimes to the point of consciously sacrificing their lives, an alternative to the fascist religion and corrupt Christianity of the church. When in 1932 Croce published *Storia d'Europa nel secolo decimono* (*The History of Europe in the Nineteenth Century*), which opened with a chapter on the religion of liberty, the fascists insulted and would rather have burned it, while the Vatican immediately put it on its index of prohibited books.

Of course, not all of the antifascists were animated by the religion of liberty. Those who experienced their antifascist choice as a command of their moral conscience—felt as an absolute and hence religious command—were few in number, I believe, although I have not counted them, and I doubt that such a count could ever be done. And yet the essential point is that there were men and women who were antifascist, and committed themselves to the Resistenza in the name of the religion of liberty. The influence exerted by Croce's book is extensively documented. If fascism established itself because the Italians were not religious, or practiced a religion that did not advocate liberty, it eventually was defeated because a new religion that commanded people to fight for liberty was born. It could not be otherwise. As fascism sought to dominate the people's conscience, and in part succeeded, the liberation from fascism could not help but be, in the first place, a liberation of the conscience—that is, a religious emancipation thanks to the rediscovery of the moral law of liberty. For this reason the Resistenza, besides being a civil, class, and patriotic war, was also a religious war as well as a religious experience, as Piero Calamandrei perfectly understood. Ferruccio Parri, the man who represented the antifascist ideal in all its purity, left us a testimony that in and of itself is worth more than a book:

> There is regret, another one, almost personal, almost secret, and it is about the scarce or imperfect knowledge of the Resistenza on the part of the political leaders of the near past, which has caused

mistaken historical judgments. I already said something about the damage that resulted from the minority position of those struggling for freedom. The many who were distant from it could not understand the profound labor and pain of the spirit of a generation of youth, the discovery of an enlightening truth, the call of a new religion that one cannot disobey.[11]

Today, more than seventy years have passed since the religion of liberty left its mark on the Constituent Assembly of 1946–47. But instead of cultivating it as the soul of the republic, Italian politicians and intellectuals have gone to great lengths to destroy it in the name of other idols (like modernity, which knows only rights and interests, Communism, the Catholic religion, and that simple banality that grows out of an inner void), or merely let it die by means of silence. The results of this devastating assault against the religion of liberty are before everyone's eyes: Italy is inhabited by a majority of individuals who have the mentality of courtiers or slaves, without a sense of duty or love of country, incapable of loving ideals and suffering to realize them, happy under the grin of the demagogue. Without morally free persons, Carlo Rosselli has taught us, there cannot be free countries, and the story I recount in this book warns us that true liberty is always sustained by a religious spirit. But these warnings and teachings are doomed to remain a dead letter or to be understood by only a few—and the consequences for Italian liberty are thus all too easily foreseen.

Without claiming to rewrite the history of Italy, I try here to rediscover a tradition of thought and religious life that has remained alive throughout the centuries, from the ancient republics to the Republic of Italy, always in conflict with other forms of religious sentiment, and especially with the indifference and irreligiosity that are perhaps the most tenacious aspects of Italian national identity. Spending a few years outside Italy is sufficient to enable one quickly to realize the degree to which the Italians are persistently irreligious and lack, with few exceptions, a true moral temper. The absence of a religious spirit has conditioned Italians' conception of the fatherland to the point of creating perverse forms of nationalism, to the detriment of a true civic patriotism.[12] Instead, Italy's best patriotism has been theorized and practiced by men and women who shared the religion of liberty in various ways—thinkers such as Machiavelli, Mazzini, Carlo Rosselli, and Croce, to name only the most famous.

I use the same methodology in this book that I have always followed in other works: Skinner's contextualism, which teaches us to place texts of political thought within the proper historical and linguistic context, then to examine them with the most careful philological attention in order to determine, as closely as possible, to what extent an author accepts or modifies the conventions of his or her time. I have also tried, however, to enrich the contextualist method by studying, in addition to the linguistic and conceptual conventions, the concrete moral and intellectual personality of the authors under exploration. For this purpose I have extensively used biographies, diaries, and private correspondence—all sources that follow the historical contextualist approach, yet are rarely used by scholars. My goal is to reanimate this history, along with the concepts and persons within it, and give my work the character of not only a reconstruction but also a narration. In a few cases, I have also tried to integrate contextualism with the history of books in order to suggest to the reader that concepts and theories indeed circulated, thanks to books that had a particular shape, illustrations, and dedications; in short, the form of the medium helps us better understand the historical significance of the text. Since I would like this book to be accessible to general readers as well as scholars, I have tried to avoid specialized language and have limited bibliographical references to a minimum.

The story I have tried to reconstruct is incomplete and still has many strands that should be further explored in other studies. My work singles out important differences and discontinuities in the history of the relation between religion and political liberty. What emerges is not a philosophy of history with the civic Christianity of the republics as its point of departure and Croce's religion of liberty as its terminus. Rather, what emerges is a body of reflections that political writers, historians, public intellectuals, poets, and men of letters and the arts developed over a long period of time in order to respond to different historical and political circumstances. And yet the intellectual links among the various authors are clearly evident. These authors often outline a true tradition, in which the reflections of one author are connected to those of previous centuries, or at least show strong analogies.

To cite one example, the republican Christianity of Salutati is remote from Mazzini's religion of duty in a number of important ways, but their interpretation of the love of fatherland and their conception of liberty as a religious principle draw them together. Similarities can be found between the religiosity of the Risorgimento and the religion of liberty, or duty, of many antifascists. A religious conception of liberty has been an essential part of Italy's religious and political history, and as such it has been a crucial component of its identity, with important effects on the dramatic history of Italian liberty.

One can draw several lessons of political wisdom from the history of the religion of liberty. The first is that liberty can be neither attained nor defended without religious men and women, for liberty demands a spirit of sacrifice, and those who live according to their interests let others sacrifice on their behalf. The second is that the Christian conscience possesses a profound aspiration to liberty, as evidenced by the many instances of people who have fought against tyranny, foreign domination, social oppression, and fascism in the name of their Christian principles. In many cases they were Christians and Catholics; in others, they were Christians but not Catholics, and were extremely critical of the Vatican. The fact that Croce and Luigi Einaudi, the two greatest masters of Italian liberalism, agreed that Christianity was the origin of liberal liberty is more eloquent proof than any other consideration. After all, the most powerful moral principle of the Christian tradition is perhaps the idea of rebirth, or resurrection. And indeed an idea of rebirth—resurrection through a return to the true principles of human living—has inspired the Renaissance, the Risorgimento, and the Resistenza. Five centuries ago, Machiavelli observed that Italy seems to have been "born to resurrect dead things."[13] It is difficult to sustain this belief today. But when we Italians have fervently believed in this idea, we were reborn in liberty.

PART I

A Republican Christianity

1

REPUBLICS PROTECTED BY GOD

IN THE ELEVENTH AND TWELFTH centuries, the assemblies of citizens that gave birth to the communes in northern and central Italy gathered in churches. Even when public authorities built their own palaces, public council meetings were always preceded by religious ritual. Furthermore, the communes contributed to consecrating the city through paintings and sculptures of the saints, especially those patron saints who had defended the community from external or internal enemies, and hence had an explicitly civic meaning. The cities were religious, and so were the communes.

The religious dimension of the Italian communes was further reinforced by the shift from a government of consuls and podestà to the experiment of real popular governments—that is, governments held by the people's councils. Whereas the first communal statutes, until the beginning of the twelfth century, contained few references to God, Christ, and the saints, the later ones offer plentiful mentions. In Vicenza, to cite but one example, the statutes of 1264 open with an oath invoking God, celebrating the divine creation that brought mankind into existence, and exalting the commune as the arrival point of God's project in the world. The religious, military, and professional associations that constituted the people scrupulously retained as well as promoted both religious and civic dimensions, and held their meetings in churches, after mass, diligently attending to the worship of the patron saints. The communes' religious identity and republicanism went hand in hand, and together engendered a republican religion.[1]

One can already find evidence of this in the treatises that explained the functions and duties of the podestà. These texts insist on the virtues that the podestà and other communal magistrates must possess so that the city can live in peace and flourish in liberty. Although these texts often have the character of practical handbooks that teach the podestà how to speak on various occasions, and how to behave at home and in the public palace, their authors also emphasize the religious significance of the supreme magistrate's office and communal government. The most ancient of the handbooks for the podestà, the anonymous *Oculus pastoralis*, written around 1220, stresses the sacred dimension of the republican regime and the authority that administers justice. After quoting the canonical "There is no authority except from God" (Rom. 13:1), the author adds that such a principle also holds for the city's governor. He then adapts the verse "A king enthroned on the judgment seat / with one look scatters all that is evil" (Prov. 20:8) to the republican podestà, and finally paraphrases Paul's letter to the Romans, to argue that subjects must revere with sincere faith those who have been elected to govern.[2] In his first speech, the podestà must invoke God's grace to discharge the task that the citizens have entrusted to him, and that he gladly accepted. The handbook also recommends that at the end of the speech, the podestà should utter words of praise and reverence for "our Lord Jesus Christ, true son of God, and to his holy mother, Our Lady Saint Mary" as well as the revered saints of the city. The republican government comes from God, and to God, to his glory and praise, it must be primarily dedicated.[3] If the city that the podestà is going to rule is lacerated by civil strife, as was often the case in thirteenth-century Italy, he must appeal to the Gospel in order to urge peace and concord, and cite the famous passage "Glory to God in the highest heaven, / and on earth peace for those he favors" (Luke 2:14).

The republic needs God's help. Hoping to obtain it, the ruler must have a sincere fear of God and must observe the Catholic faith, remembering the scripture "But Yahweh's face is set against those who do evil, / to cut off the memory of them from the earth" (Ps. 34:16). From the Bible, the author of the *Oculus pastoralis* draws the admonition that the council must deliberate the weightiest issues and, once a decision has been made, must execute it firmly, despite any popular uproar.[4] Within the council, he who rules must above all heed the advice of the wise and elderly, as again the Bible teaches us: "Do not dismiss what the old people have to say, / for they too were taught by their parents; / from them you will learn how to think" (Sir. 8:9). The ruler must also always recollect that wisdom keeps cities free: "There was once a small town, with only a few inhabitants; a mighty king made war on it, laying siege to it and building great siege-works round it. But there was in that town a poverty-stricken sage who by his wisdom saved the town" (Eccles. 9:14–15). If instead the ruler mistakenly trusts foolish councillors, he will bitterly regret it, for "sand and salt and a lump of iron / are a lighter burden than a dolt" (Sir. 22:15).

Finally, the ruler must always remind the magistrates appointed to the civil tribunals, in the words of the Book of Wisdom, to "love uprightness you who are rulers on earth" (Ws 1:1).[5]

One of the ruler's most important duties is to address the people when soldiers die. On such sad occasions, the podestà must reemphasize to the citizens that man's life on earth is composed of just conscript service (Job 7:1), and that it is men's duty to fight against pride, vainglory, avarice, and envy. The podestà must then explain that the soldier who falls for the country emigrates from earth to God (*ad Deum*). In order to assuage the suffering, he must quote the Bible's admonition that "everything goes to the same place, / everything comes from the dust, / everything returns to the dust" (Eccles. 3:20), and that man is "fleeting as a shadow, transient" (Job 14:2).[6] Weeping is human, and Jesus himself wept before the suffering of Mary, Lazarus's sister (John 11:33–35). But the ruler of a city must teach with humane words that persistent weeping will not make the beloved come to life again. It is wiser, once more, to ponder the Old Testament's words: "Yahweh gave, Yahweh has taken back. Blessed be the name of Yahweh!" (Job 1:21).[7] In public rites, an essential moment of republican religion, the Bible teaches the fittest words to instill within the citizenry both the courage and the wisdom indispensable to a life of freedom.

The work closes with an invective against bad rulers, who, longing for earthly glory, break human and divine laws, unmindful of the sacred principle of compassionate justice. Their bad conduct offends not only men but also God: it violates the principles of human justice and exemplifies a way of life antithetical to Christian principles. The ruler who oppresses his subjects out of an excessive desire for power instead spreads darkness on the earth, and extinguishes the love of God in his heart—the highest and most sacred good.

In a republican government justice must be sacred.[8] Even in the most pragmatic of the handbooks on the podestà, the *De regimine et sapientia potestatis*, written in verse by the magistrate Orfino da Lodi (ca. 1195–1251), one finds precise religious dictates: that God and Christ teach chiefs and kings to "institute the laws"; and that not only wisdom and philosophy but also theology regulate the creation of civil laws. The first precept of the art of governing is that the podestà "fears God and observes the commandments of the law." When the podestà sits as a judge in civil and penal proceedings, he must be a "sharp interpreter of the laws, following Heaven's precepts."[9]

Much more ambitious and refined, the *Liber de regimine civitatum*, written by Giovanni da Viterbo, probably in 1240, is another eloquent example of republican religion. The author begins his treatise with an invocation to God, and adds that he intends to address, with the help of divine grace, the topic of republican cities, government, and magistrates, with a special focus on their mores. When he explains what he means by "government," he quotes, after Horace, the Psalms (124:1) to emphasize that only God can protect cities. To clarify what he means by "podestà," he mentions, following Marcus Tullius Cicero's *De Officiis*, the Gospel of John (19:11)—"You would have no power over me at all if it had not been given you from above"—as well as Old Testament sources that attest to the divine foundation of sovereign power. Aware of the sacred character of his office, the podestà must solemnly swear on the Gospels and invoke God's help to honorably perform the difficult task that he has agreed to undertake.

Da Viterbo assures the podestà that he can count on God's help, but only if he sincerely fears him. The Book of Wisdom affirms that "by me monarchs rule and princes decree what is right" (Prov. 8:15). If God did not help them, all men's efforts would be vain. This concept, of the utmost significance for the republican ideology of the thirteenth and subsequent centuries, is drawn from the Bible: "If Yahweh does not guard a city / in vain does its guard keep watch" (Ps. 127:1). This implies that the podestà must have a sincere Catholic faith, must be religious, and must never forget that "like flowing water is a king's heart in Yahweh's hand" (Prov. 21:1). If the podestà is instead disloyal to God, he will forfeit righteous reason and fall slave to degrading passions (Rom. 1:26). Corrupt rulers, blinded by pride, seek glory, but do not realize that all they obtain is merely vainglory, which does not come from God.

After a lengthy treatment of the podestà's virtues, da Viterbo makes it clear that the sovereign's power, similar to that of the priest, is a gift from God, greatly elevating the condition of the one who receives it. He then explains that Christian, pagan, and Jewish authors all agree that sovereign power is good inasmuch as it comes from God, who is perfect goodness. The exercise of sovereign power, however, can be bad: "They have set up kings, / but without my consent, / and appointed princes, / but without my knowledge. / With their silver and gold, / they have made themselves idols, / but only to be destroyed" (Hosea 8:4). Leaving aside the tricky question of the obligation to obey corrupt sovereigns, da Viterbo strongly reaffirms that the podestà must always have God and justice before his eyes.

A widely distributed encyclopedia in the Middle Ages, the *Livres dou Tresor* (ca. 1260), written by the magistrate and master of rhetoric

Brunetto Latini (ca. 1220 to 1294–95), contains what is perhaps the most influential treatment of republican religion. In the third book, Latini begins by invoking the Aristotelian idea that city governance "is the noblest and highest science, and the noblest occupation on earth," and then cites Cicero's definition: "the city is an association of men who live in the same place and in accordance with a single law."[10] As he goes on to explain the pillars of government, he relies on biblical sources to emphasize that "all dominions and dignities are conferred on us by our sovereign Father, who, in the sacred order of earthly things, wanted the cities' government to be founded on three pillars, that is, justice, reverence, and love." Justice, in particular, must be fixed in the ruler's heart so firmly that he shall guarantee everyone's right, and shall "turn neither to right nor to left" (Prov. 4:27). He then quotes the apostle to prescribe that our Lord should be loved, as reverence is "the only thing in the world that augments the faith's merits and overcomes every sacrifice."[11]

Among the ruler's virtues, besides the political virtues of justice, fortitude, prudence, and temperance, Latini identifies the theological virtues of faith, hope, and charity. About faith, he observes that "God is well praised and glorified when he is believed in accordance with truth, and that only at that point can God be rightly entreated and prayed to." Without faith, he adds, no one can please God. Faith must be translated into deeds, but many Christians, Latini laments, greatly depart from Christian truth in their lives. Man must trust that God will pardon him, but "must take great care not to persist in sin." About charity, Latini writes that it is "lady and queen of all virtues and represents the bond of perfection, for it binds together the other virtues." As the apostle Paul teaches us, a man has no virtues at all "if he lacks charity and love for men." Charity means loving God and one's neighbor. Jesus Christ, Latini remarks, "is God and man, and hence whoever hates man does not truly love Jesus Christ."[12]

When Latini expounds on the qualities that the ruler must possess, he carefully stresses that the ruler "shall have pure faith in God and in men, for without faith and loyalty justice cannot be preserved." Governing well is a task that offers great honors, but is also demanding: "Only Jesus Christ's nobility makes man worthy of such offices." Whoever agrees to govern in full liberty and awareness must confide in Christ and the sovereign father, must be religious, and must respect God and the holy church. The law also states that the judge is consecrated in God's presence and "like a God" on earth. As soon as he arrives in the city, the ruler must address the magistrates and the citizens, and Latini urges that in his speech, he must not forget to invoke Jesus Christ, the glorious Virgin Mary, and

Saint John, the city's patron and guide. After having sworn to serve, he must go to church, hear Mass, and pray to God and the saints. There is nothing finer for a prince on earth "than following the right faith and true doctrine." The ruler of the republic must therefore possess both a pure soul and pure intentions, and must always keep his hands "clean before God."[13]

What emerges from the first writings on government in the thirteenth century is a republican religion founded on the principle that the commune is under the protection of God, Christ, and the patron saints. Divine help is the true bulwark against sedition, discord, tyranny, and war—the mortal enemies of republican liberty. The man who undertakes the task of governing acquires a dignity that renders him godlike while also compelling him always to follow a virtuous path, in both the political and the theological domain. Charity, love for God and men, is prominent among these virtues. In addition to charity, the ruler must respect justice, understood as God's command. The principles of republican government are thus not only moral and political maxims dictated by reason and prudence but also religious principles.

2

IMAGES OF THE CIVIL RELIGION

Through the treatises on government, the concept of civil religion spread within republican cities' culture and customs. But even more effective were the images that embodied those concepts. Whereas the concepts expounded in the treatises spoke first and foremost to reason, paintings struck the eyes, and from the eyes touched the passions. The rulers of republics were aware of the images' strength, especially when they were accompanied by clear words, written in large, legible characters, preferably in the vernacular. For this reason, rulers commissioned skilled artists to produce a great number of works explaining the principles of republican good government to the magistrates and citizens. The message conveyed by the walls of the city government's most important halls was at once political and religious. That is, their imagery taught people to view civic duties as if they were real religious duties—God's and Christ's commandments, not just human advice.

In Simone Martini's wonderful *Maestà* (1315), in Siena's Palazzo Pubblico, Christ holds a scroll containing words from the Book of Wisdom: "Diligite iustitiam qui iudicatis terram" (Love justice, you that are the judges of the earth). The Madonna, too, uses exigent language. More than flowers, the Virgin says that she loves good advice, and she suffers because men too often prefer their own advantage to the common good: "The angelic little flowers, roses and lilies, / with which the celestial meadow is adorned, / delight me no more than the good advice. / However, sometimes I see the one who, for his own advantage, / disregards me and deceives my land, / and the worse he speaks the more he is praised. / Look, anyone who condemns this."[1] Siena is the Virgin's land, and whoever offends or deceives the republic also offends the Virgin, and behaves as a bad Christian.

The Virgin herself commands people not to follow men who speak against the common good. The fresco's political and religious teaching is rendered even clearer by its inscription, titled "Responsio Virginis ad dicta santorum," which is the Virgin's reply to the pleas of the four saints (Ansano, Savino, Crescenzio, and Vittore) who address her on the city's behalf. The four saints' words are lost, but the Virgin's are still readable within the frame's lower border: "My beloved, bear in mind / that as you wish I will meet / your pious honest prayers. / However, if the powerful will oppress the weak, / by burdening them with disgrace or harm, / do not pray for them / or whoever else deceives my land."[2] Christ's Mother is saying to Siena's magistrates and citizens that she sides with the unfortunates who have been offended, molested, and oppressed by wicked citizens. She is unwilling to listen to the prayers of those in positions of power who deceive her and her land. If they want to be heard, even the saints, like other citizens, must take justice's side. This is a perfect civic warning, but also a religious one, both because it is the Virgin who is speaking, and because her words set a specific condition for those who would receive divine help: "You can count on my protection and my benevolence if, and only if, you behave like good citizens."

The principles of republican religion also shine forth from the great painting by Ambrogio Lorenzetti (1258–1348) in the Palazzo Pubblico's Sale dei Nove, where the city's supreme magistracy met. In this work, the artist draws from the Greek and Roman traditions as well as from biblical sources. This is immediately evident in the image of Justice, which is the foundation of the common good and of good government. She draws inspiration from divine Wisdom, which is in heaven, at the same height as the theological virtues—faith, hope, and charity. Between Justice and Wisdom, as an ideal link between the two, lie the Book of Wisdom's words, as in Martini's *Maestà*: "Diligite iustitiam qui iudicatis terram." Because she descends from divine wisdom, justice itself has a quasi-divine status. Lorenzetti defines it as a "holy virtue." It is this concept of justice that endows republican government with its distinct religious dimension.

Republican religion also emanates from the majestic figure that dominates the central part of the painting. This figure represents Siena's commune: its dress features the city's colors, and at its feet one sees the twins suckling the she-wolf—a clear indication of Siena's boasted Roman origin. The figure is an old man—that is, a *sena* person; the letters CSCV (Commune Senarum Civitas Virginis) encircle his head, and the image of the Virgin with the baby Jesus appears on his shield. The old man's head is as high as the theological virtues and celestial figures. Lorenzetti wants to impart the teaching that a well-governed commune is under the Virgin's protection and respects the principles of justice. Besides representing Siena's commune, the majestic figure is a judge and as such acquires a further religious significance. As we have already seen, the treatises on civil government maintain that the judge is "like a God on earth," for by judging in conformity with justice, he brings divine wisdom to the city. Even if he is the supreme judge, the judge is bound by laws and statutes, which he has solemnly sworn to respect and apply. The sovereign and free commune is thus the opposite of tyranny, which is not subject to any laws or statutes but instead crushes justice under its heel. Because of the judge's quasi-divine character, the commune and its representatives must be accorded a devotion similar to that owed to God, as is depicted in the fresco by the citizens who walk in a procession toward the ruler (especially those who are closer to him).

Another aspect of republican religion concerns the principle of the common good, sparking a quarrel about the majestic figure's meaning. In 1958, Nicolai Rubinstein argued that the image is the pictorial translation of the Aristotelian notion of the common good, as the basis and criterion of good government "in its Thomistic-Aristotelian meaning." In Rubinstein's view, Lorenzetti wanted Siena's governors and citizens to have a perpetual visual reminder that the common good must at all times prevail if the city is to enjoy the benefits of good government.[3] Contrary to this interpretation, Skinner has claimed that the proper intellectual context for understanding Lorenzetti's painting's meaning is not the Thomistic-Aristotelian tradition but rather the prehumanistic treatises on city government of the thirteenth century. According to Skinner, the majestic figure is not a representation of the common good but instead the symbolic representation of the kind of ruler that the city needs in order to live in justice and enjoy the common good.

Consequently, Rubinstein and Skinner offer different interpretations of the key inscription that Lorenzetti placed at the base of the fresco's central section: "WHEREVER IT RULES, THIS HOLY VIRTUE [justice] INDUCES TO UNITY THE MANY SOULS. AND THESE, GATHERED FOR THIS REASON, MAKE A COMMON GOOD FOR THEIR LORD."[4] According to Rubinstein, the sentence affirms that wherever the holy virtue of justice rules, it draws many souls into unity, and that these people, thus gathered, take the common good as their lord. Skinner, on the other hand, maintains that the sentence affirms that wherever the holy virtue of justice rules, it draws many souls into unity, and these people create a common good through their lord.[5] In my own judgment, in addition to representing the sovereign commune and supreme judge, the majestic central figure represents the common good. The most important proof of this is the inscription Lorenzetti placed at the base of the depiction of tyranny. It describes what happens when justice is crushed and tied up, and citizens pursue private advantage instead of aiming at the common good: "WHEREVER JUSTICE IS TIED UP, NO ONE EVER WITH THE COMMON GOOD / IS IN KEEPING. NOR DOES HE FOLLOW A STRAIGHT WAY. BUT TYRANNY IMPOSES ITSELF."[6]

When justice is sovereign, the citizens agree on the common good and enjoy good government; when justice is oppressed, the citizens do not act in accord with the common good and tyranny emerges, with its dreadful succession of vices. The message could not be clearer, and in order to retain this clarity, we must interpret the majestic figure as the representation of the common good, and read it as the pictorial rendering of a political principle deriving from the Aristotelian tradition. This interpretation allows us to grasp a further meaning of the majestic figure that has great relevance for the study of republican religion. Once more, the Aristotelian context is a precious guide. In the first pages of the *Nicomachean Ethics* (1094, 1–10), Aristotle in fact writes that the common good is not only better but also more divine than the individual good: "melius vero ac divinius," as proclaimed in William of Moerbeke's Latin translation, which circulated during Lorenzetti's times. In his comment on this, Saint Thomas Aquinas explained that Aristotle meant that the city's common good is more divine than the individual good because it resembles God in its being the universal cause of all goods.[7] The idea that the common good is divine became almost a commonplace in fourteenth-century republican political thought. In turn, the conviction that magistrates who serve the common good make themselves godlike derived from this idea.

Lorenzetti renders these concepts figuratively by placing the central figure at the same height as the theological virtues, and putting *caritas*, as a guide and inspiration, on the figure's head. In the Aristotelian tradition, caritas is the passion that encourages us to put the common good above the individual one. Remigio de' Girolami (1235–1319), who was Thomas Aquinas's disciple and Santa Maria Novella's prior, writes in *De bono pacis* that charity does not involve seeking one's own good but instead entails placing the common good before one's own good.[8] In *De bono communi*, he points out that charity is the foundation of civil life, and emphasizes that love of country is a Christian duty founded on man's natural inclination and God's love.[9] Inasmuch as the common good, as Aristotle teaches us in the *Nicomachean Ethics*, is the best and most divine good, those who love the common good become closer to God. Another disciple of Thomas Aquinas, Tolomeo da Lucca, affirms in *De regimine principum* that the love of country is a charitable love of the common good, which renders one's soul strong, and is perfectly coherent with God's love; indeed, it is a necessary consequence.[10] Unlike Augustine, Tolomeo does not acknowledge any difference between the pagans' and the Christians' *caritas patriae*. He ranks charity highest on the hierarchy of virtues, and assigns the same rank to the love of country. In the most influential texts of medieval political thought, the love of country therefore assumes the meaning of a charitable love of the common good, bringing man closer to God.

After having explained the nature of charity, Tolomeo expounds on its political and moral effects. Charity for the fatherland inspired the Romans to govern well ("ad bene regendum"), and for this reason, in Tolomeo's view, they deserved to become masters of the world. He also adds the noteworthy specification that the love of country shares to some degree in divine nature ("partecipabant quandam naturam divinam"). As God is the universal cause of all things, a love of country is directed toward the good of the community and its people. In support of his thesis, Tolomeo quotes the classic tales of Marcus Curtius, who hurled himself into the abyss; Attilius Regulus, who preferred to save his country rather than his own life; and Fabricius, who was not corrupted by gold. He who really loves his country and diligently fosters the common good becomes God's deputy, and shares in divine nature, thereby fulfilling God's commandment to love God along with one's neighbor with all one's heart, soul, and strength.

The concept of the love of country as a love that renders man godlike resurfaces in Dante's *Convivio* (4, 5.13–14). For Dante, the love of country is a love that God instills in some men, rendering them divine:

> If we consider, then, [Rome] in its adolescence, after its emancipation from royal tutelage , from the time of Brutus, first consul, to that of Caesar, first supreme prince, we find her exalted through citizens not human, but divine, in whom a love not human, but divine, was inspired in loving [her]. And this could not be but for a special end, intended by God in such a celestial infusion. Who can affirm that it was without divine inspiration that Fabricius could reject an almost infinite quantity of gold because he did not want to abandon his country? And Curtius, tempted by the Samnites' corruption, who for charity of country rejected a great quantity of gold, stating that Roman citizens wanted to possess not gold, but the possessors of gold? And Mucius, who set fire to his own hand, as he had failed in his attempt to free Rome? Who will say of Torquatus, who condemned his own son to death for love of the common good, that he could endure this suffering without God's help?[11]

Returning to Lorenzetti's painting, we notice that caritas is the highest of all virtues, and although it is a theological virtue, it has a worldly content as well as strong erotic meaning. Lorenzetti paints caritas red, love's color, perhaps after Dante's inspiration "tanto rossa / Ch'a pena fora dentro al fuoco nota" (*Purgatorio*, 29.121). Charity is veiled, to be more seductive. In her right hand she holds an arrow, pointed downward—one of the most typical symbols of love piercing someone's heart. She carries a burning heart in her left hand, to suggest that charity is *amor concupiscentiae*, a real erotic passion.[12] Lorenzetti admonishes that in order for the common good to triumph and save the city from the horrors of tyranny, the ruler must be guided not only by political virtues but above all by a charity that makes him love the common good with intense passion.

The same principles of republican religion emerge from the *Cycle of Famous Men*, which Taddeo di Bartolo (1362–1422) painted between 1413 and 1414 in the Anticapella; the paintings are placed between the Hall of the Nine and the Council Hall. Like Lorenzetti's *Buongoverno*, the cycle lies at the center of the Siena's institutional space. Aristotle, as the entire cycle's guide, demonstrates how to preserve liberty and become godlike.[13] Great Romans, represented in the pictorial cycle, reinforce Aristotle's words. Cicero is first among them, and next to him is Cato, who asserts the principle that liberty requires devotion, even at the cost of one's life.[14] The sacred republican principle of serving both one's country and the common liberty meets a spectacular divine confirmation through the representation of "Religion," placed on top of an arch that leads to a chapel. Underneath lies a map of Rome, signifying the link to the civil ethos that pagan religion was able to instill in the Romans' hearts. Yet its message is unmistakably Christian: "Whatever you do, in words or deeds / Do it in the name of Jesus Christ" (Omne quodcumque facitis in verbo aut in opera / In nomine domini Iesu Christi facite). If the republic's magistrates follow the example of Roman and biblical heroes, and if they always act as good Christians, they will be able to serve the common good, defend liberty, and rise to heaven in glory.[15] This is Aristotle's and the Romans' lesson, but above all it is the lesson taught by the Christian religion. Serving the common good is, in Bartolo's cycle, the true path to being a good Christian and a fine citizen.

If we turn from Siena to Florence, the artistic representations meant to give a religious significance to republican liberty are equally splendid and meaningful. One of the most important examples, because of its artistic value and the eloquence of its political message, is the statue of David, which Donatello began to sculpt in 1409, and which was transferred to the Palazzo Vecchio's Sala dei Gigli in 1416. As mentioned above, David single-handedly confronts and defeats Goliath. The religious character of the statue's message emerges not only from the choice of a biblical hero,

David, but also from the explicit reference to God's helping those who fight for liberty, as seen in the inscription placed at the statue's base: "Pro patria fortiter dimicantibus etiam adversus terribilissimos hostes deus prestat auxilium" (God helps those who fight for their country even against terrible enemies).[16]

Equally striking is the pedagogical message carved into the statue of Judith and Holofernes, completed by Donatello in 1464 (the year that saw the death of Cosimo il Vecchio, the founder of the Medicean regime). The Florentines—who, in 1494, inspired by Savonarola's preaching, had established a republican government—understood the strong civic message in the statue, and decided to transfer the work to the Palazzo Vecchio's podium, where everybody could admire it. They were quite familiar with the biblical story of Judith, Manasseh's wonderful wife, who wore a sackcloth garment next to her skin after she was widowed, "without anyone finding a word against her, so devoutly did she fear God" (Jth. 8:8). Judith invoked the "God of the humble, / the help of the oppressed, the support of the weak, / the refuge of the forsaken, / the Saviour of the despairing" (Jth. 9:11), entreating God to help her free the people of Israel from the oppression of the Assyrians and their chief, Holofernes. She then "removed the sackcloth she was wearing and taking off her widow's dress, she washed all over, anointed herself plentifully with perfumes, dressed her hair, wrapped a turban round it and put on the robe of joy she used to wear when her husband Manasseh was alive. She put her sandals on her feet, put on her necklaces, bracelets, rings, earrings and all her jewellery, and made herself beautiful enough to beguile the eye of any man who saw her" (Jth. 10:3–4). Admitted to Holofernes's presence, she was invited to his table, and made him drink far more wine than he had drunk on any other day in his life. When he collapsed completely drunk on his bed, she beheaded him with his own scimitar. Judith brought his head to her fellow Israelites, who found the strength to attack the Assyrians and regain liberty. The Florentines decided to exalt Judith's deed as an example of a heroic action aimed at a country's salvation, thereby teaching citizens that it is their duty toward God to protect the republic from enemies and tyrants.

Around the end of the fourteenth century, a *Cycle of Famous Men* was installed in the Saletta (it was destroyed in 1470). This cycle was illustrated with epigrams composed by Salutati, the Florentine Republic's chancellor from 1375 to 1406. The republican content of the inscriptions was strong. Especially powerful were the references to Brutus, who, by expelling the kings, founded Roman liberty; Cicero, who died by the same sword that killed liberty altogether; and Cato, the implacable enemy of vice, who committed suicide rather than submit to the tyrant.[17] The use of biblical and classical themes to exhort people to love liberty with a religious devotion is particularly evident in the paintings that Domenico Ghirlandajo made in 1482 for the Sala dei Gigli. At the center of the painting one finds images of Saint Zanobio, flanked on the right by a lion carrying the people's banner and, on the left, another lion carrying the banner of the city of Florence. Higher up in the painting, there are two big lunettes with portrayals of Brutus (the first consul), Mucius Scaevola, Scipio Africanus, and Cicero. The inscriptions placed under these Roman heroes have a more generic republican content than those composed by Salutati about a century before. Salutati's Brutus founds Roman liberty by expelling the kings; Ghirlandajo's Brutus defends the country. Cicero, who died together with Roman liberty, becomes Catiline's triumphant flogger.[18] The difference can be explained by the Medicean dominion over Florence. Nevertheless, the simultaneously religious and republican character of the paintings' teachings is clear enough. This character rests not within the inscriptions but instead on the juxtaposition of a saint and Christ with the symbols of the commune of Florence and the republican heroes.

During the popular government of 1494–1512, Florentine authorities dedicated themselves with renewed eagerness to decorating the Palazzo Vecchio with artworks of civic and religious inspiration. Not all of these projects were realized before the republic's fall in 1512, above all because of the financial straits imposed by military commitments. One of the works, comissioned to Fra Bartolomeo, that did not see the light was a painting of Saint Ann, which was supposed to represent the saint in an important position, for, during her feast day, the Florentines had rebelled against the duke of Athens, who was tyrannizing the city. In the Consiglio Grande's hall, the seat of the popular government, two marble epitaphs inspired by Savonarola were installed. The first, in the vernacular, clearly referred to the rallying cry "chi vuol fare parlamento vuol torre al popolo e' reggimento" (those who want to summon the parliament want to destroy popular government), used more than once in Florence's history to call people into the squares to destroy republican liberties. The second, in Latin, admonished that God had established the Great Council, and anyone who tried to dissolve it would come to no good.[19] The religious dimension of the republican government was plainly visible at the center of Florence's institutional space, and from there it radiated outward, to the whole city.

3

REPUBLICAN AND MONARCHICAL RELIGION

Republican religion was born and spread in a late medieval Europe dominated by monarchies that, from the thirteenth century on, had endowed themselves with a sacred dimension similar to that of the church.[1] Jurists and political philosophers transferred the concept of *corpus mysticum*—intended to designate the church community as a body that cannot be seen by the eyes but can only be grasped by the intellect—to the state. Applied to the state, the concept of a mystical body referred mainly, but not exclusively, to the monarchy, where the king is at the head of the mystical-political body, just as Christ or his vicar on earth is at the head of the mystical body of the church. Republics, too, however, are mystical bodies. The jurist Baldus de Ubaldis (1327–1400), for instance, uses the phrase "mystical body of the people" as the equivalent of *politia*—political community, or any other multitude ordered by laws and political institutions. The "breath of incense" and sacredness that invested the state when it began to be considered a mystical body also invested republics.[2]

The spread of Aristotelianism further reinforced the state's sacred dimension. From the Aristotelian perspective, the state is a moral and political body that pursues the goal of the common good—that is, as we have already seen, a divine good. Thanks to Aristotelianism, a new sacred aura thus descended on the political community. Of course, that aura was different from the church's aura, yet it was not incompatible with it. Later on, adding to the quasi-sacred character of the political community, jurists created the metaphor of the moral and political marriage between the prince and state: just as men are spiritually united in the mystical body whose chief is Christ, they are morally and spiritually united in the *respublica*, whose chief is the prince. The crowning of a king symbolized the marriage between the prince and the political community, analogous to the divine marriage between a prelate and the church, with God as the witness.[3]

The centrality of holy oil within rituals testifies to a basic tenet of monarchical religion: the transformative event of God's descent to man, as opposed to the republican idea of man's elevation to God through his virtues. The ancient custom of anointing catechumens, priests, and bishops became the essential character of the royal religion. Through it, medieval kings became "Christs du Seigneur," divinely protected from the devil.[4] Kings acquired quasi-priestly character through anointing, without ever properly becoming priests. Inasmuch as he has not taken holy orders, the king obviously cannot be a clergyman. Having a wife and a sword prevents him from being a friar; therefore, he must be a layman.[5] This logical argument was little appreciated by kings, even though they were eager to expand their power so as to undertake priestly functions. The use of holy oil was the quintessential royal act, to the point that not even the great feudal lords, who were constantly seeking to imitate other aspects of the kings' sacred character, ever dared to arrogate such a prerogative.[6]

The concept of a royal religion (*religion royal*) emerges with particular clarity in the *Traité du sacre*, written in 1372 by the Carmelite friar Jean Golein. The author insists above all on the rite of disrobing, as a symbol of the passage from a mundane condition to royal religiosity.[7] From the point of view of a more rigorous theology, like that established at the Council of Trent, such a doctrine would have been scandalous. How could the anointing of a king, which was not a sacrament, pardon a mortal sin? Still, starting in the thirteenth century, one witnesses an effort to assimilate the condition of the temporal chief of Christianity into that of a deacon or a subdeacon.[8] In the Middle Ages, kings always strove to appear to their subjects as men illuminated by the glory of priesthood. As one can read in a text written in 1430, the king who has been anointed is not merely a layperson but also a person of spiritual significance.[9] Besides the disrobing, the anointing, and the conferral of the ring, the royal religion's signs were—especially in France—the healing of the scrofulous, Charlemagne's relics, and the tradition of the Crusades. The king of France was called a holy king in a holy land, as witnessed by the royal lily, the fleur-de-lis, a symbol of holiness, with the three petals representing faith, doctrine, and military power. In the thirteenth century, when republican religion emerges in Italy, the idea of the holy king in a land devoted to the true Christian faith was generally accepted in France. At the beginning of the fourteenth century, commonly used terms included "most Christian king," "champion of faith," and "defender of the Church."[10]

We can now rather easily grasp the difference between the royal and the republican religion. The former celebrates an individual mystical body—the king; the latter celebrates a collective mystical body—the republic. Even in Venice, where the doge had a quasi-royal dignity, public ceremonies were aimed at celebrating the republic's excellence along with the doge, as its representative.[11] From the eleventh century onward (according to sources), the new doge's investiture evolved—from the simple civil ceremony that it had been—into a religious one, but even then there was no trace of anointing, not even when the doge's chancellery, after much debate, adopted the formula "Dei gratia dux" (duke by the grace of God).[12] Some of the doge's symbols, such as the ducal horn and the pope's cap, evoked royal religiosity. Nevertheless, the Venetian doge was not a sacred person and was neveranointed. In 1485, by the decree of the Maggior Consiglio (Great Council), the ducal coronation was instituted; yet it was a strictly secular ceremony. In certain phases of Venice's history, the doges were inclined to imitate Byzantine dress and customs, but this tendency soon faded away and never translated into a true sacralization.

Although the doge was not a sacred person, like the Byzantine emperor or the kings of France and England, he nonetheless had a more solemn status than did the communes' governors, who assumed office immediately after taking a simple oath. Propitiatory rites accompanied the doge's election. In the case of Domenico Selvo's election, at the end of the eleventh century, all the bishops of the region headed to the monastery in San Nicolò al Lido to pray to God with litanies, masses, and supplications, entreating the divinity to grant Venice's people a doge who would protect her.[13] The prayers sung for the doge were meant to summon God's protection, but they did not transform him in turn into a God. With respect to Venice, it is more accurate to speak of the subordination of religion to the republic than of the sacralization of the doge. Venetian humanists went so far as to subordinate all values, theological virtues included, to the republic. Giovanni Caldiera, a fifteenth-century humanist, regarded the republic as the "living embodiment of all perfections." In his judgment, republican virtues were the same as divine ones. God and state, patriotism and religion, harmoniously merged.[14] Once again, the republic, not the doge, attained a sacred value.[15]

Public processions were the fundamental expression of republican religion. Both Florentine and Venetian ones recognized the sacredness of secular authorities, and endeavored to bestow a sacred character on their republics. The doge was, for Venetians, a mystical and holy figure—not a relic but rather a living being, elected and made sacred by the political system.[16] The Florentines, deprived as they were of a central sacred symbol, had to seek alternatives: adolescents' confraternities, miraculous images, and charismatic priests. The Medici were able to satisfy the Florentines' need for a ritual and symbolic center, but only after they had buried the republican government. The Venetians instead succeeded in making religion serve the republic. As Francesco Sansovino remarks, "Accompanying temporal matters with religion has ever been our custom"—accompanying, indeed, as a servant.[17] Even in the republic that expressed the highest sacredness, no man could attain divine status by virtue of God's grace. Rather, a citizen attained sacred dignity insofar as he represented the republic, and retained such sacred dignity as long as he performed his duty of serving the common good.

4

A RELIGION THAT INSTILLS VIRTUE

THE MOST REFINED ELABORATIONS of republican religion are to be found in Quattrocento political thought. Politicians, prophets, historians, and philosophers of that time explained that the men who serve the common good render themselves godlike. Salutati, for instance, stated several times that a good Christian has a duty to serve his fatherland with all his energies. He also noted that charity toward the fatherland must comprise as well as surpass any other affection, bond, and interest.[1] For him, caritas was the foundation of patriotism and the ideal of the Christian citizen. In his early writings, Salutati elaborated on a form of charity without any religious implications; during his chancellorship years, however, he gave charity a pronounced religious meaning. Inasmuch as all men have a natural inclination to live in society, Salutati argued, it is against nature to cause harm to other men or to refrain from helping them. Christians have a duty to love their neighbors as themselves, and even love their enemies—private enemies, of course, not the enemies of their country.[2] Christ, too, experienced the sentiment of love of country, and his example teaches that Christians have a stronger obligation toward the common good than other men.

For Salutati, Christians' love of country is far superior to the much-celebrated ancients' love of country. The ancients did not know true charity (*vera caritas*), which originates from Christ's love and Christians' love of him, and commands us to love our neighbor as we do ourselves. A society of true friends was impossible among the ancients and can exist only among Christians.[3] Christian ethics are, in his view, the perfection of Cicero's ideal of civil virtue. Those who live in the world, and fulfill their duties toward family and fatherland, are truer to the Christian spirit than are the anchorites, who seek salvation in solitude.[4] A good citizen who serves his country operates much as does divine Providence, because providence acts for the good of the universe and desires the good of civil communities. The true Christian who serves his fatherland is thus an instrument of Providence, and thereby becomes *imago dei,* the image of God.

Christian religion teaches us that earthly life is a struggle, in which man employs his will in pursuit of the good. Precisely because he was "religious, endowed with an austere and profound faith, lived with all his soul," Salutati considered it his primary duty as a Christian and citizen always to place the struggle for liberty above all else.[5] In Salutati's religion, Cicero, Seneca, and the Gospel spoke the same moral language, and the ancients' moral and political wisdom acquired, in light of the Christian faith, new and more fulgent splendor.[6] When man seeks to render himself similar to his creator, he obeys the divine will, but within the limitations of human nature. Man's end is not to know God but rather to obtain eternal beatitude by means of his good deeds on earth. Laws serve as a safe guide to acting well. They lead us to live according to virtue, show us the way to achieve earthly happiness, and disclose the path toward eternal beatitude.[7] Through good laws, legislators make political happiness (*politica felicitas*)—which evolves into eternal happiness—possible on earth.[8] Obeying the law and serving the common good is a duty toward God, and the right way to behave for a man in whom God has instilled the sentiment of caritas.[9] This is why those who found states and serve as legislators are not only loved by God but also obtain his friendship: "Is it predicated of anyone else besides legislator Moses that he talked to God face-to-face, as a man with a friend of his?"[10]

Bruni, who served as chancellor of the republic from 1410 to 1411, and again from 1427 until his death in 1444, also thought that the good Christian should be a good citizen, ready to serve his fatherland, because Christ's word does not conflict with a love of country.[11] In his *Libri della famiglia*, Alberti presents caring for one's country as a difficult and demanding job, but one that a good citizen must accept to prevent the arrogant from dominating the republic and making all others their servants. Defending the public good, even when it requires strictness, is therefore *cosa piissima* (a most pious deed) and dear to God.[12] According to Matteo Palmieri, author of that true compendium of civic humanism *Vita civile*, civic duties are religious duties. The passion spurring republican Rome's heroes to give their life for the liberty of all, Palmieri explains, was "pietà della patria [piety for country]," or "civile pietà [civil piety]." "Attending to the fatherland's well-being, preserving the city, and maintaining the union and concord of the well-assembled multitudes" are the most meritorious among human actions.[13] Justice, in particular, is the highest among virtues, so welcome to Almighty God that, throughout the holy scriptures, God calls the righteous blessed and the blessed righteous. Not just the scriptures but all divine and human laws as well, together with the common interest, command that justice be honored. The actions of those rulers of republics who honor justice are dearer to God than anything else. This is why they shall receive, as a reward for their labor, eternal beatitude.[14] Man can render himself divine and eternal through the search for perfection in all arts and deeds. Thus he realizes his true nature, lives in accordance with God's will, and obtains glory on earth.

Authentic Christianity requires every person to fulfill his own task in life, without escaping risks and pains. Giannozzo Manetti, a man of profound faith, explains in his oration *De dignitate et exellentia hominis* (1451–52) that escaping pain is acceptable not for the strong and magnanimous but rather, as Aristotle says, for the weak and feeble. We cannot abandon our place in life, except at "the chief's, that is to say, God's, command." Wisdom and faith command us to face with virtue the labor, struggles, and pains that torment the earthly city. Manetti exalts the virtue that translates into a strong and magnanimous approach to civil life—the virtue that one loves with the body and the soul, and that renders those who practice it godlike: "Love it, observe it, I pray you, follow it, embrace it so that, by practicing it at all times, you will not only be happy and blessed, but you will also become almost similar to Almighty God."[15]

Lorenzo Valla (1405–57) provides solid philological grounds for the interpretation of Christianity as the religion of virtue. He starts with the assumption that Christianity's central tenet is charity, which he defines as love toward God and one's neighbor, and the chief of all virtues that make men morally strong.[16] Fortitude, Valla notes, is a kind of affection that supplies strength. When the apostles received the Holy Spirit, which is the charity of the Father and the Son, they became strong so that they could spread the word of God. According to Valla, the idea of virtue as power and strength can be found in the Gospel.[17] If charity offers strength, and strength is virtue, it follows that Christianity cannot be a religion that preaches weakness and humility before the powerful of the world, but is rather a religion of virtue.[18] The conviction that true Christianity teaches us virtue will play a fundamental role in later republican political thought.

Christian religion and political virtue also go hand in hand for Bartolomeo Sacchi, named the Platina (1421–81). He fervently supports Christian religion as the moral foundation of republics, and restates the conventional idea that virtue—the virtue of republics' rulers in particular—makes men godlike and opens the way to true glory. He explains that the people love and adore as demigods those who excel in virtue. The good citizen who rules a city carries a heavy burden on his shoulders; the reward that awaits him is true, perfect glory (*vera ac integra gloria*) assured by God.[19] Marsilio Ficino (1433?–99), too, argues that religion enjoins civil virtues and commands a love of country.[20] Civil virtue, he clarifies, consists of the following elements: prudence, which helps us to understand what the country's common good is; justice, which teaches us to bestow honors on the basis of merit; fortitude, which triumphs over fear; and temperance, which assists us in our effort to moderate the passions.[21] The Christian religion commands us to exercise virtues ardently, not out of ambition, or for pleasure or to find repose, but only to fulfill God's ends and attain salvation in the afterlife. Christ embodied the divine idea of virtue, exemplifying notions of upright justice, magnanimity, temperance, and meekness.[22]

Ficino's ideal of a religion founded upon caritas, and that in the name of caritas commands people to love and serve one's country, was also spread widely in the laic confraternities of the late Quattrocento. Proof of this can be found in the orations of Giovanni Nesi, who served several times in Florence's highest magistracies and was one of the most typical exponents of a "popular" Platonism, with strong republican aspirations.[23] In the *Oratio de Caritate*, delivered on February 25, 1478, Nesi emphasizes that "Deus caritas est et caritas est Deus" (God is charity, and charity is God), and that charity made "God descend from heaven to earth, become a man, change from immortal to mortal, and from master to slave." Likewise, charity alone "lifted man from earth to heaven, and, whereas he was mortal, bestowed eternal life on him; and, although he was man, made him God."[24] Charity makes us "similar to our Creator," commands us to love our neighbor, and gives us strength, so that we can comply with God's command. Thanks to charity, cities enjoy peace and unity. It therefore deserves to be called the "madre [mother]" and "forma [form]" of all virtues and, as such, should be honored and pursued with all our strength.[25]

A religion founded on charity prevents human beings from seeking salvation in contemplation and solitude, and exhorts people instead to serve the public good with wisdom and courage. For Nesi, religious faith is one with civic humanism's ideals. In the *Oratio de humilitate*, which he delivered before the "Reverendi Padri et dilectissimi Frategli" of the confraternity of the Nativity on April 11, 1476, Nesi affirms that Christianity—if correctly understood—requires us to serve the fatherland. Nesi's ideas were echoed by Giovanni Pico della Mirandola in his oration *De dignitate hominis* (1486). Only to man did God grant the possibility of elevating himself to the point of imitating his creator.[26] In these words lies republican religion's heart: it is not that men are rendered divine by God; rather, men become divine as they serve liberty with their souls augmented and strengthened by charity.

5

SACRED LAWS AND SACRED REPUBLICS

FOR CIVIC HUMANISTS, laws are sacred as long as they reflect divine wisdom, and because their object is not just whatever is good but rather the divine good, which is the public good.[1] In order to ignite and sustain loyalty within a citizenry toward laws and statutes, a republic must foster its religious system with great diligence. Furthermore, a republic must educate its citizenry to love justice and the fatherland, through both the teaching imparted by good and revered priests, and ceremonies that strike and move the multitudes' sentiments.[2] Palmieri, for instance, elaborates on these ideas of republic and religion in the *Libro della città di vita*, written between 1455 and 1464. The work's circulation was troubled by the suspicion of heresy—a notion that gained strength immediately after Palmieri's death, in 1475.[3] For Palmieri, religion instills a sense of duty and reinforces within men's souls the will to live in accordance with justice.[4] A city structured according to this religion would be a perfect republic, like the one imagined by Plato. Since human corruption does not allow for such perfection, civil wisdom suggests that men try to realize not necessarily Plato's republic but the one depicted by Cicero instead, such that "come in terra dar si puo più netta [on earth, nothing more upright can exist]." In earthly republics, too, men can live and rule according to justice, and the reward for those who live thus, Palmieri assures us, is salvation.[5]

As other political writers focusing on civil humanism had done before him, Palmieri emphasizes that God loves the decent life and wants to preserve it, and therefore rewards men involved in the excellent deeds of "extirpating tyrants for the good of the many" as well as "establishing good and peaceful governments."[6] Platina believes the same thing. In *De optimo cive*, a model text of Florentine political thought in the Quattrocento, he reaffirms that religion is necessary for preserving republics, and that the Christian religion is among the fittest to educate good and strong citizens.

Platina assumes that the republics' ultimate end, as Aristotle teaches us, is to allow citizens to live well. No man can govern something as large and important as a republic without God as his guide.[7] Since religion is the true foundation of civil government, a ruler must ensure the pious and saintly observance of the worship of God and the Christian religion.[8] After all, the necessity of religion and piety is evidenced in the fact that people who preserve religion and respect divine worship, as the Romans did, realize admirable achievements. If this is true with regard to the false religion of the ancients, it must with greater reason be true for the holy and chaste Christian religion.[9] Christianity, Platina continues, urges us to pursue justice, fortitude, and humility; it teaches us the meaning of modesty, shame, respect for promises, constancy, and honesty; it commands us to avoid carnal violence, fraud, villainous actions, fury, turpitude, lust, injustice, concupiscence, indolence, and temerity. Much more than the ancient pagan religion, founded on fables, Christian religion is suited to sustain republican life. The ruler's duty is thus to carefully encourage Christian worship and discourage superstition—that is, the cult of false gods. Consequently, the prince must beware of hypocrites and dissemblers, who have no faith whatsoever yet employ every stratagem to seem utterly religious.[10]

At the end of the Quattrocento, the idea that a republic needs Christian religion as its moral essence found its most convincing, but also most extreme, elaboration in Savonarola's sermons and *Trattato circa el reggimento e governo della città di Firenze* (*Treatise of the Regime and Government of the City of Florence*), written in 1494 at the instance of the Signoria elected after the Medici's expulsion and the establishment of a popular government. Savonarola hoped that the republican government would devote itself to making Florence into the new Jerusalem, united in the love of God and mutual love of citizens, which would become the inspirational force for Italy's and the world's moral and religious reform.[11] He urged that Florence must choose Christ as her king: not only because, insofar as Christ was the divine king, no one else could become prince of the city, but also because choosing Christ as the king implied assuming the solemn commitment of living according to the divine law.

Savonarola repeated over and over again that he was preaching religious reform and the establishment of a civil government inspired by God. The new republican government that Florence had established was part of God's design to save the city. Its principles and institutions agreed in all respects with natural law and the church's teachings.[12] Both natural law and Christian doctrine agree on condemning tyranny as an enemy of true religion, and as such, the foremost political and moral evil. The tyrant simulates piety and religiosity, but he cultivates only the superficial aspects of religious ritual while rewarding bad priests and punishing the good ones, thereby destroying true religious sentiment.[13] Civil government instead leads a city toward that beatitude that Christ has promised men, and it encourages the good life even as it sustains religion, understood not as a collection of exterior practices of worship but rather as a truth felt and lived with sincere faith.[14]

Civil or republican government proceeds from God, and receives from God all good things. Religiosity and the citizens' good customs make the city's government perfect, both because they bring divine favor on it and because the citizens selected for government can, through God's illumination, offer good counsel.[15] At the same time, Savonarola stresses that true religion is a good government's first duty and the safest bulwark against tyranny. Tyranny offends all cities, especially those in which citizens cultivate Christian piety. Florence, in Savonarola's opinion, is profoundly Christian. If tyranny is finally defeated, Florence can perfect itself as a Christian city. But as long as tyranny dominates the city, its citizens will not be able to live according to the true religion. The admonition that Savonarola launches from the pulpit as well as the pages of his treatise is clear: the choice is either true religion or tyranny.[16]

Savonarola wanted the citizens of Florence to think of the Consiglio Maggiore (Great Council) as the republic's soul, as a special gift of God, and hence as the proper object of their profound devotion. Citizens must feel that it is their duty, as an obligation that each of them owes to God, to make the republican government ever more perfect:

> Every Florentine citizen who wants to be a good member of his city and wants to help her, as everyone should, must first of all believe that this Council and this civil government are sent by God, as it is true, and not only because every good government derives from Him, but also because of the special care that He has for the present condition of the city of Florence: anyone who has been in Florence during the last three years, and is not blind or totally without judgment, will find it clear that, without God's intervention, such a government could never have been established, given the many and powerful obstacles, nor could it have been preserved today in the midst of so many plotters and so few adjutors.[17]

Republican political writers would repeat this argument many times in the centuries to come: republics are so difficult to establish and maintain, and so precious, that they seem like gifts of God.

If Florence is just, Savonarola contends, it will also be great and powerful, for its people will then happily agree to be ruled by a just republic that follows Christian precepts. Rome was not Christian, but it was just, and God, who wants people to be ruled according to justice, gave her dominion over the world. If she wants to do so, Florence can follow Rome's example. The most precious goods follow from civil government: true liberty, the security of goods and person, the honor of women and children, progress in arts and trade, prosperity, free marriage, and the wish to beget children. The treatise's conclusion epitomizes Savonarola's idea of the republic's divine value:

> Therefore, the good ruler being (as we have proven) happy and similar to God, and the bad ruler being unhappy and similar to the devil, every citizen must abandon sins and his own passions and interests [*le proprie affezioni*], and must strive to rule well, and preserve and augment and perfect this civil government, for God's honor and the salvation of souls. Indeed, such government has been given to us especially by Him, because of the love He has for this city, so that she may be happy both in this world and in the other world, by grace of our Savior Jesus Christ, king of kings and lord of lords, who lives and reigns, with his Father and the Holy Spirit, *in saecula saeculorum. Amen.*[18]

Savonarola urged the Florentines to cultivate a religion of virtue.[19] In the third *Predica sopra Aggeo*, for instance, he explains that charity "renders man valiant and able to accomplish any great thing for love of God." To extol charity's power, he almost literally repeats Saint Paul's words: "Charity minds not persecutions, or opprobria, or scourges, she minds not death; charity fears nothing at all; charity is stronger than death is; charity separates man from all the things of the world more than death does; death takes away from you the things of the world, against your will; charity takes them away in accordance with your will, and the entire world cannot triumph over charity." Savonarola keeps reiterating that men must act well "for God's honor, and then for zeal towards the fatherland and the common good," and even affirms that "if you have no charity, you are no true Christian."[20] Egoism diminishes "when everyone can have what is common to all, and you are content that everyone has his lot, and therefore every good citizen is bound to love the common good." Charity unifies the people and the church, just like the mortar "that conjoins and binds the stones together." In order to be genuine, charity must be untainted by self-love. For this reason, Savonarola underscores with a clear polemical purpose that there was no charity among the Romans: "Although they did notable things, they did them for their self-praise and out of self-love."[21]

As an example, Savonarola points to the ancient Romans, who "greatly loved the city's common good." He reiterates that good magistrates will obtain from God both glory and an extraordinary reward in eternal life.[22] Finally, it is worth noting that he insists that God loves in a particular way the ruler who governs for the common good, for he recognizes him as his equal:

> *Item*, like loves like, and the more one is loved by his like the more the two look alike: hence, all creatures being similar to God, they all are loved by Him; but since some are more similar to Him than others, these—those who are more similar—are loved by God more: and inasmuch as the ruler is much more similar to God than the ruled, it is obvious that if he rules justly, he is more loved and rewarded by God because he is exposed to greater danger and more tiring efforts of mind and body than ordinary citizens.[23]

Precisely because the republic must be religious, it must expel bad priests, and establish a "most perfect worship" and the "best Christian way of life."[24] Florence will resurrect the ancient Christians' way of life and become the "New Jerusalem," a mirror of true religion in the world, "a terrestrial heaven" that lives "in jubilation and songs," where children will be like angels.[25] In Savonarola's millenarian vision, republic and religion are two aspects of the same reality. The city as a whole, with its institutions and way of life, must become a true church and place itself in the service of good Christian living. At the same time, the church is fully actualized in the republic, into which it pours out its spiritual patrimony. The union of religion and republic signifies the victory of the divine plan on earth as well as the end of the clash between heaven and earth, between the human and the divine. Savonarola seeks not only a new republican leader but also a redeemer, politician, and prophet who can realize religious and moral reformation. Against the irreligious cynicism that destroys both civil and Christian life, Savonarola strongly emphasizes that the more a republic is spiritual, the stronger it becomes, and that those who govern become true political rulers only if they obey the dictates of Christian morality.[26] He specifies, however, that electing to public office men who are good but foolish is equivalent to undermining "the honor of God, the common good, and the honor and reputation" of the city.[27]

The Florentine political elite only partly shared this vision of Florence as a New Jerusalem. It did accept, albeit with important qualifications, the ideas that the republican constitution of 1494 was a divine gift, that God had a special love for Florence, and that respect for divine law and religious worship assured the city of God's friendship. When the most respected and influential citizens of Florence took the floor during the Pratiche and Consulte (the republic's advisory bodies) to offer their carefully thought-out advice on problems of domestic politics and international affairs, they stressed the idea that Florence was a religious republic. For these Florentines, God was seen as all-powerful, intervening in human affairs at his own discretion. Fortune was often malignant, but God "can modify fortune," as an orator explained in the Pratica of August 19, 1505.[28] One must turn to God because he has wise advice. At times of grave danger, furthermore, Florentines thought that priests should organize processions, the republic should increase its charity to the poor, and the miraculous image of the Madonna dell'Impruneta should be solemnly carried to the city. During the crisis of spring 1512, which led to the dissolution of the republican regime, some Pratica members proposed postponing all deliberations so as to concentrate on prayer.[29]

The Florentines held that governing for the public good and protecting the common liberty was a religious duty, in the precise sense of a duty toward God. The failure to perform that duty resulted in divine punishment. On the other hand, if someone worked for a just cause, God would have to "favor him."[30] Even when the republic's defense was entrusted to men who had erred through sin, God would still remain on their side. For Savonarola's followers, but not for them alone, it was necessary in all public deliberations that men always put Christian principles above those dictated by human reason.[31] They called the Great Council the "soul" and "the very life of our city."[32] Since it was a gift of God and dear to God, the Great Council could withstand the attacks of the enemies of of civil freedom. Because republican institutions and civil life were a gift of God, they must originally have been perfect, and hence the only way to reform them was to draw them back, now and again, to their original principles.[33]

Another significant document of republican religion in Florence in the early years of the Cinquecento is the speech by Lamberto del Nero Cambi in favor of the law imposing a tithe on priests' revenues. Cambi's oration is entirely inspired by the religion of the fatherland, meant not as an alternative to the Christian religion, but rather as the true and right interpretation of it. After a short preamble, he explains that

republics and kingdoms, and more generally all states, as they are established, thus they are maintained, either by force through arms, or by love through religion, or with both one and the other thing taken together; and, if one of the two things were to be absent, I would prefer to be deprived of the force of arms, rather than of religion, as I judge entrusting oneself to God's will to be not only more pious but also more secure than placing oneself in the power of men. Religion, just like arms, needs—or rather requires—not so much good laws, of which there is no shortage, as good men, who create those laws in the first place, and who ensure that the laws are justly and inviolably observed and executed.[34]

In order to reinforce his argument, Cambi invokes the Romans and urges people to follow their example:

If the Gentiles so greatly revered their own religion, which was manifestly false—as one sees in the Roman republic, better ordered than all others—then what should we Christians do with respect to our own, which is undoubtedly true? And if they punished so harshly those who violated or vilified their ceremonies, then what chastisement can be administered that is not too small to those who violate or vilify ours? It seems to me, from reading the ancient histories, that men have been not quite better but greater and more prudent, the more they have prioritized and always favored religious matters; nor do I believe that there is a greater sign or better argument that any city and region must choose between either quickly changing itself or falling into ruin, than seeing there either changes in or scorn of the divine cult.[35]

Moving to his conclusion, Cambi charges the papacy with having corrupted Christian religion and provoking the end of Italian liberty:

Those who say that the popes have been and still are absolutely the first and foremost cause of our ruin and miseries, as well as of the servitude of Italy, do not speak the truth; for it was not the popes, but the popes' ambition, and avarice, and their infinite lust and cruelty that have caused and continue to cause all of our ills. Their vast greed and incredible wickedness, and not the popes themselves, have annihilated and nearly extinguished the Christian Faith, which is, at once, holy and good in and of itself, and also, undoubtedly, highly useful, nay absolutely necessary, not only for living in beatitude in the other world, but also to live securely in this one.[36]

In the peroration, he praises Florentine republican Christianity for being the most effective support for freedom:

Read your histories, and you will find that eight men, who in those times, which were much more religious and Catholic than these, the most religious and Catholic men to be found, having had greater respect for the common good of all than for the private interests of a few priests, won so much favor among the populace, and so much benevolence among all, that they were generally called, and are still called when we talk of them today, the Otto Santi (Blessed Eight).[37] Those magistrates who for love of country, felt as a Christian duty, fiercely opposed the popes' temporal power were the perfect example of republican Christianity.[38]

6

REPUBLICAN RELIGION AND
RELIGIOUS REFORM

THOSE WHO LIVED LIBERTY as a religious faith felt a deep revulsion for the corruption of the clergy and the temporal power of the pope. The former corrupted customs and extinguished civil virtues; the latter was a constant menace to republics and hindered the rule of law from within, through the vindication of exemptions and privileges. For this reason, republics intensely felt the need for a religious reform that would eradicate the church's temporal power and bring Christian religion back to its focus on poverty and charity.[1]

The advocates of religious reform drew inspiration and arguments from biblical and classical sources.[2] In Latin texts, the words *reformatio* and *regeneratio* are equivalent. Ovid calls Iolaus, who is rejuvenated in order to be once again fit for battle, "reformatus primos in annos" (alive again, with the look of his early years).[3] He also writes in his *Metamorphoses* that times change ("et nova sunt semper"). As an example of the capacity to be reborn through one's own power, Ovid cites the phoenix.[4] The paradigmatic example of resurrection was Christ, but every human soul is also reborn, if it is able to find its way back to the right way of living.[5] In the New Testament, *reformari* means to transform oneself on the model of the Christian ideal, and the force or efficient cause impelling this transformation is caritas.[6] In the First Epistle to the Romans, Saint Paul urges his readers not to adapt to the corruption of the world but rather to transform themselves, to regenerate their entire ethical and spiritual life: "be ye transformed by the renewing of your mind" (Rom. 12:2). Whereas in the Epistle to the Ephesians the rebirth is not directly equated with a heavenly afterlife, in the Epistle to the Colossians renewal means becoming once again similar to God.[7]

The ideal of the twelfth-century religious movements was a reformation aimed at returning to the authentic form of the Christian religion.[8] In the *Convivio*, Dante explains the fundamental character of the *reformatio*: "The supreme desire of each thing, and the first given by Nature, is to return to its first source."[9] To be reborn, for Dante, means returning to an ideal, original, pure form. Dante begins a collection of poems that express his internal renewal through the spiritualizing and purifying force of love with the words "INCIPIT VITA NOVA" (a new life begins). In the *Commedia*, he reformulates with great expressive power the ideas of rebirth and renewal as well as the ideal elevation of man and humanity: "The ages turn new again; / Justice returns and the first time of man, / And new progeny from heaven descends," he writes in *Purgatorio* (22.70–72), translating Virgil almost to the letter.[10] The poet then describes the significance of the inner renewal, achieved through "passi tanti [so many steps]," which took him to the threshold of paradise: "Remade as are new trees / Renewed with new-sprung leaves, / Pure and prepared to rise up to the stars."[11]

During the Middle Ages, the Christian ideal of rebirth through faith became a myth of social and political reform. An eloquent example is the republican restoration that Cola di Rienzo (1313?–54) attempted in Rome. In spite of its brevity, his experiment had vast repercussions. Rienzo was animated by a love of glory, the cult of the sacred Roman people, and the fervent desire to restore Rome, and with it all of Italy, to ancient greatness. He himself presents his rule, after the expulsion of the Roman barons, as the beginning of the new era and an awakening from a fossilized life. The power that drives the moral rebirth is charity: just as soil is prepared by a plow, the church of God is renewed through acts and seeds of charity.[12] Reviving justice cannot be merely the act of a prince but instead must be the achievement of an entire people, which is then reinvigorated and can realize a new, higher form of life.[13] Morally deformed by tyranny, the people must be reformed, liberated, and returned to the ideal form that is proper to it. The reform, therefore, is liberation from corruption and redemption from decadence.[14]

Petrarch, too, felt and forcefully expressed the myth of rebirth.[15] In a poem that was perhaps dedicated to Rienzo, he describes Italy as a lazy, sleepy, befuddled old woman; she does not respond to the cries of men, until a new redeemer seizes her by the tresses, lifts her out of the muck, and helps her regain her former beauty and vigor. Petrarch portrays Italy as a "gentil donna" (gentle lady) who awaits rescue at the hand of a husband or father, and he promises her redeemer everlasting glory. Rebirth is a renewal of the spirit that takes place when men rediscover devotion, charity, and virtue. Petrarch's sources are the Psalms ("When you send your Spirit, / they are created, / and you renew the face of the earth" [104:30]) and Revelation ("Then I saw a new heaven and a new earth, for the first heaven and the first earth had passed away, and there was no longer any sea.... And he who was seated on the throne said, 'I am making everything new!' " [21:1–5]).[16] Petrarch also resorts to prophetic language to herald the rebirth of virtue and the return of the golden age: "Beautiful souls, and should that are friends of virtue, / shall hold the world; and then we shall it become / all golden, and full of the ancient deeds."[17]

Salutati, who in many ways was a disciple of Petrarch, perceived the signs of the new age in Florence's victorious war over the papacy.[18] Bruni, in his turn, adopted the cycle of birth, growth, perfection, and decay to interpret human affairs. A people decay and die because of the corruption that dissolves its original virtue, and especially because of the loss of liberty.[19] They are reborn when they learn to rediscover virtue and regain liberty, as testified to by Florence's example. After endowing herself with a free republican government and becoming the protector of Italian liberty, this city became the providential locus for the rebirth of literature and the arts, the rediscovery of the ancients, and the reattainment of civil living.

One of the texts that better expresses the Italian aspiration to political and moral reform is Nesi's *Oraculum de novo saeculo* (1496), which interprets the new century as a political rebirth for Florence and a rebirth in general of Christianity:

> What does the new age mean if not the conversion and the renewal of the church?... Indeed, after many different cases, I summon you to that golden age.... Whoever is a follower of Christ, come into the kingdom of Christ.... Do you want the prophet? Here he is, truthful in announcing the future, admirable always and everywhere.... Italy will be devastated by the barbarians; the Florentine government, today in crisis owing to the ambition, the perfidy, the frivolity of its citizens, will extend its name and its powers, augmented in wealth, power, and glory. Rome will soon come to ruin, invaded by foreigners; but the church will save itself through divine aid and will triumph; the Mohammedans will very soon convert to the Christian faith. And, finally, one will be the flock, and one the shepherd.[20]

The demand for religious and moral reform drew special strength from the comparison between the bad customs of the Italians and the good customs of the free German cities. Poggio Bracciolini, who served in the Roman Curia and was chancellor of the Florentine republic, has left us an illuminating testimony of the "pleasant way of life due to the extreme freedom of customs" that he noticed at the baths of Baden. As Bracciolini explains, everyone there strives to live happily and enjoy pleasures. They are not concerned with "splitting up common goods" but rather with "sharing those things that have been split up." In the diverse crowd at the baths, "there are never quarrels, disorders, divisions, murmurings, calumnies." Everyone is contented with the little he has, living one day at a time and not pursuing unattainable riches. The contrast with Italian customs is sharp: we "indulge in libels and slanders," entirely focused on gains and appetites, never satisfied with what we have, always miserable, always frantic.[21]

In Constance, Poggio witnesses the trial of Jerome of Prague, a pupil of Jan Hus, and admires the defendant's eloquence, worthy of the masters of classical oration. Poggio has serious doubts about the validity of the heresy charges again Jerome of Prague and finds nothing wrong in Hus's faith: "He said nothing that would be unworthy of an upright man, and if his faith was truly that which he professed, then one could not find any ground even for the slightest punishment, let alone a capital sentence." Poggio quotes the words of Jerome of Prague in defense of Hus with evident approval: "He said that he had not held anything against the Church, but against the abuse committed by the priests, and against the pride, ostentation, and pomp of the prelates," as well as against all those things that were "unworthy of the religion of Christ." Poggio, a Catholic, sees in Jerome of Prague, about to be burned at the stake as a heretic, a man "eminent beyond all belief," who knew how to die like a philosopher.[22]

Even before they began to hear about Martin Luther, the Florentines conceived of Germany as a land of people who lived in accordance with a sincere Christian faith, in keeping with the origins of Christianity, which translated into a powerful civil conscience. Francesco Vettori observes this as early as 1512, when he recounts his diplomatic mission to the court of Maximilian I from June 1507 to March 1508. Vettori's account is an impressive and vivid documentation of the corruption of the priests and monks. In nearly every tavern at which he stops, Vettori hears tales of clergymen guilty of every sort of infamy. In the region of Verona, Vettori hears, in the testimonies of several Germans who are returning home, the disgust with which true Christians judged the papal court:

> If you ask me the reason that I am leaving Rome, I will tell you that
> we from the Rhineland are good Christians, and we have heard and

read that the faith of Christ was founded on good customs with the blood of the martyrs, and strengthened by many miracles, so that it would be impossible for someone from the Rhineland to question the faith. I have been in Rome for several years, and I have seen how the prelates and others live, such that I was afraid that if I stayed there any longer, not only might I lose faith in Christ, but I might become an Epicurean and lose my immortal soul.[23]

Years later, in his *Sommario della istoria d'Italia*, Vettori observes that the Roman papacy has in fact created "a new religion" that shares nothing with the Christian faith but the name: Christ "commanded poverty, and they desire wealth; commanded humility, and they pursue pride; commanded obedience, and they want to command everybody."[24]

In the lands through which he travels, Vettori also meets quacks, charlatans, and cheats, like the one near Verona who claimed that he had miraculously survived a hanging in Bologna and was going to see the Blessed Simon of Trent to fulfill a vow. With this tale, he managed to get money from "poor men," which he then cheerfully spent in the nearest tavern. The episode makes Vettori think about the countless methods, arts, industries, and tricks that men, first and foremost religious men, employ to deceive others.[25] Alongside the corrupt prelates and quacks, however, are those heralding new religions aimed at restoring the authenticity and simplicity of the evangelical message, and dissolving the wicked religion that popes and priests have established through deception and force. In Mirandola, for instance, Vettori hears the story of Piero Bernardino, who "was sowing a certain new religion" and thus was burned at the stake.[26]

Vettori discusses worldly and religious concerns in a cold, detached manner. But as he walks toward Germany, he notes that the message of Christ is quite another matter from the casuistry of theologians: "In our religion, the theologians are the first who have made and continue to make so many books, disputations, syllogisms, and subtleties that not only all the libraries are filled with them, but also the booksellers' shops. And yet, our Savior Jesus Christ says in the Gospels: 'Love the Lord your God with all your heart and with all your soul and with all your mind, and your neighbor as yourself.'[27] In these two precepts, all the laws of the prophets are contained. What need have we, then, of so many disputations over the Incarnation, the Holy Trinity, the Resurrection, the Eucharist—all things that we Christians must believe by our faith, and by believing become worthy of them, and reasons do not add anything to this?"[28]

Prelates who met in Pisa to take part in the Gallican Council, held at the king of France's behest in opposition to Pope Julius II, had been talking about the church's reform, too, but with political objectives. In the session on November 7, 1511, the abbot Zaccaria Ferreri read a passage from the Gospel of John—"Lux venit in mundum et magis dilexerunt homines tenebras quam lucem" (This is the judgment, that the light has come into the world, and men loved the darkness rather than the light; for their works were evil) (3:19)—all about the "reformatione della Chiesa" (reform of the church), and concluded that "before attempting to reform the Church, all the most reverend cardinals and prelates should first reform themselves."[29]

But the text that, more than any other, reveals the hope for a religious and moral reformation is the *Dialogo della mutatione di Firenze*, which Bartolomeo Cerretani, a moderate pro-Medici, wrote around 1520. The protagonists of the dialogue, Lorenzo and Girolamo, both fervent followers of Savonarola, set off on a journey to Germany to meet "Martino Luter," and explain to Giovanni Rucellai, whom by chance they meet near Modena, the reasons for their pilgrimage: "Since you are like a brother to us, our desire need not remain secret from you: we are going to Germany, attracted by the fame of a Venerable Religious called Brother Martino Luter, whose writings—published in Italy and especially in Rome, as I know you are aware—suggest that this man must be extremely valiant in customs, doctrine, and religion. It seems to us that his conclusions are quite proper and in keeping with the doctrine and practice of the early church militant." Rucellai replies to the wayfarers: "So you are still victims of the same superstition that used to center on Fra' Girolamo from Ferrara."[30] At that time, Luther was conflated with the memory of the monk burned at the stake twenty years earlier, thereby becoming the prophet of a *renovatio* that some yearned for, others feared, and still others mocked. "Don't you in Rome," asks Girolamo, "have a great fear of this renewal of the Church because of love for your temporal possessions?" Even if "everyone is calling for a renovatio," Giovanni replies, "and indeed your nuns and peasants and friars and other petty prophets talk about it all these days, everyone laughs at it in Rome, and you are living on dreams."[31]

Despite some significant differences, all those calling for religious reform were in favor of a regeneration of the body of the church through a return to the authentic principles of the Christian religion. Savonarola, as we have seen, preached the need to renew and rebuild the church with "poverty and simplicity and unity and peace." His renovatio had above all a moral and spiritual importance, founded on a rediscovery of justice and a return to the principles of the apostolic life, along with the republican and communitarian political values that Florence preserved by divine will: "Thus the church of Christ, which was founded by His apostles in poverty and simplicity and unity and peace: you see today how one could say it is destroyed, as was the temple of Jerusalem. And yet God wants to renew and rebuild it, and wants Florence also to be renewed, whence comes the renewal of many other places."[32] To draw the church or city back toward its beginnings means correcting distortions, so that the institution will be consistent with the purpose for which it was instituted.[33] Reviving a people deadened through sin requires not only natural wisdom but also the aid of God, prophetic words, and the warmth of charity.[34] Mirandola, who followed Savonarola's sermons with fascination, summarized the meaning of the aspiration to renovatio when he wrote that man can degenerate to the lower things, "the brutish," or regenerate in accordance with his will to the higher things, "which are divine."[35]

7

A RELIGION TO LIVE FREE

MACHIAVELLI WAS THE POLITICAL writer who, better than anybody else, elaborated on both republican religion and the need for a religious reform. In the last pages of *The Art of War*, which he wrote in order to revive the ancient orders and ancient Italian military virtue, he reveals his conviction that Italy "seems to be born to resurrect dead things, as one could see in poetry, painting, and sculpture."[1] In the *Canto degli spiriti beati*, Machiavelli harks back to the myth of the return of the golden age and the revival of ancient virtue with words similar to those of Petrarch: "Throw away fear, / Enmity and hate, / Avarice and pride and cruelty, throw them away; / Let love of the just and noble honors rise in you once more / And the world go back to that ancient day: / This way, the path to paradise / Shall be opened up for the blessed / And the flames of virtue shall never die."[2]

Machiavelli harshly criticizes the corruption of the church with words similar to those used by many others before him. He accuses the church of Rome of keeping Italy divided, bringing about the death of "all devotion and all religion," and instilling in the minds of the Italians the especially malign wickedness of those who have no religion: "Thus we Italians have this first obligation to Church and priests: that we have become without religion and wicked."[3] Because they have no fear of God, nor the sense of modesty that arises from true religion, the Italians are convinced that they can always escape, in one way or another, the just punishment for their misdeeds and therefore can be frivolously wicked. Fra Timoteo, the friar in Machiavelli's *La Mandragola* who is only superficially religious, is ridiculous, but after all good-natured. The bad moral education that the Christian religion diffuses, though, deserves serious condemnation, in Machiavelli's view. "Our religion," writes Machiavelli, "has glorified humble and contemplative more than active men"; "it has then placed the highest good in humility, abjectness, and contempt of things human";

and if "it asks one to be strong, it wishes one to be strong in suffering rather than in doing something strong."[4] The church of Rome thus must take the grave responsibility for having suffocated the love of republican liberty in modern men, rendered "the world weak," and given it "in prey to criminal men, who certainly can manage it, seeing that the collectivity of men, so as to go to paradise, think that they have to endure their beatings rather than avenge them."[5]

Machiavelli contrasts pagan education to Christian education. The former taught men to esteem the honor of the world and find in it "the highest good"; beatified only "men who were full of worldly glory, as were captains of armies and princes of republics"; and celebrated "greatness of spirit," strength of body, and "all other things capable of making men strong." Some critics therefore held that Machiavelli was a pagan.[6] They failed to notice, however, that Machiavelli also found examples in modern Christian peoples of a religion that instills good moral and political customs. Like others before him, Machiavelli admired Germany, and when he traveled there in 1508, he passed through some of the same villages and towns that Vettori mentions in his *Viaggio in Alamagna*. Machiavelli emphasizes that in the "province of Germany," there is still a great "goodness" and "religion" similar to that of the Romans; thanks to their good customs and good religion, those peoples live safe and free. The contrast between Italy and Germany is sharp: on the one side, there is irreligion and wickedness; on the other side, there is religion and goodness. The contrast was not between Christianity and paganism but rather between two ways of being Christians.[7]

Machiavelli finds in the Christian religion those moral and political principles that he admires, and that he yearns to see reborn in the modern world. The principles are not themselves wicked; the wickedness lies in the interpretation that the church has given those principles: "Although the world appears to have become effeminate and heaven disarmed, this derives without doubt more from the cowardice of the men who have interpreted our religion according to idleness and not according to virtue."[8] It is necessary, then, to return to the principles of the Christian religion, not to abandon it in order to revive paganism, nor to invent a new religion from scratch, as other republican political theorists would attempt to do after Machiavelli. Neither a pagan nor the creator of a new religion, Machiavelli seeks and discovers in the Christian tradition a God who teaches us to love the fatherland and liberty. He points to that God as the foundation of a religious and moral reform.

In Machiavelli's view, the religious reform should be a renovatio—that is, a return to the original principles betrayed by bad interpreters and violated by corrupt followers. "If one wishes a sect or a republic to endure, it is necessary to draw it back often toward its beginning," he writes in the first chapter of the third book of *The Discourses*. Those changes "that lead them back toward their beginnings" are beneficial to republics and religions because "all the beginnings of sects, republics, and kingdoms must have some goodness in them, by means of which they may regain their first reputation and their first growth."[9]

As examples of religious renewal, Machiavelli cites Saint Francis and Saint Dominic, who, "through poverty and the model of the life of Christ," revived "in the minds of men" the Christian religion "that was already extinguished there." He adds, though, that both saints' reforms ended up leaving the corruption of the clergy completely unrestrained. This happened not because they preached and practiced a return to the principles of Christ but instead because they taught in their sermons that "it is evil to say evil of evil," and that it is good to obey the prelates. When prelates are in the wrong, one should "let God punish them," with the consequence that "they do the worst they can, for they do not fear the punishment that they do not see and do not believe." Whatever the negative effects of Saint Francis's and Saint Dominic's renewal, the fact remains that if the two preachers had not drawn the Christian religion back toward its beginning, it would have died.

The renovatio that Machiavelli defends and sets forth as a religious and political ideal is a return to virtue—first of all a return to justice and a love of country. He has no interest in issues of dogma. This is the difference between his idea of religious and moral reform and the Protestant Reformation. Machiavelli knew about Luther and the Lutherans, but that reform is not his reform.[10] He is not concerned with indulgences, predestination, grace, free will, or the presence of Christ in the Eucharist. He wants a God who would help the men of his own time, and those of times to come, to rediscover their love of liberty and the inner strength demanded by a free way of life. He is seeking not a new theology but rather a new way of living in the world. For that reason, Machiavelli speaks of a God capable of entering into the hearts of men and giving them the strength to overcome moral corruption. Bad religion has rendered the Italians wicked, capable of doing evil as well as defrauding and oppressing others without shame. Only a good religion could change Italians, even if the cure, given the seriousness of the disease, was almost hopeless.

Just like the political writers associated with humanism, Machiavelli was convinced that a good religion is indispensable for the birth of republics. Although some founders, such as Romulus, did not have to avail themselves of the "authority of God" in order to establish new civil and military orders, many others, "such as Numa Pompilius, Lycurgus, and Solon," resorted "to God" to persuade the people to accept their extraordinary laws. Numa, in particular, "pretended" to "be intimate with a nymph, who counseled him on what he had to counsel the people," and thanks to this pretense he succeeded in persuading the Romans to accept the new laws. Savonarola, similarly, succeeded in persuading the citizens of Florence, who were neither ignorant nor simpleminded, to accept the new republican order of 1494 because he also convinced them that he "spoke with God."[11]

Founders obtain the friendship of God thanks to their remarkable virtue, and with divine aid they accomplish the exceedingly difficult task of founding a state. Lawgivers succeed in the almost equally challenging endeavor of introducing new orderings because they, too, possess extraordinary qualities, like Numa's "goodness and prudence" and Savonarola's "way of life and learning." Thanks to their qualities, they are believed when they claim to be inspired by God. If they possessed similar qualities, other men could also do what Numa and Savonarola did: "No one, therefore, should be terrified that he cannot carry out what has been carried out by others, for men…were born, lived, and died always in one and the same order."[12] The founder who through his virtues succeeds in persuading the people that he is inspired by God, and hence achieves his goals, is for Machiavelli not an ancient myth but rather an actual possibility of modern politics, provided that men, or at least some in their midst, rid themselves of the mistaken belief that imitating the great founders is impossible.

According to Machiavelli, both founders and lawgivers are often sent directly by God, as was the case with Numa. In his narrative, Livy writes that "when the senators heard the name of Numa, although it was clear that the balance of power would incline to the Sabines if a king were chosen among them, yet none of them ventured to prefer to such a man either himself or any other member of his class or any of the senators or of the citizens, unanimously resolved that the kingdom should be conferred on Numa Pompilius." When he reached Rome, Numa determined that the gods should be consulted. But Livy says nothing of divine inspiration.[13] Machiavelli, in contrast, focuses on the divine influence on the senate's decision: "Heaven," he writes, inspired "in the breast of the Roman

Senate" the wise counsel to elect Numa as Romulus's successor "so that those things left behind by him, might be by Numa ordered." Since men who are friends of God, or are inspired or sent by God, give birth to and order states, states have a religious character, prompting reverence and veneration. All states, Machiavelli observes, "have some reverence in their beginning," and the founders of states who succeed in making their people "observe their constitutions for long" obtain "veneration."[14]

Necessary as it is to the founding of republics, religion is also indispensable for maintaining them in good condition. Indeed, customs depend on religion. Even the best political orders established by the wisest lawgivers are incapable of protecting a free life if the customs are corrupt: "As good customs need laws to maintain themselves, so laws need good customs to be observed."[15] Machiavelli also remarks that "hunger and poverty make men industrious, and the laws make them good"—that is, disposed to perform their civic duties. The task of the law is therefore to correct custom: "Where something works well on its own without the law, the law is not necessary; but when good custom is lacking, then the law is necessary at once."[16] Laws "make" men good through fear of human punishment or hope of human reward; religion keeps them good through fear of divine punishment or hope of divine reward. Good customs upheld by religion remain alive even when laws and political orders lose their vigor. Religion is thus stronger than laws and even the virtue of the rulers. For that reason, it is "a thing altogether necessary to maintain a civilization," be it a kingdom or a republic.[17]

When it is not corrupt, the sovereign people of a republic has a special kind of wisdom that makes it godlike: "A people is more prudent, more stable, and of better judgment than a prince. And not without reason may the voice of a people be likened to that of God: for one sees a universal opinion produce marvelous effects in its forecasts; so that it appears that it, by a hidden virtue, foresees its ill and its good."[18] Machiavelli recognizes in the sovereign people of a free republic a divine aura that he never attributes to the prince unless the prince is a redeemer. He also believes that religion is more necessessary in republics than in monarchies. In the former, the people is master of the laws, and as such there is no fear of a prince to restrain men from their natural insolence: "As the observance of the divine cult is the cause of the greatness of the republics, so disdain for it is the cause of their ruin. For where there is no fear of God, one must rely on the fear of a prince which supplies the lack of religion."[19] Such fear, though, would in any case be extinguished on the death of that virtuous prince. By contrast, the fear of God survives independently of the prince. To ensure that a republic endures, it is then wiser to rely on religion than on the fear that a virtuous prince is capable of instilling.

As a consequence, a people lacking good religion can only live under a prince or under a tyrant. And as we shall see, republics need a certain moral content to their religion. Machiavelli, however, believed without a doubt that a free life is impossible without a religious underpinning. All the free peoples of antiquity were profoundly religious. The first was the Roman people; for centuries, "there was never so much fear of God as in that republic."[20] Another such people were the Etruscans, one of the "very free peoples" of antiquity, who lived "for a long time secure, with the highest glory of empire and arms, and with the greatest praise for customs and religion."[21] Yet another were the Samnites, who "had recourse to religion" as a last "remedy from which they could take hope of recovering the lost virtue," thereby proving "how much confidence can be gained through religion well used."[22] Among the moderns, the free cities of Germany stand out as exemplary: "In the province of Germany, this goodness and this religion are still seen to be great among those peoples, which makes many republics live free there, and they observe their laws in such a way that no one from outside or inside dares to attack them."[23]

Peoples without religion are instead corrupt and enslaved. The Italians, who, thanks to the church of Rome, were in Machiavelli's view "without religion and wicked," are the most corrupt and servile of all.[24] The French and Spanish, likewise Catholic, were second in the ranks of the corrupt, according to Machiavelli, but without the religion and goodness of the ancient Romans and modern Germans. They live in servitude inasmuch as they are subjects of kings, and are less corrupt than the Italians not so much because of their goodness, "which in good part has been lacking," but because they have "one king that maintains them united, and not only through his own virtue, but through the orders of those kingdoms, which are not yet spoiled."[25]

Religious peoples can live free; irreligious ones can live only in servitude. In order to fully understand the significance of this alternative, one should keep in mind that Machiavelli refers to a religion that educates people concerning virtue and condemns idleness. The following verses from *L'Asino* effectively summarize his thoughts about how religion makes people free: "To think that, you being lazy, for you God fights, / While you are on your knees and do nothing, / Has ruined many kingdoms and many states. / Prayers are necessary, / And he who forbids the people rites / And devotions is utterly a fool; / for truly it seems that from these derive union and good order, And on good order / good and happy fortune ultimately depends. / But let no one be of so small brain / so as to think that, should his house crumble, / God would soon save it with no man's support; / For he would die under its ruin."[26]

Machiavelli calls for a religion that educates people about a genuine goodness of heart. He explains what he means by *goodness* with two examples drawn from the history of the peoples that he admires for their religiosity and good customs: the Romans and the Germans. The Roman example is an episode from the war against the inhabitants of Veio. The spoils of war, destined to be shared with Apollo, instead fell into the hands of the Roman plebs. In order to recover the booty, the Senate issued an edict ordering all those who had taken the loot to return a tenth of it. This edict proves that the Senate had full faith in the plebs and was certain that nobody would refuse to return what was due. And yet that restitution did not take place, because the plebs rebelled against the edict with "open indignation." The rebellion, coupled with a rejection of the fraud, demonstrates, in Machiavelli's view, "how much goodness and how much religion were in that people, and how much good was to be hoped from it."[27]

The German case is even more eloquent, proving that ancient goodness was still present in these peoples. Such goodness "is so much more to be admired in these times as it is rarer; indeed one sees it remaining only in that province." Machiavelli adds that

> when those republics need to spend some quantity of money for the public account, they are used to having those magistrates or councils that have authority for it assess on all the inhabitants of the city one or two percent of what each has of value. When such a decision has been made, each presents himself before the collectors of such a tribute according to the order of the town; and having first taken an oath to pay the fitting amount, each throws into a chest so designated what according to his conscience it appears to him he should pay: of this payment there is no witness except him who pays.[28]

To perform one's duties in accordance with "conscience," eschew "fraud," and possess a sense of individual responsibility regarding the laws and the common good—this is the goodness that an uncorrupted Christian religion teaches, and that Machiavelli considers necessary to "a free way of life." In order to find such goodness, he does not need go back in time to ancient paganism, or think of reviving it. Those citizens of the free German republics were Christians, not pagans. And yet the civil ethos of religion lived on in them. The same ethos survived, though more feebly, in Machiavelli's own Florence. He laments that ancient goodness has not survived in the principles of the Christian religion: "Such religion [of the Romans]," he writes in a significant passage of the *Discorsi*, "had been maintained by the princes of the Christian republic as was ordered by its giver, [so] the Christian states and republics would be more united, much happier than they are."[29]

On the contrary, Christianity did all it could to destroy not only the pagan religion but even the memory of it: "When a new sect—that is, a new religion—emerges, its first concern is to extinguish the old to give itself reputation; and when it occurs that the orderers of the new sect are of a different language, they easily eliminate it. This thing is known from considering the actions that the Christian sect took against the Gentile: the former has suppressed its orders and its ceremonies, and extinguished every memory of that ancient theology."[30] Along with orders, ceremonies, and theology, it also extinguished—and this is what Machiavelli deplores—the civic virtue that religion kept alive.

To be able to teach men to be good, and thereby effectively aid a civic way of life, religion must keep its distance from political power and not become a slave to the powerful. Machiavelli draws this teaching from the religion of the Romans, too. "The life of the Gentile religion," he observes,

> was founded on the responses of the oracles and on the sect of the diviners and augurs. All their other ceremonies, sacrifices, and rites depended on them; for they easily believed that that god who could predict your future good or your future ill for you could also grant it to you. From these arose the temples, from these the sacrifices, from these the supplications and every other ceremony to venerate them: through these the oracle of Delos, the temple of Jupiter Ammon, and other celebrated oracles that filled the world with admiration and devotion. As these later began to speak in the mode of the powerful, and as that falsity was exposed among peoples, men became incredulous and apt to disturb every good order.[31]

The history of the church confirms the same teaching. In the first centuries of Christianity, the pontiffs had authority and veneration "for the holiness of their lives and for the miracles" as well as "reverence for their customs and their learning."[32] When they became powerful through the weakening of the emperor and barbarian kings in Italy, and above all through their arms, censures, and indulgences, they were "terrible and awesome," but lost their moral authority and the devotion of the people. In subsequent centuries, they also saw their temporal power diminish, and after having rendered the Italians unbelievers and without religion, were reduced "to the discretion of others."[33]

Like others before him, Machiavelli wanted to see the end of the popes' temporal power. Evidence can be found in his account of the unsuccessful conspiracy of Stefano Porcari, who attempted to free Rome from the "hands of the prelates" and restore it "to its ancient way of life." Even though Porcari failed—remember that Machiavelli is commenting on this while writing a work commissioned by Pope Clement VII—his intention is praiseworthy.[34] The desire to punish corrupt popes and prelates also emerges in his narration of Julius II's visit to Perugia. Machiavelli recounts that when Julius reached the city, from which he intended to expel Giovanpagolo Baglioni, he "did not wait to enter that city with his army, which would guard him, but entered it unarmed, notwithstanding that Giovanpagolo was inside with many people that he had gathered for his defense." Although he was a man capable of all sorts of wickedness, Baglioni did not take advantage of the pope's mistake. If he had, Machiavelli observes, everyone would have "admired his spirit," and he would have left "an eternal memory of himself as the first who had demonstrated to the prelates how little is to be esteemed whoever lives and reigns as they do. He would have done a thing whose greatness would have surpassed all infamy and danger that could have proceeded from it."[35]

The state must be able to use religion for the common good, but popes cannot command kings. A private individual, Machiavelli writes in the *Istorie fiorentine*, would have been ashamed to subject himself to the conditions that Pope Alexander III imposed on the king of England.[36] Machiavelli is indifferent to the question of whether the church is run as a republic or as a monarchy. What matters for him is whether the prelates are good, and whether they nourish and sustain religious sentiment, or instead corrupt it with their bad example. In turn, princes and republics must maintain "the foundations of the[ir] religion" and support "all things" that encourage religion, even if they judge it false.[37] Machiavelli does not want a religiosity, reduced merely to the exterior practices of worship, that absolved those who do evil—a religiosity much like that of Timoteo, who is concerned with processions and statues, but is false, greedy, mean, and shameless. Nor does Machiavelli want a religion that inspires admiration for cowardly men, who do not know how "to be honorably evil or perfectly good," and are incapable of performing that noble, great-spirited evil necessary for the success of great political under-takings.[38] What Machiavelli wants, in sum, is a religion made up of faith and the fear of God, instilling sincere devotion, penetrating into the soul, teaching a sense of duty and love for a free way of life, and helping men find the moral strength within themselves to defend that free way of life. He let others worry about the details of the rites, the forms of worship, and the internal organization of the church.

8

⚏

WITHIN THE SOUL

MACHIAVELLI SPEAKS OFTEN about God. In the last chapter of *The Prince*, he writes that Italy "prays God to send her someone who will redeem her."[1] In the *Florentine Histories*, discussing the religious wars that roiled Africa at the time of Arcadius and Honorius, he observes that "living thus among so many persecutions, men bore the terror of their soul written in their eyes, for, besides the infinite evils they endured, a good part of them lacked the possibility of seeking refuge in God, in whom all the miserable are wont to hope. As most of them were uncertain as to which God they should turn to, they died miserably, deprived of all help and all hope."[2] Flavio Biondo (1392–1463), who is in all likelihood his source, mentions religious conflicts only in passing.[3] Machiavelli instead feels the need to write that in times of war and religious conflicts, the unfortunate are denied even the last, scanty consolation of asking God for help, as they do not know to which God they should direct their prayers. Machiavelli himself, on his deathbed, confessed his sins to the friar Andrea Alamanni, cousin of Luigi Alamanni, to whom he had dedicated his *Vita di Castruccio Castracani*. Of Machiavelli, that friar "used to speak a world of good."[4]

In his private letters, Machiavelli speaks of God saving the innocent from the malice of men. On June 26, 1513, a few months after being released from prison, he confides to his nephew Giovanni Vernacci:

> I have received several letters from you, most recently one from last April in which you complain that you have not received any letters from me; I answer that since your departure I have had so many troubles that it is no wonder I have not written to you, and rather it is a miracle that I am alive, for my post was taken from me and I was about to lose my life, which was saved by God and by my innocence; I have had to endure all sorts of other evils, both prison and other

kinds: and yet, by the grace of God, I am well and I manage to live as I can, and so I shall strive to do, until the heavens appear to be more favorable.[5]

Thirteen years later, in his dramatic letter to Guicciardini dated May 17, 1526, Machiavelli calls on God three times in order to persuade Guicciardini (and the pope) to openly wage war against the horde of lansquenets (foot soldiers) that have crossed over the Alps: "This opportunity, for the love of God, shall not be lost"; "see to it now with such measures, for the love of God, that His Holiness does not fall back into these same perils"; "now God has brought things to such a pass that, if this moment is not lost, the pope is in time to take the emperor." He again invokes God, twice, in his last letter to Vettori, dated April 18, 1527: "And, for the love of God, since this treaty cannot be made, break the negotiations off immediately"; "whoever profits from war, as these soldiers do, would be crazy to extol peace. Yet God will make them have more war than we would like."[6] Perhaps they are only customary phrases, or perhaps Machiavelli, in the saddest moments of his life and amid the tragedy of the fatherland, invokes God because he believes God is the last hope of the just.

He rarely speaks of Christ. In letters to his family, he sometimes writes, "May Christ watch over you" or "May Christ watch over you as He should."[7] He opens the *Decennale primo* with a reference to Christ, who came to earth and shed his blood in order to free men from sin: "One thousand and four hundred ninety-four…/ since the time Jesus came to earth for the first time / and, with the blood He shed, extinguished / the diabolical evil sparks."[8] Cesare Borgia deserved his grim end "as a rebel against Christ."[9] Make sure you're good with Jesus "and scoff at the saints," he has Nicomaco say in the *Clizia*.[10] In his more developed political work, the *Discorsi sopra la prima deca di Tito Livio*, Machiavelli straightforwardly acknowledges Christ as the founder of the Christian religion, and insists that had that religion been maintained in keeping with its founder's teachings, Christian republics would have greatly benefited.[11]

The earthly glory that makes men immortal is a human achievement, but it in no way detracts from God. In Machiavelli's view, the "heavens," or God, give men the opportunity to become immortal: "Heaven indeed cannot give man a greater gift than this, nor can it point to him a more glorious path," he writes to de' Medici, exhorting him to restore a transition to a popular government in Florence. He adds that "among other blessings that God has bestowed on your house and the person of your Holiness, this is the greatest: providing it with power and the occasion to make yourself immortal."[12] God loves those men who garner glory on earth, and immortality on earth, when it springs from true glory, opens the door to immortality in the heavens.

Machiavelli scoffs at hell: "After all, the worst that can happen to you is to die and go to hell; and how many others have died! And how many excellent people are in hell! Why should you be ashamed to go there?" he has Ligurio say in *La Mandragola*.[13] Apparently, on his deathbed he even asserted that he wanted to go to hell, where he would be in the good company of the great men of antiquity, rather than to heaven, where he would get bored with the saints and the blessed.[14] Machiavelli makes fun of those who believe in purgatory, indulgences, and masses on behalf of the souls of the dead. Concerning this, the dialogue between a woman and Timoteo in *La Mandragola* is more eloquent than any treatise:

> WOMAN: Now take this florin, and make sure that every Monday,
>   for two months, you will say the requiem mass for the soul of
>   my late husband. Even though he was a terrible man, still, flesh
>   is flesh; I can't help feeling that whenever I remember him. But
>   do you think he is really in Purgatory?
> TIMOTEO: Absolutely![15]

The favorite targets of his scorn are the pious souls who spend hours in prayer, and are constantly bustling off to Mass or church. The virtuous Lucrezia in *La Mandragola*, who "insists on stringing out prayers down on her knees for four hours before she'll get into bed," is portrayed as an idiot.[16] In *Clizia*, Nicomaco mocks his wife, Sofronia, who goes to Mass even during carnival times: "Think what you'll do during Lent!" Even worse than women are old men, Nicia states, who stick "their head" into every church they find and "mumble an 'Our Father'" at every altar.[17] Machiavelli is an even sharper critic of confession and other religious practices. In his *Capitoli per una compagnia di piacere*, he prescribes that "no gentleman or lady of that circle may go to confession except during Holy Week," when "a blind confessor should be chosen, and if hard of hearing, too, all the better." In the same text, as a punishment for anyone breaking the rules of the confraternity, he orders the offender "to attend every single pardoning, religious feast, and all the other church-like things."[18]

Machiavelli has a cyclic vision of history; unlike the Christian conception, his notion does not foresee the final triumph of good over evil.

Rather, he holds that human affairs are linked to the movement of the heavens: "You see the stars above and the sky, you see the moon, / you see the other planets wandering / now high and then low, without any rest." Nations and peoples are subject to alternating cycles of virtue and vice: "Virtue quiets regions down: / and then from quietness, weariness derives, / and weariness soon burns lands and towns. / Then, once a region has been hit / by disorder for some time, virtue is back / to dwell in it. / This is the way Order is told to run / by Him who governs us, so that nothing ever / may remain still beneath the sun. / So it is, and always was, and ever will be, / that evil will follow good; good, evil; / and the one cause of the other will ever be." God gave man free will so as not to strip him of the possibility of achieving glory, but his actions are always under the influence of the heavens: "From here [the heavens] peace and war are born, / from here the hatred between those / who encircle themselves with walls and ditches."[19]

In the *Decennale primo*, a verse account of Italian history from 1494 to 1504, Machiavelli writes: "I shall sing of the struggles of Italy / in the last five years and five, / beneath stars inimical to her prosperity."[20] In the dedicatory letter to Alamanno Salviati, he reiterates that Italy's disasters were caused by the inevitability of fate, whose strength cannot be resisted.[21] The heavens exert either benign or malignant influence over individuals as well. In *L'Asino*, Circe's damsel explains to the story's unfortunate protagonist, who is none other than Machiavelli, that "heaven has not changed its mind / yet, nor will it change till fate / will not abandon its hostile intention against you. / And those humors which have been / so adverse and so inimical to you / they are not, alas, not yet cleansed. / But as soon as their roots will be dried up, / and the heavens will be merciful once again, / times happier than ever will return."[22]

The universe is inhabited by occult spirits, which dwell in the air and help men to foresee future events.[23] Everyone was well aware, Machiavelli remarks, that Savonarola foretold "the coming of King Charles VIII of France into Italy."[24] Machiavelli is keenly interested in astrological and celestial signs. In June 1509, before allowing the Florentine commissioners to enter Pisa to take possession of the city, he consults an astrologer in order to obtain a detailed reading of the stars.[25] In November 1526, when he senses looming tragedy for Italy, he consults a soothsayer in Modena.[26] If he needs special assistance, he isn't picky about the difference between the Christian God and pagan gods:

And if God does not help us with the wind from the south, as He has already done with that from the north, then there are few remedies left to us: for, just as He interfered with the reinforcements from the Germans to this army [the lansquenets who were marching on Rome] with the destruction of Hungary, so he would have to interfere with the reinforcements from Spain with the destruction of the armada; hence we would be in need of Juno to go and pray Aeolus on our behalf, and promise him the countess and every lady Florence has, so that he might push the winds in our favor.[27]

In Machiavelli's cosmos there are the heavens, Fortuna, and God. Every power plays a role of its own, though not a neatly defined one. The heavens govern the cycles of decay and progress, death and rebirth, and corruption and regeneration of all things on earth, especially the "mixed bodies"—that is, the republics and religious sects—and also cause periodic purifications of the nations by means of plagues, famines, and floods. Whereas the heavens govern orderly and necessary movements, Fortuna is the mistress of casual and contingent events.[28] She exerts her immense power over terrestrial affairs in an arbitrary manner, "without mercy, without law, and without reason." Often "she keeps the just beneath her feet, / while raising the wicked, and, if ever she promises you / anything, never does she keep the promise."[29] Fortune is particularly happy when she strikes down good-hearted men, as in the case of Antonio Giacomini Tebalducci, one of the few valorous military commanders who ever served the Florentine Republic.[30]

Fortuna is as ferocious as she is discerning. She clearly distinguishes the good, whom she punishes with servitude, infamy, and sickness, from the wicked, whom she rewards with power, honor, and wealth. Not even the strong and daring can escape her clutches. To triumph against her, men should know how to adapt their conduct to fit the times and order of events: "And truly, anyone wise enough to understand the times and the pattern of events and adapt to them, would always have good fortune or would always keep himself from bad fortune, and it would come to be true that the wise man masters the stars and the fates." Machiavelli adds, however, "since such wise men do not exist, in the first place because men are shortsighted, and in the second place because they are unable to master their own nature, it follows that Fortune is fickle, masters men, and keeps them under her yoke."[31]

When Fortuna wishes to abet great undertakings, she selects a man capable of seizing the chance that she offers him; but when she wishes to bring a nation or republic into ruin, she supports ambitious men, and if there is someone who might be able to hinder her plans, "she either kills him or deprives him of all the faculties of doing any good." Machiavelli concludes that men "can second fortune but not oppose it, and can weave its warp but not break it. They should indeed never give up; for, as they do not know her end and as she proceeds by oblique and unknown ways, they can always hope and, through hope, they should never give up, in whatever situation and in whatever trouble they may find themselves."[32]

Machiavelli acknowledges God as the creator of the universe, but he does not entirely rule out the pagan idea of the eternity of the world.[33] He also hints at an occult power concealed in the heavens.[34] Machiavelli's God, who allows the presence of another, occult force in heaven, with enormous power over events on earth, is different from both the Christian God who governs nature and the human world through divine Providence, and the heterodox God who governs nature and the human world by means of the heavens and Fortuna.[35]

Machiavelli's God seems to compete with the heavens and Fortuna for the honor of influencing world events rather than making use of the heavens and Fortuna. In the *Istorie fiorentine*, for instance, God intervenes in order to help Florence: "But God, who in such emergencies has always had a particular care for her, made an unhoped-for accident arise that gave the king, the pope, and the Venetians something to think about greater than Tuscany." In the same work, Machiavelli attributes a similar intervention in human affairs to the heavens: "He [the duke of Athens] arrived in Florence precisely at the time when the campaign at Lucca was completely lost, as the heavens willed which were preparing things for future evil." In yet another passage, he chooses to cite Fortuna: "And although the nobility had been destroyed, nonetheless fortune did not lack for ways to incite new troubles through new divisions."[36]

And if all this were not enough to persuade us—with the prudence that this kind of research requires—that Machiavelli was hardly an orthodox Christian, we have letters unequivocally revealing that Machiavelli did not care about the salvation of his soul, as any good believer should have done. The first of these letters, written by Guicciardini, governor of Modena, on behalf of the pope, is dated spring 1521. Machiavelli, then over fifty years old, is working with the Minorite friars of Carpi, carrying out the difficult mission of finding a preacher and resolving an issue of jurisdiction over monasteries: "My very dear Machiavelli," writes Guicciardini,

> it was certainly a good decision on the part of our reverend consuls of the Wool Guild to have entrusted you with the duty of selecting a preacher, not otherwise than if the task had been given to

Pacchierotto, while he was still alive, or to Ser Sano [two well-known homosexuals in Florence], to find a beautiful and graceful wife for a friend. I am sure you will serve them according to the expectations they have of you, and as is required by your honor, which would be stained if at this age you started to think about the soul, for, since you have always lived in a contrary belief, it would be attributed rather to senility than to goodness.[37]

According to Guicciardini, who knew him well, Machiavelli had *always* lived in a manner "contrary" to—and not just different from—those who "think about the soul." In view of the manifest absurdity of the very idea, Machiavelli does not ever reply to the insinuation that, surrounded by so many friars, he might be turning into a devout and practicing Christian. What he does respond to instead is his friend's reference to the fact that he was still in the service of the Florentine Republic, however minor the matter at hand: "And since I never failed to help that republic whenever I was able to—if not with deeds, with words, and if not with words, with signs—I have no intention of failing to do so now."[38] His answer represents a double standard: concerning the reference to his soul, he wastes not even a word; concerning the allusion to his fatherland, he replies with grave, almost resentful words.

The second exchange of letters that shows us directly how little Machiavelli cared about his soul and the religious practices required for salvation culminates in his renowned letter of December 10, 1513. In a letter dated November 23, 1513, Vettori had written: "On Sundays I go to Mass, unlike you, who sometimes do not."[39] For men like Vettori, the nourishment provided by Christ's word was vital. We can gather this from the letter that Machiavelli writes Guicciardini from Carpi on May 19, 1921, where he apologizes for having failed in the assignment to find a priest, as requested by Vettori and Filippo Strozzi, two important friends of his, therefore leaving them without that vital nourishment.[40] Now how does Machiavelli respond to Vettori, who had openly reproached him for not going to Mass to obtain the spiritual nourishment of Christ's word? He says that he lives on another food, which, just like Christ's word, has the power to free him from anguish along with the fear of poverty and death:

When evening comes, I return home and enter my study; on the threshold I change, out of those workday clothes, covered with mud and dirt, and put on royal and curial clothes; and, dressed in this dignified way, I enter into the ancient courts of the ancient men, who receive me lovingly, and there I nourish myself on that food that belongs to me alone, and for which I was born; in those courts, I am not ashamed of speaking with those venerable men, and ask them about the reason for their actions; and they, out of their great humanity, respond to me; and for four hours I feel no boredom, forget all troubles, fear not poverty, am not anguished by death: I simply give myself over to them completely.[41]

Vettori, who is "religious," seeks the salvation of his soul in the food that he receives at Mass—that is, the word of Christ.[42] Machiavelli, who is religious in a different sense, finds nourishment for his soul in dialogue, inspired by love of country, with the great men of antiquity who, through their greatness, knew how to defeat death and achieve eternity. That food alone has the power to redeem him, and only by means of that food can he again be himself.

Machiavelli's dialogue with the ancients is not just an intellectual act; it is also an experience of redeeming love: love of country, glory, and beauty. For him love, not the intellect, keeps the soul alive and opens the path to eternity. What Machiavelli describes in this letter is the authentic religious experience of redeeming love. As Ficino explained in his edition of Plato's *Symposium*, love is the desire for immortality ("Amor est immortalitatis desiderium").[43] A lover often "wishes to give himself over to the person he loves," and yearns thereby to "become God."[44] The best men, such as founders of states and legislators, do all that they do "because they love immortality."[45] Out of love of immortality, they turn to great works of creation through wisdom, and of all the forms of wisdom, political wisdom is the highest. The creations of the soul, like the works that Lycurgus bequeathed Sparta and Solon bequeathed Athens, engender greater glory than natural procreation.[46] What "takes us to Heaven is not knowledge of God, but love."[47] Like Ficino's lover, Machiavelli "gives himself over to them" and feeds on the same spiritual food that was theirs. Since he is a "true lover," he is religious, and he writes his political works to teach the young to exert themselves on behalf of the fatherland, in a never-ending effort of moral and political generation and regeneration. He cultivates the idea that the passion that inspired the great founders of states and the great legislators is love of immortality and beauty. He would like to be the creator of political orderings himself, and hopes that there will be men, in his own time as well as in times to come, who feel a passionate desire to establish political orderings admirable for their order and beauty, and capable of surviving through the ages. To overcome the misery of the human condition and attain immortality, Machiavelli needs neither God the creator of the universe nor the God who puts an end to human history and rewards the good with eternal life. Even if the history of the world has no beginning or end, even if it is an eternal alternation between good and evil that does not terminate with the final victory of good over evil, "true lovers" can save themselves by becoming gods.

In a letter to Vettori dated April 16, 1527, Machiavelli seemingly reveals to us a few months before his death that he is a true lover, but also what he loves beyond anything else: "I love my fatherland more than my own soul." This is a conjectural reconstruction, since in the text copied by Giuliano de' Ricci there is an emphatic erasure after "I love my fatherland more." But all of the editors of Machiavelli's letters believe that the blotted-out words were indeed "than my own soul." "To love one's fatherland more than one's soul"—*Amare la patria più dell'anima*—was a common mode of expression in Florence. Machiavelli himself had used the phrase in the *Florentine Histories* in his account of the war between Florence and Pope Gregory XI.[48] But if what de' Ricci actually read was the common and innocuous expression "I love my fatherland more than my own soul," which Machiavelli had used in that historical work, published with the authorization of Pope Clement VII in 1525, why would he have furiously struck out the words "than my own soul"? The fact is that de' Ricci had been working hard to produce a new, "expurgated" edition of the works of his great forebear, which had been placed on the index of prohibited books in 1559. Well aware as he was that the current times were different from those of Clement VII, it is entirely understandable that he censored a phrase that would have caused no scandal a few decades earlier. And yet it is possible that the erased words were such as to make the sentence far more heterodox or scandalous. Giorgio Inglese, who has closely examined the apograph, notes that "with a great deal of effort, one can make out the letters '*st.*' On the basis of this piece of flimsy evidence, in the spirit of conjecture, we might hypothesize that the censored word was 'Christ.' Machiavelli therefore would have actually written the sentence 'I love my fatherland more than Christ.'"[49]

For Machiavelli, the saying "to love my fatherland more than my own soul" had two different meanings. First, it meant placing the good of the fatherland above the practices of religious worship; second, it meant loving a common good (the fatherland) above an individual good (the soul).[50] An example of the first meaning is the praise of the Florentine magistrates known as the "Eight Saints" who administered the war against Pope Gregory XI, serving only the city's liberty: "The war lasted three years and did not end before the death of the pontiff; and it was administered with such virtue and with such satisfaction of all that the Eight had their magistracy extended every year; and they were called Saints even though they had little regard for censures, had despoiled the churches of their goods, and had compelled the clergy to celebrate the offices: to this point did those citizens then esteem their fatherland more than their souls."[51] An example of the second meaning is the praise of Cosimo Rucellai at the beginning of the first book of the *Art of War*. In this context, "the soul" is a reference to the most personal and precious good of any individual: "For I do not know of something that was so much his (not even excepting his own soul) that he would not have willingly spent for his friends; I do not know of any undertaking that would have frightened him, if he had perceived in it the good of his fatherland."[52] Whether one is speaking of the soul in the context of religious worship, or in the sense of an individual's greatest and most personal possession, to place the fatherland above one's own soul, as Machiavelli does, means elevating the fatherland to a principle of faith and redemption. Love of country was the core of Machiavelli's republican religion, and this religion was his life.

9

THE TWILIGHT OF REPUBLICAN RELIGION

WHEN, AT THE END OF THE THIRD decade of the sixteenth century, the Florentine experiment with republican government was on the wane, the conviction that Christian religion and republican principles were tightly interconnected was declining, too. The idea that to serve the republic one must depart from God, or that to save one's soul one must put aside republican ideals, was more and more widely spread. Evidence of this decline can be found in Guicciardini's reflections in *Le cose fiorentine* (1528). Guicciardini reports that the belief that God loves the freedom of peoples is commonly held in Florence, but he cautiously abstains from adopting that opinion as his own.[1] While he censures neither confiding in God nor expressing gratitude to him, he exhorts people to be wise and hope for God's help as a reward for wisdom, rather than as a remedy for recklessness and madness.[2] Guicciardini's harsh criticism, especially noteworthy as it came from a strictly observant Catholic and clear-eyed realist, is directed against the religion of indolence. Nevertheless, whereas Savonarola had repeatedly declared God a friend of the just, Guicciardini stresses that this faith in divine aid—although it can supply hope—has no ground whatsoever.[3] He questions not only the idea that God helps the just but also that he intercedes at all in human affairs with punishments and rewards: God's justice does exist, but men cannot grasp divine verdicts.[4]

In the *Dialogo del reggimento di Firenze*, written in 1521 but languishing unpublished in a desk drawer, Guicciardini questions the fundamental principle of republican religion—that serving the fatherland is the true way of complying with God's will and winning his friendship. He explains that those who truly wish to serve the fatherland must be ready and willing to depart from God and break his commandments, without hoping for his pardon. After mentioning Gino Capponi's warning that rulers must love their fatherland more than their soul—a genuine synthesis of Florentine civil religion—Guicciardini has Bernardo del Nero say that simultaneously living according to Christian conscience and working for the good of the fatherland is impossible:

> How, according to conscience, will one ever be able to wage war from a lust to expand one's territory, thereby committing so many killings, sackings, violations of women, burnings of houses and churches, and an infinite number of other evils? And yet, if someone, for this reason and for this reason alone, stood up in a senate and argued against undertaking some feasible and advantageous enterprise, he would be repudiated by everyone. But let's continue: how, according to conscience, could you accept even a war in order to defend the lands you already possess? ... All states, if one thinks carefully about their origins, are violent; and excepting republics, just inside their own territory and not beyond them, there is no power whatsoever that is legitimate, even less the power of the Emperor, who enjoys such authority that he administers judgment to others; nor do I exempt from this rule the priests, whose violence is double, for they use both temporal and spiritual weapons to keep us under.[5]

One lives either according to the reason of state or else according to the law of God:

> You see the position to which someone who wanted to govern states strictly according to conscience would be reduced. However, when I talked of murdering or keeping the Pisans imprisoned [as the Genoese did after the battle of Meloria], I didn't talk as a Christian, but according to the reason and practice of states; nor would his counsel be more Christian than mine who, after rejecting such cruelty, would recommend making every effort to take Pisa, since this means in effect nothing else than being the cause of infinite evils to occupy something which, according to conscience, doesn't belong to you.... I wanted to say this not to pronounce verdicts on these difficulties, which are immense, since anyone who wants to live in total accordance with God's will had better remove himself totally from the affairs of this world, as it is difficult to live in the world without offending God.[6]

If it is hard to follow the law of God when one is ruling a republic, it is even more difficult to renounce God when one is facing death. When in February 1513 the chief constable informs Capponi and Pietro Pagolo

Boscoli in a short note that they have been sentenced to death for their failed plot against the Medici, who had returned to power in September 1512, Boscoli abandons himself to despair. He asks to receive comfort from someone of great standing and suggests Friar Zanobi Acciaiuoli, a renowned follower of Savonarola. But since the friar was then in Rome, Boscoli says he will content himself with someone else, provided he is "learned and good-hearted." On the other hand, Capponi, a sincere believer, faces death with greater serenity and invites his friend to follow his example, confiding in God's infinite mercy. Luca Della Robbia, too, the sculptor's brother, exhorts Boscoli to seek comfort in divine mercy. To his words the poor sentenced man replies: "Oh, Luca, I have been always ungrateful to God, and have offended Him in all sorts of ways: and yet, yes, I hope for His mercy."[7]

Robbia's account provides us with an illuminating testimony about the separation between republican ideals and Christian faith. Whereas Capponi does not feel the need to renounce his republican beliefs when approaching the fatal moment, Boscoli is tormented by the thought of having offended God by believing in Brutus and the greatness of tyrannicide. He has confidence in God's mercy, but needs someone who "would move his feeling" and prepare him for a full encounter with God. He reveals to his friend Robbia that he is afraid of not being able to approach death in a fully Christian way, for he still feels attracted to the figure of Brutus, the tyrannicide who attempted to free Rome from Caesar's tyranny, just as he himself had tried to free Florence from the Medici: "Please, Luca, get Brutus out of my head, so that I may walk this last step fully as a Christian."[8]

For Boscoli, approaching death as a wholehearted Christian means feeling God inside, being one with him not merely through intellect and faith but rather with all of himself. Religious practices do not suffice for this. When they offer him the *tavoluccia*, a religious image, he refuses it: "I don't need the *tavoluccia*. It will mean that I will be doing very badly, if I won't recognize Him without it." He barely knows the most basic prayers, such as the Hail Mary and the Our Father—further evidence of his previous distance from any practices of religious worship.[9] The classic arguments used for serenely sustaining oneself at the moment of death annoy him. When Fra Cipriano, the prior of the monastery at San Domenico di Fiesole, advances such assertions, he bluntly replies: "Father, don't lose time with this, for philosophers suffice me for it: help me instead so that I die for love of Christ. I would like to approach death intrepid, with so much faith that I'd submerge my senses. I still feel a struggle inside that troubles me more than death itself, as I am resolved to die."[10] His last words are inspired by the purest Christian spirit: "I submit myself to the faith of Jesus Christ, and want to die according to it; and although I have innumerable times offended the divine goodness, *tamen* [nevertheless] I do hope to save myself in Christ's blood, and in nothing else. And since, my Jesus, it is your will that I face this death, I accept it willingly, for my love of you."[11]

A few months later, Robbia meets Cipriano in the Dominican monastery of Prato. The clergyman tells him how Boscoli had saved himself, and indeed had been a martyr, for he was animated by a "good and stout intention." According to the friar, republican ideals would certainly not preclude the salvation of his soul. He explains that in certain cases, tyrannicide itself is permitted: "Saint Thomas makes this distinction: either the peoples have burdened themselves with the tyrant, or they have to stand him by force, against their will. In the first instance, it is not permitted to plot against the tyrant, but in the second it is a merit."[12] We cannot be sure about it, but Cipriano probably said the same things to Boscoli when he heard his confession. In order to die as a Christian, it was not necessary to forget about Brutus, as Boscoli believed. Brutus and Christ could continue to live side by side within the conscience of men who loved republican liberty. The story of Boscoli shows us how the balance between Christian faith and republican principles was shaky, and could tilt so as to favor either the republic or God, but it still had force. Cipriano, a follower of Savonarola, and hence someone who knew much about purgatory and republican liberty, assures us that Boscoli has not undergone the apotheosis that would have elevated him directly to God, like pagan heroes, but he does not have to pass through purgatory either.

In the same prison where Boscoli and Capponi were beheaded, Machiavelli, too, was detained, charged with being involved in the plot against the Medici. He heard the prayers of the comforters who accompanied the sentenced to the gibbet: "What annoyed me most / Was that, as I had fallen asleep, towards dawn, / I heard saying in songs—We are praying for you— / Now, to hell with it! / On condition that your piety turns towards me, / Good Father, and untie these chains." These words are drawn from a sonnet that Machiavelli composed for de' Medici in hopes of being pardoned. They express no pity for the young men sentenced to death, only the determination to show that he is the same man now as he was before imprisonment, as well as the desire to save his life on this earth, which is the only one he is interested in.

The pagan ideal of a glorious death in the name of liberty, with no need of any comfort from God's love, resurfaces in Antonio Brucioli's *Dialogi,* published in Venice in 1526.[13] Brucioli is forced into exile because of his ideas about religion—first in 1529, and again in 1548. In 1555, the Inquisition subjects him to an interrogation; his books are all condemned and then burned, and he is put under house arrest. Brucioli dies on either December 4 or 5, 1566, as noted in the file "in materia heresis" that the Inquisition diligently maintained.[14] Brucioli was a friend and admirer of Machiavelli. He met him during the gatherings in the Orti Oricellari, where the project of a new plot against the Medici took form in 1522. Those involved, besides Brucioli, who fled to France, were Iacopo del Diaccettino, Luigi Alamanni, Zanobi Buondelmonti, Niccolò Martelli, Giovanni Battista della Palla, and Bernardo da Verrazzano. Diaccettino and Alamanni were sentenced to death. With a clear reference to this case, but using false names of course, Brucioli writes the dialogue *Che non è da temere la morte*, focusing on the theme that death is not to be feared. Here, too, as in Robbia's recount, two youths sentenced to death for their love of liberty are comforted by a third person—in this case Filolopo, who is actually not a human being but instead an apparition from the afterlife. God is always present in the dialogue, but the arguments that Filolopo adopts in order to comfort the unfortunate youths are not Christian; they are of explicit classical derivation—namely, Platonic.

While Robbia helps poor Boscoli renounce Brutus and the republican ideals that incited him to tyrannicide, Filolopo reproaches the doomed Eufronio and Leutideno for having forgotten republicanism, and in particular the classical doctrine that death is but a "false fear," a "light thing" to be despised.[15] Eufronio concedes that the classics were right and that death for liberty is to be preferred to the "vileness of the servile condition." Nonetheless, he still feels the fear of death, rendered even more bitter by the consciousness of having failed in the attempt to free Florence from the Medici tyranny. Filolopo then tries to comfort the two by explaining that God does not judge deeds, like their actions, as "good" because of the result but instead based on the intention. The two youths, however, fear the complete disintegration of their beings into nothing, or the fall into an even worse condition. At this point, Filolopo does not resort to the Christian doctrine of the immortality of the soul but rather appeals to Platonic themes. He explains that the body is an "earthly prison," and when freed from the body, one's soul returns to its full originary liberty and thereby resumes its divine condition. The body, too, carries the imprint of divinity, but in an imperfect fashion. The soul's "great thirst" for "seeing God and enjoying the sweet conditions and happiness of the supernal life" originates from just such a state of unhappiness.

Brucioli reaffirms the principles of republican religion in other works. In the dialogue *Della Repubblica*, one of the characters explains that it is difficult to govern cities in the absence of a fear of God, "for many who care little for the laws of man yet fear those of God." If the priests are like those of our own times, "wicked and without any religion, so much the worse become the people." True lawgivers must be lovers of God's wisdom and capable of interpreting the "intimate mind of God," which is the foundation of the rational order of the world. A lawmaker who wishes to establish the best republic must ensure that "everyone piously understands all of God's matters," for "man cannot be good, nor can anything good happen to him, unless he lives with the love and the fear of God." In accordance with Plato's and Aristotle's doctrines, "our religion," says Brucioli, instills in men "great hopes of immortality," and men, because of that hope, achieve great things and are willing to face "the danger of dying for their fatherland."[16] The true greatness of the republic consists not of strong city walls, riches, splendid palaces, and arms but abides rather in the customs of the citizens. Republics are powerful and flourishing only if their citizens are "learned, wise, good, upright, justly educated and pleasing to God for their good actions."[17]

Before approaching its twilight, republican religion flourished in Florence for a short but quite intense season during the three years of the last Florentine Republic (1527–30). Born on the wave of dismay over the sacking of Rome (May 6, 1527), the revivified republic had since its inception faced two obstacles, which finally were fatal to its survival: hostility from the Florentine dignitaries, and, above all, the international context, dominated by the rise of Charles V, a strong supporter of the Medici, who wanted to return to Florence as rulers.[18] In this framework, characterized at once by great hopes for a moral and civil rebirth, and equally great fears of a return to the Medici's regime, the political elite committed itself with zeal to rediscover and reinforce republican religion. On June 25, 1529, the Great Council proclaimed Christ as the king of Florence. It was a tribute to Savonarola's memory, in the hope that the religious sentiment would work the miracle of saving the city from its powerful enemies. A few days later, in the same spirit, the Signoria had some open books placed on the altar of the Sala dei Cinquecento—books on which citizens could affix their signatures to a solemn oath of faith in Christ and in the republican regime.

Preachers inspired by a prophetic spirit, such as Zaccheria da Treviso and especially Benedetto da Foiano, also contributed to shifting hearts toward republican religion. Foiano, who was away from Florence when the Medici were expelled, was called back by the popular government to take over the prior's office in Santa Maria Novella. Venerable and dignified, eloquent and learned, he attracted great masses of people to listen to his sermons, and exerted considerable influence on political deliberations as well. During the siege, he spoke in the hall of the Great Council, which was exceedingly crowded. The historian Benedetto Varchi recounts that the master declared,

> by reference to passages of the scripture, both in the Old and in the New Testament, when, how, and by whom the city of Florence could survive so many misfortunes, and then enjoy forever, together with her most desired liberty, endless happiness; and he said this with such grace and such eloquence that he made all the listeners cry and rejoice, from moment to moment, according to his rhetorical intention. As anyone had been allowed to enter the hall, the listeners were an incredible number. In the end, with indescribable gestures and words, saying *cum hoc et in hoc vinces* [with this and under this you win] he gave the Gonfalonier a standard, one side of which depicted a victorious Christ with soldiers lying on the ground, and the other a red cross, ensign of the Commune of Florence.[19]

The faith that God would protect the reborn Florentine liberty from internal and external enemies inspired many of the citizens who participated in the public debates. Those who were not allowed to go to the Palazzo Vecchio, women and children in particular, prayed in churches while men were fighting. On November 2, 1529, the Signoria solemnly issued a decree that alone suffices to enable us to understand the character of the civil religion of the last republic:

> Considering how in every human action we should always and principally seek divine aid, and hoping that the arms of the militia, when accompanied by prayers and divine help, will always achieve victory and every good result, we do therefore proclaim and notify all persons not adapted and fitted for arms, such as priests, friars, monks, nuns, children and women of whatever age, that every time our soldiers go to battle with the enemy, this sign shall be made from the Palazzo, viz. the sounding of the Ave Maria by the great bell of the Palazzo,…all the above-mentioned persons not adapted or fitted for arms shall be held and obliged to kneel, both in churches and in convents and in their houses, and to make continual oration while the battle aforementioned shall continue, and to pray the Omnipotent

God to give strength and courage to the arms of the Florentine soldiers and militia, and to give them victory against the enemies of the city of Florence, hoping that through the infinity of the mercies of Our Lord Jesus Christ, King of our city, and through the intercessions of His most holy mother, our aforementioned city shall obtain the abovenamed grace.[20]

Equally eloquent is the law of June 2, 1529, meant to promote peace, moral reform, and the unity of the city. The text opens with a preface that solemnly declares that the magnificent and excellent dignitaries of Florence intensely wish to confirm and reinforce the current free and popular government, conscious of the truth contained in the sacred scriptures, which affirm that the efforts and the diligence of the men who govern and guard the city are completely useless, unless the city is protected and defended by the divine goodness with its divine compassion. This law proclaims that the exceedingly precious gift of liberty which God has given the devout Florentines, can be defended only if the city is firmly established and founded on the square and irremovable stone of Jesus Christ, and if the whole Florentine people are forever and in the most special way subordinate to Christ, king and lord of all things, who, together with the Virgin Mary, has been elected lord of Florence.[21]

The Florentines promised to observe the Christian religion as well as preserve the present popular government and "most holy liberty" with utmost diligence, as the most special gifts from the Divine Majesty. In order to put into effect what had been established by the law, the Signoria decreed that a crown of thorns would be affixed to the Palazzo della Signoria's door, as a symbol expressing the Florentine people's will to be subject only to Christ, and to serve only the "true and immortal king." Finally, to compel the Florentines to love Christ, the Signoria took strict measures against those who would curse or offend God in any way, as well as any who committed homicide. It also asserted that since Christ was the king of Florence, he who rebelled against the popular government would be betraying not just man but also God, and for this he would incur punishment both before the magistrates of the popular government and at the final judgment.

The Signoria then summoned the Great Council to take a solemn oath. All the citizens, starting with the gonfaloniers (high ranking officials), were to take an oath too, as a sign of loyalty to the "sacred foundations of this just, political, and popular government on the firm and irremovable rock of Jesus Christ." Nobody could become a member of the Great

Council without first taking this oath. In order to reinforce republican religion, the Signoria also decreed every November 9, "the day on which God the Almighty restored the welfare of this republic" (it was the day on which the Medici had been expelled from the city, in 1494), a solemn holiday. May 16, the founding date of the popular government in 1527, when "our immortal king was pleased to restore Christian religion and free us from the exceedingly hard yoke of tyranny," was to be celebrated in perpetuity with solemn festivities, including a parade by the Florentine army. A century earlier than England, Florence, too, had its own revolution of the saints—republicanism sustained by a profound religious spirit drawing inspiration from the ideals of authentic Christianity, but at the same time sustained by the force of the state.[22]

The strongest expressions of republican religion emerged in public ceremonies and especially speeches before the army. An eloquent example is the oration that Francesco Carducci delivered in 1529 when he assumed the office of gonfalonier. Carducci insisted on the concept that God loves liberty, and the corresponding duty of men to work with all their means to defend it: "It was God's work that tyranny was expelled from this city, in contrast with the wishes of many, and it will be God's work to keep tyranny away, despite the will of more than a few: but we cannot conclude from this that we may or should feel that we are secure and can do nothing." At the oration's conclusion, he masterfully links the ideas that God loves those who do good deeds on behalf of the fatherland more than he loves other men, and that man, by working on behalf of the fatherland, becomes godlike, thereby winning perpetual glory on earth and eternal beatitude in the heavens:

> I cannot think of anything that is more welcome to God nor more desirable to men than to work in such a way that those who write histories will have our names placed in their books, and the things that we have done, either through prudence or valor, celebrated in bright and perpetual inks; for this is nothing other than avoiding death and preserving oneself alive for a long age; indeed, nothing other than never dying at all, and eternally living in glory. What the Gentile philosophers and theologians wrote is therefore not completely wrong, nor actually far from our own most true and most holy religion: that after death the souls of those who have administered republics well and loyally live a sempiternal and blessed life, separate from all the others, in the highest and brightest region of Heaven. For no praise is greater or finer among mortal beings, nor

can any praise make men more godlike, than to do good to the other men, and be the cause of the liberty and safety of their republics.[23]

The most eloquent document of republican religion at the time of the last Florentine Republic, however, is the speech that Piero Vettori delivered to the army on February 5, 1529. He begins his talk by stating that the army was created "by divine instinct," and that, if allowed to grow, it will ensure the fatherland "eternal fame and secure rest." If the army, sent by the "Almighty God," had not aided Florence, the city's demise would have been unavoidable. Solemn prayer should therefore be directed to God:

O glorious and supreme God, you who have always particularly cared about this city of yours, one can clearly see that you do not want to destroy this poor people, as you have reignited in these valiant soldiers' hearts that ancient virtue which for long had been hidden and buried. This is a sign that the ancient valor that cured this beloved country of yours from its own mortal wounds and freed it from the shameful sores of servitude could rise again; for you have generated such frank souls and such resolute hearts in this beautiful youth that they throw themselves in any danger in order to save our sweet liberty and unleash a just wrath against the enemies. I certainly do not see adequate rewards that can be found for such merits, but the most beautiful will be given them from God the Almighty and their own virtue, nor will this fatherland fail to recognize them with great benefit, a fatherland that never ever forgot any merit or service she received.

Precisely because serving in the army is a religious duty, citizens "would gravely offend the Almighty God" by using arms to "oppress the good and serve their own personal hatreds and interests." Mindful that perjurers inescapably face just punishment, all citizens who serve in the army thus must solemnly take an oath before God, and mindful that no cause is more just nor more saintly than defending sweet liberty and the blessed life of the citizens, the soldiers can serenely trust in victory, as "Jesus Christ of the armies" will be their infallible guide. Furthermore, when facing danger, they will be comforted by the thought that those who die for the fatherland have awaiting them in heaven "a seat among the blessed spirits where they will then enjoy eternally the face of their Redeemer."[24]

Another significant instance of republican religiosity is the speech that Bartolomeo Cavalcanti delivered to the reconstituted Florentine militia on February 3, 1530. He first of all insists on the importance of religion for armies.[25] He then repeats a typical theme of republican Christianity when he emphasizes that the people must have religion if they are to count on Christ's help:

> Your King [Christ] desires nothing more from you than that your souls be inflamed with his love, and joined together and bound by the most holy bond and the indissoluble knot of charity. O Florentine people, this religion is such that, if it will reign among you, you not only will be always defended by him [Christ]—as his devoted and faithful servant—as well as freed from your enemies, but you also will be exalted victorious and triumphant above all other peoples: otherwise let none of us confide in our own virtue and hope to achieve anything successfully; because our works will turn out wrong, if we are devoid of the light of divine religion, which guides us along the right path; the daring will be reckless, if it depends on confidence not of divine help but of our own valor; the forces will be weak if they are not supported by the immense power of our King; and ultimately any hope will be vain unless based on him who governs the universe.[26]

In another oration, Cavalcanti maintains that liberty is a gift from God—another fundamental concept of republican religiosity:

> On that day, 16 May 1527, the tyranny of the Medici left, and not because they were expelled, but out of the great fear that God instilled in them in order to fulfill the prophecy uttered through the prophet Friar Girolamo, which stated: "The next time that you regain your liberty, you will regain it from God, and not through your own industry and strength, lest the citizens grow proud in the glory of that liberty, as they did the first time, in the year 1494, when they were unwilling to recognize it as a gift from God, as it was; and they therefore lost it."[27]

Orations, fasting, and processions were of no avail to save the republic from the imperial forces that attacked, and then demanded surrender, on August 12, 1530. Guicciardini wrote that Florence's resistance to the imperial army demonstrated the strength of faith, not because of its specific precepts, but rather because those who have faith become stubborn and are not afraid to undertake the most desperate enterprises. Although Guicciardini thought that the Florentines, who were determined to resist until the end in order to defend their liberty, were crazy, since he would never have advised adopting such conduct, his words express respect for the republican religion that sustained his fellow citizens.[28] He showed respect for people who were defeated because they ignored the rule that destiny guides those who submit to it and destroys those who contest it. Cecil Roth's *L'ultima repubblica fiorentina*, published in 1927, concludes by emphasizing that such lunatics deserve the most sincere admiration. Might this have been meant as an exhortation to the Italians of his own day to defend their liberty in a spirit similar to that of the Florentines of the Cinquecento, instead of fearfully and "reasonably" standing by as fascism assailed it?

As the republican experiment came to an end, the criticisms of republican Christianity inspired by Savonarola became increasingly harsher. An instance is the dialogue between Francesco Capponi and Piero Vettori that Luigi Guicciardini, Francesco's brother, composed in 1530. In this dialogue, Capponi reiterates the traditional components of republican Christianity—first of all the conviction that in the presence of extreme danger, Florence will not be left without divine aid, because its liberty is "welcome to the one and Almighty GOD." He then goes on to stress that in order to defend liberty, one must "put up happily with any harm, and anyone who believes otherwise, can be neither a good citizen, nor a true Christian." Vettori drily replies that concerning events proceeding from "the will of the Almighty GOD, we have no way of knowing whether they will occur or not." Experience shows that hopes of divine aid have frequently been disappointed. Vettori adds that true liberty deserves to be defended, but the liberty proclaimed by the republican government established in 1527 was only a simulacrum concealing a tyrannical power.[29]

Traces of the persistence of civil religion are also present in other republican cities. In the incomplete and virtually unknown text titled *Trattati nove della prudenza*, probably written between 1530 and 1540 by the Siennese nobleman Bartolomeo Carli Piccolomini, a follower of the ideas of the reformer Juan de Valdés, we can clearly see the idea of religion as perfection and human greatness as well as the foundation of the true civil way of life. Like other Italian intellectuals, Piccolomini experienced the religious reformation above all as a demand for moral rebirth. He calls for a religion that does not encourage resignation and idleness, relying on God for help, but rather exhorts its followers to operate wisely and with strength of spirit. In this connection, he quotes a passage from Sallust: "Neither by vows nor by women's entreaties is the help of the gods secured, but through watchfulness, action, and good counsel do all things occur propitiously. Inasmuch as you abandon yourself to laziness and baseness, you call on the gods in vain, as they will be offended and hostile."[30]

In addition to laws, "fear of God" is needed in order to sustain the goodness and unity of a republic. For this reason, if they want to maintain good customs and civil peace, princes must respect the cult of the divine and preserve religious ceremonies uncorrupted, even at the cost of feigning a devotion that they do not feel.[31] Through religion, the ancients achieved great things that would otherwise "not have been possible." Those men considered worthy of speaking with the deity were themselves divine, like Scipio Africanus, "who was considered to be such divinity that he could speak to god." But if men, or at least certain men, have divinity within themselves, then religion becomes synonymous with moral virtue, as Piccolomini explains: "Under this heading [of religion] I mean a virtue of the soul that consists of the fear of god, in a perfect conscience and in an effort to preserve the honor of religion." If these elements are found in a prudent man, they will afford him reverence from all, because good men will love him, while wicked men will hesitate to offend him in order not to be considered enemies of religion.[32]

The notion that the Christian religion teaches civic virtue was also present in the context of the Genoese aristocracy during the first half of the sixteenth century, as shown in Ludovico Spinola's *De reipublicae institutione*, written between 1528 and 1530 to praise the ruling republican oligarchy, which claimed to represent the entire civic community.[33] Despite its apologetic intentions, the work argues for a civil philosophy founded on the principle that a true Christian and human life is one spent in the service of the fatherland and the common good. Political action on behalf of the republic's good is "man's way of saying yes to the divine plan." The *civis genuensis* must act to defend the free republic as an actualization of God's plan.[34] Since God loves those who serve the republic, the citizens who aid and preserve it will, after death, ascend to a seat in heaven where they will enjoy eternal beatitude.[35] From this interpretation of the civil content of the Christian religion, Spinola derives not only an admonition to preserve and uphold religious worship but also an exhortation to a full-fledged moral reform based on the principles of charity and justice as a response to divine love.[36] Spinola harmonizes the municipal religiosity based on the idea of a God who protects and loves the republic of Genoa with an Erasmian religiosity based on the idea of a Christ "who is nothing other than charity, simplicity, and patience."[37]

The same harmony between civic spirit and Christian authenticity emerges in the meditations of Agostino Giustiniani, the Dominican bishop of Nebio in Corsica who lived in Paris for many years and traveled extensively to visit the learned men of Europe, such as Desiderius

Erasmus in Flanders and Thomas More in England. Giustiniani claims that he has always been faithful to a sober ideal of piety and averse to superstition. He reiterates that loving one's fatherland and serving the republic are entirely consistent with a Christian way of life.[38] In the "Epistola al Duce, al Senato, e a tutto il popolo di Genova" that begins his *Annali della Repubblica di Genova* (1537), he writes that "if those who examine and frequently reread holy texts are religious, then what could be more religious and divine than to have given instruction—as those very books do—to educate our people to be lovers of the republic, so that they attempt not only to maintain it in existence and true unity, but also to increase it in power and glory?" "God commands" that people set aside a disorderly love of their own private good and instead dedicate themselves to caring for the public good.[39]

In sixteenth-century Venice, republican religion was torn between the ferments of Catholic reform and heretical movements.[40] At the beginning of the seventeenth century, one can still find texts supporting a religious and moral reform in keeping with political liberty and a true religious spirit.[41] For the Brescian friar Fulgenzio Micanzio, a disciple and friend of Paolo Sarpi, the great historian of the Council of Trent, political power requires the support of religion, because over the centuries religion has proven to have the power to influence people's minds and passions.[42] From this principle Micanzio derives a harsh critique of the church for having attempted to subjugate temporal power to spiritual power, and for having "formed a religion no longer indifferent to all states, but shaped to one's own state and for that state's furtherance."[43]

Micanzio contrasts a religion that claims to subjugate secular power, and those princes who allow religion to be corrupted out of self-interest or ignorance, with an interpretation of religion that harmonizes the Christian and classical ideals, and teaches us how to translate the lesson of Christian piety into political engagement in service of the common good. "But man," he writes,

> was born not just for himself, but principally for the fatherland and for the common good. Let the question as to whether or not a wise man should become involved in governance be left to others. Our father [Sarpi] will give us the example of turning away from neither labor nor danger in the service of God and the fatherland; and that an upright and wise man is far from the mistaken doctrine invented by a mob of seditious deceivers who never speak of the secular power except as a bad thing, even though it is an institution established by

God in which an upright man can well serve his divine Majesty with so pious and excellent a vocation that either has no equal, or certainly is not outdone, as in homage to the greatest piety, which can be exercised in the Church, and to which God has summoned from time to time the greatest heroes of the entire ecclesiastical order.[44]

Further proof of republican religion's survival in Italy in the first half of the sixteenth century is the plot that Francesco Burlamacchi, an eminent citizen of Lucca, tried to hatch in order to free Tuscany from the Medici's dominion and unite it in a federation of free cities following the ancient Etruscan model. When, during the night spanning August 26 and 27, 1546, the conspiracy was detected and Burlamacchi was brought before the elders, the highest magistracy of the republic of Lucca, he stated:

Having read many books of history, and considered that, when a country is united in concord, in that country one lives both securely and happily, and having also read that Tuscany was in remote times united precisely in such a union as the one I intended to bring about, it seemed to me that, if it had been possible, it would have been something that would greatly benefit the city and consequently the whole of Tuscany. And so I began to like thinking about it, and as I liked thinking about it, I began to consider whether there was a way to do it.[45]

Alongside the unification of Tuscany through a league of free cities, Burlamacchi was intent on religious and moral reform. On September 3, 1546, he confessed that, if he had succeeded in the task of uniting Tuscany, he would have then gone to the emperor, or would have sent him a letter, "to ask him to come here, so that he could have the Church's many misuses reformed, and its many different strands reduced to unity."[46] His action plan, therefore, was inspired by the two ideals that had characterized republican religion ever since its inception in the thirteenth century: love of republican liberty, and religious and moral reform. These were the last gleams of a religion on the wane, however. Another religion had started to take root in Italy—that of the Counter-Reformation. It taught people not to serve liberty as a Christian duty but rather to accept servitude with Christian resignation.

PART II

Religious Rebirth and National Emancipation

10

WITHOUT GOD

THE PUBLICATION, in 1762, of Rousseau's *Du Contrat Social* opened a new chapter in the history of republican religion. Like Machiavelli, Rousseau was well aware that republics need religion to come to life and endure.[1] Rousseau notes that great lawgivers had to place the rules of civil life in God's mouth in order to "entraîner par l'autorité divine ceux que ne pourroit ébranler la prudence humaine." He also stresses that only men with great souls can persuade people that they have been inspired by God and hence can establish enduring laws. At the same time, he charges the Christian religion with inculcating in its followers a servile mentality: "Loin d'attacher les coeurs des Citoyens à l'Etat [so far from binding the hearts of the citizens to the State]," the Christian religion "les en détache comme de toutes les choses de la terre: je ne connois rien de plus contraire à l'esprit social." His invective concludes with a condemnation that admits of no appeal: "Le Christianisme ne prêche que servitude et dépendance. Son esprit est trop favorable à la tirannie pour qu'elle n'en profite pas toujours. Le vrais Chrétiens son faits pour être esclaves; ils le savent et ne s'en émeuvent gueres; cette courte vie a trop peu de prix à leurs yeux." Inasmuch as both past and present religions are ill suited for founding a civil morality, Rousseau recommends a new religion, to be instituted and preserved through the force of laws, founded not on dogmas but rather on "sentiments de sociabilité, sans lesquels il est impossibile d'être bon Citoyen ni sujet fidelle [sentiments of sociability without which it is impossible to be either a good citizen or a loyal subject]."[2]

Rousseau's ideas on civil religion had considerable impact not only in France but also in Italy during the "Jacobin years" (1796–99), when, in the shadow of French armies, republican governments were formed. Everywhere, with greater or lesser conviction, the patriots tried to corroborate the new political institutions with a republican religion. The Florentine Girolamo Bocalosi, an active supporter of revolutionary ideas, supplies one of many possible examples with his *Dell'educazione democratica da darsi al popolo italiano* (1797). The book, following in Rousseau's footsteps, theorizes a full-fledged religious revolution: not just a new interpretation of the Christian religion, but rather an entirely new religion, intended to completely destroy the principles, language, and rites of Christianity. Insofar as the Christian religion was incapable of shaping republicans as well as regenerating and reconstituting a people, it was necessary to elaborate new principles capable of educating good citizens. For a radical political revolution, there should be an equally radical religious and moral revolution.[3]

Another Jacobin, Enrico Michele L'Aurora, offered an even more detailed treatment of the project of a religious revolution, which should, in his view, envisage a new theology of a supreme being and new forms of worship. In appeals published under the title *All'Italia nelle tenebre l'aurora porta la luce* (1796), L'Aurora denounces "the wickedness and ignorance of the ecclesiastics," who were guilty of having deceived people for centuries with countless falsehoods and also of preaching resignation. In contrast to the temporal power and corruption of the church, L'Aurora exalted the figure of Christ.[4] From his praise of Christ, L'Aurora did not derive the idea of a reformation that might draw religious practice back to its first principles, but instead the dream of a rational religion founded on the idea that God is the supreme being, both good in the highest degree and the creator of heaven and earth. The calendar was to be divided into ten-day units. A specific holiday with its specific temple would correspond to each day: the first day would be dedicated to justice, the second to peace, the third to charity, the fourth to virtue, the fifth to liberty, the sixth to equality, the seventh to unity, the eighth to truth, the ninth to love of country, and the tenth to the supreme God. To help the believers of all religions identify with the new God, the altars would display no images—just a painting of a cloud emitting thousands of rays of light. There were to be no priests (existing priests younger than fifty were to throw their robes away and become citizens; those older were to go to convents erected for this purpose), and obviously no pope (he was to be sent to Sardinia with all the cardinals, or, should he foment rebellions, to China).[5] L'Aurora believed that such a religion would replace the old one, educating people about peace, toleration, and a respect for republican values.

The Salernitan Matteo Galdi (1765–1821), enlisted in Italy's army where he became captain, expressed similar thoughts. A friend of the great conspirator Filippo Buonarroti, Galdi received honors in the Cisalpine Republic, and then under Joachim Murat, in Naples, where he died in 1821. Like the other Italian Jacobins, Galdi builds his argument on the consideration that Christianity cannot be reformed:

> However pure and innocent this cult may have been in its beginnings, it is now too corrupt to be drawn back to its proper boundaries; too many factions and religious wars would be ignited between the reformed and the reformers; too insolent, avaricious, and ignorant are its ministers to be able to be summoned back to the right way. Christianity, ultimately, as a human practice, is too deeply flawed; it has caused too much bloodshed, encouraged too many wars and civil strives; it has been too closely attached to despotism, ignorance, and error; and therefore it always was and ever will be the same—an enemy of truth and the republic.[6]

From this observation, Galdi concludes that it is necessary to establish a completely new religion, which he calls *teofilantropismo* (theophilanthropism), founded on the principle of the love of God and our neighbors. The only way to destroy superstition and end Christianity's political influence is by means of such a theophilanthropic system. Begotten by the republican revolution, the new religion was the only one consistent with the progress of the human spirit and capable of rendering the republic universal.[7]

Vincenzio Russo (1770–99), a man of great moral and civil merits as well as a martyr of the Neapolitan Republic, supported a civil ethics without religion. He theorized about the possibility of uprooting superstition through the action of a censor, who would demonstrate to the people, with unequivocal facts and luminous words, that a morality different from that produced by theology was possible. He was even convinced that people would love the new morality as soon as they perceived it as being truer and more in keeping with human faculties than the old religious one. The only religion that should exist in the republic was a civil one. Russo explains that he has nothing against those who, in good faith, adore "a God of peace"—that is, a God who teaches people to love their neighbor. He also concedes that religion can have great political effectiveness and stimulate men to act in ways that are beneficial to civil life. He forcefully emphasizes, however, that good social institutions can obtain the same results with less danger by setting religion aside—indeed, by trying to extinguish religion and replace it with a rational ethics.[8]

Giovanni Antonio Ranza (1741–1801), founder of the republic of Alba (April 1796), was a proponent of religious reform as an indispensable condition for republican liberty. In his appeal "Per la Lombardia repubblicana," he spoke explicitly of the need for a "religious reform" that would correspond "to the simplicity and dignity of the democratic government." Such a reform should consist of a return to the equality and apostolic democratic liberty of the earliest centuries of the Christian church, and set itself the task of "reforming abuses, uprooting errors, banishing superstition, and preserving only truly Catholic and apostolic dogmas." It should also replace casuistic morality with evangelical morality; the ridiculous mess of ceremonies, multiplied endlessly over the course of sixteen centuries, with primitive simplicity; the Latin language of the liturgy, incomprehensible to the people, with the Italian vernacular; and luxury and pomp with the modest propriety "of the democratic Christians of the good old days, when the ministers of the sanctuary, married with hearts of gold and pure hands, sacrificed with clay vases and woolen garments; and the people, in unison with their sacred ministers in the social virtues, were the object of the admiration and envy of the sternest philosophers of Gentilism!"[9]

Gaetano Filangieri (1752–88), a proponent of Enlightenment ideas, also theorized about the necessity of a civil religion, following Rousseau's path. In Filangieri's view, religious experience is not a superstitious fraud but instead a powerful force for social unification and response to the demands of the multitudes. Religion is a powerful political force because it is "so inherent in the nature of man, so necessary to the formation, perfection, and preservation of society, and so terrible in its degeneration." Filangieri distinguishes the realm of religion from that of politics. The former belongs to the internal forum—that is, individuals' inner convictions; the latter belongs to the external forum—that is, actions. From these premises, Filangieri derives the idea of a civil religion proceeding from the lodges of the Freemasons to the elites and populace at large. Such civil religion should fight against fanaticism and irreligiosity, and put an end, through legislative measures, to the privileges enjoyed by the clergy as well as the existence of a church separate from the civil power and hostile to it.[10] In contrast with the Jacobins, who supported religious reform, Filangieri theorized about a gradual transition from the old superstitious religion to the new civil one. In his project, too, reform would not be a return to the original principles of the Christian faith but rather the construction of a new theological and moral edifice. Once civil power discredited the old religion and its superstition, it could introduce new rites and new ceremonies "controlled by the concealed hand of the legislator," and could finally declare the new religion of the state and government.[11]

During the same years, alongside more or less fanciful proposals for a republican religion, a wealth of sermons and appeals flourished, all meant to explain that Christian religion is a friend of democracy. These texts elaborate on commonplaces, adorned to a greater or lesser degree with historical arguments and biblical references, but nearly always cold, as if they had been written—and indeed this was often the case—by the order or solicitation of either the French authorities or patriots who governed the republics born under the French armies. They lacked, in short, the sort of warmth that derives from a full inner conviction and is an essential quality of religious preaching. An example is the leaflet *La Religion cattolica amica della democrazia: Instruzione d'un teologo al clero e al popolo romano*, printed in Perugia in 1798, whose author seeks to instruct the multitude about the perfect agreement between religion (summoned back to its pure principles) and democratic government (rightly represented). Since religion and politics share the principle of divine order, they must support each other and be loyal to republican institutions.[12]

The advocates of despotism maintain that monarchy is the form of government more in keeping with Christian religion. Yet on the basis of the sacred texts, democracy is the form of government more consistent with Christianity. The democratic government is a state in which the people freely elect their magistrates, determine their own laws, and choose their presidents and ministers. In sum, it is a form of regime where the government depends on the absolute will of the nation. Christian religion precisely supports and elevates the fundamental republican principle of liberty.[13] In fact, Christ taught liberty in its truest sense: liberty of the spirit as well as liberty from bad laws and bad customs. He also taught people to love virtue, which is, together with liberty, the basis on which republican government rests. Terror, force, and violence, along with a vile and shameful licentiousness, all support despotism. Virtue alone creates and preserves democracy. Religion, moreover, recommends a respect for laws, and wherever the customs of the people are informed by the majestic and divine morality of the Gospel, there will certainly be a happy democracy. Finally, the perfect concord of principles between religion and democracy can be seen as far as equality is concerned—the third basis of a popular government:

> Such civil natural equality of men consists of being all equal before the law: that is to say, the laws indiscriminately apply to each and every person, and regulate the conduct of the rich just like the poor, the magistrates just like the people: all have since the beginning an equal right to magistracy, to the public, civil, and military functions, merit

alone discerning among candidates and deciding about who shall be chosen; the government does not recognize persons who are privileged by birth or fortunes; all are, to put [it] in one word, at once people and citizen, everyone enjoying an equal right in elections and in assemblies, save always the respect due to the established authorities.[14]

For the author of this pamphlet, no one was more democratic than Christ. He condemned the haughty aristocracy of the Pharisees, avoided royal halls, never sought the favor of princes, and, "superior to the scorn, the malignant mockeries, and the calumnies of the aristocracy," led a wholly popular life. His fellows, table companions, and followers were from the vilest strata of the populace and represented the roughest people. To offer an example of unparalleled humility, Christ kept himself at the margins, even though he knew of the people's desire to declare him their sovereign. He showed his followers that popularity "shall not aim to win the favorable attitude of the greatest number of people, but only sincere charity and fraternal love." Christ banished from his own vocabulary any pompous titles as well as any symbols of imperious despotism. With his disciples, he used only the name of friend, "a sign of the dearest equality." The leaflet concludes that the great protagonists of the age should not disdain "imitating the majestic humility of the Man-God, fraternizing cordially with the people and declaring one's friends those whom perhaps they previously considered of quite another stock, but who, too, are the first benefactors and the firmest basis of society." Christian priests must "impress in the soul of the citizens the simple truth of Gospel's morality, showing them how perfectly in keeping the principles of such morality are with respect to a republican government."[15]

Riccardo Bartoli (1747–1806), a Catholic priest, embarked with particular enthusiasm on the work of preaching republican religion. "Give me a people religious in this manner," he writes in *I Diritti dell'uomo: Catechismo Cattolico-democratico del cittadino*, "and I will give you back a population of excellent citizens, for, as I will show to you when we treat of the duties of man in society, there can be no true virtue without Religion."[16] Bartoli insists with particular eloquence on the idea of Christ as a perfect democrat, and he, too, proposes an interpretation of Christianity as a religion that can instill virtue. Charitable toward the humble and the suffering, Christ was uncompromising with the arrogant and the corrupt:

> Easy to prove is his [Christ's] inflexibility in resisting, correcting, and
> discrediting the insolence, haughtiness, shrewdness, and detestable

deceit of the Pharisees, the scribes, the pseudo-pontiffs, and all the other proscribed race of the chiefs of the Sanhedrin and the synagogue, who were the most domineering and overbearing aristocrats of those days. They always kept apart from the people, conferred on themselves a grand air of dominion, and thought they would have vilified themselves, had they mingled with the people.[17]

In the pamphlet *La libertà e la legge considerate nella libertà delle opinioni e nella tolleranza de' culti religiosi* (Genoa, 1798), Vincenzo Palmieri insists with equal strength on the inseparability of virtue and religion:

Religion! Majestic virtue, which, starting from the inalterable foundation of every morality, and from the eternal rule of the honest and the just—which is God—fixes in men the true idea of every virtue, and renders it more sublime and more noble to the extent that more sublime and more noble is the principle from which it starts. Religion! Majestic virtue, which, speaking that noble language which is so worthy of man—and of God—does not compel, but rather invites, entices, allures: religion that does not spur violent, boastful and excessive actions, but teaches sweetness, charity, benevolence, voluntary subjection to the laws; and not for the fear typical of slaves, but for the sweet pliability of a reasonable and free soul; religion simply forbids acting through violence, and promises pure and sublime contentments, and the peace of the heart. I wonder if this Religion might be proposed, adopted, established as the foundation and wall of defense for the virtues that are so necessary to the State.[18]

Homilies and sermons in churches also contributed to the construction of a republican religion. Preachers could reach a broad audience, and profited most richly from the consummate mastery of religious eloquence. As for the contents, some homilies just reiterated ideas and arguments similar to those used by preachers of the fourteenth and fifteenth centuries in order to reinforce the civil religion of the ancient Italian republics. The *Omelia del cittadino cardinal Chiaramonti vescovo d'Imola diretta al popolo della sua diocesi nella Repubblica cisalpina nel giorno del santissimo Natale l'anno MDCCXCVII* (Homily by citizen cardinal Chiaramonti, bishop of Imola, directed to the people of his diocese within the Cisalpine Republic, on the day of holy Christmas, year 1797) was particularly important owing to the eminence of its author and the repercussions it had as a statement. "Explain to the people," Chiaramonti urged, "the true nature of liberty and equality, so as to animate them towards their duties, while you make them know their rights. In this way we will have good Christians for heaven, and wise, useful, and generous citizens for the fatherland, and for the whole of our Republic."[19] In the righteous Christian understanding, liberty is not libertinism, nor is it an unbridled license to do what one wills, be it good, bad, honest, or abject. Such an interpretation destroys all the divine and human order, and disfigures humanity, reason, and all the beautiful qualities that God equipped us with, according to Chiaramonti. Liberty, the cardinal continues, is a faculty that was given to man by God; it is thus the power to do or not do, but always under divine and human law. The man who, proud and rebellious, opposes the law, is not exercising his liberty in a reasonable way; neither do those who contradict God and the secular sovereignty, and those who wish to pursue pleasure and set aside honesty. The man who cultivates vice and abandons virtue is a monster who does not put the powers that God gave him to use, and therefore is "friend neither of God, nor of men."[20]

After clarifying the true meaning of liberty, Chiaramonti restates his belief that democratic government is not in opposition to the Gospel. By contrast, it requires all those sublime virtues "that cannot be learned but at the school of Jesus Christ." In addition to Christ's example there is the equally dazzling case of the ancient republican heroes. Jesus Christ, however, was more of a teacher of brotherhood and civil union than were the ancient heroes. In the religion that he brought to men one therefore finds the most effective aid to democracies.[21] Catholic religion must be the object of solicitous care, for it teaches men to fulfill their civil duties and serve *il comun bene* (the common good). By means of the Lord's grace, the citizens will perform their civil duties. "Yes, my dear brothers," the cardinal concludes,

> be good Christians and you shall be excellent democrats. Imitate the humility and the obedience of the Savior and you shall be wise and obedient subjects. If you see that any of your brothers stray from the path of virtue and the Gospel, pray tirelessly also for them, for the hope remains that they will convert in order to enjoy our God. Do so that they may learn, if only by mirroring themselves in your deeds. Avoid imitating the error, but regard with indulgence the erring brother, and think of how you could bring him to repentance, and to the state of health. And you, my dearest brothers, to whom particular portions of my Christian flock are entrusted, you, supporting with me the spiritual burden of the people of God, join me

to preserve the Catholic religion pure within it; take every effort to make the followers of Jesus Christ piously faithful to the authorities and to the republic.[22]

In the *Lettera pastorale* published on February 12, 1799, Naples's archbishop Giuseppe Maria Capece Zurlo insisted instead on the obligation instituted by the French Army to obey the republic, on the basis of the principle that all power comes from God, and that being respectful subjects is a duty that God himself prescribes. The archbishop carefully notes that liberty should not be confused with libertinism, incivility, injustice, and vice. True liberty consists of being subject only to the law: "To this law you are hence indebted for your obedience and loyalty; therefore, you must also grant your subjection and respect to those who are singled out to be the guardians and protectors of the law. And this, my beloved brothers, not quite out of fear of punishments—as too vile and equivocal would your respect be—but rather out of the conscience, love, zeal, and character that are proper to a Christian, and of a generous and faithful heart." Reason and faith agree in highlighting the citizen's duty to defend the fatherland with zeal, to serve with loyalty, to live under the laws, and to respect the established authorities. Anyone who rebels against the laws or the fatherland is guilty of abomination and worthy of death.[23]

During the revolutionary period, some priests recommended bringing Christianity back to its original principles. One of these priests was Francesco Conforti (1743–99), an eminent theologian, formerly minister of the kingdom and then a martyr of the Neapolitan Republic.[24] He believed that a religion cannot be reformed except by means of another religion. For him, a Christian religion gradually redirected to the Gospel's simplicity was better suited to a moderate and liberal government. In Conforti's view, no other known religion has better sustained the principle of liberty. The pagan religion produced unruly slaves and tyrannical masters. The Christian religion, by contrast, was the first to teach men that God does not approve of slavery. Thanks to it, modern Europe enjoys a sort of liberty quite different from that of the ancients. The first Christians, at their origin, were none other than people who, in the most corrupt of times, wanted to reduce, on the one hand, the most superstitious idolatry to the simplicity of pure and eternal reason, and, on the other hand, to transform the most horrible despotism that ever oppressed humankind (Rome) into a government that abided by the norms of justice.[25] Conforti concludes that a people cannot remain without a religion. If a republican government provides a religion, then people will have a religion that concurs with the good of the nation; otherwise, if people try to build a religion by themselves, such a religion will more likely be inimical rather than amicable.

Among those who tried to build a republican religion in Italy, special mention should go to Eleonora de Fonseca Pimentel because of the purity of her faith and the strength with which she faced martyrdom. Pimentel was a woman of true Christian faith, by no means dogmatic, imbued with charity, and intent on alleviating the human condition in the world. This can be seen in *Fuga in Egitto*, a sacred oratorio that she wrote in 1792.[26] True, in this text there is no trace of a critique of the Roman Catholic orthodoxy, and yet there is also no trace of the traditional Counter-Reformation apparatus: no glories of Mary, no thaumaturgy, and no exaltation of the church as *mater et magistra*, or the vicar of Christ. There is, instead, such a full adherence to the principle of *sola scriptura* that it may seem a Protestant work, and, above all, one with an intense focus on human nature. Pimentel describes Mary's reaction to the angel's command—to depart from Egypt immediately—as the human expression of a "shaking femininity."[27] Pimentel was herself a mother, and knew what maternal love and anguish were all about, and therefore portrays Mary as compassionate, as a mother who lives her charity. In addition to this religiosity, one finds in Pimentel the colors of Jansenism in, for instance, the following verses: "Thank you, Father in Heaven; among your maidservants you chose me, the humblest, for such a gift, / So that ever more will / Your Omnipotence be admired; it is a gift of you / This valor that is descending within me, / And from above renders me strong." Her God is not a "God of revenge" but "only of love."[28]

Once the republic had been proclaimed, Pimentel committed herself to passionately explaining in the pages of the *Monitore Napoletano* that Christian religion commands people to defend liberty. In one of the first issues of the paper, on February 5, she states that the republican government must exhort the clergy to teach the people republican principles with the same zeal they used to teach the word of Christ:

> We invite the Government to establish civic missions, as beforehand there were simply religious ones; and we invite the great number of our clergymen, who are no less civic and zealous than they are learned, and already have practice with popular persuasiveness, to lend themselves to such a work, even without order and invitation by the Government. The man who commits an offense because he is ignorant is never fully guilty; justice therefore requires us to educate

the people, before condemning them, and not a minute should be wasted before we start such education.[29]

Pimentel deceived herself about the civic conscience of the Neapolitan clergy, but was right when she wrote that the religious and moral education of the people was the most dramatically urgent task, if one wanted to save the republic. Urgent, indeed, but almost impossible, for the time was short and the number of priests willing to become preachers of liberty was exiguous. The Philanthropic Society was founded with the purpose of "democratizing" the people, and it held its gatherings in the market square. Friars like Michelangelo Ciccone translated the Gospel into the Neapolitan language, "adapting to democracy all the maxims of the Christian doctrine." Curates and priests distinguished themselves by their commitment to use their sermons to spread the principles of civil Christianity. One example is Father Giuseppe Carlo Belloni of S. Maria Nuova, described in the chronicles as a "learned and persuasive" man who, before the tree of liberty, with a crucifix in his hand, "charged with the most boorish injuries the King, his family, and all the followers of the Monarchy," and struggled to prove that Jesus Christ and the saints "had preached with Religion equality and brotherhood."[30] In spite of the generous efforts of the patriots, the other religion, which taught people to obey kings, accept injustice, and await saintly miracles, reacted with all its might and monstrous ferocity against the republic, thereby destroying it.

The counterrevolutionaries called Pimentel "a Jacobin." Actually, her faith was a Christianity consisting of charity and love of country, the true spirit of brotherhood, as she herself explains in an article titled "Gli ecclesiastici e la repubblica," published in her *Monitore* on February 19, 1799. She argues that the duty of the priest is to provide an example of loyalty and obedience to the laws of the fatherland, and that the brotherhood commanded by the Gospel is the brotherhood and equality imposed by the republic; in short, such brotherhood is true democracy.[31] Pimentel defines the religion of priests who oppose liberty as false and the fruit of private passions; she affirms that the Bourbons' monarchy deluded people with the help of bad priests, while the republic exalts the good ones. The principle of a true priest—to a higher degree than for other citizens—must be charity, and charity is due above all to the fatherland. Finally, she insists that the brotherhood and equality of the democratic republic are nothing less than the political expression of the brotherhood that Christ has taught us. The Gospel is therefore the ideal foundation of the republic.

That same religion that had sustained Pimentel in her fight for liberty also helped her face martyrdom on the gallows, on August 20, 1799. Her only religious comfort was the Bible that a priest, Gioacchino Puoti, brought to the convicts. Probably it was the Bible translated by the Genevan Protestant Giovanni Diodati (1576–1649). On the one hand, there was the religion of Cardinal Ruffo and the king; on the other hand, there was Pimentel's religion, which came directly from the Bible, and was understood as well as loved for its truest meaning. "She believed in Jesus Christ, and acted for what she was convinced was the good of her fellow men, destined to bring about a more just and less oppressive society. For this faith, that cannot be described but as evangelical, she lived and fought. For this faith she also died, as a martyr, according to the meaning that the term '*màrtyr*' has in the Greek of the New Testament: 'witness of truth.' "[32]

The religious establishment unleashed particular fury on priests who had embraced and spread the new faith, such as Michele Natale, bishop of Vico Equense, guilty of having preached that the Christian faith is perfectly consistent with democracy, or Andrea Serrao, bishop of Potenza, slaughtered by the Sanfedists. Of 120 people sentenced to death, more than a dozen were men of the church, distinguished for their faith and doctrine, like Marcello Scotti, a professor of rhetoric, about whom Vincenzo Cuoco (1770–1823), the historian of the Neapolitan revolution of 1799, observes, "It is difficult to think of a more evangelical heart." The tide of popular hatred against the French and the patriots also overwhelmed the few Catholic priests who sincerely believed that republican liberty was the form of government most suited to the Christian religion. Michelangelo Cecconi, a priest who supported the revolution, for instance, was derided right before his own execution by the hangman, precisely because he had tried to explain to the people that religion is a friend of republican liberty.

The Bourbons' reaction was to crush both republican democracy and antipapal reformism. In the tragic events of the Neapolitan Revolution of 1799, two conflicts overlapped: that between the Bourbons' regime and republican liberty, and that between a Christianity of liberty and a fanatical Christianity that supported oppression. The dreadful savagery of the repression cannot be understood if one does not keep in mind that for the loyalists to the throne, the patriots were enemies of both the king and God. The Jacobins made the mistake of believing that the institutions and laws of the republics born out of revolutions—and with the help of foreign armies—could have the force to uproot traditional religious beliefs from the people's minds, and replace them with new dogmas, symbols, and rites. They did not account for the fact that armies can create new states, but not new religions. The words and arguments were right, but the prophets who announced the new religion often had little credibility among the people. They wanted to talk to the people, but they did not quite understand either the poor laborers of the town or those of the countryside. Republican sermons had too strong a French accent, and "French," to the manual laborers of the town and the rural proletariat, meant taxes, requisitions, and the appropriation of the precious and revered items in the churches. In the text *Catechismo repubblicano per l'istruzione del popolo e la rovina dei tiranni*, written by Naples's Archbishop Michele Natale (1751–99), one finds an impeccable republican eulogy of artisans and farmers, except that in the Neapolitan Republic, the vast majority of artisans and farmers were not full citizens, and hence did not belong to the population that the cardinal meant to educate.[33]

In the eyes of the people, republican priests and friars behaved in a scandalous manner, especially when they were celebrating Republican weddings under the tree of liberty. Equally harsh was the people's judgment about the friars who enrolled in the civic militia, boasting republican arms and symbols. Concerning the republican priest Ignazio Falconieri, who had become a militia captain, reporter Carlo de Nicola wrote that "while this fellow thinks that he is rendering a good service to the republic, such a thing looks scandalous to the people."[34] As for the French, they did worse; they did not show respect for churches and religious symbols. During a benediction given by a missionary in the marketplace, a French soldier made a sacrilegious gesture and was massacred by the people. In such a context, forging a republican religion was simply impossible.

In the provinces of the Kingdom of Naples, progress was not any better. The priests strove to demonstrate that the principles of the republic were in keeping with the Gospel and the epistles of Saint Paul, but the people considered these priests to be noblemen, or friends of noblemen—that is, rich and profiteers, if not quite heretics. When Andrea Serrao, bishop of Potenza, participated in establishing the republican municipality, the people showered him with abusive words. They called him a Jacobin and an atheist, and wanted to kill him, which they eventually did, with ghastly brutality. In Molfetta, a priest who tried to explain republican religion drawn from the Gospel was not able to conclude his sermon because the audience vehemently interrupted him. The following Sunday, he was so afraid of the menacing multitude that he could not even open his mouth and precipitously ran away.

Cuoco left us with a portrait that needs no further comment:

> Inexperienced youth who had no knowledge whatsoever of the world flooded the provinces with a "charter of democratization," that the central committee conceded to whoever requested it. They were not accompanied by any title whatever; rather, they were lucky when they were not called unbecoming names! They had no notion of the government: each operated in his own village according to his own ideas; each believed that the reform was going to be the one he desired: some were at war against prejudices, while others were against the simple and strict customs of the provincials, which were called "roughnesses": they started by contemning that very nation that was to be elevated by the republican vigor, and this occurred because a foreign nation was instead too much praised, a foreign nation that as yet was known just because it had been the winner; everything that the people held most sacred—their gods, their customs, their very name—was badly hit.[35]

The people of the provinces, and those of Naples itself, were not hostile to a religiosity that was amicable to republican religion. As soon as the people of Picerno heard that the French were coming, they dashed to church, led by their priest, to thank "the God of Israel, who had visited and redeemed his people."[36] But all in all, the southern populace practiced a religion that was, more than anything else, a festival. As long as they had the festival, they were content, and nothing was more remote from their outlook than a religious war. Notwithstanding their excellent intentions, the republicans made the mistake of deluding those who believed in the God of Israel who frees the peoples, and irritating those who practiced the old religious rituals as a festival. There was nothing wrong with wanting to dispossess the priests of their material goods. The damage was done when the republicans, while wanting to do so, also wanted to destroy—or at least gave the impression of wanting to destroy—"the gods" in which the people believed and the ceremonies that the people loved.[37]

11

AFTER THE REVOLUTION

THE DEFEAT of the revolutionary experiment made the most perceptive political writers aware of the fact that Italy lacked a public spirit capable of sustaining republican institutions. These thinkers realized that the true enemies of republican liberty, rather than reactionary governments and the papacy, were Italy's bad customs and bad religion. The revolutionary initiative could change governments and institutions, but only education could improve customs and religion. Cuoco understood better than anybody else that the Italian problem was above all one of public spirit. In a letter to Giovanni Battista Giovio on March 7, 1804, Cuoco explains that no better order would arise as long as Italians remained "sluggard and fainthearted," especially weak in spirit rather than just in politics and arms. "It is time," he writes in the letter's conclusion,

> to add to the glory of being able to say beautiful things the other glory, of being able to accomplish great things; for nations who are unable to accomplish the latter sooner or later will no longer be capable of even say[ing] them; the people's minds get narrower, and so do their hearts, and since they no longer have the true ideas of the beautiful and the great, they create a mannered beauty, typical of rhetoricians and schools, and they fall into the faint, the lacquered, the fake: just like the Greeks before and then the Romans, today it is happening to us.[1]

Cuoco believed, or at least hoped, that Italy was "born to resurrect dead things," as Machiavelli had written three centuries before. But that sort of rebirth could happen only if a public spirit arose in Italy that was founded on a love of country and virtue. Without virtue, Cuoco observes, "neither cities nor men can ever be great." The problem was that no trace of that virtue survived, and Italians were weak and "vilified by sluggishness." They had been educated to sluggishness by that holy religion that, "given by heaven in order to better mankind," had become "the source of new corruption, because of its abuse by some who preached it." God wants to see an eternal war waged on vices—above all, the vice of abandoning one's country amid perils; this is why God does not help the cowardly and fainthearted. In order for Italy to resuscitate itself, it was necessary to return "to the ancient ideas and ancient virtues," and substitute for the God of a corrupt religion the God who commands people to be strong, so as to be able to defend the fatherland.[2]

Ugo Foscolo was one of the first to express a new religion of the fatherland and liberty. In some of the most powerful verses of the *Sepolcri* (1807), he praises Florence for bringing together, within the church of Santa Croce, the tombs of the great Italians and in particular Vittorio Alfieri (whom I will discuss later), whose bones "vibrate with the love of country"; from that "religious peace," "a God" speaks who sustained the virtue that allowed the Greeks to defend their liberty at Marathon.[3] In his prose works during the years between 1811 and 1816, Foscolo emphasizes the necessity of religion for the achievement of liberty.[4] Unrestrained by the fear of God, people fall into despotism.[5] The problem of Italian liberty is first of all moral and religious in kind: Italy "cannot have liberty because there is no liberty without laws, nor laws without customs, nor customs without religion, nor religion without priests." As long as Italians experience religion as an "external ceremony," they will remain serfs. Political rebirth will take place only if Italians, and the clergy in particular, understand that Christian religion needs to be brought back to its founding principles.[6]

Precious suggestions aimed at rediscovering a religion that could contribute to the attainment of liberty came from France in the first decades of the nineteenth century, as a remedy of sorts for the damage done by Jacobin religion. The most important work in this regard was *De la religion*, published by Constant (1767–1830) in Paris in 1824 to denounce the perversion of religion allied with political despotism. Constant writes that during the Napoleonic regime, the prince took command of religion, which served as an indulgent and zealous auxiliary.[7] The lack of a true religious spirit was one of the most serious causes of the failure of the French Revolution, which indeed had been capable of acquiring liberty through the force of the Enlightenment, but not of maintaining itself on the right path through the force and restraint of religion. The revolution unleashed an unrestrained and unruly multitude of individuals, who had no adequate moral preparation, upon all existing institutions. Religion eventually supported the most execrable persecution, and the Restoration was a cure worse than the disease, for the men who stood up in defense of religion were as ignorant as the antireligious revolutionaries.[8] Both the revolution, with its Napoleonic epilogue, and the Restoration had therefore perverted Christianity's true meaning, and had put it in the service of ends repugnant to its nature. Precisely because a true religious spirit supported neither the French Revolution nor the Restoration, neither could ensure a stable liberty.

The difficult path toward liberty could be reopened only if the best minds and most generous souls understood that the religious spirit is always in agreement with the principles of liberty. Considered separately from the religious institutions that came into being over the course of history, the religious spirit is a defining characteristic of the human soul. Liberty, equality, and justice are its dearest conceptions. All the beings created by a good and Almighty God, submitted to the same destiny in their earthly life, and equipped with the same moral faculties, should have the same rights. Where religious sentiment has triumphed, there liberty was its companion, as the example of the early Christians shows. In contrast, the lack of religious sentiment promotes all the pretensions of tyranny. When the religious sentiment fades from men's souls, the time of their enslavement is always close at hand. Constant's words were a sharp warning that could not but touch the hearts of those who cared about liberty: "Des peuples religieux ont pu être esclaves; aucun peuple irréligieux n'est demeuré libre" (Religious peoples may have been enslaved; no irreligious people has been able to be free).[9] The conquest and defense of political liberty require disinterestedness to the point of a willingness to sacrifice oneself. Any morality that is alien to the religious sentiment, on the contrary, can by no means motivate the sacrifice of one's life. For one who sees nothing beyond life, what is more than life?

For Constant, not utilitarianism, but an authentic religious spirit can help men gain liberty. A well-conceived interest, the dogma of the best utilitarianism, defeats all passions, both base and noble: it triumphs over the raptures of the senses, the longing for money, and the fury of revenge, but it also suffocates piety and compassion along with the most generous passions that bring us a lasting good. How could an individual who follows the rule of a well-conceived interest as his maxim in life sacrifice himself for liberty? Yet without individuals who are prepared to sacrifice themselves, the people can never wrench liberty from the hands of the despots, nor can they defend it, once gained. They are bound to remain serfs. Thus, the real guide to be followed is not a well-conceived interest but instead the inner sentiment with which nature endowed all men.

Whereas well-conceived interest shows us what is advantageous and disadvantageous, the inner sentiment teaches us what is good and bad.[10]

In order to maintain this sentiment, one must cultivate religious feeling. France under Napoléon again offers evidence of this principle: "So long as they were rich in spirit, they contented themselves (under a moderate government) with some sort of opposition. So long as there was no danger, well-conceived interest had allowed vanity to indiscriminately criticize the good and the bad. But when danger came, the well-conceived interest advised [men] to prudently applaud the bad as if it were the good: so that one has proved himself in the opposition under a moderate government, and vile under a violent power." The natural outcome of utilitarianism is that the individual feels himself to be "his own center." But, Constant intelligently notes, "when everyone represents his own center, all are isolated. When all are isolated, there is only dust. When the hurricane comes, dust turns into mud." Constant exhorts us to recover the religious idea of liberty that animated the first Christians: "Friends of liberty…, be the early Christian of a new late empire. Liberty lives on sacrifices: return the power of sacrifice to the enervated race that has lost it. Liberty always implies citizens; sometimes, heroes. Do not extinguish the convictions that are at the basis of the virtues of the citizens, and that create heroes by giving them the strength to be martyrs."[11]

One year later, in 1825, Saint-Simon (1760–1825) published *Le Nouveau Christianisme*, in which he proposed the authentic spirit of Christianity to all men who feel the need to purify and perfect their moral and religious life. For Saint-Simon, the foundation of the new Christianity consisted in the principles that men should treat one another as brothers, and that society must be organized in the most advantageous way for the greatest number, especially for the poorest.[12] The spirit of the new Christianity is composed of goodness, charity, and grace. Its arms are persuasion and demonstration; its strength lies in its moral superiority.[13] When society has distanced itself from the true Christianity, it has fallen under the dominion of force. Returning to the Christian principle was thus the only way to resurrect society. The prophet of this new humanity was Saint-Simon himself, who felt he was explicitly endowed with divine inspiration and protected by God.[14]

In 1835, ten years after the author's death, Saint-Simon's loyal disciple Berthélemy Prosper Enfantin (1729–81) published *La Nouveau Christianisme* in an edition that comprised also *Die Erziehung des Menschengeschlechts* (*The Education of Humankind*) by Gotthold Ephraim Lessing (1729–81). This other text also heralded a new Christianity, meant to open up a third era in the world: one in which humanity was morally redeemed by the new religion. Lessing explains that the Christian religion has historically demonstrated the superiority of its principles. For this reason, it can still lead humanity to rediscover the true ideas about the "divine Being," human nature, and our relationships with God. Summoned by a well-understood Christianity, the time will come, Lessing assures us, when man will do good just for the sake of the good, and will appreciate the inner recompenses for virtue as the most coveted reward. That shall be the time of the "new eternal Gospel" promised by the books of the new alliance and guaranteed by Providence.[15]

Likewise for François Guizot (1787–1874), an eminent historian and politician, Christianity is a moral force that works for liberty and, from liberty, draws ever-renewed energies to fulfill its mission. Unlike Constant, Guizot argues, in his famous lectures of 1828, that Christianity is not merely an internal individual sentiment but also an institution and association. He recalls how, by the end of the fourth century, Christianity was no longer just a religion but also a church, and precisely because it was a church too, it could survive the fall of the Roman Empire and barbarian invasions. Where it could not become a church, as in Asia and northern Africa, it disappeared.[16] In order to defend itself, Christianity affirmed the principle of the separation of spiritual and temporal powers, even though, once it gained its autonomy, it tried to dominate temporal power as well. The impulse to form a community of faith, proselytize, and create a religious society with an ecclesiastical government is inherent in the religious nature of man. The church becomes an obstacle to religious sentiment when it turns into a caste, pursues and tolerates privileges, cultivates social immobility, and exercises compulsion over believers and nonbelievers, with the result that it negates the rights of individual reason and affirms "priestly tyranny." In order to properly fulfill their task in the world, all religions—Christianity first and foremost—must be models of liberty, and must require that those who submit to their norms do so freely. Religion must therefore disabuse itself of the mistake of seeing liberty as an obstacle rather than as the indispensable condition for carrying out its mission in the world.

An article by Théodore Jouffroy (1796–1842) titled *Comment les dogmes finissent*, which appeared in May 1825 in the *Globe* and then in the volume *Mélanges philosophiques*, published in 1838, contributed to the search for a religion of liberty. Jouffroy, who had lost his Catholic faith when he was about eighteen years old, describes in this article, rich with autobiographical references, the progression toward the crisis of dogmatism and, afterward, the rebirth of a true religious faith. After tracing, in an idealized fashion, the different phases of the clash between old dogmas and skepticism that foreshadows the triumph of the new faith, Jouffroy concludes with the prophecy of a world restored by a new faith, laboriously gained. He argues that the new generation feels a new faith that rejects both fanaticism, which always tries to reemerge, and skepticism, which corrupts the soul. The new generation has faith in truth and virtue, and from this a legitimate kingdom of truth originates that arouses "an indescribable love and enthusiasm" within people's souls. A new ideal man is born and a new faith is spread, and, thanks to both, the new generation triumphs over both dogma and corruption.[17]

Even more influential were the writings of Hugues-Félicité-Robert de Lamennais (1782–1854), whom many in Europe considered the prophet of a new religious and moral reform. A supporter of reactionary Catholicism, he later became a fervent defender of the alliance between Christianity and political liberty. Together with the other contributors to the journal *Avenir*, Lamennais defended both liberty and Christianity even when, during the Restoration, France was divided between those who wanted Christianity without liberty, and those who wanted liberty without Christianity. Lamennais held that Christianity and liberty had a common root, and one was the necessary condition of the other. Evidence of this was the fact that the French liberal party, hostile to Christianity, was also hostile to liberty, whereas the monarchy, hostile to liberty, was also hostile to Christianity, and indeed the monarchy degraded it into an official religion—bastardized, vilified, and enslaved.[18] Although Lamennais was aware of the disgraced condition of French Catholicism, he hoped for a religious and moral rebirth through a new alliance between the principles of order and progress, faith and science, Christian religion and political liberty. Inasmuch as its fundamental principles are truth and love, Christianity cannot live without liberty—first of all the liberty to examine the sacred scriptures, and openly discuss religious, moral, and political issues. Over the centuries, human reason has become accustomed to liberty, and hence it would be impossible to destroy liberty. Even if it were possible, what value would a religion have that was an obstacle instead of an encouragement to the progress of humanity?[19]

By its nature, Christianity demands liberty. The evangelical law proclaims the equality and brotherhood of men. Just as it contributed to the dismantling of ancient slavery in the past, Christianity must in modern times fight for the termination of modern slavery—that is, political oppression. Only by returning to its roots as a religion that practices charity can Christianity live again in the hearts of millions of men, rather than vegetate in the shadow of a throne or present a sad image of itself in public pageantry. Within the conflict between political absolutism and liberty that dominated the European scene in the first half of the nineteenth century, the place of the Christian should be on the side of liberty. Whereas absolutism could count on its material force, liberty was a moral force, and therefore was destined to win, even, if necessary, at the cost of revolutions, to affirm right over arbitrary will and establish a happier life for humanity. Although they inevitably bring suffering and grief, revolutions that are animated by a true spirit of liberty must be considered as gifts of Providence and signs of God's presence on earth.[20] The greatest revolution ever realized, after all, was Christianity itself. Its effects were still alive in the great effort to substitute the principles of liberty for those of the ancien régime. According to Lamennais, this great effort was nothing less than the spreading of the spirit of Christianity from the realm of the religious community to the realm of politics. Political and civil equality tended to be realized in the religious equality of all men before God, which in turn required political liberty for the simple reason that it repudiated any power of man over man. The earthly city was to be conceived of as a "free association," whose end was to guarantee the liberty of all.[21]

During those same years, Jean Charles Leonard Simonde de Sismondi (1773–1842), a man of Protestant faith, reminds Italians, in his *Histoire des républiques italiennes du moyen âge*, about the patriotism and religion of the citizens of the ancient republics. He insists on the destructive effects of a bad religious education on citizens' moral sense.[22] Because of the education they received from the church, Italians had become masters in the art of silencing the voice of conscience and replacing it with a superficial devotion, a lack of true moral sense.[23] Simonde de Sismondi emphasizes that such a moral and religious perversion is the main reason for the Italians' servitude, and so long as they will not emancipate themselves morally, they will not be able to emancipate themselves politically either.

The most complete and coherent lesson on the relationship between republican liberty and Christian religion, however, came from *Démocratie en Amérique* by Alexis de Tocqueville (1805–59), published in two volumes in 1835 and 1840. During his journey through the United States, Tocqueville immediately noticed that the alliance between religion and political liberty was the basis of the democracy. In the United States, religion taught rigorously republican and democratic principles. It could instill the conviction in its citizens' souls that Christianity and liberty were inseparable, and that the true Christian must love his or her country.

The alliance formed in the New World was a radical novelty as contrasted with Europe, where Christian religion and political liberty, instead of being allied, were sworn enemies. The United States, where, in Tocqueville's view, religion is stronger than in any other Western country, is also the freest nation: "Nonetheless, America is still the place where the Christian religion has kept the greatest power over men's soul; and nothing better demonstrates how useful and natural it is to man, since the country where it now has the widest sway is both the most enlightened and the freest."[24]

The religious and moral legacy of the Puritans was fundamental for realizing the encounter between Christianity and political liberty. The Puritans went to the New World in order to be able to pray to God in liberty, and maintained the most radical democratic and republican theories—first among them an interpretation of liberty as a sacred principle:

> Nor would I have you to mistake in the point of your own *liberty*. There is a liberty of corrupt nature, which is affected by men and beasts to do what they list; and this liberty is inconsistent with *authority*, impatient of all restraint; by this *liberty Sumus Omnes Deteriores*, 'tis the grand enemy of truth and peace, and all the ordinances of God are bent against it. But there is a civil, a moral, a federal *liberty* which is the proper end and object of authority; it is a liberty for that which is just and good; for this liberty you are to stand with the hazard of your very lives.[25]

In the United States all religious confessions, the Catholic one included, teach people to love and serve political liberty, and support the struggle of peoples that want to emancipate themselves from colonial and imperial domination.[26] Tocqueville's account of a rally convened to collect money in support of Polish liberty is worth more in its own right than a treatise:

> I found two or three thousand people in a vast hall prepared for their reception. Soon a priest dressed in his ecclesiastical habit came forward onto the platform. The audience took off their hats and stood in silence while he spoke as follows: "Almighty God! Lord of Hosts! Thou didst strengthen the hearts and guide the arms of our fathers when they fought for the sacred rights of their national independence! Thou who didst make them triumph over a hateful oppression and didst grant to our people the blessings of peace and of liberty, look with favor, Lord, upon the other hemisphere; have pity upon a heroic people fighting now as we fought before for the defense of these same rights! Lord, who hast created all men in the same image,

do not allow despotism to deform Thy work and maintain inequality upon the earth. Almighty God! Watch over the destinies of the Poles and make them worthy to be free; may Thy wisdom prevail in their councils and Thy strength in their arms; spread terror among their enemies; divide the powers that contrive their ruin; and do not allow that injustice which the world has witnessed for fifty years to be consummated in our time. Lord, who holdest in Thy strong hand the hearts of peoples and of men, raise up allies to the sacred cause of true right; arouse at last the French nation, that, forgetting the apathy in which its leaders lull, it may fight once more for the freedom of the world. O Lord! Turn not Thou Thy face from us, and grant that we may always be the most religious and the most free nation upon earth. God Almighty, hear our supplication this day, and save the Poles. We beseech Thee in the name of Thy beloved son, our Lord Jesus Christ, who died upon the cross for the salvation of all men. Amen.[27]

Religion in the United States performs its task of moral education well precisely because it stays away from political power. Tocqueville candidly confesses that he was profoundly struck by his discovery that US priests did not hold political office and were not even represented in the legislative assemblies. Priests even loudly proclaimed that politics was not their business. On the contrary, when religion seeks the aid of governments, it loses its power, which consists of teaching and educating by words as well as example. On US soil, religion teaches citizens to view their republic as a gift from God and liberty as a sacred principle. Religion therefore becomes an active force that merges with patriotism to become the true faith of the Americans.

Religion shapes customs, molds the profound convictions of citizens, and purifies the pernicious passions of egoism and the search for material well-being—the latter being a particularly necessary task in an egalitarian society where individuals aspire to achieve prosperity and well-being without being hindered by hierarchical orders, as had happened in the aristocratic societies of the Old World. In the US democracy, where individuals furiously pursue their own interest, religion performs the invaluable function of moderation and education. For this reason religion is "the first of their political institutions."[28] Precisely because in democratic republics the people are sovereign, society must be subject to the superior law of God: "Despotism may be able to do without faith, but freedom cannot. Religion is much more needed in the republic they advocate than in the monarchy they attack, and in democratic republics most of all. How could society escape destruction if, when political ties are relaxed, moral ties are not tightened? And what can be done with a people master of itself if it is not subject to God?"[29]

In a democratic society, constantly changing and full of conflicts, where individuals form their own convictions about what is just and what is wrong, religion is also necessary because it offers a firm and constant moral reference. Tocqueville emphasizes that moral uncertainty exhausts souls and disposes people toward servitude:

> When a people's religion is destroyed, doubt invades the highest faculties of the mind and half paralyses all the rest. Each man gets into the way of having nothing but confused and changing notions about the matters of the greatest importance to himself and his fellows. Opinions are ill-defended or abandoned, and in despair of solving unaided the greatest problems of human destiny, men ignobly give up thinking about them. Such a state inevitably enervates the soul, and relaxing the springs of the will, prepares a people for bondage. Then not only will they let their freedom be taken from them, but often they actually hand it over themselves.

The conclusion, once more, is that democratic societies need the moral aid of religion more than do monarchies and despotic regimes: "For my part, I doubt whether man can support complete religious independence and entire political liberty at the same time. I am led to think that if he has no faith he must obey, and if he is free he must believe."[30] Tocqueville's admonition was clear, and this time it derived not from abstract principles but rather from his observation of the concrete experience of a great republic: those who really love their republic and liberty must sustain Christian religion.

An even more precise admonition not to separate political from religious reform came to Italians from Edgard Quinet (1803–75), a convinced republican and militant in the revolution of 1848 (the revolution that overthrew Louis-Philippe I, who opposed Prince Charles Louis Napoléon Bonaparte, who would become Napoléon III). In *Les révolutions d'Italie* (1848), Quinet argues that Savonarola alone attempted to realize religious reform in Italy. The friar from Ferrara, according to Quinet, made the mistake of applying the remedies of the primitive church to the evils of Italy. He preached that people should look for God's help and arm themselves with prayers while waiting for the miracle.[31] Machiavelli tried instead to resurrect Italy from moral death by means of a politics "without God, without providence, without religion, neither pagan nor Christian." He tenaciously strove to "found and conserve the fatherland without God and notwithstanding God."[32] Owing to the bad example of the papacy, Italians were morally corrupt as well as devoid of remorse and shame. Against this moral depravity, Machiavelli did not bear the standard of religious and moral reform but instead appealed to a redeemer who could revive Italy by force. His notion for Italy's rebirth was exclusively political, and hence it failed.[33]

In *La Révolution* (1865) Quinet turns, at greater length, to the relationship between political and religious reform. He maintains that England, the Netherlands, Switzerland, the Scandinavian countries, the United States, and "all the peoples that were children of the Reformation" could give themselves "a soul," and therefore achieve "the only revolution that deserves this name." The French Revolution, by contrast, was not the result of a religious reform. The reform of political institutions without religious reform, Quinet counseled, has fragile bases, and thus can be easily overturned, or can degenerate, as it did in France (first with the Terror and then with the Restoration). The Latin peoples, who missed the opportunity to reform their religious ideas, thought they could achieve the same results in a different way: without changing their dogmas, they changed their civil laws. But experience demonstrates that this solves nothing at all, "for it leaves untouched the ancient mold by which the future eternally reproduced the past."[34] The true example to follow is that of the republic of the United States, where liberty is founded not on atheism but rather on a divine idea.

Only a religion can extinguish a religion. Quinet explains that the French Revolution

> might have corroded the ancient religion only by opposing it with a new positive faith. But since this was not possible, all the efforts of modern France, and of some half-million people, were dissipated; they could not but demonstrate their powerlessness on the fundamental questions.... The farmers of Vandea obtained that for which they had taken up arms. They assured for their posterity the supremacy of their religion, the real dominion of their priests and their altars; not only for themselves, but for the whole of France. Where could one look, instead, for the cult of liberty of their republican adversaries...? Where are their rites, their altars, their trophies? The religion of liberty has disappeared from the souls even more than from the things.[35]

From these reflections about the French Revolution, Quinet drew general lessons about the political effects of the religious spirit and saw in liberty the religion of the future: "Only religion makes men achieve great things. At the origin of religions, when these were still alive and sincere and they wholly filled the human soul, they led the soul to superhuman actions. The saints and the political martyrs of the Reformation and of the French Revolution provide exemplary evidence. Indeed, since liberty is the new religion, the religion of law and justice is eager to found its kingdom by replacing the old, corrupt Christianity."[36] These words arrived in Italy when the Renaissance had already reached, for better and worse, its epilogue; rather than outlining a program for action, these words underscored that even the pursuit of national unity—great as that deed might have been—was incomplete and therefore fragile.

12

THE NEW ALLIANCE

THE IDEAS COMING FROM France helped Italian intellectuals seek a civil religion different from the Jacobin one, which had revealed all its flimsiness and had not been able to weaken the traditional religion. In various writings, Terenzio Mamiani (1799–1885), who participated in the riots of 1831 and 1848, invoked a religious reform that would abolish the temporal power of the pope, and offer a new religion capable of educating people—in accordance with science and civilization—about civic virtues and love of country.[1] During those same years, Giacomo Durando (1807–94) wrote, in *Della nazionalità italiana* (1846), that civilization and nationality were irreconcilable with the church and Catholicism, and that a secular civilization required reducing the church's power to a mere spiritual patriarchate. Moreover, church reform had to be accompanied by a reform of Catholicism that reduced it to a pure religious sentiment.[2] Other voices, like that of Giuseppe Ferrari, argued for a humanitarianism to replace Christianity.[3]

The prevailing position, however, was that of promoting a civil religiosity in Italy within Christianity. The most refined intellectual reflections originated in Tuscany, where four centuries before, as we have seen, a republican Christianity was born and took root. The most influential personality of the reform movement, despite his solitary life, was Raffaello Lambruschini (1788–1873), who was imprisoned because of his involvement with the refugees of the Neapolitan Revolution, and had a prominent role in Tuscan cultural and political life at the beginning of the 1820s. Commenting on Constant's *De la religion*, Lambruschini writes that the greatest merit of religious truths consists in their practice, and the influence they can exercise "on the public and individual well-being."[4] He concedes that in certain cases, fear and authority might be useful for spreading and defending religion, but adds that in his times, only "reason and benevolence" are adequate means for reviving the ancient religious spirit. To persist in deploying authority and fear only has the effect of compromising religion, and yet the ecclesiastical teaching is gradually substituting command for persuasion: "Whereas formerly one would pray, now one was starting to threaten. Spiritual chastisements are waived, and the King's arm is invoked. In the past, one justly wanted the people to acknowledge that Religious truths are not in the least inconsistent with the many truths that all the sciences are revealing to us. Now, the enlightenment is being despised, and one tries to disseminate disfavor on all branches of human cognitions, and to warn men's minds against their progresses." From the sincere sentiment it represented in the past, religion had become a cold practice and shrewd simulation.[5]

Lambruschini's stand in favor of the alliance between religion and liberty is straightforward: "The point is to reaffirm the spirits in the sound Religious disposition to which the experience of evil had led; the point is to prevent Religion from becoming the enemy to the enlightenment, an instrument of slavery and persecution, and the servant of human interests and passions; the point is rather to bind in indissoluble friendship all the truths grasped by the human intellect with the simple, unchanging and touching truths of Religion." Religion requires liberty. In order to make religion an act worthy of human intelligence and liberty, it is also necessary that those who support authority realize that religion is a form of persuasion and sentiment that must enter into men's minds and hearts. Disputes and exaggerations originate from an overly vague definition of the borders between politics and religion. On the one hand, men want to shake off the yoke of any authority; on the other hand, they want to close their eyes to understanding, suffocate the voice of their inner sentiment, repress the impulses of their most irresistible tendencies, and have authority determine their thought and action.[6]

Liberty is a command and gift from God. For Lambruschini, God himself demands that men live free—that is to say, in accordance with moral law. Man's real elevation above other creatures resides precisely in this particular condition of the human soul.

> In nature, from the most impalpable molecules to the stars, from light to clay, from alga to rose, from the insect that lasts a day and from the stupid polyp to the ancient lion and to the intelligent beaver, everywhere an invisible hand bridles the forces, determines the actions, inspires life and directs sentiment: everything is movement, order, beauty, pleasure; but movement is set in motion, order is inviolable, beauty is passive, pleasure is blind; everything, that is, mutely

serves an Eternal Legislator. By contrast, to man God assigns the place that suits him in the great series of beings, by attributing to him a mode of existence, a grade of perfection of his own; He grants man the forces that allow him to pursue such a mode of existence, and does not reserve to Himself the direction. For this reason man cannot live without moral and civil liberty: the civilly best man, as he is also morally best, gives all of himself to other men; only one thing he keeps, which his conscience tells him he cannot give up to anyone but to God: his independence. For the human soul gets equally corrupted whether man rejects God's lordship or accepts the lordship of other men; indeed, when man obeys other men, and should do so, it is because he is obeying God; and if man transfers any part of his own independence to God, he does so in order not to violate the independence of other people—that is, to assure independence to all, just as he wants such independence assured for himself. The triumph of liberty.[7]

Gino Capponi, a descendant of one of the most distinguished Florentine families, also supported a religious reform capable of rendering religion an effective instrument of civil education. In his view, Christianity is an indispensable foundation for internal liberty, for it had called man back from the external world to the inner part of his conscience. Capponi thus regards religion as an educator of man, and considers "any moral discourse that is not invigorated by the value precepts of the Gospel to be very insipid."[8] Since it is a source of spiritual liberty, Christian religion could serve as the starting principle of that sort of steady education that Italians—morally weakened by long centuries of serfdom—lacked. In Capponi's judgment, Italy's problem is not that it lacks ideas or culture but rather that it suffers from a weakness of character. Just like the best spirits of the romantic age, Capponi had tried ever since the first years of the Napoleonic regime to reconcile religion and political liberty, and fought against the pope's claim to a monopoly on religious truth.[9] When, in 1819 in London, he composed *Progetto di giornale* (Project for a newspaper) he extolled a clear-cut separation of religion from political power and objected to any claim of a monopoly on truth.

The Christian religion could and should undertake an invaluable educational function in modern times, provided it freed itself of that preponderance of its own ideas that were antithetical to the principles of the Gospel. A reform internal to the church was urgently required, but at the same time a return to the original principles of Christianity was impossible. Faithful to the teaching of John Locke's *The Reasonableness of Christianity*, and more realistic, was the proposition of a church freed from the priests' oppressive predominance, centered instead on the idea of Christian charity, and inspired by liberty as the guide for individual and social action. As Capponi wrote to Lambruschini in a letter dated August 14–18, 1834, Protestantism—although spoiled by individualism—amounted to immense progress as a reaction against Roman tyranny. The life of every religion, and the life of Christianity, resides in the purity of the moral principle. Thus interpreted, Christianity set itself on the road to liberty and equality, detaching itself from the Catholic spirit of conformity. Sent by God to enlighten men, Jesus had redeemed them from their double servitude as slaves and citizens, conferring on them their dignity as persons in the name of the value of their moral conscience—that is, Jesus made man, for the first time, "truly man." Purified with the help of reason, Christianity could become a new "eternal Gospel," an "eternal Religion of Jesus Christ." As such it could educate man to inner liberty, which is the foundation of all other liberties.[10]

The ethical and social content of Baron Bettino Ricasoli's Christianity was quite similar. He, too, was, like Capponi, a distinguished member of the Florentine aristocracy. Ricasoli draws a work ethic of commitment and charity from the Christian religion.[11] He considers the bond of religiosity and toil (especially in the fields) "a model of true and genuine religion," and tries to educate farmers about the ethics of work with the zeal of a Calvinist pastor, going so far as to utilize the cult of the saints:

> Since farmers have so much love for the Saints, and among them for Saint Isidore, I told myself: why not make of this prejudice of theirs, which henceforth exists and for long will exist until people will profit from it, an instrument for my plan of action? They adore many anchorites, martyrs, and others who are useless models for the life of the farmer. It would be more useful to offer examples of domestic virtues, love for work, and a wisely religious sentiment. Hence why not let them know better a farmer like themselves, one who must have endured the like of their distress and must have needed the same qualities necessary for educating and creating their own families—Saint Isidore, that is?

Ricasoli also educated his daughter to a religiosity made up of deeds of charity, readings of the holy scriptures, meditation, and the contemplation of nature in order to find signs of divine wisdom along with fostering the internal self-perfecting that leads one closer to God.[12]

Ricasoli has a religious faith in liberty because, he believes, liberty is the child of thought, and thought comes from God. He perceives in his own times the signs of the rebirth of a religious sentiment, especially among the most educated classes—although not including the priests.[13] Like the Florentines in the old days of the free republic, Ricasoli was convinced that God sides with the just and strong, not with tyrants, the seditious, and the sluggish. He was equally convinced that the Christian faith demanded a commitment toward one's neighbor and fatherland, supported by a constant effort of internal self-perfecting. For these reasons he worked for a religious reform, and even before 1870 he thought society was on the "eve of a great revolution for Roman Catholicism, which I ardently desire and would like to see before I die." In October 1870, he wrote that the next transformation of the papacy could not help but be good for true religious sentiment. The end of the temporal power of the popes, together with the church's absolute liberty, was indeed to bring a revolution, both beneficial and splendid, as the foundation of Christianity. In Ricasoli's opinion, the separation between state and church was ripe for a religious reform designed to build a true communion of believers: laity and priesthood. The religious revolution, hence, should follow the political revolution not as a mere appendix but instead as its necessary completion.[14]

Whereas Ricasoli supported religious reform within the Catholic Church's orbit, his friend Count Piero Guicciardini (1808–86), a descendant of the great Francesco Giucciardini, abandoned the Catholic religion in 1836 to embrace Protestantism, and he lived within this faith for the rest of his life. Precisely because of the seriousness of his faith, he urgently felt the need to emancipate Italy from *pretismo* (priestism), an indispensable step toward moral rebirth and the strengthening of civil liberty. In many of his writings, one can almost hear Guicciardini's great ancestor's words against the *caterva di scelerati* (mass of wicked) priests. Besides his family tradition, Guicciardini was aided in finding his way by his reading of the Bible, which he taught to schoolchildren, and by his visits to the house of the Foggi family in Pisa, under the auspices of Matilde Calandrini, born in Geneva and descended from one of the Lucca families that emigrated in the sixteenth century to find that liberty which in Italy was no longer possible.[15] Those ideas that had departed from Italy when political and religious liberty were stifled there, were returning, aiding a rebirth of both.

Guicciardini's main preoccupation was with religious liberty rather than with Italian liberty and unity. He writes about this in a straightforward way from London, a few months before the referendum concerning the annexation of Tuscany to Piedmont. Only religious liberty could abet Italy's moral rebirth.[16] He pointed to the Savoy government's failure to resolutely manage the Roman question as a threat to the survival of liberal institutions. The letter he wrote from Geneva to Cosimo Ridolfi on May 26, 1860, is an eloquent document: "But what will really debase poor Italy will be the question of the priests. You do not want to understand that they are a source of the demoralization of society and a school of hypocrisy. Because of them we will never achieve the *Risorgimento* [rebirth] of the nation." A letter written on June 9, 1860, too, deserves quotation: "I disagree with you on the idea that Italy should be granted civil liberty first, and religious liberty afterwards. I believe the other way round is possible; having both things at the same time, probable. Having civil liberty without first having religious liberty, is utterly impossible. England was never free until it broke free from the Pope. Today liberty is enjoyed only by those peoples where Romanism is either excluded or powerless."[17]

The work of moral and religious education undertaken by the Tuscan reformers was part of a broader effort intended to teach the people a religion of virtue that would support them on their road to liberty. The documents of this educational work can be found above all in the popular newspapers. Turin's *L'Alba*, initially edited by Giuseppe La Farina (1815–63), maintained, for instance, that politics should rejoin religion, recognizing all the evangelical principles of equality and brotherhood. It also contended that the clergy, for its part, should preach adherence to the new constitutional order founded in 1848. At the same time, the paper emphasized that spiritual power and temporal power were irreconcilable, and that it was the duty of the papacy and of Christians to participate in the war against Austria. All told, the Turin paper was an expression of a religious anticlericalism—and, strange though it may seem, Catholicism.[18]

Il Popolano, in Florence, went further with its anticlerical and anti-Catholic critique. An article titled "Il papa è morto" (The pope is dead), published on December 4, 1848, argued that it was necessary to replace the papacy with an assembly of bishops elected by universal suffrage, in order to purify the Christian doctrines distorted by the popes and thereby reform ecclesiastical legislation. Other articles instead advocated a Christian reform that would pick up the themes of democratic evangelism, or, conversely, a neatly rationalistic perspective that should replace religious belief in the hearts and minds of the people.[19] With tones that resounded with the republican Christianity of bygone times, *Il Contemporaneo* of Rome, which was edited by Pietro Sterbini, asserted that popular government was "most in keeping with the principles of brotherhood that are written in the Gospel," and urged the clergy to return to the right path of democratic holiness. The paper explained that the republic by no means sought the destruction of religion. Rather, it was perfectly consistent with the dictates of the Gospel. The priests thus had nothing to fear from the republic and could become, on the basis of their faith, its most zealous supporters.[20]

Il Povero, in Bologna, became a supporter of the alliance between Catholic Christianity and democracy, and advocated an evangelical socialism founded on Christian charity. An article of May 26, 1848, affirmed that the nineteenth century had replaced the irreligious liberty of the Enlightenment with a liberty that was "well-conceived and religious." That same year, Giuseppe Casati wrote that just as liberty without religion is anarchy, religion without liberty is hypocrisy. By contrast, the democratic papers of Naples, mindful of the tragic lesson of 1799, worked chiefly to win the support of the clergy for the liberal cause, and spread a democratic interpretation of Christianity. *Mondo vecchio e mondo nuovo* (Old World and New World), one of the best and most popular papers, insisted that the church must recover the democratic character that had laid the foundations of modern civilization. It also maintained that people had to realize that religion is a support to civilization, and that the alliance between religion and liberty is possible and necessary.[21] Finally, *L'Indipendente* (Independent) stated that society is a work of God and not of man, and that Christianity and the republican regime were perfectly compatible.[22]

In Piedmont, *La Gazzetta del Popolo*, founded in June 1848, was perhaps the most consistent example of an intellectual position that, on the one hand, harshly criticized the meddling, *politicien*, and corrupt priests, and, on the other hand, had a strong sympathy for Catholicism reduced to its true principles. The attention to an evangelical and democratic Catholicism was sometimes accompanied by arguments in favor of a secular, philanthropic, tolerant, and democratic religion of a somewhat enlightened derivation. Two more starkly anticlerical papers were *Opinione* and *Unione*, edited, at different times, by Aurelio Bianchi Giovini. A scholar of biblical exegesis and sacred history, Giovini maintained that the Gospels were a collection of various historical, half-historical, legendary, and mythical traditions about Jesus Christ, who had just been a man like anybody else. In sum, Christianity was the product of preexisting traditions and had degenerated into reactionary political tendencies wholly inadequate for the development of modern civilization. Notwithstanding this, Giovini declared that he believed "in God, in an afterlife, and in some mysterious revelation of God on earth."[23]

The aspiration for a religion supported by the values of liberty also existed among the laborers' mutual aid societies. According to their leaders and organizers, these societies should have become the centers of a reform capable of emancipating workers from both skepticism and traditional religion, and educating them to a wise conduct of life based on saving, order, reciprocal respect, and moderation. This educational enterprise was based on secular values that had absorbed the values of Christianity—first of all, liberty of conscience and the equality of all men before God. Religion was considered crucial in enabling moral values to penetrate consciences; what changed was the overall end of the educational effort, which aimed to produce not humble and devoted laborers but rather workers conscious of their rights and duties.[24]

The movement for popular libraries that originated in Prato (Tuscany) in 1861 had similar aims. Its statute banned those books that spread "anything against the dogmas of the religion of the State and good customs." The movement instead supported books that educated people about "the sentiment of one's duty towards God, towards the Fatherland, and towards Society"; books should also aid in uprooting ignorance, prejudices, and immorality, and should teach a love of work. With a clear conservative intention, the founder of the movement, Antonio Bruni, emphasized the appropriateness of an education that freed laborers from the vain hope of rising above their condition: "Our principle, rather, is to make the workman love his condition, by allowing him to gain the most from his labor through the concourse of both physical strength and intellectual faculty," and preventing him from falling into the traps set by sects of reactionaries and socialists.[25]

Religion, in this educational project, should point to moral norms capable of educating citizens. Evidence of the distance that separated the religious education of the movement for popular libraries from traditional Catholic religiosity was, on the one hand, the favor that the former had with Masonic lodges and the most radical proponents of free thought, and, on the other hand, the open opposition on the part of important Catholic circles. In an 1882 article, the journal *Civiltà Cattolica* defined the Lega delle Biblioteche Popolari (League of Popular Libraries) as an association dedicated to producing anti-Christian propaganda aimed at the abolition of religious education along with the tyrannical imposition, through the state, of "Godless" teaching and education.[26]

A religiosity advocating individual and civil virtue also emerged from the writings of Samuel Smiles, in particular *Self-Help* (1859), translated into Italian in 1865 by Gustavo Strafforello, with the title *Chi si aiuta Dio l'aiuta*—a book that had wide circulation among the Italian working classes. As Guido Verucci, a historian of contemporary secular Italy, has observed, the self-help theory was the secularized version of a religious and cultural tradition inspired by Scottish Calvinism. Whereas in the original English text reference to God is absent, it figures immediately in the Italian title. Protestant ethics thus entered into Italian popular culture with a starkly anti-Catholic meaning. After all, other representatives of the movement for popular education insisted on the bad effects of a Catholic education. Enrico Fano, for instance, the author of *Della carità preventiva e dell'ordinamento delle società di mutuo soccorso in Italia*, explicitly condemned the passivity—that is, waiting for help from others or counting on some supernatural intervention—instilled in the Italians by centuries of Catholic education. The clerical profession itself was idle, thereby encouraging inactivity and fatalism. The priests exalted poverty, blessed mendicancy, and preached the idea that poverty of spirit is similar to ignorance and profits from it. They completely misunderstood the true meaning of Christian charity, which does not encourage passivity, submissiveness, and weakness but rather promotes work, strength, and emancipation:

> And how, after having heard for the whole day poverty glorified in prayers, from the pulpit, in the confessional, in the few books that the people were allowed to read—how could such a people develop the sentiment of prudence, the sense of duty to live by one's industry, and the determination to redeem oneself from misery through working and saving? The people, rather, are persuaded that poverty is a virtue sanctioned by God, a virtue that shall bring future goods, and, disheartened, surrender to ignorance.

The work of religious reeducation, then, had to attempt to uproot superstition and indifference—two habits of mind inculcated in the Italians by the Catholic religion that were completely incompatible with the mentality of free citizens.[27]

In a work whose title is quite telling, *Dell'ozio in Italia* (On idleness in Italy), published in 1870–71, Carlo Lozzi, too, focuses on the malignant effects of Catholic education, as a fomenter of laziness, slothfulness, and apathy. The Catholic Church, in his view, spreads a tyrannical tendency, and blesses beggary, sloth, a poverty of spirit, the abandonment of any virile principle, and subjection to the powerful; most important, it preaches an asceticism that sacrifices the present life for the sake of the future one. Through such an education, the Catholic Church spreads among Italians an aversion toward work as well as a torpor that discourages any high and dignified purpose. Lozzi imputes the bad religious and moral education to the Catholic Church as deformed by the Counter-Reformation, but also detects roots in the Catholicism of the previous centuries and even ancient Christianity. Lozzi's intention, however, was to modify Catholic morality in order to make it more suitable to the needs of an industrial and liberal society, not to suppress religion. He clearly affirms that religion, together with family and propriety, is one of the necessary pillars of social life, also remarking that people cannot do without religion, morality cannot be independent of religion, and religion—provided it is rightly interpreted and taught—can be an antidote to idleness.[28]

In his *Volere è potere* (Will is power), published in 1869, and reaching a print run of about twenty thousand copies by 1874, Michele Lessona does not evidence either anticlerical or anti-Catholic polemical traits, but neither does he mention God or religion at all. Paolo Mantegazza, in *Le glorie e le gioje nel lavoro* (The glories and joys in work), published in 1870, made antireligious remarks, yet at the same time exalted "the religion of work," and held that work was the law of the universe, the principle of health, morality, and joy, and, last but not least, the only source of wealth. Earlier, in 1860, Mantegazza had published *Il bene e il male: libro per tutti* (Good and evil: A book for everyone), a handbook of civil and religious education in which religion is presented as a necessary support for morality, especially for the working classes. In 1864, he published *Ordine e libertà: Conversazioni di politica popolare* (Order and liberty: Conversations on popular politics), where he reiterated that traditional religion supported a morality that could not be renounced. He added, though, that in order to perform this function well, religion should relinquish any form of temporal power, instead embracing liberal, unifying, and national aspirations. Quite different content appears in *Il Dio ignoto* (The unknown God), written in 1876, where Mantegazza harshly criticizes the corruption of the clergy and atheistic materialism, to advocate a "religion of the ideal" and exalt the constant tropism toward "an unknown God," symbol of a religion of the good, the beautiful, and the true.[29]

The search for a religiosity that was consistent with civil life is also evident in the work of Girolamo Boccardo, who at first had been a free-trade economist and then moderated his stance. In 1872, he published

Prediche di un laico (Sermons of a layman), through which he launched an attack against the morality of "easily contenting oneself"—a morality that, in his opinion, was guilty of encouraging "a contemplative idleness, monasticism, social unrest, the camorra and the Mafia." The opposite morality, "never contenting oneself," has instead "replaced superstitions and errors with the achievements of the intellect, the Holy Office with toleration, and theocracy and tyranny with a free and civil regime." Tolerance and indifference with respect to dogma are, to Boccardo's mind, elements of civil progress, whereas the habits of simulating, suspecting, and plotting are expressions of the clerical mentality, similar to that of Freemasonry and the Communist International.[30]

During those same years, Giovanni Cantoni wrote on the necessity of a morality founded on duty and a politics founded on democracy. Cantoni, an admirer of the federalist Carlo Cattaneo, taught physics at the University of Pavia and became the university's president; he was also a politician and served as a member of parliament. In *Scienza e religione* (Science and religion) he vigorously argued for a civil religion that was more concrete than Mazzini's. His version was designed to oppose both a skeptical indifference toward moral and religious questions and, on the other hand, mystical and theocratic ideas; it had to be founded on work, study, the practice of charity, and a commitment to improve the conditions of the material and moral life of individuals and peoples in this world. What Cantoni entrusted to the youth in 1870 was a true secular faith, in which the best traditions of free thought, science, and tolerance coexisted.

The whole age of the Risorgimento, in sum, was characterized by tenacious efforts—different in their contents and goals as well as the ideas and social rank of their advocates—aimed at realizing a reform of the Italians' moral and religious culture. The reform projects, though, did not succeed in changing the prevailing mentality. Once the Risorgimento was over, as I will show, more than one voice lamented the failed moral and religious reform. And yet the fact remains that the Risorgimento generations committed themselves to a work of reform that no one had tried before and no one would try again. Finally, it should not be forgotten that although few respected the reformers' hopes, there were indeed Italians who developed a religious conception of life inspired by the principle of liberty; these reformers did their part, whether large or small, to aid the struggle for national unity.

13

LITERATURE AND HYMNS OF THE RELIGION OF LIBERTY

A RELIGION must have hymns and music that move hearts and impel action, even when reason admonishes people not to run risks. Alessandro Manzoni composed the poem and the novel that taught people to love liberty as a religious principle. In the ode "Marzo 1821" (March 1821), the patriots, "certain about the ancient virtue within their heart," take a solemn oath: "The sacred words are already given; / either fellows on a deathbed or brothers on a free soil." Their guide was God, who "rejects the foreign force," wants to assure that "every people is free," and hopes that justice wins out over the unjust reason of the sword. Manzoni directs the Italians toward a biblical God who listens to the invocation of the oppressed peoples: "If the land on which you moaned oppressed / pushes the bodies of your oppressors, who told you that sterile, eternal / will the mourning of the Italian people be? / who told you that God, that God who heard you, / will be deaf to our moaning?" This is the God of Exodus, the God of redemption against the tyrant: "Yes, that God who enclosed in a ruby wave / the cruel who were chasing Israel / that God who put the mallet into the vigorous Jael's hand / and guided the blow; / that God who is Father to all the peoples, / and who never told the Germans: / Go, reap where you have not sown; / Spread out your claws, Italy is yours." As Manzoni writes in *Pentecoste*, this is a "living God" who operates in the world, supplying inspiration to a church that suffers, prays, and fights. The divine word that operates in the world to comfort the aggrieved is a "signal to the peoples," edifying the city on the hill so that it will not only be an example of moral redemption and liberty but also a force of rebirth that heralds a new time to come: "Heaven promises a new freedom, and new peoples; / new conquests, too, and a glory / attained in the most beautiful ordeals; / also, a new peace, unmoved by any terrors / and by any treacherous allurements; / a peace which the world derides, but cannot take away."[1]

The God of *I promessi sposi* (*The Betrothed*), too, speaks the language of liberty and courage. Fra Cristoforo, the novel's true exemplary figure, reacts with great determination when Don Rodrigo offends the principle of human liberty, affirming that he could bring Lucia under his protection:

At this suggestion, the friar's indignation, which he had taken pains to hold back until then, overflowed. All those fine resolutions to remain calm and patient were cast to the winds: the new man he had become joined up with the old man that he had been; and, in such cases, Fra Cristoforo really counted for two. "Your protection!" he exclaimed, moving back a couple of paces, fiercely positioning himself on his right foot, putting his right hand to his hip, lifting the left with the forefinger pointed towards Don Rodrigo, and fixing on his face two blazing eyes: "your protection! It is better that you have spoken like this, that you have made to me such a suggestion. You have gone way too far; and I am not afraid of you any more."[2]

Cristoforo is indignant because, as a true Christian, he considers the domination of one man over another to be an offense against God. This indignation gives him the strength to oppose Rodrigo's threats without any fear: "I talk as one should talk to one who is abandoned by God, and can no longer frighten anyone. Your protection! I already knew that that innocent girl is under the protection of God; but now you make me feel this with such a certainty that I no longer need to take care saying this to you. Lucia, I say: and you see how I can pronounce this name with my head high and with steady eyes." Cristoforo knows that Lucia is under God's protection because his God, like the God invoked in the ode "Marzo 1821," is the God of Exodus, who smites the powerful, those whose hearts are hardened, and uplifts the oppressed:

I pity this house: the anathema hangs over it. You will see if God's justice will show respect for these few stones, and will be frightened by a bunch of bullies. You have believed God made a creature in His own image in order to give you the pleasure of tormenting her! You have believed God wouldn't be able to defend her! You have despised His warning! You have judged yourself. Pharaoh's heart was hardened like yours; and God knew how to crush it. Lucia is safe from you; I, a poor friar, can tell you that.[3]

Another character in the novel, the unfortunate Gertrude, who was forced into the cloister by her father, the prince, represents a completely different religion: "Religion, as they had taught it to our poor girl, and as she had received it, did not ban pride but rather sanctified it, and proposed it as a means of obtaining earthly happiness. Thus deprived of its essence, it was no longer religion, but a phantom just like the others."[4] This phantom religion struck terror in her heart, and taught her to be submissive to paternal and all other authorities: "In the intervals when this phantom took first place and towered in Gertrude's imagination, the miserable girl, overwhelmed by confused terrors, and seized by a confused idea of what her duties were, would fancy that her aversion to the cloister, and her resistance to the insinuations of the elders with regard to her choice about her future status, were a fault; and she would promise herself to expiate it by entering the cloister of her own will."[5] The God that dominates Gertrude's mind makes the weak submit to the will of the powerful, while the true Christian God instead makes the powerful yield to the invocations of the poor.

In the face of Lucia's supplication to be freed in the name of God, another character in the novel, the Innominato (the Unnamed), reacts with resentment: "God, God,…always God: those who cannot defend themselves, those who haven't got the strength, always bring in this God, as if they had spoken to him. What do you expect to get from this word of yours?" But that night, the Innominato recalls words that he heard as a child—words about the other life—and those words echo Lucia's words, which the Innominato remembers as uttered not with a tone of supplication but rather "with a tone full of authority."[6] He starts feeling hopeful about a remote but possible redemption, and the next day presents himself to Cardinal Borromeo, asking for help to completely change his life. The God who changed him was not the God who inspires through threats and chastisements but instead the one who speaks a language of charity, forgiveness, and hope.

Manzoni describes Borromeo as a more ambiguous religious figure than Cristoforo, as Borromeo is incapable of completely distancing himself from the prejudices of his times. Borromeo, however, is able to say to the confused but unrepentant Don Abbondio—who, out of personal fear of Rodrigo's threats, had not celebrated the marriage of the betrothed in the first place—that the Christian faith demands and is able to offer the courage that derives from charity:

> And why then, I might ask you, have you committed yourself to a
> ministry that compels you to be at war against the passions of the
> world? But I will rather ask you: how, why can you not consider
> that, if in this ministry—regardless of how you found yourself in
> it—courage is necessary in order to fulfill your obligations, there is
> always One who will infallibly give it to you when you ask for it? Do

you believe that all those millions of martyrs were naturally courageous? That they naturally held life of no account? So many youths who were just beginning to enjoy life, so many elderly used to regretting that it was so near its end, so many young girls, so many wives, so many mothers? They all had courage; for courage was necessary, and they had faith.[7]

In another work, *Osservazioni sulla morale cattolica* (Observations on Catholic morality), Manzoni affirms that the Christian religion requires courage to defend justice from the arrogance of the powerful: "The spirit of the Gospel" is "all frankness and dignity," and "in the conflicts that will inevitably arise with other men in defense of justice, what wins most of the time is a conduct that requires courage." When Manzoni published *I promessi sposi*, the cause of justice was the redemption of Italy from foreign domination. The religion that Manzoni depicted to the Italians required serving that cause with the courage that comes from Christian charity as well as faith in the help of a God who sides with the oppressed.

At the beginning of the Risorgimento, Niccolò Tommaseo (1802–74), a patriot and writer close to Manzoni, openly maintained that the Christian religion was most suited to inspiring the fight for liberty. In the dialogue "Delle rivoluzioni secondo il Vangelo" (Of revolutions according to the Gospel), he emphasizes that if one closely examines the word of Christ, one sees that the Christian religion encourages "courage and the conscience of magnanimous things." It is a Christian's duty to

spare others grief, and remove it or relieve it even at the risk of one's own grief and danger; the duty of a Christian is to impede evildoing. The consequence of this principle is the duty of uplifting the oppressed, suffering with them, and fighting for them, as long as certain or at least very probable mitigation of their suffering derives from our own suffering and fighting. Another consequence is this: one shall point out and reprimand injustices, regardless of who perpetrates them, be they plebeians or princes; and, when it is necessary and possible, one shall repress them. My sacred duty as a Christian is to attain public liberty, as an alleviator of sorrows and terminator of injustices. Patience teaches me to endure my own ills, but not to tolerate the others; and patience, which teaches one to bear misfortune, does not teach one to endure misdeeds.[8]

Against those who hold that the religion of virtue betrays the spirit of the Christian religion, Tommaseo suggests that the Gospel, the apostles, the church fathers, and an endless series of other sources demonstrate how the Christian faith teaches to love liberty. The Italian revolution cannot help but be a "war of religion"—one that originates from love and faith, not from hatred and false judgment—because only a revolution supported and restrained by the true Christian faith will result in liberation, rather than producing a new tyranny.[9] Tommaseo affirms (and he was a good prophet) that if the Italian revolution is successful, the true difficulty will lie in preserving liberty. Italians must first of all liberate themselves from the corrupting consequences that centuries of oppression have had on their minds and thoughts. Revolutions led by leaders without religious faith may be suitable for other peoples, but the Italian revolution can only and must be a political revolution animated by the moral and religious ideal.

Giacomo Leopardi's reflections on the religion of virtue are equally revealing of the new sensibility toward the problem of the moral revolution that spread in the first half of the nineteenth century. As a starting point, he asserts that if virtue is to be resuscitated, it is necessary to return to the true principles of man—that is, the ideals that spur people to virtue, heroism, and the good customs of the ancient republics, and in particular those of the Greeks before the Persian Wars as well as those of the Romans before the Punic Wars. In those republics, merit and virtue received just reward, and the desire for glory was a powerful trigger for great actions. Love of country, too, being the true root of virtue, was one among the principles that mankind should rediscover. "There is no virtue in a people without love of country," he notes in his diary—the "Zibaldone"—on July 21, 1822, and adds: "Wherever a true and warm love of country has existed, and especially where it was more strongly felt—that is, with free peoples—the customs have always been as fierce as they were grave, steady, noble, virtuous, honest, and full of rectitude." Although it may be difficult for those who came afterward to conceive, to live inspired by a love of country made citizens of those ancient republics happy.[10]

Along the path to reaffirming the principles of virtue and love of country, however, the Christian religion represented a formidable obstacle. The ancient religion taught people to love the public good, live for their country, and seek glory.[11] It educated men to elevate themselves "just a little below the gods" as well as to hold a high opinion of human nature.[12] Christianity, in fact, has debased man with respect to God, countered the idea that great men are divine beings, and rendered men inactive, contemplative, and willing to accept despotism. It calls the man who suffers blessed, and deems misery useful and necessary.[13] Leopardi clarifies that in principle, Christianity neither praises nor forbids fighting against tyranny. Nevertheless, men who consider their earthly life to be a sort of exile and care for nothing other than "a country situated in the other world" are more inclined to bear tyranny than those who were educated by the ancient religion to see earthly life as their true fatherland.[14]

Leopardi does not conclude from this diagnosis that the Christian religion itself must be fought and replaced with another one. Rather, he proposes a return to its original principles. Although Christianity, like any other religion, is for Leopardi an illusion, and is responsible for rendering the world feeble and weakening love of country, any rebirth of or return to the natural principles of a proper human life requires illusions—that is, rationales about the reality of things, which can "be real and important only in a different form of life."[15] Religion is necessary to generate and sustain illusions. Religion alone "establishes many of those qualities that were proper to the ancients, or to those men who were closer to nature; pleases our imagination with the idea of the infinite; preaches heroism; gives life, body, reason, and foundation to a thousand of those illusions which constitute the condition of a well-balanced civilization—the happiest condition of the social and incurably corrupt man."[16] A pure Christianity, indeed, has beneficial effects on a peoples' virtue, as demonstrated by the heroic resistance of the Spanish people against the French armies.[17] In order to gain redemption, Italians needed illusions, and they could find them only in religion.

A religion that inspires the struggle for liberty was the central theme of *Confessioni di un italiano* (Confessions of an Italian), a novel composed by Ippolito Nievo between 1857 and 1858. Nievo was born in Padua on November 30, 1831, sailed with Giuseppe Garibaldi from Quarto to take part in the Expedition of the Thousand, and died in the *Ercole* shipwreck when returning from Sicily. Himself a model patriot-writer, he presents Carlo Altoviti and la Pisana, the two protagonists of his novel, as exemplars of a faith in liberty lived with a religious devotion. When his fatherland—the republic of Venice—falls, Altoviti gives expression to a thought that makes the religious conception of liberty almost palpable:

> My life started to ramble among ruins; my intellect got every day reinforced by longer and furious studies; together with the vigor against grief, the strength and the will to do something also grew within myself; love was torturing me, I missed my family, my fatherland was dying. But how could have I loved her? Or better, how could that torpid, marshy, powerless fatherland have awakened within me a dignified, useful, industrious sentiment? Corpses can be lamented, not loved. The liberty of the rights, the sanctity of the laws, the religion

of the glory that together grant the fatherland a quasi-divine majesty, for a long time had not been dwelling under the Lion's wings. Only old, uprooted, and contaminated limbs of the fatherland remained; her spirit was gone, and those who felt in their hearts the devotion to things sublime and eternal looked for other simulacra to which they could dedicate hope and the faith of their souls.[18]

Nievo emphasizes the stark contrast between a religion that teaches liberty and the slimy religious hypocrisy of the Jesuit father Pendola. At a dinner, Altoviti (the narrator), in love with la Pisana (who instead is falling in love with Giulio dal Ponte), says, "Father Pendola glanced Giulio dal Ponte and la Pisana; then he winked at me; two eyes like his did not move for nothing, and every time I met them I felt to the bottom of my soul the cold creeping of their glances." With great pity on his face, Father Pendola offers Altoviti advice to help him cure the piercing pain that is lacerating his soul: follow your duty and remember that you are not only a man but also a "citizen and Christian."[19] His notion of being a Christian means being a militant for the true faith and legitimate governments against subversive ones, ready to use any means in such a war:

> One must seek the good, one must do it so that it will really triumph. One must completely give himself to those who sweat, work, fight for this; one must use the enemies' own weapons to damage them; one must gather in one's heart all the steadiness of which one is capable, and arm one's hand with force, one's mind with prudence, and never fear anything and always remain vigilant in the same place; driven away, one must come back; despised, one must suffer but dissimulate in order to return to eventually win; if necessary, one must also yield, but to rise up again later; and come to terms, but only to gain time. In sum, one must believe in the eternity of the spirit in order to sacrifice this earthly and temporary life for the sake of a future and better immortality.[20]

As far as being a citizen is concerned, the reverend Father Pendola explains with vehement and inspired words that the duty of a Christian citizen is to obey the laws and defend the political order sanctioned by tradition against all its enemies.

Despite the fact that it assumed a cloak of patriotism, Pendola's religion teaches obedience and submissiveness:

> The fatherland, my son, is the religion of the citizen, and the laws are his *creed*. Woe to those who touch them! The inviolability of her decrees—wise heritage of twenty, thirty generations—must be

defended with word, pen, example, and blood! Unfortunately, how-ever, a latent and unwearied phalanx of destroyers tends to doubt what the tribunal of the centuries has decreed as true, just, and im-mutable. One must oppose such barbarity that is bursting out, my son; one must return to the enemies the very damage they are trying to bring us by seeding corruption and discord. Evil against evil must be used courageously, in the manner of the surgeons. Otherwise, we will certainly fall; we, friends and enemies, will fall into the power of those wicked ones who preach an insane liberty in order to impose on us a real servitude; the servitude to immoral, foolhardy, tyranni-cal codes! The servitude to the passions, ours and others; the servi-tude of the soul to the benefit of some greater enjoyment, worldly and transitory. Let us be strong against pride, my son. This is why it is better to be humble; and obey, obey, obey. Let the law of God com-mand, the law that used to be, the law that still is; not the arbitrary will of a few possessed ones who think they are innovating but do nothing other than devouring! My son, do you understand what I am saying?…In this way religion and fatherland go hand in hand; and they prepare for you a beautiful battlefield where you may sacri-fice yourself more worthily than in the guilty idolatry of an affection or of a private interest.[21]

The good Altoviti thus goes to the lawyer Ormenta of Padua in order to inform the Venetian government about subversive students. At the law-yer's house, Altoviti finds a good example of the effects of the religious education imparted by the Jesuits. The lawyer's son, who in his father's eyes is a "little prodigy of wisdom and holiness, who had spontaneously consecrated himself to Saint Anthony," looks to Altoviti like "a yellow-ish, filthy, ruffled little boy," dressed like Saint Anthony, who "amused himself with some sort of sacristy toys," and whose hair was "shaved like a crown on his head and disheveled like the hedgerow of an abandoned orchard, the eyes dim-sighted and bleary, the hands covered with pitch and every filth, and the clothes torn and greasy in all their holiness—all this made a particular contrast with the panegyric woven in a low voice by the lawyer."[22]

The contrast between the religion of Pendola and that of the true Venetian patriots was radical. One of these patriots, Leopardo, as por-trayed in Nievo's novel, represents a particularly shining example of a strong soul who seeks death, overcome by too much disillusionment and discouragement—the last being the end of his fatherland, which had sur-rendered to Napoléon without dignity. Leopardo, too, is a Christian and wants spiritual consolations on his deathbed. But when Pendola appears at the door, Leopardo chases him away: "I don't want him!" To the weak insistence of the priest, Leopardo replies with harsh words: "Better no one than you, Father," and throws all the strength of his religiosity and moral integrity back at him:

> From the threshold of the grave, Father, a last spiritual memory for you, who usually commend the souls of the others. You see how I am dying: calm, happy, serene!…Now, in order to die like this, one must live as I have lived. You see, you will long for such a fortune in vain: you will remember me in that final moment, and will pass to the other world trembling and frightened, like one who feels in his flesh the devil's scratches! Good night, Father; at dawn I will be sleeping calmer than you.[23]

Leopardo knows that God forbids suicide. But, for a republican, once the fatherland is dead, once the liberty of Venice is lost, life is no longer worth living. Death is preferable to servitude: "You see, my friend? Until yesterday, I was thinking about it, but valorously defended myself. I had a fatherland to love and hoped that some day I could serve it, and forget all the rest. Now even that illusion has vanished." To try to save his friend from a death that had already entered into his flesh, Altoviti appeals precisely to the religion of the fatherland and invites Leopardo to become its apostle: "No, Leopardo, not everything is over!…And if it is like that, recover, return to live with us: we will carry the fatherland in our heart wherever we will go, and we will teach and disseminate her holy religion. We are young, better times will smile on us." But Leopardo cannot accept his friend's exhortation because life has left him already. He prays that Altoviti, though, will never abandon their common faith: "Preserve your candid faith, my friend; I urge you thus, for such a faith is, if anything, an incentive to beautiful and honored deeds…. As for me, I depart without any regret…. I am sure I would have waited in vain."[24] Leopardo dies as a true Christian. Attending his friend, Altoviti understands how much religion can achieve "in a high and manly soul," and for the first time envies "those sublime convictions" he does not feel.[25]

The religion that brings Clara, la Pisana's sister, to the cloister is as miserable as Leopardo's republican religion is great. Clara freely chooses the cloister, although she was strongly encouraged by her mother, who by this means could squander her daughter's dowry in card games. She freely decides to reject Lucilio's love for her and abandon his ideals to spend her life in a cloister. Society is a work of God, Lucilio exclaims, "and those who withdraw from it bear the guilt of a crime or the cowardice of fear, or the ineptitude of inertness in their soul!" Neither these words nor the most heartrending supplications, though, shake Clara's resolve to take final vows. For Lucilio it is a searing defeat; for Clara's mother, Redenta, and the cloister, it is a great triumph: "The old nun rejoiced so much that she wouldn't have traded that joy for the grandest abbey of her order. It was the joy of pride satisfied, and there is no pride greater than the pride of the humble. But it was also the joy of revenge, the joy, that is, that comes of avenging oneself on others for one's own unhappiness, and this, too, had no limits."[26] Clara's decision affirmed all the old nun's power, to take away the man Clara loved, and the power of the religion that had corroded Venetian liberty. It is impossible to better delineate the features of a religion that must be despised by everyone who loves liberty.

Truly Christian, by contrast, is the religion that animates la Pisana's love of fatherland. When Altoviti visits her for the last time, at her deathbed, la Pisana tells him that the heavenly fatherland is now more important to her than the earthly fatherland—their most beloved Venice: "O Carlo! Don't talk to me about Venice, my fatherland is so much closer, or farther away, if you will, but one gets there with a much shorter journey. Up there, up there, Carlo!"[27] But immediately afterward, she encourages Altoviti to work for the fatherland that they have both loved: "That's true; I will not at all die if you will live; if you will honor my memory by making those few sacrifices—which, if badly, I've yet made for you— profit! If you think…of the children that you begot and to whom you owe sacred and inviolable duties, if you think of your fatherland, my fatherland, Carlo, for which this little heart of mine has always beaten, and for which, wherever God's will shall take me, I will never cease praying, and hoping!" La Pisana knows that Altoviti has always loved her, ever since they were children. In the name of his love for her, she asks him to swear that he will live fighting faithfully for their ideals: "Now, I want and demand that my death, to me so easy and sweet, shall not cause a whole family despair, and shall not deprive a whole country and all of mankind of all the good that you still can and must do!…Carlo, are you strong and valiant? Do you have faith in virtue and justice? Swear to me then that you shall not be a coward, that you shall not abandon your outpost, that you, miserable or happy, accompanied or alone, shall fight for justice and for virtue, to the utmost!" When Altoviti eventually swears to her that he will live for the good of his family and the honor of the fatherland that they together loved, she feels that she has fulfilled her religious duty and is ready at last for her encounter with God.[28]

For la Pisana, the love of God and the fatherland are one and the same thing. After having exhorted her beloved Altoviti to live for the fatherland, she invites him to revere with her the clemency of God, "who surrounds with the most splendid colors the setting sun," and thank him for granting men a foretaste of the unutterable happiness that he prepares for them in the other life. La Pisana's faith in God and in liberty is so deeply rooted in her conscience that she is indifferent to all ritual. She accepts last rites, but only because her sister Clara, the nun, "would suffer a great deal to know that I have died without a priest." But those rites look like a funeral conducted with gloomy and dreadful pomp at the bed of the sufferer. Rather, for la Pisana, religious observance comprised such acts as Altoviti's cutting a lock of hair from his dead beloved and putting it side by side with another lock of hair that he had taken from her when she was a young girl, so that the two little objects would hold their love. And religious observance comprised above all the obligation that he had solemnly assumed to dedicate the rest of his life to Italy's liberty.

The religious spirit of the Risorgimento also had its music and hymns. The words and notes of *Va', pensiero* capture the sense of liberty understood as a religious aspiration that comes from God. This God helps men to transform suffering into virtue, and to resurrect themselves and become free again. Such was the religiosity that was being revived, and Giuseppe Verdi's expression of it is unsurpassed.[29] The hymn of the Risorgimento did not come about through a deliberate plan or according to any theory, as the Jacobin religion had. For the opportunity given by destiny or Providence to be seized, what was needed was a man who loved to read the Bible (even though as an adult he did not go to Mass). Verdi himself reveals to us that his source was the Bible:

One winter evening [1840], just as I was leaving the De Christoforis Gallery, I bumped into Merelli [the impresario of La Scala], who was on his way to the theater. Heavy snowflakes were falling from the sky and Merelli, grabbing me arm in arm, invites me to accompany him to the box-office at La Scala. On the way we start chatting, and he tells me he was in difficulties because of the new opera he had to present: he had commissioned Nicolai to write the opera, but the composer was dissatisfied with the libretto. "Just imagine," cries Merelli, "a libretto by Solera, astonishing!!…magnificent!!…extraordinary!!…The dramatic situations work perfectly well, grandiose: beautiful verses!…And yet that obstinate Maestro doesn't want to hear about it and declares the libretto is impossible!…"I don't know where on earth to turn to get another one for him quickly." "I can help you," I comforted him. "Didn't you have the *Proscritto* written for me? I haven't composed a single note of it: I put it at your disposal." "Oh bravo…this is what I call luck!" Thus talking we had got to the theater: Merelli summons Bassi—poet, stage manager, call-boy, librarian, and more—and bids him find out immediately whether he can find a copy of the *Proscritto* in the archive. A copy is there. But at the same time Merelli picks up another manuscript and shows it to me, exclaiming: "See, this is the libretto by Solera! Such a beautiful theme, how can you possibly to turn it down? Take it…read it." "What should I do with it?…no, no, I have no will whatsoever for reading librettos." "Eh…you won't get hurt!…read it and then you will bring it back to me"—. And he hands over the manuscript to me: it was a big folder written in large characters, as was the style then: I roll it up and take leave of Merelli, heading back to my place. On the way, I felt some sort of vague uneasiness, a profound sadness, an anguish that gripped my heart!…I got home and, with an almost violent gesture, I threw the manuscript on the table, remaining standing before it. In falling on the table, the folder had opened of itself: without knowing how, my eyes are gazing at the page before me, where this verse faces me: "*Va', pensiero, sull'ali dorate.*" I skim through the following verses and am deeply impressed by them, the more so since they were almost a paraphrase of the Bible, which I always loved to read.[30]

The music of *Va', pensiero* originates from the soul of a severely tried, defeated man, who finds within himself, though, the strength to create music for a people that can redeem itself with the help of the same God that Machiavelli, three centuries before, had invoked in the solemn conclusion to *The Prince*. Verdi immediately understands that behind the words of the *Va', pensiero*, there lies the biblical narration of Exodus: the slaves who become a nation through the long trek that is simultaneously a journey toward a place and an internal transformation. None of the slaves who departed from Egypt got to the Promised Land. Many physically died; all spiritually died, for they had to get rid of their servile mentality to acquire a consciousness of the duties that are the soul of liberty. Verdi wanted to write a music of redemption, and for this reason he demands that the librettist highlight the prophecy:

This reminds me of a comical scene I had with Solera some time before: in the third act he had put a little love duet between Fenena and Ismaele: I didn't like it, for it cooled the action and, it seemed to me, detracted from the biblical grandeur that characterized the drama: one morning when Solera was at my place, I pointed this out to him: but he wouldn't say I was right, not so much because he didn't agree as because it bothered him to redo a finished work: we argued back and forth: I stuck to my point and so did he. He asked me what I wanted in place of the duet, and I suggested he could write a prophecy of the prophet Zechariah. He did not think the idea was bad, and, through "ifs" and "buts," said he would think about it and write something. That was not quite what I wanted, for I knew that many days would pass before Solera would resolve to write a verse. I locked the door, put the key in my pocket, and, half joking, half seriously, told Solera: "You don't get out of here if you've not written the prophecy: here is the Bible, you've got all the words ready in there. All you have to do is to put them into verse." Solera, whose temperament was quick to anger, didn't appreciate that idea of mine. A flash of fury gleamed in his eyes. I passed an uncomfortable minute, for the poet was well-built and could have made quick work of the stubborn maestro that I was. But all of a sudden he sits down and, a quarter of an hour later, the prophecy was written![31]

It was the prophecy needed for an enslaved people that could be redeemed by its own strength with the help of God: "Oh who weeps? / Who raises lamentations / of cowardly women to the Eternal God? / Oh arise, anguished brothers, / The Lord speaks through my lips! / I discern in the darkness of the future…/ The ignoble chains shall be broken!…/ The wrath of the Lion of Judah / Already falls on the treacherous sand!" It was a prophecy addressed to a people that had been afflicted and was mournful, but wanted to return to a dignified and powerful stance, and rise to virtue again:

> *Va', pensiero, sull'ali dorate;* / Go, thought, on wings of gold;
> *Va', ti posa sui clivi, sui colli,* / Go, settle on the slopes, the
>   hills,
> *Ove olezzano tepide e molli* / Where soft and mild smells
> *L'aure dolci del suolo natal!* / The sweet air of the native
>   land!
> *Del Giordano le rive saluta,* / Greet the banks of the Jordan,
> *Di Sionne le torri atterrate.* / Zion's toppled towers.
> *Oh mia patria sì bella e perduta!* / Oh, my country so beautiful and lost!

> *Oh membranza sì cara e fatal!* / Oh, memory so dear and
>   lethal!
> *Arpa d'ôr dei fatidici vati,* / Golden harp of the prophetic
>   seers,
> *Perché muta dal salice pendi?* / Why do you hang mute from
>   the willow?
> *Le memorie nel petto raccendi,* / Rekindle the memories in
>   the heart
> *Ci favella del tempo che fu!* / Speak to us of the time gone
>   by!
> *O simìle di Solima ai fati* / Either similar to Solomon from
>   the fates,
> *Traggi un suono di crudo lamento,* / Draw a sound of sad
>   lamentation,
> *O t'ispiri il Signore un concento* / Or else let the Lord inspire
>   you with a harmony
> *Che ne infonda al patire virtù* / Which shall instill virtue in
>   our suffering![32]

A God that instills virtue: in Solera's words and Verdi's music, the religion of virtue that Machiavelli had imagined and hoped for finds its song and prayer; it becomes religion in the full sense of the word, with that force of moving souls that the Risorgimento had been waiting for. There is no better explanation of the religious power of Verdi's music than Massimo Mila's remark:

Every hint was immediately grasped. Imagine when they were sung *coram populo* by the chorus of La Scala, and emphasized by such music, which upset the soul of the audience, brought a lump into their throats, and made their eyes grow dim with tears, instilling even in the laziest a new warmth of national brotherhood and solidarity in the devotion to a common ideal. This strange Italian fatherland, which had existed in poetry and in the arts long before it was born as a geographical reality and within the conscience of the citizens, found in Verdi's melody one of its most plastic and concrete ways in which to stir the imagination of the people.[33]

14

APOSTLES AND MARTYRS

"Imagination," "illusions," "faith," and "devotion" are all words that often loom large in the writings of the Risorgimento's protagonists, from the greatest leaders to the more modest militants. In the previous centuries, such words were detached from any profound sentiments. This time, though, there was a correspondence between sentiment and language, since the words had been a site of laborious struggle. They drove action, to the point of self-sacrifice. Silvio Pellico, to cite the obligatory example, received an education based on love of family, country, and humanity.[1] Pellico discovered his faith in prison, although he was already convinced that if God existed, another life also should exist as a reward for those who suffered unjustly. Guided by his vision of Christianity, Pellico decided to commit himself to teaching—in spite of the pretentious philosophy that claimed to be a substitute for religion—the true Christian message: "It will have to be love of God and of one's neighbor; namely, it will have to be just what Christianity teaches.… Be therefore coherent! Be a Christian! Stop being scandalized by the misuses! And do not cavil about some difficult issues of the doctrine of the Church, for the central point is this, and it is exceedingly terse: love God and your neighbor."[2]

Pellico read the Bible in prison. This reading did not incline him at all to bigotry—that is, that "misunderstood devotion that renders one pusillanimous or fanatical." On the contrary, it taught him "to love God and men, to long ever more for the kingdom of justice, and to abhor iniquity, forgiving the iniquitous." Instead of contradicting the teachings of philosophy, for Pellico, Christianity reinforced them with higher reasons. Because he was firmly convinced that God is always close to or in us, or rather that we are in him, Pellico was able to face his daily solitude without dread. The faith that Pellico finds in prison is composed of charity and compassion for those who have veered from the path of Christ, such as, for instance, the poor women who, from his prison cell, he hears talking and quarreling, and especially a woman named Maddalena, who he imagines is more beautiful and pitiful than the others, and reminds him of the passages in the Gospel where Christ offers his forgiveness to the sinners and welcomes them among the souls that he honors the most. "As soon as I could sincerely pray for everyone and no longer hate anybody," Pellico writes, "the doubts about faith vanished away: *Ubi charitas et amor, ibi Deus est*." When he says good-bye to the imperial inspector who had accompanied him to Milan, he remarks: "I passionately love my country, but have no hatred for any other nation. Civilization, wealth, power, and glory are different in the different nations; but in all there are souls obedient to the great vocation of man—to love, and to pity, and to do good."[3]

Luigi Settembrini also embodied a model of religiosity that inspired generous actions for one's country. In his *Ricordanze della mia vita*, he describes the contrast between the prejudiced religiosity that dominated the life of the subjects of the Kingdom of Naples, and the religion of virtue and liberty that his father taught him, with reference to classical and Christian examples. Like Leopardi, Settembrini vindicates the value of religious faith and the illusions of the fools who work for great ideals: "Without that faith, that ardent fever, and that enthusiasm, the wise would still be debating and would not have actually done anything." Settembrini blames the church for having imposed "three centuries of foreign and clerical servitude" on Italy, and argues that precisely because Italy was a slave to political and religious tyranny, Italian unity could never be a mere political achievement but had to be "also a religious fact." And religious indeed was the commitment of Settembrini and the other youths who adhered to the patriotic movement: "It was a wonderful evening, the stars were shining brighter than ever, we had been reasoning for a long while about the miserable condition of the fatherland, and I spoke to them openly for the first time about *Giovane Italia*, as a new political religion of which we had to be the apostles and the martyrs."[4]

After being arrested, Settembrini awaited the court's verdict from his prison cell. Fearing a death sentence—which was imposed but later commuted to life imprisonment—he writes his wife to explain how, in his soul, Christian faith and love of liberty sustain one another:

> If I am sentenced to death, I can promise on our love, and on the love we have for our children, that your Luigi will not betray his principles; I will die with the certainty that my blood will bear good to my country; I will die with the serene courage of the martyrs; I will die and my last words will be for my country, to my Gigia [his wife], my Raffaele, my Giulia.... You will tell them that they shall remember the words I said in court on the day of my defense. You will

tell them that I, blessing and kissing them a thousand times, leave three precepts to them: to recognize and adore God; to love work; to love, above anything else, the fatherland.... True virtue produces only bitterness. My enemies do not feel the beauty and dignity of this grief. In my place, they would tremble: I am calm because I believe in God and in virtue. I do not tremble: those who sentence me should tremble, for they offend God. My dear Gigia, I will always be myself. God sees into my soul and knows that I am calm not out of my own strength, but out of the strength that comes to me from him. Look, I am writing to you with no tears, with a steady hand, with a serene mind, and my heart is not upset. My God, I thank you for what you are working within me: even in these moments I feel you, I recognize you, I adore you, and I thank you. My God, comfort my most discomforted wife and give her strength to endure this sorrow: my God, protect my children, guide them toward the good, draw them toward yourself, as they have no father, they are your sons: preserve them from vice: they have no help whatsoever from men: I entrust them to you, and pray for them. O God, I commend to you this country: give wisdom to those who rule it; may my blood appease all the anger and hatred of all sides; may it be the last blood that is shed on this afflicted earth.[5]

A love of liberty also pervades the testimony of the martyrs of Belfiore—the patriots put to death in Mantua by the Austrian government between 1851 and 1855. Three of them, Enrico Tazzoli, Giovanni Grioli, and Bartolomeo Grazioli, were Catholic priests; the others held to a fervid Christian faith. Father Luigi Martini narrated and documented the last days of their lives. With the strength of faith and great human charity, Martini helped them face the gallows. His account exalts the Christian faith of the sentenced men, and also emphasizes that these martyrs' love of fatherland was fully in keeping with the Christian message. Tazzoli, the organizer of the anti-Austrian plot, stresses that a Catholic priest must be ready to sacrifice himself for the fatherland and edify it with virtue. Although a Catholic priest is obligated to remain uninvolved in politics, he can and indeed must "love his fatherland, his brothers, and pursue the public and the private good." In fact, by committing himself to the service of God and the church, a priest does not cease to be a citizen as well as a member of human society.[6]

The layman Bernardo Canal displays a similar religiosity. Born in Venice on August 4, 1824, he suffered from a serious illness as a child to which he lost his right eye. He studied law at the University of Padua and went on to become an esteemed journalist. As he wrote on the wall of his prison cell, he lived "28 years, 3 months, 28 days." Before heading to the gallows, he engraved the last four stanzas of Manzoni's poem "Cinque maggio" on his cell wall. He modifies the text in several places, perhaps because he is quoting it by heart, but the conclusion is an explicit adaptation of Manzoni's invocation to his own situation, as if God is particularly close to the man who dies for liberty: "From the exhausted ashes / Scatter every guilty word, / That God who knocks down and rises up, / Who wearies and comforts, / On the deserted bed / Next to me descended." Canal does not repudiate a love of liberty in order to rejoin God; he invokes God, the Christian God depicted by Manzoni, so that God will be close when he gives his life for the fatherland. Commenting on the verses transcribed and adapted by Bernardo, Martini observes: "And will anybody now continue to hold that the Catholic religion degrades and annihilates man, and kills the patriot, and makes one refuse to recognize the fatherland and the nation? For once, let us render unto Caesar the things which are Caesar's, and unto God the things that are God's."[7]

For other patriots, religion was above all a faith in the moral ideal. This is certainly true of Carlo Poma, born in Mantua on December 7, 1823. His father was Leopoldo Poma, a tribunal councillor and learned jurist, and his mother was Anna Filippini, a woman of impassioned patriotic sentiments. He became a physician and surgeon, and distinguished himself as a man of letters and a polyglot. Poma died in Belfiore on December 7, 1852. He conceived of national emancipation as the outcome of the strength of a moral ideal. That ideal, he says to his comforter, "does not withdraw," in the same way that a river, "which, grown bigger by the addition of the many waters coming down from the mountains, departs from its river-bed, overcomes its embankments, overflows and drags with its flood those very embankments, the houses, the plants, the flock, and whatever else obstructs its flow or does not abet it." With words and living examples of brotherly charity, the Italians will gain liberty. The strength of morality and education will prevail over the strength of the cannons.[8]

Grazioli, a priest, understood with great clarity that Italy's redemption would never have occurred in antagonism to religion; rather, it was achieved thanks to religion. According to Grazioli, if Italy drives away the religion of Christ—and hence good faith, justice, and loyalty to our fathers—it will not be able to attain the crown of glory and honor, nor will it be great and admired, as is befitting Italy's position.[9] Grazioli's Christianity was enriched by classical themes, to the point that Socrates and Jesus were for him conflated in a single ideal, offering what could be seen as Socratic Christianity. Socrates was convinced that by philosophizing even at the point of death, he performed an action appreciated by the gods. He was eminently religious, as testified to by his reflections on truth and justice as well as holiness and the soul. His dialogues cannot be read without wonder and some moral gain. And if Socrates was able to philosophize about such ideals in prison during the last days of his life, a priest should be able to consecrate his life to doing good; for doing good is an eminently religious work, in keeping with the most sublime moral philosophy. Full of goodness, Socrates loved his disciples and educated them; a true priest must love his parishioners and educate them in the Christian faith and morals in order to render them true Christians as well as upright citizens. For that charity that he regarded as the core of a Christian life, Grazioli plotted to liberate Italy and, as a result, faced the gallows with great dignity.

Tito Speri, the most famous among the Belfiore martyrs, approached capital punishment in the spirit of a Christian martyr, Martini recounts. Speri found great consolation in reading the Gospel, and said that he endeavored to carry within his heart both God and the people, both religion and the fatherland. He did not believe in the materialism and sensualism that had conquered the minds of many young men of his time, and instead maintained that only the religious spirit could supply the strength necessary to the nation's Risorgimento. Italy needed great ideas and concepts in keeping with the Italian genius as well as in agreement with Italy's historical tradition, and such ideas and concepts could be found in the Catholic faith. For Speri, the religion of Christ was not a human creation but rather an idea, a divine revelation. One cannot love the fatherland in the right manner and reject Christ's religion.[10]

Pietro Domenico Frattini, the tenth victim of the Austrian repression, put aside his love of fatherland in order to concentrate on his love of Christ. As Martini explains: "All my family—he said—is Catholic, in the footsteps of our forefathers. In our house religion is simple, frank, and ruled by love of God and love of the neighbor. My mother used to repeat to us that we have to demonstrate our faith through our good and holy deeds, rather than with vain clamor and through lengthy prayers said without any concentration and without one's heart. Therefore *I, born, educated, and raised as a Catholic, want to die as a Catholic as well.*" True love for the fatherland and liberty originates not from opinions but instead from an idea that is "innate in or incarnated by man, and that advances through the years and develops itself, without ever stopping, notwithstanding all the efforts of the powerful to stifle it in embryo, or to kill it as soon as it blooms or gives any sign of life."[11] These words illustrate the difference between the new religion of liberty and Rousseau's old idea that liberty requires the repudiation of Christianity.

15

MASTERS

THE MARTYRS' RELIGION was consistent with the teachings of the Risorgimento's moral and political leaders. Albeit in quite different ways, all of them—Vincenzo Gioberti, Giuseppe Mazzini, Camillo Benso Count of Cavour, and even Giuseppe Garibaldi—lived by a religious conception that regarded Italy's liberty as the fundamental principle of life. They were aware that national emancipation required a religious sentiment. Gioberti, the main advocate of the project of national unification under the aegis of the pope, fought against the religion of idleness in the name of the religion of virtue. For him, idleness contradicts the will of God, "who created man to act, rather than merely take pleasure from things," and idleness "eradicates morality from the roots." Virtue, by contrast, is in keeping with God's will, as it glorifies and deifies man by rendering him—within the limits of his finite nature—similar to God.[1]

The causes of Italians' malignant inclination toward idleness and "cowardly indolence" were "bad rulers" along with a religion misunderstood as an "ascetic quietism" that heavily betrays the "evangelical principles":

It is no surprise that Christianity, understood and misunderstood as if inertness were its essence, is conducive to idleness; it is equally not surprising that patience—which is a sublime virtue when it is joined with evangelical activity, with faith animated by work, with an ardent love of one's neighbor, and with the cult of anything that might make one's neighbor happier and better off—becomes vicious when it departs from such a virtuous track. Machiavelli, who also criticizes the corrupt asceticism that *wants you to be ready to suffer rather than capable of accomplishing something strong*, adds that this disorder does not derive from Christianity as such, but from the vileness of men, *who have interpreted our religion according to idleness and not according to virtue.*[2]

On the contrary, the religion of Christ exalts any acts that are motivated by goodwill, are magnanimous, and require one to work for the triumph of liberty and justice in the city of man: "[Christ] passed on earth benefiting and accomplishing in an extraordinary and immediate way, worthy of his creative power, those same wonders of charity that are achieved through the process of becoming civilized over the centuries in a natural and gradual way. By improving the legal, judicial, and governmental orders; by abolishing the dominion of man over man, and any form of violent, fickle, and despotic mastery; by making wars rarer and more moderate; by unifying and uniting the nations; by promoting and increasing knowledge." This civilizing process glorifies and elevates to heaven the sincere and upright cooperators for the common good on earth.[3]

Mazzini, the most influential apostle of the religion of the fatherland, taught a theory of political emancipation based on the principle that a people can resurrect themselves only by means of virtue and the "religion of truth"—that is, not by means of Machiavellian devices or Jesuitical reticence.[4] Rather than a disillusioned Florentine secretary, for Mazzini, the true masters to follow were Socrates and Jesus:

> No; one cannot resurrect with Jesuitism, as one cannot regenerate a people with lies. Jesuitism is the instrument of religions that are about to die; lying is the art of peoples doomed to serve others. By the hand of executioners, Socrates and Jesus died in their bodies, but their souls live forever, transfused century after century in the improved life of the generations. Every moral and philosophical progress accomplished for the past two thousand years bears the name of that first progress, and a whole age of emancipatory civilization drew for fourteen centuries on the auspices of the sacred name of Jesus.[5]

For him, religion is a faith that gives men the strength to translate moral ideals into action, and, as such, it regenerates a people. It is the principle urging men to find new political and social forms; it is the concept elevating the individual, purifying him of egoism and rendering him capable of acting in history to actualize a moral ideal. For this reason, religion is the source of the impulse for achieving harmony between thought and action.[6]

Mazzini was profoundly convinced that in the absence of a religious sentiment, there has never been, and can never be, any redemption or emancipation:

> Man is higher up than the earth that sustains him. He lives on its surface, not in the middle of it. His feet touch the ground, but his

forehead faces the sky, as if he wanted to set out for it. Up there, in the highest, splendid clear sky or hidden in the midst of stormy clouds, lies his polestar. From the bottom of his soul he aspires to a future that he at present cannot hope to reach, but that is the goal of any activity of life, the secret of being, the guarantee of progress; and every great epoch of humanity makes that aspiration more intense, and spreads a new light on the concept that man forms about that future. To that light, corresponds a social renovation—a new earth in the image of the new sky. Historically speaking, I do not know of a single conquest of the human spirit, of even one important step on the way to the improvement of human society, which is not rooted in a strong religious belief; and I say that any doctrine in which the aspiration to the ideal remains neglected—in which, that is, a solution to this supreme necessity of some faith is not found, as the times allow for, and a solution to the eternal problem of the origin and the fate of humanity—is and will always be incapable of actualizing the concept of a new world.[7]

For the emancipation of a people, religion has a much greater value than philosophy.[8] The French Revolution is the prime example. Mazzini interpreted it as a victory of an ideal lived as faith over dead institutions, as a manifestation of the most genuine religious spirit. He writes that the French Revolution was "Luther's work in the political sphere," and the revolution's glory and power resides precisely in this aspect.[9] Mazzini points Italians to a religion of truth and of duty:

Truth! The rising Italy asks but that, and cannot live but with that. The rising Italy seeks her end in the present and the norm of her life in the future—a moral criterion, a method of choice between good and evil, between truth and error, without which no responsibility, and hence no liberty, can exist for her. Centuries of servitude, centuries of egoism (which is the only foundation for the life of a slave); centuries of corruption, slowly and shrewdly instilled by a Catholicism deprived of any sense of its mission, have spoiled, perverted, nearly erased the instinct for the great and sacred things that God bestowed on Italy.... The resurrecting Italy needs to fortify herself by acquiring an awareness of her duties, of her strength, of virtue animated by sacrifice, and of the certainty about the next triumph, which is in the logic of things: and you just give her a theory of interests, opportunities, fictions; you just give her a misconceived Machiavellianism, presented by pupils of his to whom he, if he could come back, would say: I had the grave in front me; you, fools, the cradle of a people. The rising Italy needs men who embody that truth with which she has to identify herself; let them preach that truth loudly, let them represent it in their deeds, let them confess it—should it happen—till their death.

Without like-minded people, Mazzini concludes, Italy will fall "under the yoke of the first foreign or domestic master who will want to inflict tyranny on her; a slack Italy, irresolute, disheartened about herself and others, without any stimulus of honor and glory, without any religion of truth and without any courage for translating it into action."[10] Although intolerant of Mazzini's prophetic language, Cavour, too, was sensitive to the religious problem, and considered Christian religion a support for the construction of secure liberal institutions, but only if religion emancipated itself from the superstition and profound corruption that rendered it a prop for reactionary regimes. An eloquent document about Cavour's thought on this issue is the letter he wrote on August 8, 1829, to his uncle, Count Gian Giacomo de Sellon, a Calvinist publicist who fervently supported initiatives for civil and humanitarian progress. His wife, Cecilia de Budé, also a Calvinist and catechist, had long striven to convert Cavour to religion, but without success.[11] "After my last trip to Geneva," Cavour writes, "a great change has occurred within me: I have several times departed from the paternal house, I have traveled throughout Piedmont, I have read the books that had been presented to me as impious, and I could not but become aware of the fragile foundation of our religious beliefs. A stay of six months on the Riviera of Genoa made me become cognizant of how seriously corrupt a population can be rendered by ignorance, by superstition." In this same letter, Cavour reveals the readings that distanced him from the religious convictions he had absorbed during his childhood and early adolescence: "After having read Guizot and Benjamin Constant, it is impossible for me not to open my eyes. And believing in the pope's infallibility is as difficult for me as believing that two plus two equals three. We must keep up appearances, though; but pretending is exceedingly painful when one is convinced of being right."[12] A rationalistic crisis sharply distanced Cavour from the practice of worship and the prevailing religious customs in Italy—specifically, in his Piedmont region—"thronged with monks of hypocritical religiosity," but did not destroy his own religious sentiment, or his belief that such a religious sentiment is the foundation of liberty.[13]

Evidence of this can be found in another letter that Cavour wrote, this time to his aunt, Cécile de Sellon, in which he repeated that religious faith is not grounded in rational arguments but rather is a sentiment proper to man that finds in Christianity the form most adequate for the modern world. Cavour is convinced that religious truth is of a completely different order from common truths grasped by the human spirit. Consequently, to try to prove religious truth with the same methods employed by the social and physical sciences is irrational. Reason cannot lead us to firm religious convictions. The true guide for that is religious sentiment, which exists in different degrees in all men, and drives them to seek a relationship with the unknown force that "rules the universe and acts on our hearts." Cavour considers the action and development of the religious sentiment to be "an urgent duty of our nature," and believes that this sentiment could operate in a right way in his own times, "both in the most elevated and in the most modest souls," yet only within the horizons of Christianity.[14]

Besides Constant's ideas, Cavour also appreciated Guizot's remarks about the importance of religion as an association of believers. He did not doubt, however, that religion had everything to gain from not confining itself to a system of dogmas and remaining far from political power. After having recognized the sublime quality of evangelical morality, Cavour notes that he is inclined to think that the Supreme Being, who placed within us an emanation of his divine nature, has left us, despite the fact that he showed us the way to salvation, the liberty to use our reason to change the forms of worship, and the principles of morality.[15] When the religious sentiment is linked to an earthly authority, it ends up becoming simply an exterior practice, an almost mechanical habit that coexists with all vices and sometimes with all crimes. Liberty instead helps the religious sentiment restore itself through the conflict of ideas and open discussion. When religious liberty is fully guaranteed, it will grant religion an invincible strength and aid in constantly trying to perfect itself.[16]

For Cavour, advancements in the religious spirit are products of the Enlightenment. This is why he hoped for the development of a Christianity guided by reason that would unite religion, morality, happiness, and philosophy. And this is why he fully agreed with Alphonse Lamartine's words at the Académie française:

If I look at the next generation, I would say to them…happy are those who come after us! Everything announces for them a great century…. A pure and scholarly generation advances through life with gravity.... Philosophy, embarrassed for having craved death and claimed nothing,...reclaims divinity by acknowledging her God. History is extended and clarified, and she writes of a full-fledged man.... Poetry is born again, child to enthusiasm and inspiration.... A religious breath invests human thinking, and this intimate and sincere religion rests only on conscience and faith. Politics ceases to be the shameful art of corrupting and deceiving in order to enslave.... Morality, reason, and liberty finally do away with the vagueness of theories.[17]

Although Cavour did not experience religion as faith in revelation, he felt that it was a profound moral force working for liberty, but only if it is not altered by dogma and superstition. In a January 9, 1834, diary entry, he writes: "For those of us who have no religious faith, it is necessary that the tenderness of our soul is deployed for the good of humanity." Francesco Ruffini, one of the finest scholars on Cavour, has identified the source of this passage: a letter from Victor Jacquemont, an eighteenth-century writer. After the words quoted by Cavour, Jacquemont adds, "It must be our religion."[18] Cavour omits these words but accepts their meaning. All his endeavors to achieve national unity and create a secular state are supported and inspired by a religion lived as a moral teaching. Notwithstanding his stark aversion to the fantasies of religious resurrection and waiting for new eras, Cavour saw Rome as the capital of Italy not only as the completion of the great political project of national unification but also as a task of universal significance that Italy should fulfill before and for the world. This task amounted to resolving the century-long conflict that had opposed the church and modern civilization, and signing in the Campidoglio a "new peace of religion, a treaty that will bring to the future of human society much greater effects than those brought about by the Peace of Westphalia!" This dream captured his imagination so thoroughly that the diplomats who listened to him were dismayed "when they saw that economist, that shrewd politician, and such a practical mind express himself with such warmth about the possible, nay near alliance between Catholicism and liberty."[19]

The same inspiration that animated Cavour also guided Marco Minghetti, the prime minister of the Kingdom of Italy between March 1863 and September 1864, and again between July 1873 and March 1876. Minghetti interpreted the separation between state and church, and the formula "A Free Church in a Free State," as the most effective means to contribute to both the reinforcement of the liberal state and the flourishing of a new religious and moral life for Italians. In the conclusion of "Stato e Chiesa" (1878), which he wrote in a spirit of "reverence and gratitude" for Cavour, Minghetti remarks:

> Finally, considering the effects of this arrangement, it seemed to us that they are to be propitious to civilization. When religious confessions coexist with equal rights, and when they are joined by critical thinking—which not only will invigilate over them but also will strive to sweep away dogmas—they will have to search within themselves for the reason for their existence and the impulse for finding adherents. It will be a race of wisdom and virtue, and victory will go to those who better instill their spirit into the souls, and give more benefits to mankind. This is our hope. Therefore the true believers must not fear the separation of church and state but rather should long for it in the faith that liberty will bring to the triumph of their doctrine. Men who above anything else seek and love science also cannot oppose such a separation, aware of the fact that no prejudices will anymore come in their way. But those who must appreciate it most are the ones who are animated by a vivid religious sentiment, and whose needs cannot be satisfied by any of the current forms [of relationship between politics and religion, state and church]. They are yet convinced that the protection by the government and other governmental devices would have no power for renovating the beliefs. An initiative that might offer again, to the generations that are eager for faith, the symbol upon which to focus can only originate from the spontaneity of a free conscience. But the highest achievement of humanity will always be in its aspiration for a supreme ideal not restricted within the limits of this mortal life and capable of connecting man, society, earth, universe, and God.[20]

Garibaldi, who was not only a military chief but also an inspiring moral figure, disdained the pope and clergy for their immorality and for their aversion to the cause of liberty. Yet he possessed a strong religious sentiment. Raised in Nizza (Nice), a town that oscillated between a rigorous Jansenism and a papalist Counter-Reformation religiosity, Garibaldi accepted the moral content of Christianity, but completely rejected the dogmas, rites, and politics of the Catholic Church. When he went to Rome for the first time, in 1825, he called it the "capital of the world,…cradle of that holy religion whose first apostles were masters of the nations, emancipators of the peoples, but which was then handed over to foreign domination by their fallen, debased, and merchant-like successors—real scourges of Italy." Garibaldi distinguished true priests from false ones, noting, for instance, that Don Giovanni Verità, the parish priest of Modigliana who helped him escape to Tuscany, and hence saved his life after the fall of the Roman Republic and his failed attempt to reach Venice, was a "true priest of Christ, and by Christ I mean here the virtuous man and the legislator, not that Christ made God by the priests and used by them to cover the fallaciousness of their existence."[21]

Garibaldi had drawn the idea of Christ as a man, legislator, and emancipator from Saint-Simon's *Le nouveau Christianisme*, a book he discovered in 1831 and kept with him until the last days of his life in Caprera. Saint-Simon interpreted Christianity from a social perspective. He claimed that Christ is not so much God's son as, rather, the charismatic leader of the liberation of peoples, and affirms that the kingdom of heaven is, on earth, the outcome of the struggle against all forms of tyranny. Garibaldi places the God of truth and reason next to this Christ-as-man. At the Congress of Peace in Geneva, on September 9, 1867, Garibaldi presented a motion for the adoption of the "religion of God," explaining that he meant "the religion of truth and reason." At the same time, he emphasized the necessity of destroying religious tyranny. Acclaimed by all the congress participants, he still faced the hostility of the Geneva Catholics, who organized a protest in front of his hotel. Reflecting on the congress, Garibaldi once more remarked that the new religion would open a new chapter in the history of liberty: in Geneva, "the representatives of the honest part of the peoples shook their hands, and they laid the foundations of the cult of justice and truth, which finally must prevail on earth, [and this will be] when the nations understand that their money must be invested in useful works and not for buying cuirasses, bombs, mercenaries, and spies."[22]

All in all, the Italian Risorgimento was an experience of political emancipation made possible by a twofold process: a departure from the republican religion introduced by the Jacobins, and the rediscovery, in the great riverbed of Christianity, of a religious conception that pointed to moral and political liberty as the supreme duty, and therefore openly opposed the doctrine and practice of the church—although the Catholics who became witnesses and apostles of the new faith were neither few nor unimportant. Different in the goals it pursued, the new religion of liberty was linked, though, to the civil religion of the old republics: Gioberti quotes Machiavelli's great pages on religion; the martyrs of Belfiore associate Socrates with Christ; and Mazzini chooses the pseudonym "Filippo," in honor of Filippo Strozzi, one of the last adversaries of the

Medici's regime, for his battlefield name. Thus the name Risorgimento is appropriate not only because it was first of all—whatever its limits—a religious rebirth but also because it is linked to the Rinascimento, a cultural renaissance. Of course, crucially, once the Rinascimento was concluded, the Italians found themselves under the double dominion of foreigners and the church of the Counter-Reformation. Once the Risorgimento was completed, by contrast, they found themselves united and independent, with the church deprived of its centuries-long temporal power.

16

REGRETS AND THE QUEST
FOR NEW FAITHS

AFTER ROME had been taken and national unification had been achieved, concerns about the future of Italian liberty were strong among the Risorgimento patriots. They understood that the new state lacked a civil religion, and that liberal institutions were, as a consequence, fragile. The educational projects inspired by Mazzini were directed against clericalism and the power of the Catholic Church, but they also urged a religious revolution in the name of the ideal of "God and people."[1] Genoa's paper *Il Dovere* published harsh articles on the religious problems, but always in favor of a humanitarian religiosity, and including a clear rejection of "that material skepticism that negates the role of any moral law in human affairs, any relationship between rights and duties, seeing nothing but the bare *fact*."[2] *La nuova Europa*, a paper associated with the Associazione Democratica Italiana, affirmed in an article in 1862 that it was necessary to go to Rome and remain there in order to bring about a European revolution in the people's consciences capable of achieving the triumph of thought and reason over faith, thereby accomplishing "the next work of the Risorgimento, the Reformation, and Philosophy, inaugurating the divinity of thought in the basilica disencumbered of the Roman God."[3] In an article in 1863, the paper maintained that religion and liberty are irreconcilable, and attacked Mazzini's philosophical and religious theories, which it labeled a "strange confusion of national religion and free conscience and true and false authority." Alberto Mario took a similar position in his *La questione religiosa di ieri e di oggi* (1867): "One must choose between liberty and the authority of divine right, between reason and church, between science and theology. Only liberty, reason, and science will wither away the Catholic religion forever." Arcangelo Ghisleri, one of the foremost representatives of the new republican generation, engaged in anticlerical and antireligious polemics aimed at educating consciences to a "new faith in man, in his progress, in science, and in a secular vision of life and society."[4]

When Rome was eventually released from papal dominion, some commentators hoped that this event signaled the victory of science over Catholicism. One of these critics was the prominent statesman and financier Quintino Sella, who believed that the God of the Christian religion should retreat before the advances of science, but not disappear. God should rather find his proper place again: moral conscience. "The infinite, the principle, the end of things, God, the concept of God," Sella writes, "does not fall into the observation of the naturalists; what is certain is that the freedom we feel within ourselves, if it corresponds to a continuation of one's responsibility even beyond life—that is, the issue of the immortality of the soul—cannot be captured by any goniometer, any dynamometer, any microscope or telescope.... [I]t is therefore clear that the concept of God and that of the immortality of the soul do not belong to the dominion of the positive sciences." The advance of the sciences might belittle and even shatter Catholicism and superstition, but it did not threaten the true essence of religion. The admiration for the sciences and the scientific mentality should not impair the religious sentiment, which curbs the unrestrained appetite for mere material pleasures.[5]

Francesco De Sanctis (1817–83), one of the most eminent public intellectuals of the Italian Risorgimento, understood the issue of religious reform, and treated it with special clarity and passion. The problem of a religion that might translate into effective morals operating in the world and a defense of free institutions runs through De Sanctis's *Storia della letteratura italiana*, completed in 1871. De Sanctis sees in Dante and the great saints, such as Francis of Assisi and Catherine of Siena, the prophets of a religion that descends from the contemplative to the active life. He is troubled by the licentious customs of priests and friars as well as the corruption of the Roman court, and instead loves "così bello / viver di cittadini" (such a fair / life of the citizen).[6] De Sanctis remarks that Dante merges, in the figure of Cato, the ancient ideal of the wise man and the Christian ideal of the saint. Resembling an ancient philosopher, calm, grave, and with a long beard, Cato is sanctified despite the fact that he is in purgatory, the place where the spirit disentangles itself from the body and searches for its liberty: "libertà va cercando, ch'è sì cara, / come sa chi per lei vita rifiuta" (he is in search of liberty, which is so dear / as one well knows who gives his life for it).[7]

Dante's world is, for De Sanctis, great and mystical, and his religion is exceedingly elevated, representing the true soul of a civil life. But neither such a world nor such a religion has any parallel in reality. In Dante's time, the invectives against the corruption of customs and the clergy were a commonplace that stirred no indignation. The most corrupt individuals proclaimed themselves good Christians, fought against the heretics with all their might, and then never failed to engage in due penance. Already back then the real, vicious Italian malady manifested itself: indifference and the "darkening of the moral sense." Culture did not cure but rather only disguised moral and religious corruption: "The cultured classes started to part from the common people and to laugh at their credulity. To be a believer used to be a title of glory of the best intellects; now, to be an unbeliever becomes a sign of a cultured soul." Thus, instead of reforming the mentality of the people and educating them about their responsibility and hence about liberty, the intellectual elite dedicated itself to the pleasures of erudition and art. Religious indifference ("better leave it to the pope") and political indifference ("it is none of my business") went hand in hand, and a long period of decadence ensued.[8]

In De Sanctis's view, Giovanni Boccaccio exemplified the moral and civil decadence of Italian life after Dante. Boccaccio lacked not only "religious sentiment" but also that moral elevation that at times may worthily be substituted for the former. In Boccaccio, the Christian and the citizen had at once disappeared: "It never occurred to him that serving the fatherland and giving it one's intellect and one's property and one's life are as strict a duty as the very act of seeing to one's subsistence." Not that Boccaccio scorned religion, virtue, and the fatherland; he just lacked any passion and true faith. With him, and the Italy of his time, the character of the people has fallen into a mediocrity that is not quite vulgar but does not express greatness either: "Still present were the forms of liberty and of the ancient man, but their spirit was gone." By this time everything in Italy smacked of courtly life and a servile mentality.[9] People amused themselves, in the name of God and Mary, in a cultured society "void of any religious and moral sense."[10] Nothing changes in the next century, the Quattrocento, either: the religious sentiment, which no longer dwells in the people's conscience, transforms itself into an artistic sentiment; it moves the spirit, but only in the form of architecture and music. Alberti's description of the religious atmosphere of the cathedral in Florence is exemplary:

This temple possesses grace and majesty, and it delights me to see conjoined within it a charming frailness and a robust and full firmness: such that on the one hand every part of it seemed situated with a view to amenity, and on the other I understand that everything here is made with a view to perpetuity. Here you can hear in these voices a sacrifice, and in these that the ancient called mysteries you can hear a wonderful suaveness. These chants and hymns of the church trigger in me what they were originally intended for: they exceedingly soothe me from any other perturbation of the soul, and they move me to some sort of—I would not know how else to call it—slowness of the soul full of reverence to God. And can so stout a heart be found that does not soothe itself while hearing ascend and then descend in beauty those whole and true voices with such tenderness and such suppleness? I confess this to you: that never do I hear the invocation of God's help for our human miseries in those mysteries and funeral ceremonies without crying![11]

According to De Sanctis, when the winds of the Reformation shook Europe, Italy was merely grazed by them. Too cultured, too accustomed to laughing at the corruption that was consuming it, but that had caused indignation within the German world, Italy had already passed "the theological age"; it believed only in science, and regarded Luther and Calvin as "new scholastics." For this reason, De Sanctis remarks in a deservedly well-known passage, the Reformation "could not take root among us, and remained alien to our culture, which developed through its own means." Sinking into the ruins of the Middle Ages, Italy could not forge the foundations of a new edifice from theology, but rather had to turn to science: "Her Luther was Niccolò Machiavelli," a man who sincerely loved the liberty and independence of his fatherland, and possessed a strong soul, reinforced by offices and political struggles, and eventually refined by forced inaction and solitude.[12] Amid the many "mercenary men of letters" who plagued Italy in his time, Machiavelli's figure stands out sharply for the sincerity of his love of fatherland, manliness, and dignity. De Sanctis composes, with vigorous words, the hymn that Machiavelli deserves for his human greatness: "Let us thus be proud of our Machiavelli. Glory to him whenever any part of the old edifice falls down. And glory to him whenever any new part is being built. In the moment in which I am writing, bells are ringing, announcing the entrance of the Italians into Rome. The temporal power is tumbling down. And hurrah is cried to the unity of Italy. Glory to Machiavelli." But Machiavelli, for De Sanctis, is not quite a religious man; he "does not believe in any religion, and hence accepts them all." This is why he was unable to promote a religious reform that would have opened up the road to modernity for Italy.

De Sanctis admires Machiavelli the patriot but is more cautious about his religion of the fatherland and his elevation of the state to a divine principle:

> Machiavelli's fatherland is a divinity, superior even to morality and to the law.... Divinity had descended from heaven to earth.... Liberty was the more or less encompassing participation of the citizens in public life. The rights of man were not yet comprised by the code of liberty. Man was no autonomous being, an end in itself: he was the instrument of the fatherland, or, even worse, of the State.... These ideas are stated by Machiavelli not quite as identified and analyzed by him, but rather as they had been introduced by a long tradition and fortified by the classical culture. The spirit of ancient Rome lies in there.... For the ancients, liberty meant participation of the citizens in the government, and in this sense it is understood also by Machiavelli. For the moderns, besides such political liberty another liberty lies, the intellectual liberty or, as it has been called, the liberty of conscience.[13]

Machiavelli's fatherland is a divinity of a sort that "absorbs religion, morality, and individuality within itself"; and his state is not content to be merely autonomous but aspires to take autonomy away from all the rest.[14] With such a state and leader, Machiavelli believed the Italian nation could be founded. He did not realize that one also should "build the people, the thought, and man itself anew—the Roman man he dreamed of." For political reform to become a reality, it should have been accompanied by a religious reform that unambiguously recognized the worthiness of the individual. What remained, though, and it was no minor thing, was Machiavelli's smile, so different from that of his contemporaries. Their smile stood for buffoonery and frivolity, whereas Machiavelli's had "something sad and serious to it, which is different from the caricature they made of him."[15] That smile teaches us that when a people is morally ill, and has lost its sincere religious spirit, the likes of a Machiavelli—after having written great pages to try to resuscitate a love of liberty—was left with nothing but the ability to laugh at the world and men.

Whereas Machiavelli still hopes and struggles, Guicciardini, according to De Sanctis, asserts his personal interest as his God (and it is an all-encompassing God, like that of the ascetics and like Machiavelli's state): "All ideals disappear. Any religious, moral, or political bond—the sort of bonds that keep a people together—are broken. On the world scene nothing is left but the individual. Everyone by himself against all others. This is no longer corruption, which one could criticize: this is wisdom, an inculcated and predicated doctrine, the art of life."[16] Such an art was well suited to the religion of passive obedience and the infallible authority of the church, which had been proclaimed at the Council of Trent. Interest, docility, and submission blended in a mix that had, by then, nothing to do with the republican religion; in effect, it was its most radical antithesis. "Religion Italian-style," De Sanctis calls it: dogmatic, historic, and formal, possessing the letter but not the spirit of a religion. Its adherents indeed "believe, go to confession, pray, go in procession," but do so in appearance only. Religion in Italy was nothing compared to the austere and profound republican religiosity that was flourishing during those same years in England. The English had Milton; the Italians had Ludovico Ariosto, who attempted to compose religious poems, but did not succeed, for "religion lies not in a dogma, nor in history, nor in mere forms, but in the spirit." And the religious spirit, inasmuch as it is an experience of internal life, cannot originate through one's will or a project. The Italy of the Counter-Reformation was a servant twice over: politically, since it was dominated by foreigners; and morally, because it had adopted a religiosity that taught docility and submission in relation to the powerful.[17]

Three centuries were necessary for the blossoming in Italy of a religion that instead taught a love of liberty. In De Sanctis's view, the authors of the rebirth were neither the religious people who, during the three years of Jacobinism, had theorized about the alliance between religion and democracy, nor Alfieri, Giuseppe Parini, or Foscolo. The warnings of the former were too heavily linked to the short-lived experiment of the republics supported by the French armies; the poetry of the latter carried a strong moral and political message of liberty, but had little religious content.[18] For De Sanctis, Manzoni was the man equipped to inform liberty with religious meaning and rediscover the emancipating force of Christianity. He "did not take the Christianity that was then rising as a Romantic reaction, in opposition to a patriotic content, but as its seal and consecration." What was true for Manzoni according to natural law was also true according to God and the Gospel: "The Gospel consecrates democracy, which becomes Christian democracy; the Gospel consecrates liberty, which becomes Christian liberty." The old ideas of the eighteenth century returned under the mantle of the Virgin and God; thus baptized anew, those ideas acquired new forms, colors, motives, and tendencies, and, more important, strength. Whereas the preachers and educators of the Jacobin period had been unable to bring Italian religiosity toward the side of liberty, and had suffered revolts against liberty in the name of the Virgin and the holy faith, Manzoni outlined a religiosity through his poetry and prose that was profoundly Italian as well as friendly to liberty and the redemption of the fatherland.[19]

The religion espoused by Manzoni remained a literary work, incapable of becoming a real religious movement that could deeply change Italian society. According to De Sanctis, Manzoni brought the Christian religion back to the side of liberty and its purely evangelical principles—like the communion of the believers, the poverty of the clergy, and the spirit of charity—but did not declare war against the corruption of the clergy and the superstition of the multitude. It elevated the Christian church to a high moral and poetical ideal, but largely left the degenerate Catholic Church untouched. Although it exalted the past "against the vices of the present," it accepted the modern world, seen as already shaped by the Christian idea. Democracy, liberty, and equality were, for Manzoni, already in the Gospel, but he never really involved himself with the most heated religious and political issues of his time: "Trapped in the past, when his soul of a sincere patriot is shaken by the Italian movement, he composes a canzone on the occasion of the Rimini proclamation by Gioacchino [Murat, 1800]; he then composes another beautiful canzone in 1821; but these works remain unknown until events change, and his spirit always remains reserved and contemplative."[20] Manzoni could not or did not want to be the proclaimer of a religious and moral reform. Therefore, notwithstanding all his admiration for him, De Sanctis offers a strong expression of regret: "A like movement can be found in Germany, where it was a revolt against the French, and can be also found in France, where it was—if not religious—political; in Italy, instead, it was purely literary."[21]

Instead of repairing the separation between religion and liberty, Manzoni's followers made it worse. They, and Cesare Cantù (1804–95) in particular, assimilated Christian religion into Catholicism—censorship, Inquisition, and the whole medieval spirit included. Rather than connecting the religion of liberty to the modern world, they returned to a religion that taught humility and submission.[22] Cantù presents society as it is, with all its injustice, as if it were the best society, and urges people to love and respect it, convinced that in this way Italians will become good citizens. To those who feel humiliated and oppressed, he says: "Rejoice, as before God we are all equal and free." Since those in both the lowest and the highest classes of society have their troubles, everyone should stay where God has put him; otherwise, the whole social fabric will be severely damaged, with no real benefits for any individual. Should we suffer from injustice, our reaction must be "tameness, humility, prayer, forgiveness, and turning the other cheek"—that is, all the trite virtues of a Christianity for serfs.[23] The old republican religion had striven to form youths after the examples of Attilius Regulus and Cato, who sacrificed their lives for the fatherland; the religion of the Manzonian school proposes the examples of Saint Aloysius Gonzaga, Saint Carlo Borromeo, Saint Alexis, and all the virtues that teach people to pardon their oppressors. This had the obvious consequence that with the exception of a few heroes and saints, youths became either serfs or hypocrites, or else, as is often the case, serfs and hypocrites.[24]

According to De Sanctis, Italy needed a different religion. What should be taught was that humility, patience, discipline, and forgiveness are not at all virtues, if they are presented in an abstract and absolute way, just as indignation, wrath, resistance against arbitrary actions, and dying for the fatherland are not virtues in and of themselves. In order to be such and also serve liberty, virtue has to have a limit, and has to include its opposite. Teaching people the sentiment of duty is a blessing; but taken in isolation, "the sentiment of duty becomes [a] sentiment of servitude." It is instead a true virtue only when conjoined with the sentiment of one's right. Only in this way can man, "by feeling that he has a right, fulfill his duty." The same holds for humility, which is a virtue when it is reinforced by a just sentiment of pride; otherwise it is vileness. Obedience is a virtue when those who obey know that they can also command; virtue certainly consists in respecting authority, provided that maintaining one's dignity is a sentiment of equal value; believing in a life after death is a noble conviction, if those who have it experience with equal seriousness their terrestrial life as a mission. Christ himself, a true example of meekness, knew how and when to be indignant. He drove the desecrators of the temple away with a whip. This was the religion to be taught to the Italians living under foreign domination. Christian mildness does not at all prohibit responding to injustice with force.[25] A religion that preaches peace, docility, humility, and prayer might suffice in barbarian times, De Sanctis concludes, when force is in excess. This was not the case in nineteenth-century Italy, where the problems were, in fact, the suppression of individual moral forces, the discouragement of the multitudes, the oppression of the weak, and violence by the rulers.[26] In order to come to the aid of Italian liberty, a religion was needed that rendered the weak strong as opposed to making the weak submissive.

Even when the Risorgimento epic was over, some writers unfailingly continued to try to educate the Italians about a religiosity reinforced by strong civil ideals. A prominent example is the novel *Cuore* (Heart), by Edmondo De Amicis (1846–1908), published in 1886. The religion that Enrico—the novel's protagonist, who writes a diary—learns from his father is simultaneously a source of hope and a stimulus for acting well. "We will see each other again in the afterlife," Enrico's father tells him, "where those who suffered much in this one will be rewarded, and where those who loved much on earth will meet again the souls they loved, in a world without guilt, without tears, and without death." But he adds that we must deserve such a new life by behaving well in this one, which entails having a noble, brave, and sincere soul, and being ready to serve the fatherland with devotion. The religion of the fatherland that De Amicis outlines reveals a Mazzinian root in its solemn affirmation of the duty to fight injustice and inequality; however, it also expresses the expansionism—with nationalistic and imperialistic overtones—that started to spread in Italy at the end of the century.[27]

The religion of the fatherland also brightly illuminates Antonio Fogazzaro's *Piccolo mondo antico* (*The Little World of the Past*), published in 1886. In his masterpiece, Fogazzaro starkly opposes different religiosities. One pole is the inhumane religion of the cold marchioness Orsola, a fervid philo-Austrian, who every night says the rosary together with guests and servants, and adds further prayers of Ave Maria and Gloria in Excelsis when her conscience is particularly pricked because of her many and serious nefarious activities. To punish her nephew Franco Maironi for his patriotic intemperance, first she notifies him that none of her immense riches will go into his pockets after her death, and then she remarks that he will have to account to God for his behavior. For the old marchioness, Maironi was accountable first to her and then to God: "If one is a Christian," she says to her nephew, "it is his duty to obey his father and mother, and in this case I represent your father and mother."[28]

The religiosity of Piero Ribera, uncle of Luisa, whom Maironi marries against her grandmother's will, is completely different. Uncle Piero provides hospitality to the couple and their child, Maria. Piero's religiosity lies in his honesty, goodness, and the customs inherited by his parents. His was a "good-natured God," who did not care much about prayers and rosaries, and even less about those said by people like the marchioness. His God was content "to have as friends good-hearted men, regardless of their being gourmands and hard drinkers, lifelong devotees of the *tarocchi* [card games], unashamed tellers of obscene stories—not dishonest, though—in order to release the nasty hilarity that everyone has within." Although he has little esteem for religious practices, he believes in the afterlife and above all charity—a charity he does not preach but practices.[29]

Franco Maironi's religion is more intense. Fogazzaro describes it as the "simple, calm faith of a child." Not the least proud, and distant from philosophical reflections, he is also exempt from the desire for intellectual freedom that captures youths when their senses and passions cannot stand the bite of dogmas. Equally remote from mystical and ascetic fervors, Maironi has never questioned his religion and has scrupulously observed worship practices, without even asking himself whether it was reasonable to do so. Precisely because he has neither to search for nor to achieve his faith, he has never carefully focused on it, and conversely his faith can never really penetrate to the bottom of his being. Religion is for him "like science was for a conscientious student who has school at the center of his thoughts, is assiduous at it, has no peace of mind unless he has finished his homework, has not prepared himself for the exams. And yet—once he has fulfilled his duty as a conscientious student—gives no further thought either to the master or to the books, and feels no need to continue to govern his life according to scientific ends or school curricula." Maironi follows the impulse of his ardent heart and the passionate inclinations of his loyal nature. He despises everything that is mean and false, and is as incapable of any pretensions as he is incapable of translating faith into action.[30]

By contrast, the religion of his wife, Luisa, is profound and completely turns on action:

> From her fourteenth year on, she had determined more and more to care only about life on earth and about other human beings under the guidance of a strong and fierce sense of justice. She went to church, performed the outward acts of worship without incredulity but also without any personal conviction that they pleased God. In fact, she had a vague conception that God was so lofty and great that no direct contact was possible between him and men. If at times she thought she might be mistaken, her error seemed to her of a kind that a God who was infinitely good could not punish.[31]

Luisa considers the story of life after death to be nothing but a mean invention of men so as to make God satisfy their wishes: a reward for the good that one has done to others, and the trust that someone will punish the evil that others have done to us. For Luisa, instead, the right way of thinking and living is to accept the idea of death while serving justice in life, without expecting any reward. She actually does not need God to live according to the moral ideal. And yet in addition to reason, a love of justice distances Luisa from religion. She admires the resignation with which her mother has been able to endure extremely painful misfortunes and disappointments. She also thinks, however, that if all the good souls of this world were similar to her mother in their religious gentleness, the earth would become the kingdom of the rogue and the oppressors.

Bound by an intense love, Luisa and Maironi are separated by their religious differences. In one of the most dramatic dialogues of the novel, Luisa sincerely confesses to Maironi that she thought he was religious in the way her mother had been, and that she married him in the hope of becoming—religiously speaking—like the two of them. But she eventually realizes that his religion does not translate into action:

> I understood that you were goodness personified, that you possessed the warmest, most generous, noblest heart in the world, but that your faith and your practices rendered these treasures almost useless. You did not act. You simply were content to love me, the child, Italy, your flowers, your music, the beauty of the lake and the mountains. In so doing you followed your heart. Concerning any higher ideal, you found it enough to believe and pray. But without faith, without prayers, you would have dedicated the fire that is in your heart to what is really true, really just here on earth—you would have felt the urge to act in the world that I felt.

Acting in the world meant, for Luisa, resisting oppression and preparing for a war against Austria. Instead of a God who teaches gentleness, Luisa felt within her a God who commands the law of duty. Her religious concept was that God exists, and is mighty as well as wise, but the fact that men adore him or speak to him is of no significance to God. What he wants of us "one can understand according to the heart he has made in us, the conscience he has given us, and the situation in which he has placed us. What he wants is for us to love all that is good, hate all that is evil, and act with all our strength according to this love and this hate; and he wants us to concern ourselves only with the earth, with those things we can comprehend, those things we can feel!"[32]

Maironi finds a new religiosity first during his exile in Turin and then, more intensely, after the tragic death of his beloved child, Maria. It is a new religiosity that urges him, this time, to live his faith in the world. In his child's death he sees God's will to save the baby from this world, and to punish him and Luisa for their mistakes. Through grief, he understands all his responsibility for the life he has lived—"wretchedly devoid of works" and just "full of vanity." He wants to correct and redeem himself, so that God will one day consider him worthy of joining Maria again. He understands that he can be redeemed only through action, in his sacrifice to Italy: "To live and work and suffer and adore and ascend! That new light wanted just this." He voluntarily joins the Piedmont region's army, which is about to cross the Ticino River and wage war against Austria. In her grief, Luisa instead definitively abandons the Christian religion. When others try to take the dead body of Maria away from Luisa's breast, Luisa bursts into a desperate cry: "No! no! Not in Heaven! She is mine! God is wicked! No, I won't give her to Him!" For if God does exist, he has to be blamed for the death of that innocent. Luisa can no longer believe in divine justice. All that exists for her now is "the ally of the Throne, the Austrian God, partner of all injustices, of all oppressions, author of grief and of evil, slayer of the innocent and protector of sinners."[33] Whereas Franco's Christian faith gets transformed into a commitment to redeem Italy, Lucia's desperation will perhaps find some consolation in the new child she conceives during the last night she spends with Franco.

In contrast, the love of fatherland championed by Giosuè Carducci, called by Fogazzaro the "fierce barbarian poet [who] had beheaded God, and said very unpleasant things about princes," was vehemently pagan. Carducci paid him back in his own coin, with a harsh invective against the Catholics and Jews who "wash their hands in attar of roses to remove the stench of Christ's blood."[34] Fifteen years later, when Carducci composed his hymn "A Satana" (To Satan), his ideas had not changed much. He still admired reason and nature, "the two divinities" of his soul, and all the generous and good souls whom a solitary and uncivil asceticism abominates under the names of *flesh* and *world*, and which theocracy excommunicates under the name of *Satan*.[35] For Carducci, Satan is "the avenging force of reason" that hurls itself at the priests; it is human thought, matter, and the king of forms. And it is also a symbol of the struggle of liberty against tyranny, the guide for religious reformers such as John Wycliffe and Hus, Savonarola and Luther. Satan, moreover, is the energy behind the revolutions that have opened the road to modern liberty: the Italian communes, Arnaldo da Brescia, Cola di Rienzo, Francesco Burlamacchi, and the German Reformation, "which preaches and writes liberty"; Holland, "which embodies liberty in fact"; England, "which vindicates and revenges it"; France, "which extends it to all orders and all peoples, and makes of it the law of the new ages."[36] On the whole, Satan is the mysterious force that inspires those men who fight and suffer for an idea, justice, and liberty; it is the great idea that has driven the difficult evolution of modern liberty; it is the divinity of man—the conviction that he not only can but also must render himself similar to God, and hence free. This indeed is what Satan taught, and this is what the philosophers taught too: "In fact, what did he—generous tempter—say to the companion of man? He suggested to her, in Jehovah's garden—a closed and uniform garden—that mystical tree that bore the fruit of knowledge and life, and of good and evil;—Eat of this one, he said to her, and you'll be like gods—. And, pray, what else did Pythagoras, Anaxagoras, Socrates, Plato, Aristotle say to man? What else did Galileo, Newton, Kepler, Descartes, Kant say to him?"[37]

Man should be free because divinity lives in him: "I am a ray of the eternal truth / That draws forth the spark of freedom." God is in the heart of man, and man is an expression of the divine light.[38] Carducci's God is an austere God, similar to that of Alfieri and Mazzini. Such a God makes him exalt Christ but also abhor the hypocrisy of the Catholics: "And drunken on their benches / Snore the canons, / And the devotees whisper / About bills and money, / And the beautiful penitents / While singing the litany / Engage new servants / For the entry to the vestry, / Invoking the Virgin / While lifting their gown."[39] In the face of this Catholic religious ambience, Carducci extols the pagan sentiment of life and the religion of the fatherland. Italy's unity, he writes, "is the love, the faith, the religion of my life." Through his poems he tried to instill the religion of the fatherland in the souls of the Italians, who, once they achieved unification and independence, fell back to the ancient vices of hypocrisy and vileness. It was a hopeless task, he realizes: "I will bring to you sad news: / Our fatherland is vile."[40]

The idea of reforming customs outside the Catholic religion was especially hopeless. After 1870, many people were convinced that without a religious education, at least in primary school, cultivating good citizens was impossible. The supporters of free thought risked creating an Italian people divided into followers of Voltaire, on the one hand, and clerics, on the other, as Pasquale Villari affirms in a speech to Parliament on May 6, 1875.[41] But a letter of October 16, 1894, from Ferdinando Martini (1841–1928), a writer, politician, and professor at the Scuola Normale of Pisa, to Carducci, is even more straightforward on this point:

> Political revolutions that do not also bring about a religious renewal lose sight of their origin and first motives, and end up unleashing every wicked instinct of the mobs; I have been sure about this for a long time. But, after the evil that *all* of us have done, are we able to provide remedies? To whom could we preach them? We, a Voltaire-minded bourgeoisie, we have created people who did not believe, while the pope took care of those who believed in a bad way; and

could we now go back to speaking about God, whom yesterday we negated, to the mobs that demand a *poule au pot* as they no longer believe in the *after*life? They would not listen to us: I am speaking of the mobs of the towns and the villages, for the rural people, in any case, wouldn't know what to do with a God without churches, rites, and priests. For all the evil that we (not you or I in particular, but we as a class) have done because of our thoughtless pride, the grave is too scanty a reward: we wanted to destroy everything and have been able to edify nothing. According to the pedagogues' chatterings, the school was to replace the church. What a beautiful substitution! I recommend it to you.[42]

Neither the Risorgimento nor efforts to educate the people morally and religiously had really changed traditional Catholic religiosity. As Alfredo Oriani (1852–1909) notes in *Fino a Dogali* (Up to Dogali) (1889):

The hatred for the priests and the contempt for religion have so far been very superficial: in the people's feelings, true marriage is the religious one, and the sole religion is Catholicism; nearly all the children are baptized, entrusted to the clergy for their first education, and initiated in all the religious practices. There is little, if any, confidence in nonreligious boarding schools, whereas, though, convents have become "institutes for girls"; all the Virgins and miraculous saints are more alive than ever in the people's illusions; a double standard divides all the consciences: one wants the liberty of one's public life, while still subscribing to the servitude of spiritual life. Science—uncertain about its methods, dubious in its results, contradictory in its statements—remains high above, the property and the cult of the few: philosophy is almost unknown; literature—having abandoned the realms of the ideals in favor of an unreflective scientific passion—is little more than a surface painting. The revolution, born and lived according to instinct, has not yet become reflection. The great majority of those who supported it, disavow it when they die, of which the priests are boastful, affirming that its truth cannot resist death. The real dream, espoused by the few but cherished by the many, is of a reconciliation that, by reconciling religious conscience and political conscience, may lead to that calm that other centuries have experienced.[43]

The youths who developed in the intellectual climate of the 1880s found a new faith in positivism. Italian Socialist Party founder Filippo Turati, who was born in 1857 and died in exile in Paris in 1932, has left us a precious document describing the state of mind of many in his generation: "When we, young, and just freed from the Christian-Catholic mythology, inclined by the impetuosity of our juvenile reaction to the most nihilist negations, still kept searching for that psychological *ubi consistam* that is an inescapable necessity for all those who are disposed by nature to 'take life seriously,' it was Roberto Ardigò who laid some of the most solid foundations of our mental and moral edifice—moral, above all."[44] Ardigò, though, despite the fact that he became the reference point of the new positivist and socialist faith, had completed his education, after his father's death in 1849, under the guidance of Luigi Martini, author of *Confortatorio dei martiri di Belfiore*, and was an example of liberal Catholicism and hence unpopular with the Holy See.[45] Ardigò's most influential work, *La morale dei positivisti* (The morality of the positivists), published in Arcangelo Ghisleri's *Rivista repubblicana* from April 1878 onward, announces a form of morality wholly independent of Christian religion and denies that God is the source of right. Viewing God as the source of right, in fact, renders man subject to the law that God imposes on him, so that he has no actual rights but instead only duties. Furthermore, when this idea takes the form of theism and the vulgar doctrine of divine Providence, it acknowledges and legitimizes the existence of unjust and arbitrary powers and authorities that have their origin only in force. The supporters of such a conception of the law are actually without religion, but defend religion as a means capable "of containing the people in a resigned misery; and, consequently, more profitable for those who are outside of it."[46]

At the same time, however, Ardigò emphasizes that the new principle of law heralded by positivism and the evangelical message are perfectly in agreement. Two "extremely notable" evangelical teachings serve as proof: "If God commands one thing and men another, one must obey God and disobey men." If some tendency in human society is a work of God, Ardigò maintains, "opposing it is culpable and insane, for what God desires is right and no one can impede it. If, on the other hand, such a tendency is not a work of God, then there is no point in even worrying about it, as it will vanish by itself." The philosophical sense of these passages, for Ardigò, can be epitomized in a revolutionary and radically liberal maxim. The first holds that "a man not only can but *must* have what his reason (whose right is unquestionable) dictates to him respected, even by those who oppose it in the name of whatever authority"; the second teaching holds that "liberty can have problems, but these get solved by themselves—unjust and unnatural social fancies just like the imperfect species of plants and animals, which simply succumb in the *struggle for existence*. But if, on the other hand, a social aspiration is legitimate, the desire to oppose it is unjust and vain because the omnipotent nature itself wills it, and it will certainly triumph."[47] Although positivism was a philosophy that proclaimed a new morality derived from nature and not from revelation, it retained those principles of Christianity that more strongly taught faith in liberty, and exhorted people to affirm liberty in the world. Because of this intellectual continuity, *La morale dei positivisti* convinced those young people like Turati who, once the hopes and passions of the Risorgimento had passed, were searching for a better answer to their aspirations for liberty than the Catholic one, and yet one not at odds with Christianity.

Their anticlericalism, and in general the anticlericalism of the socialists, was with few exceptions directed against the Catholic priest and church as political adversaries, and not against the Christian religion.[48] Leonida Bissolati, the adopted child of Stefano Bissolati (1823–98), who had abandoned the cassock and become director of Cremona's city library, had in 1891 already outlined the guiding principle of Italian socialism with regard to the religious question. Bissolati's was a precise and convincing warning against antireligious propaganda. Recalling Karl Marx, his argument was that "the religious reflex of the real world will not go away until the conditions of work and practical life take the form of evident and rational relationships between man and his fellows, and between man and nature." At the same time, Bissolati remarked that it was advisable "to get to the people...through their own material interests," considering the issue of religious faith to be something alien to socialist propaganda aimed at improving work conditions and ultimately socializing the means of production.[49]

The fight against religious sentiment by means of invectives was instead to be undertaken by a Voltairean and conservative bourgeoisie that did not understand that an antireligious propaganda in the name of science and reason did not have any chance of scratching "the granite of psychological fatality, which desires that the poor man—to whom the joys of existence are prohibited by his social conditions, and who cannot replace his fantastical conception of the world with a naturalistic one—find in religion the satisfaction of his imperious needs of senses and intellect." In the struggle for emancipation, the popular classes were to develop a new morality that would abolish God from the routines of daily life and even from thought. Until then, however, the religious faith of the worker and farmer could remain intact.[50] What was apt to accelerate the moral and religious emancipation of the people was, instead, pointing out the example of Christ and primitive Christianity to a clergy enslaved by capitalism and monarchy. The statements that socialism is a movement endowed also "with a religious nature" and that socialists are "the true followers of the great revolution begun by Christ" appear numerous times in the socialist press.[51] Christ preached "the abolition of all injustices and social inequalities, and exhorted all men—irrespective of their race, country, or faith—to love one another and consider each other brothers. This is precisely what we, too, say to the workers."[52]

On many occasions, even Guido Podrecca's and Gabriele Galantara's *L'Asino*, the most representative voice of socialist anticlericalism, featured articles and cartoons that opposed Christ to the counterfeiters of his doctrine and true enemies—that is, the priests. Addressing a mother who is waiting for her son to return from the Casa del popolo (Socialist Party Center), De Amicis writes in the *Almanacco socialista* (1895): "Do not commend yourself, as you do every night, to that small image of the crucifix that hangs over your bed, praying that he may convert your rebel son. If that crucified man descended from the cross for a moment, large and alive in the presence of the two of you, it would not be your forehead that first would feel the sweet caress from his pierced hand." In *Socialismo popolare*, Carlo Monticelli even advanced the idea that socialism was some sort of synthesis of the Christian and pagan religions: "Like any other religious principles based on the paranormal, Christianity is but an aberration. Wise and *superior* to paganism is only its moral sanction of human equality and solidarity.... In socialism, the quest for pleasure returns on earth, as in paganism, but is informed by the concept of solidarity and equality, as in the religion of Christ."[53]

One of the most popular papers of socialist education, *Il seme*, founded in 1901 by Francesco Paoloni and intended for farmers, insisted on the contrast between clericalism and primitive Christianity. In pamphlets, too, Paoloni focused on the theme of Christ, who on returning to earth, is indignant at the odious inequalities that afflict the weak in modern societies. He even makes Christ say, "I died in vain on the cross nineteen centuries ago for the redemption of humanity, if so great a part of humanity is still oppressed by so many miseries, injustices, and infamies."[54] Giuseppe Rensi, who until 1905 was one of the main contributors to *Critica Sociale*, the most prestigious journal of Italian socialism, writes that Lev Nikolayevich Tolstoy's novel *Resurrection*, translated into Italian in 1900, proves that "at the end of every great historical time—today, just as in the late Roman Empire—a mighty moral energy presents itself as the only force capable of salvation and redemption. This moral energy is necessarily different in every period, and today only socialism has the moral energy capable of performing the task propounded by Christianity." Rensi adds that Tolstoy's theory was clearly socialist insofar as it "unites all men without exceptions,…stirs in them the idea of equality and brotherhood, which consequently is not exclusive to just a circle of men, a class, or a cult but is universal."[55]

Even when it was particularly harsh, the anticlerical polemics of the socialists did not touch the figure of Christ. In the propagandistic literature, the myth of a "socialist Jesus" emerges often, and with it a millenarian view of the social revolution as a complete and irreversible triumph of good over evil.[56] Even *La Plebe*, the avowedly republican, rationalist, and socialist journal founded in Milan in 1868, with all its tough polemics against religion and monarchy—defined as "twin sisters, firstborn of fantasy, terror, and ignorance," that should be destroyed in the name of the principle "Neither king in heaven nor king on earth"—presents its conception of socialism as the negation and overcoming of Catholicism, but also as the "actualization of the most sublime principles of the Gospel."[57] Other articles even argue that the socialists could accept from "the little son of the carpenter of Nazareth only the maxims of love, equality, and brotherhood," and that they could recognize Jesus as a benefactor of humanity, although "the most monstrous domination of all times" originated from him. Enrico Bignami, in an article titled "Il Socialismo" explains that Christianity is a great thing, but socialism will be even better, for it will realize an even greater synthesis: "It will be not only moral and religious but also political, economic, and social."[58]

Assertions on the religious dimension of socialism derived in part from propagandistic needs, especially among the peasants. They also reflected, though, the conviction of many socialists that their movement, inasmuch as it was one of human emancipation, was animated by a sincere religious sentiment, and that their work was a new way of interpreting and actualizing the true spirit of the Gospel. Giovanni Zibordi was right when he wrote, in the essay "Camillo Prampolini e i lavoratori reggiani" (1930), that the work of the "apostle of socialism" had an "ethical, human, 'religious' character, which makes it stand out in respect to all other works, and forms an inheritance of moral values that is worth knowing and useful to meditate on."[59] Prampolini also felt the influence of the easy confidence with which positivism faced the religious problem. Especially in his early propagandistic writings, his ideas evidenced a strong anticlerical and antitheist content. Yet he soon abandoned that merely negative attitude toward religion and, thereafter, was always careful to distinguish the ethical substance of Christianity from Catholic theology. He understood that within the Catholic religion, there was a widespread aspiration to transcendence and ideals—an aspiration that could and should not be extinguished. Rather, it should be directed toward convictions, and above all ways of life, that were more humane and moral.[60] Although the church had distorted the ideal aspiration at the root of the religious sentiment, it was possible to revive it in order to light a fire of sentiments and hopes.

With these convictions, Prampolini went to the villages and spoke to people returning from Mass, often facing indifference and hostility. He told them: "You say you are Christians; but do you live as such? Do you love each other, are you united, do you help each other according to the teaching of Christ? Do you actualize his precepts of brotherhood and justice? I tell you, we socialists are more Christian than you are, for we teach you to unite, to defend yourself from iniquity, to elevate yourself to a more dignified life."[61] With these words, Prampolini at once fought against the God of the priests, who preached that people should accept injustice; and endowed socialism with a clear ethical content by grafting it onto the moral lesson of Christianity. Prampolini's propaganda was religious "insofar as it was based on a 'religious' tradition, although he then channeled it toward new and different outlets. It was 'religious,' even more important, insofar as it resolved to instill a moral ideality, a sense of duty, a superior aspiration in life, beyond merely material attainments."[62]

Benito Mussolini and the revolutionary trade unionists were among those who depicted Prampolini's evangelical socialism as "emulsified in humanitarian syrup," deriding Christianity in the name of a materialistic atheism and some sort of ancient paganism. When Zibordi's little book on Prampolini came out in 1930 (*Essay on the History of the Working Class in Italy*), the former had become *Il Duce* of fascism, and many of the latter had followed him. The ideal inheritance of Prampolini and reformist socialism is to be found, in a new form, in the liberal socialism of Carlo Rosselli, which was indeed—as we will see in the next chapter—an interpretation of socialism no longer as a materialist doctrine but rather as an ethical ideal of human emancipation. As such, it was the legitimate and conscious heir of the religious spirit of the Risorgimento.

PART III

They Got Too Close to the Light

17

TWO CLASHING RELIGIONS

IN 1932, MUSSOLINI CELEBRATED the tenth anniversary of his rise to power with solemn ceremonies, climaxing in the Exhibition of the Fascist Revolution in Rome, a grand event aimed at exalting the regime's religious character.[1] While workers prepared the imposing halls and set up gigantic representations of the deified leader, Croce published *Storia d'Europa nel secolo XIX* (*History of Europe in the Nineteenth Century*) to explain to the Italians that another religion existed: the "religion of liberty." The fascist religion brought thousands of people to the squares, had state support, and offered impressive rituals; the religion of liberty lived in the souls of a few men and women, and circulated on the pages of books and reviews as well as in letters and private diaries. Less than fifteen years later, the fascist religion dissolved under the weight of the immense and unfathomable suffering that its idols and priests imposed on millions of human beings along with the force of worldwide moral condemnation. The religion of liberty, instead, helped the birth of a new Italian fatherland.

The contrast between the fascist religion and the religion of liberty was irreconcilable. In the history of antifascism, there were—as is true of all human endeavors—ambiguities, uncertainties, and simulations, but those few who opposed fascism in the name of the religion of liberty were its irreducible enemies. They bore witness to the faith in liberty by sacrificing their own affections and interests, and often facing death. No revisionist work can obliterate this historical datum. The names of the antifascists are almost forgotten because their example is almost too powerful; they "tried to get too close to the light," as Carlo Rosselli writes to his mother, Amelia Rosselli Pincherle, on September 16, 1928. This chapter recounts the history of the religion of liberty from the beginning of the fascist regime to the birth of the republic, and the stories of some of the men and women who believed in that religion.

The contrast between the fascist religion and the religion of liberty is evident from the start, in the initial years of the regime's life. It was Mussolini himself, before the king had asked him to form a government in October 1922, who proclaimed the religious character of fascism: "We work with alacrity to carry out that which was the aspiration of Giuseppe Mazzini: giving Italians the 'religious concept of the nation.'…Laying the foundations of the Italian greatness in the world, starting from the religious concept of Italianness…should become the impulse and the essential directive of our life."[2] In 1923, in a book titled *Fascism and Religion*, Piero Zama observes that

> religion is a sense of mystery manifested in certain forms. A human work on which a moral conception is imposed is religion. The dogmas that can be reduced to one single fundamental truth, and the rites that can be one single great rite, are the essential expression of religion. A people, or better an army that faces death for a command, that accepts life in its purest sense of mission, and that offers it as a sacrifice, truly possesses that sense of mystery that is the fundamental motive of religion, and asserts truths that do not descend from human arguments but rather are dogmas of faith. Likewise, the absorbed silences of "camice nere" [fascists wearing their black shirts] around brothers who have abandoned the earthly fight are rites of religion, and rites of *a* religion are the prayers that fascists say together with the priests of a church, when circumstances of special significance presuppose the public celebration of the sacrifice and the supplication to God.[3]

Giovanni Gentile, on his way to becoming the foremost ideologue of the regime, emphasizes "the clearly religious character of the fascist spirit" even in 1924. He notes that Mussolini "has expressed, with the energy that is typical of his intuitive thinking, the mystical character of fascism, as a cult rendered from the whole soul to the nation." Fascism was a religious movement because it proposed an absolute moral ideal that the individual had to recognize as a superior law, "since from it all the valor that he can ascribe to himself and win over for himself derives." A religious sentiment "analogous to the one that animated the Giovine Italia, and that was the most powerful spark of the Italian revolution for independence and unification," was particularly visible within the army. Much as Mazzini's motto in "Giovine Italia," *Dio e popolo* (God and people), "made the imperative and absolute value of the ideal rights or the people's needs depend on a religious concept, that is, on seeing in the people the living revelation of God," the fascist concept of the national state or fatherland as superior to all classes, groups, and individuals "is not a utilitarian concept, a means to be accepted if one wants to achieve the ends for which it is instrumental, but rather it is indeed the concept of something absolute, that contains its own end, and thus is divine."[4]

Gentile presents fascism as a movement of religious reform and rebirth, as the new locus of the most genuine traditional spirituality of Italy. Thanks to the grafting of the new fascist religion onto the old trunk of Italian religiosity, the latter "will revive and sprout new shoots, and rekindle into spring fronds." These shoots and fronds represented not charity but rather division and war. Gentile explains that Jesus said, "Non veni pacem mittere, sed gladium. Veni enim separare hominem adversus patrem suum et filiam adversus matrem suam," and "Ignem veni mittere in terram. Putatis quia pacem veni dare in terram? Non, dico vobis, sed separationem: erunt enim ex hoc quinque in domo una divisi, tres in duos et duo in tres dividentur."[5] Here Gentile is freely quoting from Matthew 10:34 ("Think not that I am come to send peace on earth: I came not to send peace, but a sword") and from Luke 12:51–52 ("Suppose ye that I am come to give peace on earth? I tell you, Nay; but rather division: For from henceforth there shall be five in one house divided, three against two, and two against three"). Since fascism was able to demonstrate the same determination that Jesus demanded from his apostles and followers, it could boast of being a new religion.

A few months later, in the manifesto created at the congress of Bologna, which was held from March 8 to March 30 in 1925, Gentile again stresses the religious character of fascism: fascism

> understood and championed politics as a training ground for abnegation and sacrifice, the individual before an idea in which the individual can find his reason for living, his liberty, and every right of his; an idea, which is the fatherland, as an ideal that is being historically realized without ever exhausting itself, a tradition that is historically determined and identified, but also a tradition that in the consciousness of every citizen, instead of being a dead memory of the past, becomes a conscious personality of an end to be actualized—tradition thus, but also mission. Hence the religious character of fascism. This character, which is religious and therefore strict, explains the method of struggle followed by fascism in the four years from 1919 to 1922.

By virtue of its religious core, fascism was able to attract an ever-increasing number of young people, and could present itself as the rebirth of Mazzini's "Giovine Italia." It inspired a new faith and "a religious earnestness that does not distinguish theory from practice, saying from doing, and does not depict magnificent ideals to then relegate them to a world beyond this one—where one, in the meantime, can continue to live meanly and miserably—but instead amounts to the hard work of idealizing life and expressing one's convictions in action itself, or with words that can be actions in themselves."

To dispel all eventual doubts about the nature of the new religion, Gentile took care to clarify that fascism was in no way inferior to Christianity: "Fascism is religion, political and civil, because it has its own conception of the state and an original way of conceiving life.... Christian martyrs and the young heroes of the fascist revolution have confirmed, through the ages, a bright reality: only a religion can negate and undo the attachment to mundane life."[6] This was not a Christianity of charity, as another fascist ideologue made clear, but rather that "of the great saints, the pontiffs, the great bishops, the great missionaries: politicians and warriors who brandished the sword as well as the cross, and used both the stake and excommunication, torture and poison, not in order to attain temporal or personal power, of course, but always in order to attain the might and glory of the church."[7]

Fascists admired the religion of the Counter-Reformation. As Curzio Malaparte affirms in 1923, with the bold arrogance of the Italian provincial: "We—we Italians—have no need whatsoever to renounce the whole national life from Clement VII onward, and become heretical in order to follow our fate, which is a fate of imperial power. We will be great even without passing, with a three-century delay, through the Reformation; we will be great, nay, only *against the Reformation*. The new might of the Italian spirit, which already manifests itself with clear signs, cannot be but anti-European."[8] To dispel all doubts, Malaparte writes with an utter dearth of intellectual refinement:

Luther, the fucking villain drunken on ale and pride, who, incapable of understanding the mysteries of Catholic scholarship, which alone can uphold civil peoples, assaulted odiously its foundations with bestial violence, and tried to cause the collapse of the most splendid social, spiritual, and religious edifice of the world, and evoked all the monsters that afterward would contaminate it.... Defining and preaching fascism, therefore, as an anti-Reformation movement is tantamount to conferring on it the clearest, most natural, highest, and most glorious task ever possible: it is tantamount to flinging open the doors to the total restoration of Italianness, nay, of Latinness—that is to say, universality or Catholicity.[9]

Such a clear example of a fawning spirit and moral baseness would be utterly risible, if only fascism, by presenting itself as a new Counter-Reformation, had not thereby emphasized its religious character, and had not gained the favor of the Italian clergy and Catholics, always eager to give heretics a good thrashing.

Thanks to the new religion, Gentile announced on November 2, 1931, from the platform of the second congress of fascist cultural institutes, that a new Italy had brought forth "a new citizen, a new people that has a new face, a new blink, which hadn't been seen in ages."[10] With a leader who was worshipped as a God, an ideology propagandized and imposed as a system of dogmas, and a new and entrancing ritual, fascism had become a political religion and, as such, dominated people's consciousness; fascism not only sought to control people's actions but also demanded that Italians believe in the new "word," and unify themselves with mind and heart into a single body.[11] Before a fascism that proclaimed itself a new religion, those in Italy who truly loved liberty immediately understood that it was necessary to oppose to it another religion, founded on opposite principles, but equally capable of inspiring faith and devotion. The Risorgimento's lesson had left its mark on the soul of the wisest. When fascism laid the moral weakness of Italians bare and crushed the liberty that the Risorgimento had achieved, the best Italian intellectuals remembered Mazzini's teaching: only religious peoples can achieve and defend liberty.

Piero Gobetti—even though he had severely criticized the Risorgimento and Mazzini—was among the first to reflect on the necessity of a religious reform as a precondition for the attainment of liberty. Our Risorgimento, he remarks in "Risorgimento senza eroi," "is a matter for those who have chosen the part of precursors, the lucid desperate, the losers who will never be wrong, for in the world of ideas, they know how to make even the winners of the feasts of optimism keep their distance. History is infallible at avenging the exiles, the unarmed prophets, the victims of collective hallucinations. Nay, before history, these fanatics of truth, content with solitude, know how to avenge themselves by themselves." He considered the "Risorgimento of the heretics, not the professionals," aware that heretics themselves could not attack the church on a dogmatic terrain, and thus the formation of national unity was not accompanied by the moral and religious reform that would have been necessary for building a modern liberal society in Italy.[12]

Gobetti looks for the elements of a religion that teaches people about the inner liberty in minor and marginal figures, like that of Count Alberto Radicati, who professed ideas of a Christianity hostile to the dogmas and intransigencies of Catholicism. Radicati held that while Christ had preached humility and charity, and had been humble and charitable, and the apostles had taught Christ's word and followed his example, the doctrines and customs of the church over the centuries had been completely the opposite: "Those were humble and these are ambitious; those were charitable and despised richness, these perverse and revengeful." They should therefore be called "enemies of Jesus Christ and his laws, not his disciples." With his laws, Christ rendered men free, and was the master of a free thought hostile to dogmatic orthodoxy. When he defended these ideas, Gobetti emphasizes, Radicati saw himself as the perfect Christian who counters the avarice of the ecclesiastics with the spirit of the Gospel and Christ's first followers.[13]

As his intellectual guide, Gobetti chose Vittorio Alfieri (1749–1803), the writer "who left us the most generous example of resistance against political oppressions, the resistance of the lonely individual who is not overtaken already because of the fact that he feels himself to be spiritually higher than the tyrant. Three generations were educated in Italy to his works; and for us he still represents the intransigent morals of the free man in times of servitude." He admires him for the way he lived, rather than for what he wrote: "His life and battles present an inexorable and continuous coherence, founded on an exclusive passion for liberty that remains the central concept of his polemics against tyranny and Catholicism, and the positive basis for his heroic morality." In addition, Gobetti admires him because he was instinctively anti-Catholic, and felt genuine repugnance for the dogmatism and formalism of the dominant religion. Alfieri judged the pope to be the tyrants' accomplice, and the Inquisition, purgatory, confession, and celibacy as the expedients by which free thought was impeded. He affirms that the temporal dominion clashes with the people's dignity, and that it is only because of ignorance and fear that people believe there is a man who represents God without mediation, and who can never err: "Ignorance is the antithesis of liberty, and fear, since it cannot be inspired by excommunications, clearly attests to the fact that where the thought of the pontiff is, tyranny is there; where religious dogmatism is, swords that support it are there." Any people that admits unlimited authority over the most important things, an authority veiled by the sacred mantle of religion, "renders itself forever slave," and thus, as Alfieri warns, there can never be at once "a truly Catholic people and a free people."[14]

According to Gobetti, Alfieri's creed deserved to be rediscovered, because it had not only criticized the corrupting effects of Catholicism but also indicated as an alternative, "a more spiritual religiosity, a heroic morality that guides the life and action of men and peoples," a religion and God that, under the threat of the gravest present and future punishments, commands men to be free and demands from the people a spirit of sacrifice that is evidence of revolutionary attitudes. The writer from Asti understood that Italy would never be free without strong minds, which, driven by a natural impulse, "search for glory in the highest endeavors"—without the "just and noble wrath of the justly enraged and enlightened peoples." Such a revolutionary morality supported by religious spirit was the only way to overcome fascist tyranny. Gobetti emphasizes prophetically that

> this is the morality of the revolution: "by chance, the day, too, comes in which an oppressed and disheartened one, grown free, happy, and mighty, blesses those slaughters, that violence, and that blood through which, after many opprobrious generations of servants and corrupt individuals, an illustrious and egregious one of free and virtuous men has finally come to procreate." Fight of liberty against tyranny: religious fight. Here ethics is at the basis of politics. We are not men if we are not free. The matter is not to achieve liberty by means of reforms, or through the utilitarianism of moderates and philanthropists; the political liberty of Alfieri arises from inward liberty, intended as strong feelings. This idea is the political program of Alfieri, the announcement of a revolution that one still waits for in Italian history, and is also his metaphysics, his absolute, his God. It is a position without heirs, though.[15]

In July 1922, at the University of Turin, Gobetti defended his thesis on the political thought of Alfieri. His supervisor was Gioele Solari, a meek professor whose teaching and life were based on a religious conception of life. Philosophical research, Solari writes in the *Lezioni di filosofia del diritto* (Lectures on the philosophy of right), "is integrated in a religious vision of reality" in that it refines the sense of the infinite in man—that is, what has universal and eternal value: the light before which the mean passions, egoisms, ambitions, and material satisfactions remain silent, and that confers true meaning on life. This religious conception of life impressed on Solari's gestures, manners, and deeds—as Norberto Bobbio, who also had him as his professor, recalls—a "very high sense of the earnestness of life and thus of the responsibility of every action of ours." Therefore, it was no coincidence that he supervised the theses of many leading exponents of antifascism, among them Paolo Treves, Aldo Garosci, Renato Treves, Dante Livio Bianco, Giorgio Agosti, Franco Antonicelli, and Mario Andreis.[16]

Nor was it by chance that Gobetti, while working with Solari on the Alfieri thesis, discovered the God who demands that people love liberty as a moral principle and thus a necessary precondition for political liberty. For Alfieri, "a political liberty that does not found itself on inner liberty—intended as *strong feeling*"—is meaningless. The God of Alfieri inspires the creators of religion, and lives within a Christ who is not a master of humility but rather the "creator of political liberty." Gobetti founds "the religion of liberty" on this God, set up against the religion of the servants, which must inspire people as citizens, capable of fighting for liberty because they should, and not because they are sure of victory. A religion that "is no longer a comfort for the weak but rather a certainty for the strong, no longer the cult of a transcendental activity but rather of our own activity, no longer faith but rather responsibility"; a religion that excludes interests and calculations, requiring "*fanaticism* from the initiators, enthusiasm of sincerity, that complete ardor through which no division separates thought from action."[17] Who was needed in those years if not initiators animated by a pessimism similar to that found in the Old Testament? My friends, Gobetti urges, "one needs to believe more in history than in progress, conceive of our work as a spiritual exercise, which finds its necessity within itself and not in its spreading. There is only one unshakable value in the world: intransigence, and we will be in a certain sense its desperate priests."[18]

For Gobetti, fascism was not merely an episode but instead "the autobiography of the nation," and an essential part of that autobiography was the bad religious education instilled in people by the Catholic Church. "Fascism," he explains in 1923 in an article titled "Il nostro protestantismo" (Our Protestantism), "is Catholic with perfect logic, if one considers that it enters into the Italian crisis in a moment of economic unemployment; and the school reform, essentially reactionary, indeed makes use of the teaching of religion to take away from the working class any revolutionary boldness." Whereas Luther and Calvin were the precursors of the work ethic, and announced to Anglo-Saxon peoples "the religion of autonomy and sacrifice, enterprise and thrift," "Italian pauperism goes together with misery of conscience." Those who do not feel productive in contemporary civilization, Gobetti admonishes, "will have neither self-confidence nor a religious cult of their dignity." This is why, he concludes, "the Italian political problem, among opportunistic acts, the shameless hunt for jobs, and the abdication before the ruling class, is a moral problem."[19]

Fascism's victory necessitated an intellectual and moral reform inspired by the religion of liberty. Utilizing De Sanctis's notions, Gobetti writes that "our Reformation was Machiavelli, an outsider, a political theorist. His concepts could not find a social terrain on which they could flourish, nor could they find men that would live by them. Machiavelli is a modern man because he elaborated a conception of the state that defies transcendence." In the first chapter of *La rivoluzione liberale* (The liberal revolution), Gobetti returns to the same concept, adding a significant detail: Machiavelli "professes a civil religiosity as the directness of enterprises and economy." In order to realize political reform, Italy needs this religion, which is a civil religion or a religion of liberty; the religion that Machiavelli taught Italians, with his refinement as a "citizen expert of historical contingencies," is far from the "noisy project" of the peasant Luther.[20]

Gobetti died on February 15, 1926, in Paris, where he fled to avoid further fascist aggressions. On April 7 of the same year, Giovanni Amendola (born in Salerno, in 1882) died in a hospital in Cannes, and fascists, who had cowardly assaulted him earlier, in July 1925, in Montecatini, then mutilated his dead body. Supported by a moral force that moved his family, friends, and the physicians that were close to him in the last hours, he died invoking the "God of peace" several times.[21] Thirteen years earlier, in an essay titled "Il libro non letto" (The unread book), published in 1912 in *La Voce* of Florence, he pointed to Christ as the supreme expression of the human spirit, immensely superior to the greatest men because of the incomparable strength of his will along with the definitive, eternal greatness of his action. Amendola wrote this essay while assisting a Russian émigré, a family friend. It is not just a reflection; it is a revelation of his inner world. This is why, as his wife, Eva Kühn, notes, "The figure of Christ expresses a wonderful might."[22] Amendola reads the Gospel as a nonbeliever, and finds the principle of life that he fully identifies with:

> I open the Gospel with a soul free from apostolic ends, and only yearning after reapproaching the pure expression of humanity. I do not presuppose faith, and thus do not aim to spread faith. I live in myself and for myself. I seek some not far distant relief, escaping from the aridity of the actual moment. And all of a sudden I find

something that suffices for the past, the present, and the future; an intense and invariable form of humanity, a seal of life capable yet again and forever of imprinting human generations through the profusion of centuries. It certainly is the universal form of the knot of life that man is.[23]

The religion of Christ is grace, a leap beyond the limit of the ethical life, an abandonment that is not an escape, a life of conscience that forms a unified personality, capable of operating in history. It has immense value for political action precisely because it is a call to the inner nature of moral life—a call that means nothing but this: "That the individual makes his own, and leaves to history its own. In fact Christianity teaches that 'there are not two laws—one ethical and one political—that are both in force within the same individual; but there is a single law that only appears to be different when we apply it to the individual or individuals.' "[24]

The Gospel has the secret power of conferring intimacy on everything that comes from man. It is by no means a religion of resignation and submissiveness but rather a religion that calls to "the most virile virtue." It forces the individual to choose, to shoulder moral responsibility, and to operate in the world according to a principle. Because of this, the word of Christ is sometimes similar to "a straight slope that juts out over the abyss: it rises from the depths to the most high, and firm and arduous it remains and shall remain." After the strong word that calls to the host, though, Christ offers "the cordial word of fraternal companionship," and "has all mercies on those who want none for themselves; has all hopes for those who have risked all their life to try the hardest and highest path; has all riches for those who, withdrawing from vagabond wandering, have chosen the poverty of the one and only road." Social relationships, too, if they are not yet destroyed, receive vital nourishment from it.[25]

Precisely because Amendola experienced the word of Christ as a teaching that embraces the fullness of man's life, and an exhortation at once mighty and meek to pursue virtue and responsibility, he complains that the New Testament was and is the "book not read" by Italians: "The Gospel did not find in Italy that sort of profound and continuous reading that can constitute the nourishing of society." The near and vivid intuition of the person of Christ—wellspring of an emotional tone capable of modifying life—"has not been the firm ground on which the men of our stock have moved about." Had it been, Amendola comments, Christ would have realized a real psychological revolution, or rather that moral and religious reform that was necessary for consolidating as well as continuing the Risorgimento's work. He hopes that, one day, Italians will discover the Gospel and, thanks to the Gospel, will become a nation of free men. His was the vain hope of a nonbeliever who engaged himself in the antifascist struggle with the religious sense typical of one who fights a crusade for liberty, as Croce wrote on the gravestone he dictated in Amendola's memory in 1945. The stories of Gobetti and Amendola reveal that two of the most prominent early martyrs of antifascism were, on the one hand, a man who felt himself close to the prophets of the Old Testament and rediscovered Christ, as master of liberty, and, on the other hand, a man who held to a profound religious sentiment, even though he never talked about it.[26]

18

IN THE NAME OF CHRIST

FASCISM OFFENDS Christian conscience. Don Giovanni Minzoni, parish priest in Argenta, massacred by the fascists on August 23, 1923, was among the first who understood this fundamental truth. Born in Ravenna on June 29, 1885, he took holy orders on September 18, 1909. His Christ was on the side of men who seek justice, as revealed by a moving page from his diary:

> Every night, as I return home, I pass by the Camera del Lavoro [Chamber of Labor], and it breaks my heart to see those halls, all with the lights turned on, and with the walls covered with great notices or agendas, and with men who feverishly wander about them and pass by again and again like many shadows. There, in the background, one sees workers who are waiting, and here, at the door, young men who talk, discuss…. Every time I pass by, a sentiment of envy assails me: "How much would I long to fraternize with this rising religion"; [with this movement] that is destined—no matter its present-day attitude—to become a religion, and if God wills, the religion of the future. Indeed, what does socialism lack in order to become the religion of Christ? What prevents Christ from being proclaimed the God of socialism? Only one thing: that man feels the need to improve himself. Form the responsible man, create for him the necessity, the duty of improving himself, and you will logically have a Christian socialism, a new society, Christ as the king of conscience. May the Lord—I keep repeating—convert a Marx into Paul, and the question will be solved.[1]

During World War I, Minzoni served as a military chaplain. Notwithstanding this terrible trial, he continued to understand the word of Christ as a teaching of liberty and democracy: "Feast day of the Christian Democrats! I was still young, a grammar school student, when I was carried away by the new democratic ideas proclaimed by the Gospel of Christ. I understood little, or nothing; yet my heart was beating fast. I dreamed the future struggles amid society, struggles that I would have supported with all the energies of my youth, and in the name of Christ."[2] Once the war was over, he intervened in the public ceremonies to honor the fallen, with his silver medal of honor on his chest, not to sustain the spirit of revenge but rather to render their sacrifice saintly. In the booklet that he himself edited on the occasion of the first anniversary of the victory, he writes: "The church is well worthy of cherishing the name of our fallen youth. The divine sacrifice of Christ will glorify every day their sacrifice with greater effectiveness than any human action, and religion, which decorates with flowers every joy and comforts all sorrows, and which has the power of spiritualizing and eternalizing in God all affections, will make their name shine before the eyes of the future generations."[3]

Precisely because he was a true Christian and patriot, Minzoni had no doubts about the choice to be made concerning fascism in power: "Just as one day I offered all my young life for the safety of my country, happy if this might be useful," he writes in 1923, "today I realize that a much harsher battle is waiting for me. We are tenaciously preparing for the fight, and with weapons that for us are sacred and divine, those of the first Christians: prayer and goodness. Retreating would entail renouncing a sacred mission. With an open heart, and the prayer for my persecutors that I hope will never die from my lips, I am waiting for the storm, persecution, and perhaps death for the triumph of the cause of Christ."[4] His Christian conscience compels him to remain on liberty's side, without uncertainties: "When a party—the fascist party—when a government, when men in a bold or petty manner denigrate, outrage, persecute an idea, a program, or an institution like that of the Partito Popolare and the Catholic circles, for me there is only one solution: to cross the Rubicon, and whatever happens will in any case be better than the stupid and servile life that one wants to impose on us."[5] If Italian Catholics and the high church hierarchs had been true Christians, Minzoni's death would have stirred up a feeling of indignation and resistance in Italy that would have swept fascism away. Pope Pius XI himself should have been present at Minzoni's funeral, and should have excommunicated his assassins and the instigators. In fact, even the archbishop of Ravenna, Antonio Lega, did not attend the funeral. He sent his secretary as his representative.

Whereas the Vatican was engaging in ever-closer rapprochement with the regime, other Catholics penned calls encouraging people to fight fascism. Igino Giordani, who in 1925 published *Rivolta cattolica* (Catholic revolt), with the Piero Gobetti Press, was one of these writers. In his text, Giordani openly urges Catholics to revolt, in the name of their faith, against the anti-Christian religion of fascism. "Against the deadly aspirations consciously or unconsciously aroused by the raging oligarchies," Giordani declares, "one must erect the barricade of those who believe in life—that is, Jesus, the first martyr of such an idiocy that leads to perdition; go against the current, in order to climb up to the sources, deserving (how wonderful!) the scorn and disdain of the gallant, amoral contemporaries, who lay down the law, and not only from the café."[6] Also among Catholics, "la vecchia anima vile" (the old cowardly soul) insinuates itself like the moth, in the tradition of Don Abbondio, turning prudence into pusillanimity, and affirming an abhorrence of principles because principles demand resistance. When the surrounding world is being ruined and the storm roars, that Catholic core does not fight against the enemy but instead corrupts it, "taming it, tickling it with arrangements, compromises, *do ut des*." It is necessary," Giordani asserts, "for Catholics to get rid of this mentality and check the new fascist paganism."

Fascism, Giordani emphasizes, has loudly proclaimed that its religion "does not confine itself to the Catholic dogma." Because of this, Catholics "ought to earn autonomy in culture and life; mold a character; give up rhetoric; define themselves; always take a clear-cut stand; vehemently believe, so dogmatically that their faith may be an inflexible rod."[7] They must conquer the state, in order to govern, and they must govern in order to moralize. Their duty is to rise up against the new doctrine, championed by Gentile, counterfeiting all Christian philosophy and life, notwithstanding the fact that it declared itself to be the true translation of Christian ethics.[8] In order to spur his readers to antifascist action, Giordani insists on the anti-Christian and anti-Catholic character of nationalism, and openly denounces the vile and senseless choice of many Catholics to become its supporters rather than its most resolute enemies.

This behavior is understandable, Giordani observes, "because fascism has a conservative and reactionary character, and many Catholics believe that the church has to support privilege." In light of such a menace—matter against the spirit, and instinct against reason—Catholics from all persuasions should convince themselves that it is still possible to save society.[9] The religious politics of fascism, because of its totalitarian, egocentric, and all-consuming core, like some jealous seraglio-keeper, does not tolerate forces outside its own control. It does not appreciate a church that freely proceeds along its path and carries out its apostolic work. Rather, it wants the church to be in the service of the new regime and the new religion; it wants priests to wear the black shirt, participate in the feasts, ring the bells for Mass, and accept the party card. Either in the square with the fascists, or in the privacy of the sacristy: these are the only places for church and Catholics.[10]

Giordani invokes a Christian vision that commands people to love and support liberty. Religion springs up in people's hearts and grows in churches, but should then go out "in the streets and into the squares to seek every creature in every corner." When one crosses the threshold of the house to dive into the world, faith "should not be hung like a faded skullcap on a nail behind the door but instead should be carried like a torch and sword in the whirl and fight." In another age, "one fought against Christianity in the name of religion and liberty. Today, one can no longer fight against Christianity unless one destroys reason and liberty." Whereas fascism and Gentile both sneer at liberty, we, "together with the thinkers of Risorgimento, believe in this liberty, which is a divine gift." "True Christians should not accept any compromise, nor should they abandon their ethical judgment. They should encircle this slovenly orgy with a sanitary cordon of earnestness and study; they should suffocate this recrudescence of brigandage, which rises again after every great crisis, with work and with a reevaluation of the spirit. Against dictatorship, liberty should be affirmed. It is a right presented to us by God: one shall never sacrifice it, not even for any alleged administrative welfare." The clash with fascism should be a clash of one faith against another. Catholics must therefore recover their faith in all its purity. Our opposition, writes Giordani, must be "essentially spiritual," a struggle of good against evil, light against darkness.[11]

Luigi Sturzo (1871–1959)—the Catholic priest who in 1919 founded the Partito Popolare and, in 1924, was forced to emigrate—also soon understood that fascism was a totalitarian regime and political religion. In *Italia e Fascismo*, published in Bologna in 1926, Sturzo observes that fascism has erected a Leviathan "that absorbs every other force and becomes the expression of an impending political pantheism." The goal of the state is no longer the free individual; the state is the goal of man: "The deification of the state (which is now called nation) is complete."[12] A few years later, in 1933, he explains in an even more precise way the deeply anti-Christian character of totalitarian regimes:

Idolatry presupposes that the idol is a power superior to man and that this power attains absoluteness. It doesn't matter that there are various idols: it is typical of idolatry to multiply idols, for man seeks in them compensation for his own individual insufficiency in a sign that represents a collective force. Idolatry is more collective than individual. It is the *totem* of primitive societies, the symbol of the clan, the tribe, the race, the nation; hence the duty of the individual to sacrifice himself for it, as is due to the very principle of social vitality. Apply these elements to Russian Bolshevism, German Nazism, Italian fascism, and you'll find the idolatrous reason that they contain in their being and affirming themselves as *totalitarian* regimes.[13]

To a fascist religion that crushed liberty, Sturzo counterposes the ideal of liberty, lived as a Christian value:

One thing we must wish and want, and Catholics as such must promote with every effort: that the religious precepts about the relationships between liberty and authority, and the evaluation of the highest ends (with which the merely terrestrial ones must be coordinated), and the evangelical teaching of the love for God and the neighbor—the basis of social life—shall penetrate the spirit of public institutions, and shall vivify the spirit of our civilization, which is substantially, notwithstanding the deviations, a Christian civilization. If liberty, attained by men in the forms and with the spirit of the last centuries, will not be inspired by the essence of Christianity, which alone in history laid claim to the human personality—the basis of true liberty—if liberty, that is, is not imbued with true religiosity, then it does not fulfill its very essence, as it has often happened, making room for the egoism of the oligarchies or anarchism of the masses.[14]

Giuseppe Donati, editor of the party newspaper *Il popolo* in 1923, took a stand against fascism, and for this he died in exile in Paris on August 16, 1931. In 1919, he writes that

all politics is inspired by spiritual principles and is oriented to spiritual purposes, for politics does not consist only of the will to have certain juridical institutions that regulate human conduct in civil society but rather it is above all *education* of the human spirit, individual and collective, to understand and freely want that civil order that best corresponds to making the individual man and the particular organizations not only instruments of material well-being but also instruments of the moral elevation of all society. This is why we call ourselves, besides *democrats, Christian* as well. The movement of the Christian Democrats is connected with the purest traditions of our

Risorgimento. Mazzini said that "either democracy will be religious, or it won't exist." And for us, as for Giuseppe Mazzini, religiosity is nothing other than the spirit of duty that drives us to sacrifice and complete commitment for the triumph of an ideal. These spiritual values are expressed in the purest form in Christianity, which is a law of love, liberty, justice, and charity especially for our fellow human beings; and if these maxims of the ancient and modern sage were several times expressed, only by Christ were they strengthened, for Christ died for them in the most horrible way. Because of this, we are Christians.[15]

In the same newspaper, he observes that religion is "concrete confession and profession of faith."[16] Minzoni was a good example of a Christian way of acting in society—as Donati averred in commemorating the first anniversary of his death with firm and noble words that were at the same time a relentless indictment of fascism and bad Christians: "Better than the shadows of night, the cowardly if not utterly obliging silences of those who did not witness, the prearranged ineptitude of the weak guardians of the law, and finally the tolerance of all those who, for love of a peaceful life, regularly forget the Christian duty of fortitude and courage before the arrogant and the unjust—all this protected the impunity of the assassins [and] the instigators." The cowardly, the indifferent, and the fainthearted bear heavy responsibility for fascism's victory: "Thereby, for hundreds of innocent victims, a systemic conspiracy of silence and impunity for the culprits was created that has destroyed any trust in justice, and has put the free citizens at the mercy of factious political rivals and fanatic and hired assassins." Donati scorns the alleged religiosity proclaimed by the pompous Gentile: the "moral identification of sermon and club," the new "*club-religion.*"[17] Only the religion of Christ, if correctly understood, could have defeated the false religion of fascism: "The submission preached by Christ and confirmed by his martyrdom is not synonymous with weakness, cowardice, tolerance of injustice and arrogance, as one is commonly made to suppose or believe; it is, instead, synonymous with fortitude, perseverance, courage 'to conquer evil with the good.' "[18]

Another prominent representative of the Partito Popolare, Francesco Luigi Ferrari (1889–1933), forced into exile as of 1926, wrote two letters, "To the Italian Parish Priests," for *Giustizia e Libertà* (Justice and Liberty) that were clandestinely circulated in 1931. In them, Ferrari urged the parish priests to account for the fact that fascism, by covering them with honors, had actually rendered them slaves of the regime and made it impossible for them to exercise Christian teaching:

> The governors were not content with having you as accomplices of their crimes at school; they have also put you at the side of their sergeants, their instructors, their officers called to educating the new generations for war and violence. This is the reward they have granted you for the deserted oratories, the dissolved units of scouts, the circles of Catholics subjected to the arbitrary surveillance of the police, for the fascistized welfare institutions. Generous reward indeed! Try to speak about peace and Christian love to youths, who are obliged by the orders of the authority and the "benevolent pieces of advice" of the party officials to enter the cohorts of the *balilla* and the avant-gardists. Illustrate to them that passage of the Sermon on the Mount that reads: "Love your enemies: do good to those who hate you, and pray for those who persecute and calumniate you" (Matthew 5:44). You will be chased off as defeatists, reported to your superiors as petty politicians and partisans of old-time democratic humanitarianism, set up for the contempt and hatred of the *gerarchi* [hierarchs] of the dominant party.[19]

It is the parish priests' duty to break with fascism, in order to be guardians of a law of truth as well as to combat the falsehood, deceit, and sham that the regime has spread in Italy: "Your place is with those who suffer, not at the side of those who triumph. In the name of Christ, judge, reprimand, condemn. Be indulgent toward the man, but do not condone the sin. Love justice and reprove injustice, which is all the more blameworthy when the culprit is more powerful. Be apostles of the love of Christ and ministers of his justice, and, thanks to you, the liberty of the country will be established on incorruptible bases." Against a fascism that "deifies the state" and, because of this, is "the negation of God and his law," Catholics should fight, following the examples of the "sublime rebels" who dared to challenge the tyrant "armed with their apostolic zeal," mindful of the Gospel's words: "Do not be afraid of those who kill the body but cannot kill the soul" (Matthew 10:28).[20]

Also *Elementi di un'esperienza religiosa* (Elements of a religious experience) by Aldo Capitini, published in 1936, presented a religious alternative to fascism. As Capitini himself recounted ten years later, he soon understood that Mussolini fascinated youths in a religious way: "An altogether superficial cleverness, an overbearing individuality, flaunted in a thousand picturesque ways, sporty, pseudocultural; the manner of an unscrupulous bachelor, adventurous, extremely active; a flashy smile (which we knew was cynical, and the adolescents thought was paternal)—all these elements together had given to the Italian youths the first political, nay, religious, frisson." Support for the regime began to diminish with the Ethiopian invasion, signaling "the end of the thrill, the mysticism, the religious sentiment." Capitini did not set out "to found a 'new religion' with a leader, a dogma, believers, gatherings, ceremonies, and a neat distinction between members and nonmembers." He did not want to find readers who would agree with his ideas but people who, by reading his work, would feel something opening up in the silence of their hearts.[21] For this open and liberating character, the book expresses a spirit in opposition to the fascist closed order, against totalitarianism, against the dogma of Mussolini's infallibility, in the name of free research, free contribution, *hearing and listening*.

The inspiration for those pages did not come from the desire to rebel, object, or contradict but rather from the yearning to serve a principle, a law, the truest, the most earnest, the most authentic for living the spiritual life in its entirety and richness.[22] Capitini calls his antifascist conception of life religious because it was consistent with modern European philosophy, which gives central value to the human spirit, which, in the concreteness of historical life, produces its manifestation, development, and celebration. He felt close to Mohandas Gandhi, from whom he drew the principles of nonviolence and truth in political life, as well as to Saint Francis of Assisi and Mazzini, "the great democrat of the nineteenth century." During World War I, he felt in the very fibers of his body the limitations of a civilization that valued only action, violence, and pleasure; and he felt an intimate solidarity with those who suffer, those who cannot act, and those who are overwhelmed.

His religious consciousness took on an even more definite character in 1932, when he believed that what he was living "was truly an experience of God." This inner conviction gave him the strength not to join the fascist party, even if that act meant losing his job and salary. That choice of resistance was, for Capitini, the demonstration of a way of experiencing God not as an obscure and mysterious force of inscrutable intent, but rather as "presence, conscience, light, closeness, help," an unlimited meekness and infinite nearness. The God that Capitini finds in the early 1930s is "a God who does not command because he is powerful, because He is He Himself: it is a God who persuades. He does not live on his own;

his infinitude consists not of being transcendental, above all and everyone, but of being capable of establishing an extremely profound, eternal, unlimited proximity."[23]

This idea of God inspires a religion that resides in the inner core of a person, and opens up "for all beings, all individuals, and even for things." In a time when fascists derided charity, for they equated it with a morality of the weak, Capitini encouraged "the loving and respectful care for every living creature, and every thing, and, I would say, for every word; a delicacy that, as it is so constant and vigilant in all directions, cannot be a weakness." His was a religion that thrives on "nonviolence, truth, the effort to open oneself, enthusiasm about liberty, continuous weaving of sociality"; a religion that inspired universalistic action and, because of this, necessarily brought people to the difficult practice of noncooperation with the regime, which affirmed the opposite values of appearance, contempt of the weak, exaltation of violence, and superior peoples and races.[24]

Barbara Allason, a gifted writer and translator from Germany, found the road to the religion of liberty in the Gospel, and, from this, the guide and support for her antifascist engagement. The author of valued translations from German, she lost her teaching position in 1929 for having written a letter of solidarity to Croce, after he courageously spoke in the Senate against the Lateran Pacts. In 1933, she published *Vita di Silvio Pellico*, featuring a dark gray, gloomy cover that recalled the painting *La partenza del Pellico e del Maroncelli per lo Spielberg* (The departure of Pellico and Maroncelli for Spielberg). Pellico is portrayed descending the steps that take him to a gondola. He is in chains at his wrists and feet, together with Maroncelli, and, with his left hand, clasps the hand of a man not in chains, probably an Austrian officer, who covers his face in order not to cry or show his shame. The soldiers who are waiting on the gondola have a sad expression too: one lowers his eyes and seems to be about to cry, overwhelmed with grief for the dismal duty he has to perform. The other one watches, with respect and curiosity, the prisoners he has to escort. In terms of the entire picture, Pellico's eyes are most striking, no longer turned on the men, like those of Maroncelli, but already looking toward the sky. Next to the title, one finds a portrait of Pellico, looking slight and mild. The publication date dutifully reads "MCMXXXIII–XI."[25] The table of contents leads the reader toward the religious dimension of man: first part, "L'Apostolo" (The apostle); second part, "The Martyr" (The martyr); third part, "Il Santo" (The saint). The first part is prefaced by a quotation from Cesare Correnti: "The strong peoples who have been prevented by God from fighting with the sword, fight with their thought; such was the way in which the prophets of Judea defended in times of slavery and exile their forefathers' faith and the seed of redemption." Could the exhortation to maintain the faith in liberty be clearer, in 1933 Italy?

Allason is particularly effective when she recounts that in the Milanese circle of *Il Conciliatore*, the young Pellico discovered at once a new philosophy and a new religion, in which the moral ideal takes the place of the God of revealed religions: "He never felt more religious than in that time, but of a religiosity that does not recall Catholicism or Protestantism or Judaism, a religiosity that, in his ardent letters to his brother, he calls 'philosophy,' and in which the pure and disinterested idea replaces the God of the positive religions." Such a religion supported a generous patriotism, deeply and radically opposed to "the mistaken nationalisms," and to that narrow-minded chauvinistic spirit that, "with the pretext of exalting only what is Italian, would like to prevent its country from making progress by competing with the other countries." Against this blameworthy nationalism and chauvinism, Pellico invokes the light of both reason and love, which illuminate and heat "the dream of a few, liberty."[26]

She allows the reader to feel all the strength of that invocation in Mussolini's Italy, where the nation was exalted instead of liberty and, in this way, lost the value that the true patriots of the nineteenth century had given to it. With the same mastery, she shows, through the words of one of the founders of the journal *Il Conciliatore*, the contrast between the religion that the Catholic Church taught and that of the liberty of liberalism. One of the *Il Conciliatore* writers maintains that political liberty and the Catholic religion are incompatible, and extols liberal religion: "Christianity, as it was perfected and still is being perfected through consciences, is great. Its authority resides in prayer and love. By fixing it in a dogmatic manner, however, the Catholic priestly spirit has ruined it. And Catholicism has become the platform on which despotism has been created. No criticism, hence no progress: political reaction is a fruit of Catholicism, as liberalism is a fruit of the Reformation." As a fruit of the Reformation, liberalism is "a holy religion." The priests of this religion "must strive to convert those who see in it but revolutions, massacres, atheism, dissoluteness." Like the Italians who, at the beginning of the nineteenth century, founded a movement of national and liberal emancipation, the Italians of the 1930s could and must have found in the religion of liberty the strength to resist fascism. The night of tyranny cannot be eternal; it is a trial that people must overcome in order to deserve liberty.[27]

Allason's conception of Christianity prevented her from justifying those Catholics who loved Mussolini, and saw in him the man who had finally resolved the tiring conflict between "religion and fatherland." She remembers instead, with emotion, those Catholics who condemned the corruption of too large a part of the clergy that risked replacing the Gospel with the fascist decalogue and did not hesitate to exalt the absolute negation of the Christian spirit. She admires the eleven professors who refused to take the oath of allegiance to fascism, among them Ernesto Buonaiuti, "master of religious life," who gathered around him "the best youths, mindful of their religious and moral destiny, who then, once introduced in real life, in the offices, brought with them the awareness of this moral duty, not intransigent, but extremely severe, and saw all their life linked to it, without the possibility of compromises and arrangements."[28]

When, by chance, a copy of the Beatitudes reaches her in prison, she reflects on the antifascist choice, and concludes that her "valiant fellows who had been facing persecution and death for years" were precisely those "who are persecuted because of their love for justice," those "who were outraged and insulted by the people," those who were "hungry and thirsty for justice," whom Christ calls the blessed. Weren't they those "who loved peace," and "loved it against the violent, the spreaders of the future wars, the instigators of consciences who taught even boys to take revenge and hate?" In the name of this evangelical religiosity, Allason despises the Catholicism of the fascist Giovanni Papini:

> Papini a Christian? Religion soothes, and he distressed me: religion does not foster despair, and he drove to desperation; it is compassionate to the wretches, to whom it says that God is always near them, whereas Papini is a braggart, mean, malignant, and a mocker, and for the weak, the oppressed, the poor in spirit, has no more pity than Nietzsche has, but without his torment and nobleness. I could forget that he had ignobly insulted Benedetto Croce...but I could not forgive him for having lowered, arrogating it to himself, the name of Christian.[29]

Allason's antifascism was dictated by the Christian teaching of forgiveness, tolerance, and humbleness. Because of these principles, the priests who, at the time of the fascist wars in Africa, lauded the "bloody and murderous deeds," disgust Allason. Again, because she was profoundly Christian, she has an even greater loathing for the pope, who openly sides with Francisco Franco. Notwithstanding the malignity of God's vicars and ministers, Allason still directs her prayers to God before the imminent tragedy of the war: "O Lord, keep Italy away from this conflict, from which she cannot exit but defeated, no matter the final outcome: snatch her from the fatal dilemma between a fascist victory and an Italian defeat! For, if Nazi-fascism wins, it is the end of civilization, the return to the darkest barbarian times; but if we lose the war, it will be a Sisyphean task for the next Italian generations to rebuild what will be lost; and hence we could lightheartedly accept not even this, O Lord."[30]

In those terrible months of 1940, when it seemed that the German army would bury Christian civilization, Giorgio La Pira (1904–77) insisted on the idea of God as the origin of the moral law that compels us to love and defend liberty. "The desire for liberty," La Pira writes in the supplement to the first issue of *Vita Cristiana* (Christian life), "is the most vital among man's desires. The more it is violated, the more it is invigorated; for liberty is an impregnable fortress, within which man's personality is steadily clasped." Civilization took a giant step on the day that it posed the rule-of-law principle as the basis of juridical and political constructions, a true "Copernican discovery," La Pira emphasizes, "which is essential for the maintenance of justice and order. This sacred principle has been violated by those who replaced the law with arbitrary power," and has introduced a "mysticism of the state," the gravest heresy of our time. Instead of worshipping the true God, certain men adore one thing: such as the state, race, proletariat, or nation. But in order to be adored, this "thing" must be personified, and hence the rational and strong-willed faculties typical of the human person and, in essence, God are attributed to it.[31] Behind the screen of the mysticism of the state, atheist communism and pagan Nazism banned God, persecuted the church, oppressed liberty, and destroyed the human personality of man. Therefore, Christian faith imposes, as a religious duty, the necessity to fight any form of totalitarianism.

To render his exhortation even sharper, La Pira explains that as creatures of God, Christians have the duty to assimilate into the image of their creator. Since the distinctive feature of God is liberty, they will be free in their action, and will find in their liberty the mark of their greatness, labor, and also, frequently, tragedy. Inner liberty, and consequently civil and political liberty, defines the essence of man: "It constitutes, as it were, the point of contact between intelligence and will," since liberty is the sole foundation of any human structure. What follows is that those political systems that rest on elements contrary to liberty, such as materialist and racist systems along with tyrannical systems, violate the Gospel's law, offend God and man in their most profound essence, and are doomed to meet "certain and great ruin."[32] How could one better express the principle that, for Christians, fighting for liberty is a duty, and that a true Christian religion is a religion of liberty?

La Pira's was an isolated voice, distant from the Vatican's orientation toward the regime. The Vatican did not call on Catholics to firmly oppose fascism; more important, it often openly helped the regime.[33] Why did the church and Italian Catholics avoid resisting fascism, and, crucially, why did they in many cases become its open supporters? The best answer to these questions is still the one offered almost forty years ago by Arturo Carlo Jemolo (1891–1981), a Catholic who defined himself as a Risorgimento survivor. Fascism, Jemolo explains, was indeed an exaltation of violence and war. It celebrated irrationality, the beauty of gesture, and the strengthening of the individual, praising the doctrines that precisely represent the antithesis of the Christian ideal, so thirsty for rationality that it had comprised within rational schemes, or rather in a perfect logical system, the whole divine world. It also represented the antithesis of the Christian doctrine that glorifies renunciation, patience, mildness, and humility along with the individual who dominates his instincts and, if hit, offers the other cheek. Fascism was indeed the glorification of one's own country against everyone and everything; the disavowal of the idea of justice when one of the parties at play is one's own country, because this is always right, and good and evil no longer apply when the country's interest is at stake; and the duty of citizens always to side with their country. Christianity, on the contrary, is a law of universality, where all men are brethren, and distinctions between nations and states cannot take priority over universal brotherhood and the duties that originate from it. "The precept of loving the creator more than his creatures also entails that no tie—be it a tie of blood or belonging to whatever group—can override the duties of justice, or justify the support of a bad action."[34] Fascism, furthermore, was "a church that accounted for man in his entirety, in all his works, in all his activities. Even in the field of literature and art, it prescribed what man should dislike and what he should consider beautiful." Ultimately, the party was a "church that took away from its zealots any other interest; a church that had no consideration of the other world. For, according to the fascist idea (as well as the communist), everything must be realized in this world, with no worries about a next world where the justice that has remained incomplete is perfected."[35]

Notwithstanding these contrasts, the Italian church and fascism had common enemies: first of all, liberalism, which, once it had won the battle against the papacy's temporal power, did not relieve and pacify the defeated adversary; and then socialism, another opponent of the church, stretching all the way back to the values of the Enlightenment and the French Revolution. Another deposit that had settled in the soul of Catholicism was the praise of military values and wars of conquest—not the church, but rather its enemies rebelled against militarism, nationalism, and the legitimacy of war. Near the end of the nineteenth century, a Catholic would find the socialists backing expressions of antimilitarism and the Freemasons backing societies of peace, and would see in Tolstoy the most illustrious defense of nonviolence.[36] Therefore, many Catholics, forgetting about Jesus of Nazareth and Paul of Tarsus, felt completely at ease among those fascists, who exalted the sanctity of national boundaries and venerated armies.[37] Of course, "great Christian spirits, pervaded by the teaching of he who was never more severe than he was with the Pharisees, who were taught that the manifestations of one's religious life should never be flaunted, that God should be worshipped in one's heart, and that the main outer manifestation of worship is the love of one's neighbor"—these sorts of Christians would have reacted with horror to the words and deeds of Mussolini and his men. Jemolo remarks, however, that "in all times, the great Christian spirits have been but a few."[38] This is why fascism won.

19

INNER LIBERTY

As fascism accentuated its totalitarian character and tried to infuse its domination into people's consciences, those antifascists who were intellectually more refined directed their research toward the rediscovery of an inner liberty. They were aware of the fact that once fascism became hegemonic, the last glimmer of hope for a political and civil liberation also would die. The philosopher Piero Martinetti (1872–1943) is a prime example of opposition to fascism in the name of human dignity. Starting in 1926, when fascism took on a totalitarian character, he exhorted students to that pride of character that is the distinctive trait of human beings: "[Immanuel] Kant lists among the essential duties of man that of pride, moral pride. He asserts: Never become the servant of anyone! And this means: Do not subordinate your conscience to the fear and hope of the inferior life: do not degrade your personality by slavishly subduing it before other men! Only a man who feels within himself the necessity of this moral dignity, this inflexible pride, is truly a man: the others are a herd of men, born to serve."[1]

A few years later, in 1931, he set an example, refusing to take the oath of loyalty imposed by fascism on university professors. His motivation was intensely religious, as he explained in a letter to his colleague Adelchi Baratono at the University of Genoa:

Personally, the thing in itself does not hurt me at all: I am glad to be able to return fully to my study: and I say "my" to say "made exclusively for me, for my inner personality and my life." Of course, I do feel the sadness of the thing if one considers it objectively: I did not want to swear (like many of the eleven, I believe) for a religious reason, for not subordinating the things of God to the things of the earth: where is the respect of one's conscience going? This is sad, and it darkly presages a sad future for all, the persecutors included.[2]

In 1928, he published an insightful study, *La libertà* (Liberty), which passed almost unnoticed in Italy at the time and afterward was completely forgotten. Martinetti argues that it is impossible to separate liberty from ethical and religious principles, and that the definition of the concepts of responsibility, punishment, and civil and religious liberty depend on the way in which moral liberty is conceived. By inner or moral liberty, he meant a person's capacity to live the good life.[3] The individual who loses his inner liberty—that is, the individual who no longer applies the rule of good and bad to his conscience, but leaves it up to other men—loses the divine dimension. Building a system of domination on earth that controls not only actions and will but also individual conscience therefore entails offending God.

The conclusion to this work is one of the highest and most intense defenses of the religious character of liberty and, at the same time, a call written with measured words, and thus even more moving, to remind people that liberty is a gift from God:

> The essence and principle of the liberty of man lies therefore in his divine personality, in his being absolute as it coessentially lies in the absolute reason—this is the conclusion, where we should stop. This concept explains to us the universal and human value of liberty, and the nearly religious character and function that it has in man's life. Man throws himself on all goods with passion, because in all of them he looks for the good that definitively satisfies his insatiable aspirations: however, he can stop at any of them: thus, he loves above any other good the possibility of freeing oneself from the present and turning one's heart to the desires and hopes of the future. But at the bottom of this vague love of liberty, another love burns, albeit ignored: the love for which every man desires the true and only good, and aspires to rejoin his divine nature. Because of this, love of liberty is the highest and most universal love of man: he seeks liberty under all skies, in all degrees of civilization, in all the forms of his activity: and the man who fights for liberty fills our soul with sympathy and respect, even though, because of ignorance or passion, he seeks liberty where it cannot be. This is why liberty is also the unavoidable precondition for every form of justice and social progress: without a strong sense of liberty, the human personality weakens and deteriorates; without free institutions, the economic perspective and political greatness of the peoples are but appearances, without any substance. But it is even truer as for the noblest forms of the spiritual life. Morality, science, art, and religion are the most delicate flowers of liberty: liberty, here, is identified with the very divine essence of the spirit, and the negation of liberty is the negation of God.[4]

While he was finishing *La libertà*, Martinetti taught a course on Christology at the University of Milan; it was interrupted several times by members of the fascist action squads. The class was his answer to a regime that since 1926, encouraged by the Vatican, had closed down the Sixth National Philosophical Congress in order to prevent Ernesto Buonaiuti from presenting a paper titled "La religione nel mondo dello spirito" (Religion in the spiritual world). Buonaiuti was a prominent historian of Christianity and a priest who had been excommunicated a few months earlier. Based on his course, Martinetti, who had by then retired in dignified poverty, composed *Gesù Cristo e il cristianesimo*, published in 1934 at his own expense. A second edition, edited by Maria Adalgisa Denti, came out in 1949, although the Holy Office quickly put it on the index of prohibited books. From the first to the last page, the work is sustained by an anguishing question: "Can we still be Christian?" No church, Martinetti writes, is capable today of satisfying the demands of a Christian spirit. All of them are too distant from the church of Christ, which was "a persecuted sect of the poor and the humble." The true Christian must counter the churches with the truths of Christ—first of all the affirmation of the kingdom of God and the vanity of the world, the law of charity, and the condemnation of any formalistic and pharisaical religion.[5]

And still, after writing that the kingdom of God will never be realized in history, and that there will never be a reconciliation between God and the world, Martinetti affirms that "no obstacle whatsoever can obstruct the renewal of that pure Christian tradition that rises above the history of the churches like the celestial Jerusalem, which in the Apocalypse rises from the ruins of heaven and earth. In all times, there have been men who, inspired by the sacred traditions of the gospel of Jesus Christ, have raised themselves to the eternal gospel written in the depth of the human spirit; they have not built kingdoms, nor have they founded churches, but have conserved among men the tradition of truth." The true faith is a secret treasure of the soul, the presence of the divine and the negation of the world, and hence offers a hope for liberty that no one can stifle: "The diffusion and outward triumph have no importance; only our eyes, blinded by the world, can induce us to believe that the divine truth can suffer from the darkness that sometimes seem to thicken on earth. Religion lives in the souls, not in the world, and the light that shines in a pure conscience does not experience sunsets. Therefore, it can watch earthly matters with indifference, because for it nothing really happens. The only true reality is the silent activity of the soul that frees itself from the world." It frees itself in order to commit itself, and it can commit itself with absolute intransigence because it has freed itself, as Martinetti observes in *Breviario spirituale* (Spiritual breviary) in 1923.[6]

Inner liberty was also the main concern for Adolfo Omodeo (1889–1946), one of the chief protagonists in the search for a religion of liberty during the years of triumphant fascism. Omodeo cultivated two broad interlocked themes throughout his life as a scholar: ancient Christianity and the Risorgimento—that is, the two great ideal traditions that inspired the religion of liberty.[7] Unlike Gobetti, who judged the Risorgimento a missed opportunity for religious and moral reformation, the Neapolitan historian considered it a political experience sustained by a profound religious sentiment. "Gobetti," Omodeo writes, "becomes the representative of the liberal revolution against the 'failed revolution' of the Risorgimento. Unable to let things and facts quietly speak for themselves, he comments on them before narrating them." His is "the example of a journalistic historiography," and the essay on Alfieri is an "incomprehensible scribble." Gobetti disagrees that the Risorgimento was a political revolution without a religious reformation, but the statement of the problem, Omodeo contends, is abstract:

> Whence must this Italian religious reformation have risen? For obvious reasons, one could not faithfully follow the Protestant one. Could the people of the nineteenth century propose it just like that? From which germ of a Catholic life withered and parched by Jesuitry should it have sprung? Where it attempted to burst out, amid the Tuscan semi-Jansenists, it did and could not have popular treatments: it was instead a prelude to the aristocratic modernist movement. Pure anticlericalism? That experiment was tried during the French Revolution.[8]

According to Omodeo, the Risorgimento had "a religious life of its own, such as to reduce and limit the demands of a Jesuitical Catholicism." Although they didn't pursue a religious reformation proper, the men of Risorgimento "lived a new faith" that led them to fight for the people. They worked hard to embody the nation, "just as the seven thousand Israelites who at the time of Elijah had not knelt down before Baal embodied the true Israel." They believed in the people and nation. They didn't withdraw into the oligarchic arrogance of the fabricators of history *ex professo*. They were obsessed with constructing the people. The reason why the work was not fully completed is that a people cannot be built in fifty years. Secular traditions had to be formed beforehand, whereas the Italian nation was altogether new. They limited themselves "with religious-like abnegation" to the borders within which the people and nation could be inserted.[9] The misfortunes that had afflicted Italy after unification depended not on the Risorgimento, as Gobetti maintains, but rather on the loss of the Risorgimento's spirit.

Omodeo lived his opposition to fascism in the name of a profound religious consciousness. In a letter to the young Alessandro Galante Garrone, who, in December 1930, confessed his discouragement about the moral conditions of the Italians, he replied with these words:

> My son, I understand your anguish, which is also mine and that of a thousand others, and I would like to be able to come to Turin one day or the other, and talk to you for a long time, about many things, as in a letter it is difficult. We must find comfort in one thing, though: even if vulgarity is ruthless with us, who take care with devotion of the light of culture and the religion of memories, we will finally triumph. The world cannot live without that light, even though at present it is declining due both to the invasion of the barbarians and the use of modern mechanical technology, and is enjoying only the exterior aspects of civilization and not its intimate spirit. Therefore, it will return to us, or rather, that sort of concentrated, spiritual life in which we set the value of life. It can be a matter of waiting for a longer or shorter time; the question is whether we ourselves will be called to enjoy part of the success, or whether we, like Moses, will die before touching the promised land. But this does not make any difference, and with Mazzini we will repeat: now and always.[10]

Without being a believer in the Christian religion, Omodeo felt the religious dimension in the simplest and most fundamental aspects of life, such as the relationship with the other and friendship. On April 12, 1911, he wrote to Eva Zona, who later became his wife:

> Look, when I stare hard at myself like that, everything becomes mysterious: all of my life, every act of my thought, becomes the act of an arcane will. I feel the other within myself. Why am I friends with you? This is a will of the other.... In the end, the relationship between two friends is mysterious just like the infusion of the Holy Spirit for the believer. It is the universal affirmation of ourselves, the acknowledgment that we are in everyone, that what pulsates in my spirit is the pulsation of yours and of all others; whence friendship, whence society, whence the word, whence the apostolate.[11]

Omodeo's religiosity was enriched by a profound love of country, rooted in Mazzini's ideas, allowing him to discern, when he was little more than twenty years old, the difference between a true love of country and nationalism. Concerning the news of the first Italian military triumphs in Libya, when an insane individualism began to pollute the Italians' conscience, Omodeo remarks to his wife-to-be:

You invite me to rejoice at the joy of the fatherland. O friend of mine, I love the land, the culture, and the tradition of my people, with an intensity of affection that is deeper as it is less apparent. The commonplaces of a nationalistic jingoism, the irrepressible and unrestrained enthusiasm, offend this patriotism of mine. Rather than jubilation, I feel anguish for my country; anguish in seeing that it is not yet what it should be, in seeing into what hands it has been put, in the sense of what still remains to be done. And whereas the success of these days much alleviates this concern, I make no secret of the fact that Italy still lacks a lot—a lot before it will be truly great. In how many souls does the country really live? How many men embody its aspirations, are really anxious about its destiny, strive to clutch and understand the problems that torment it in all their depth? The raging chauvinism of these days for the newspaper columns is not yet patriotic conscience in the profound sense of the word.[12]

Omodeo lived his patriotism as a religious sentiment that resulted in a steady will to act. The letter he writes to Eva from Rome on November 3, 1913, testifies to this clearly: "I see the current meanness of Rome today, more wretched than many modern Italian towns, and I feel an impulse of religious affection for this city, the impulse to bind to it all my work as a student and a teacher as a legacy. It does not matter whether small or big, provided that I could contrive somehow to give it dignity, and a new and austere life. I feel for this city a religious worship devoid of any rhetoric. I have never felt so much an Italian as here in Rome."[13] Precisely because his religiosity was inward and civil, Omodeo was disgusted by outward and servile religiosity. Evidence of this can be seen in the tale of his visit to the cathedral in Cefalù with a few friends in March 1914:

After having wandered for a long while, we went to the cathedral to listen to the sermon. The preacher was a Passionist missionary father. A wrath of God. I am not anticlerical, but I was nauseated by it. A trivial rhetoric. He was overacting: declamations with a blooming of rhetoric…, with such an utter and complete artifice that allowed one to hear the dreary void of the soul. He was talking about hell; a scenographic hell: devils, dragons, fire, flames, darkness, awful howls (uttered also by the reverend), all done not to move and convert, but to impress. And consequently shrieks of hysterical females, faints, screams of fear and desperation; and that beast who kept saying that the poor crucified one, who was looking at him with astonishment, wanted not to forgive, but to send everyone to hell; desperate yells, invocations to the Madonna; and here she was, carried along the church, and the reverend made her embrace the crucifix; altogether a nauseating farce, and the whole religion reduced to fear of hell, which made me sick. I am surprised that the bishop can consent to such jokes in church. An improbable thing, which I would have never deemed possible.[14]

The religiosity that made him abhor the bigoted and superstitious spurred him to locate the broad themes of his historical research in Christianity and the Risorgimento. "As a historian, I want to reveal a sort of life almost fully neglected by us modern Latin peoples: the life of Christianity in its great moments. I want, however, to embrace together various activities. I want to study our Risorgimento too, gaining knowledge of all the historical movement that has given us means of understanding the present moment as well. History will lead me face-to-face with the political problems of our days."[15] Precisely because he studied the Risorgimento with a religious sensitivity, Omodeo clearly saw that Italians' movement toward national emancipation was not the premise of fascism but rather its opposite. Whereas fascism proclaimed a nationalistic conception of fatherland, the Risorgimento affirmed a universalistic notion. All the men of the Risorgimento, from Mazzini to Cavour, from Garibaldi to Settembrini, Omodeo notes, "were aware that they were working and suffering for Italy and a universally human ideal, which pertained to all men."[16]

Their universalistic conception of the fatherland was an expression of their religiosity. Mazzini, Omodeo explains, had an "adamant faith, which subdued the spirits and overwhelmed them in a wave of religious enthusiasm." His mother, Maria Drago, taught him about the ideal of the austerity of life, in the strict sense of duty to the point of sacrificing every individual interest to the conviction that life is a mission without reward under a divine commandment.[17] He saw the resurrection of Italy almost as the revelation of divine assistance to the people, in recognition of its "heroic and religious faith" in its destiny. Democracy was not, for him, an exercise of popular sovereignty but instead the ethical elevation of the people. He considered the people as a means or medium, the intermediary of the "divine revelation." The duty of the young, whom Mazzini called to fight under the republican flag, was to nurture faith in the people, while at the same time educating the people, redeeming the people from political servitude and social brutishness, making examples of abnegation and sacrifice shine before its eyes, saving it from socialist materialism, and finally inflaming the enthusiasms of which a people is capable, even through martyrdom.[18]

For Mazzini,

> the whole history of mankind is the gradual revelation of divine providence. From step to step, humanity ascends to the goal predisposed by God: one civilization is the step for the next; one phase closes and another one opens up. Duty and mission are the forms through which man concurs in the fulfillment of this divine law of progress: a duty and a mission that are absolutely selfless, without the allurements of a reward or the fallacious illusions of happiness. Once the task of Christianity has been resolved in the new religion of progress, and once an era has ended rather than begun with the French Revolution, one must usher in a new era that is at once social and religious. To Italy, which should rise again as if it had "to show the miracle" of the forces that can restore faith, falls "the initiative" that will give to the world a third Italian civilization, and not with the force of arms, or with a theocratic dominion, but with the association of free peoples, who have to proceed together toward the divine end.[19]

It actually was not possible, Omodeo concludes, "to substitute Catholic religion for the vague Mazzinian religion of progress, so substantiated by philosophical doctrines. Yet this faith endowed many with the courage to take action and, instead of dismaying them in the objective calculation of the facts, exalted them to the point of martyrdom."[20]

According to Omodeo, the other eminently religious figure of the Risorgimento was Gioberti. With skillful rhetoric, Gioberti attempted to promote a "consociation between patriotism and religion," interpreting Catholicism as "the greatest effort to realize the Idea on earth." Within himself, Gioberti wrestled with the tension between a sincere religion of liberty and an insincere Catholicism:

> He did not *believe* in Catholicism in the full sense of the word. His true faith was in modern civilization, human progress, the action of the spirit within men's and peoples' life. Hence in his soul cohabitated a fossil and living faith, and he had to try to assimilate the former into the latter—that is, transform the traditional physiognomy of Catholicism, to instill a new content into it, and use it as an instrument, according to an ever more openly political calculation. As events unfolded, his liberal ideas were resurrected completely, and in

a Machiavellian way he exploited the Catholic Church and its ascendancy over the people, trying to insinuate from outside the idea of a reformation that seemed to the guardians of orthodoxy ever more manifestly heterodox.[21]

Jansenism was important, too, as an underground river resurfacing at the outset of the nineteenth century to supply a new source from which the most significant men of the Risorgimento drew—not only Manzoni, but also Mazzini, Cavour, Gioberti, Lambruschini, Ricasoli, and the whole of liberal Catholicism.[22] Omodeo explains that Jansenism was a special—archaic Christian—way of living one's religion and recognizing the content of one's faith in a vision of redemption. The religious experience as a moral force that guides human beings to achieve their redemption is therefore the true principle of the hard story of the attainment of liberty. This was the aspect of religion that had fascinated Omodeo since his first studies on Paul of Tarsus. He saw in Paul the reformer who was able to make history with the force of a moral ideal and a rigorous sense of the limits that actual conditions impose. Paul did not suffer from "the weakness typical of utopians, which is a cerebral effort that is extrinsic to the act of will." What distinguishes a fruitful apostolate from quixotic raving is the link with history, which "we can't even simply call historical sense or conscience, for then we would make of it the typical privilege of the cool, political man who studies the actual reality in order to derive the few possible conclusions from it." Rather, it's a moment of enthusiasm, arising from the identification between conscience and self-consciousness The conscience of rights and duties—the "should"—of one's inner life is the apex and climax of history and Providence. Omodeo's work, "which can present hints and flashes of politics, but comes before any politics," is a product of this premise.[23]

The need for a religious sentiment that shaped inner life drove Omodeo to carefully study the Reformation as well. Like Croce and Gobetti, he saw in it the creative force of the modern liberal world.[24] Calvin was for him one of the masters of modern liberty, one of the great educators of humanity in the modern world, as Augustine was for the ancient world. Although his theology concerning justification by faith and predestination has been surpassed, Calvin remains effective as a myth, in the sense of a narration that inspires action.[25] The *Christianae religionis institutio* is "a vigorous plan of an ideal of life and of religion."[26] Without being a liberal, the Genevan reformer "rekindled the first and foremost fire of all liberties, inasmuch as he required that religion have at its center human conscience and human responsibility." Because of this, "the authoritative, paternalistic, patriarchal Calvin must be considered the father of the spirit of modern liberty, although he maintained the dogmas of grace and predestination, and put Michele Serveto to death."[27]

Omodeo also drew important intellectual insights from his studies on French culture during the Restoration age. As early as 1928, while he was concluding his research on Saint John's mysticism, Omodeo conceived the idea of a broad inquiry into De Maistre and the church in the nineteenth century. The first step in this new project was his trip to Paris in 1932 for general research on "modern civilization and Catholicism." Recalling in 1946 the spiritual condition that oriented his studies, he notes that while he was working, "the fanatical fury of nationalisms and iron dictatorships, which were negating any form of free life, was roaring around."[28] Against that fury, a cosmopolitism, different from the cerebral one of the Enlightenment and also from the polemic one of the Socialist International, was spontaneously maturing within him. "Without repudiating my country," he remarks, "I felt a broader fatherland was arising, which comprises everything that all the peoples have acquired (also within the worship of their own countries) according to universal values—that is, according to what is valuable 'per quante / abbraccia terre il gran padre Ocèano' (Foscolo, '*I sepolcri*') [in all the lands that the great father Ocean embraces]."

One of Omodeo's earliest studies on French culture during the Restoration period appeared in May 1940, when France fell under the assault of Nazi troops, and it seemed that civilization, with "its ideals and its faiths," was collapsing with it, and that Italians were doomed to survive "in a world that was no longer ours." Born out of an age filled with deep suffering, these studies were a "testimony of faith in a fatherland that was greater, a fatherland that exceeds the old tiny fatherlands"; it was a testimony of faith in an "ideal country, imagined in the pure disinterestedness of science, beyond narrow borders, because of the effort of recognizing its value wherever it appeared, the effort of showing to everyone its source, and unifying the work of the different peoples in a common tradition."[29]

With this resolution in mind, Omodeo invited readers to pay attention to *De la religion* of Constant, published in 1824, particularly those pages in which the author lashes out at the subjection of the church to the Napoleonic despotism. "It's not been a long time," Constant writes,

> since the most complete despotism that we have ever known had seized religion as a complaisant and zealous auxiliary. During fourteen years of slavery, religion has not been the divine power that descends from the sky to amaze or reform the earth. A submissive,

subordinate, timid organ, it has bowed down before power, asking for orders, following its gestures, offering adulations in exchange for contempt: it didn't dare make the old vaults resonate with the words of courage and conscience; it just stuttered mutilated words at the feet of servile altars, far from admonishing the great leaders about the severe God who judges the kings, terrified, it sought in the haughty eyes of its master to understand how it ought to speak about its God, content because it was not compelled to command, in the name of a doctrine of peace, invasions and wars.[30]

How could one fail to see behind this passage a reference to the situation of the Catholic Church, which hailed Mussolini as the man of Providence, blessed the wars in Ethiopia and Abyssinia, and refused to call the Italians to resist against a regime that stained itself with infamous crimes, destroyed Catholic circles, and pretended that its leader was adored like a god? Omodeo also used Constant's reflections on religion to explain that utilitarianism cannot provide men with the motivations necessary to defeat an oppressive regime. "That philosophy is absolutely incapable of facing the crises of life and restoring the moral order endangered by despotism." Not interest but rather faith restores the life of humankind. The principle of the religion of liberty, which alone could help Italians achieve redemption, was embodied in this concept.[31]

In the same years during which he was studying French culture at the time of the Restoration, Omodeo also worked on a book on war, published in 1934 with the title *Momenti della vita di guerra (Dai diari e dalle lettere dei caduti)* (Moments of war life [From the diaries and letters of the fallen]). He wrote it while he was closely collaborating with Croce as editor of the journal *Critica*, with the aim of defending the last outpost of Italian culture uncontaminated by fascism. As the years passed by, our passion, Omodeo recalls, "became more acute and incisive. We truly lived liberty as a religion, at times doubtful that we would see it rise over the horizon."[32]

Precisely because it was inspired by the religion of liberty, his work was neither one of the many exaltations of warlike virtues nor a lamentation over the "mutilated victory" that abounded in the literature of the regime but rather "a spiritual history of the war." Through an edited collection of soldiers' letters and diaries, Omodeo wants to show Italians that within the army that fought World War I, there lived "a soul that supported them all; that circulated in the words whispered in the trenches; that ran against the eternal motives of egoism and self-preservation, suffered and cried for the absent family, the constant pain, the fallen fellows, raised in the elation of the attacks, that was racked with pain under the reverses."[33]

Omodeo highlights the religiosity that lived, often in contradictory forms, in many of his comrades' hearts because he cultivated the same sentiment in his soul. Only a man who had gone through the war with his religious sense of duty could produce a picture at once delicate and touching like that of Leonardo Cambini, from Livorno. Omodeo tells us that Cambini was a professor in one of the "normal schools" in Pisa. He was a spirited and jolly fellow, always ready for jokes and jests, with the typical Livornese habit of swearing oaths that seemed to be about to crack the vault of heaven. Yet he drew "a religious sense of duty" from Mazzini—a sense of religion not as a separate sphere but instead as the essence of all activities, and as an austere commandment that one does not question. "In his letters, he expresses this secular idea of religion," Omodeo explains, "in a simple, popular form, but more effective than any technical philosophical speculation." "I never utter a word of prayer," Cambini writes to his wife, "but every time one acts on an idea of duty, every time one fixes one's eyes in the domain of the supernatural, and one lives in spiritual communion with our men, who invisibly live around us, isn't this an elevation of the mind? Isn't it like raising our soul toward him who is the principle and the end?"[34]

Omodeo also understands and describes in a masterly way the religiosity of the Garrone brothers—Giuseppe (Pinotto), the older, and Eugenio—who died nearly at the same time during the First World War. Men like the Garrone brothers, observes Omodeo,

> will speak with another voice: they will express the sentiments and hopes of that large part of Italy that had embarked itself on war for a higher human justice, according to the Mazzinian-Garibaldian tradition of Italy. They will speak for all, because they offered themselves with more faith and more resolute dedication, and the light of their sacrifice will illuminate a great part of the gray and obscure events of war. Indeed, mankind must be evaluated for the heights that it reaches, and not for the roots in which it confuses itself with nature.… Human ideals are resurrected like Christ and keep resurfacing, and only in them can the peoples identify themselves. "Non de solo pane vixit homo."[35]

At the beginning of the 1930s, Luigi Russo (1892–1961), who was close to Croce and Omodeo, was also working on the relationship between liberty and religion from the perspective of a historian of literature.

In 1931, he published an essay on Machiavelli's *Prince*, in which he highlights the prophetic character of Machiavelli's thought and emphasizes the importance of a religious spirit for human emancipation. Russo explains that those who really kept alive the profound meaning of Machiavelli's teachings were men like Mazzini and Alfieri who understood that the problem of liberty in Italy was first of all a question of moral reform.[36] Savonarola, the scorned unarmed prophet, was thus ideally revenged by the anti-Machiavellian political thinkers who "bothered to assert besides a 'realtà effettuale' [factual reality] also a 'realtà ideale' [ideal reality], besides the earth, the sky, besides the being, the should, and end up purifying, brightening, and humanizing the Machiavellian centaur's ferality." Machiavelli was revenged, crucially, by Italian history, "when the unity of the peninsula was realized at the end of the eighteenth and in the nineteenth century, and this only because pure politics became also poetic and religious agitation, and the poetic pathos of the friar returns in the words of Alfieri or Mazzini."[37]

For Russo, political action that becomes prophecy and poetry for the redemption of peoples and the foundation of states was not the antithesis of the politics that Machiavelli had theorized but rather its truest interpretation: "After having coldly dissertated on the arts and skills of the lion and the fox, at the end of the little treatise…, he also talks biblically about a sea that has opened up, about a cloud that has made out the path, about a stone that spilled water, about manna falling from the sky, and calls on the assistance of a poet; because he knew that 'i poeti molte volte essere di spirito divino e profetico' [poets often possess a divine and prophetic spirit]." Machiavelli becomes a prophet because he knows that "without prophetic pathos, without moral revival, without civil conscience," the princedom, and even more so the republic, remain utopian, nothing more than another of the many imagined republics.[38]

It was the strength of Machiavelli's political realism that required him to search for and conceive of the God who commands civil virtue:

Actually, neither is Machiavelli the devil and Savonarola the saint, nor do they represent two different ages, two centuries one against the other. Savonarola and Machiavelli simply have two different temperaments, if not antithetical, deaf, and unintelligent one to the other, opposite in their logics. They are two eternal expressions of the human spirit—I would say—that only metaphorically we can call medieval, the one, and Renaissance, the other. Savonarola is pure religion, and Machiavelli science, technique, pure politics. Both aim at the same end: that of reforming Italy; one wants to be its religious reformer, the other the technical reformer; one appeals to enthusiasm, the other to science; the friar enthralls the souls with his prophetic pathos, the layman wants to control the minds in the cold and rigorous evaluation of the actual reality, in order not to just pursue its "immaginazione" [imagination].[39]

During the same year that Russo's *Prolegomeni* was published, Francesco Ruffini, a professor at the University of Turin who outstandingly kept alive the Risorgimento's moral and intellectual heritage, published (with Laterza) a broad study on the religious life of Manzoni. In this work, based on a wealth of documents and historically rigorous, he argues that the author of *I promessi sposi* held to a firm liberal political faith and an equally firm Jansenist religious faith. The two faiths "supported one another" so well that removing the one would have meant the collapse of the other. But Manzoni's political faith was never shaken, nor did it change, and the same is true of his religious faith.[40] Jansenism drove him to love liberty and instilled in him a severe, but not desperate or tragic conception of life, which taught him not to preach but rather to do good, and thus served as a "school of dignity in life, and public and private virtues."[41] Talking about Manzoni, Ruffini encourages his fellow Italians—at least those few who took his courses and read his books—to rediscover a religion and conception of life that were diametrically opposed to those inculcated by fascism. He explains with the calm, authoritative voice of the scholar that authentic liberalism was not the fainthearted practice of political plots depicted by fascist propaganda but instead a serious and austere conception of life—nay, it was a real religious vision. It was of little importance whether the source was ancient Christianity, Machiavelli, or the literature of the Risorgimento. The key point was to keep alive the inner liberty that survives even the death of political or civil liberty. These and other thinkers scoured the past for great ideas to help people believe, in spite of everything, in the redemption of the fatherland.

20

THE RELIGION OF LIBERTY

AMONG THE OTHERS, Croce's voice rose with a particular force and was able to penetrate souls. As early as 1925, he outlined the characteristics of a religion of liberty opposing the fascist religion. In his "Manifesto degli intellettuali antifascisti" (Manifesto of antifascist intellectuals), which he wrote in direct response to the "Manifesto of Fascist Intellectuals" composed by Gentile, he uses the most severe words against fascism's claim to be a new religion for Italy:

> Let us leave aside the already-known and arbitrary historical interpretations and patchworks. For the mistreatment of the doctrines and history is minor thing, in that text, compared to the misuse of the word "religion." In the view of the fascist intellectuals, in Italy we would have to rejoice at a war of religion, at a new Gospel and new apostolate against an old superstition, which is reluctant to die (which lies above it, and with which it will have to come to terms sooner or later). As a proof, they bring the hatred and malice that rage among Italians now more than ever. It sounds like a most gloomy joke to call a conflict of religion the hatred and malice that are sparked off against a party that negates the character of Italians to the members of the other parties and abuses them as strangers, and by so doing, poses itself as a stranger and oppressor, thereby introducing in the life of the fatherland those sentiments and habits that are typical of other conflicts. It sounds equally gloomy to dignify with the name of religion a suspicion and animosity that are spread everywhere, and have taken away even the ancient and trustful fellowship of the university youths in the common and juvenile ideals, and keep them opposed to one another in hostile appearance. It's impossible to gather from the words of the verbose *manifesto* what the new gospel, new religion, new faith would exactly amount

to. In fact, the reality testifies to an incoherent and bizarre mix: an appeal to authority and demagoguery; a proclaimed reverence for the laws and violation of the laws; ultramodern concepts and old-fashioned ideas; absolutist attitudes and Bolshevist tendencies; godlessness and courting of the Catholic Church; abhorrence of culture and sterile attempts at a culture that is deprived of its conditions; mystical mawkishness and cynicism.[1]

Croce proudly opposes liberalism's religion of liberty to the religion of fascism. "We oppose abandoning our old faith," he writes,

> for this chaotic and obscure "religion": for two centuries and a half, our faith has been the soul of the Italy that was rising again, modern Italy. That faith was composed of love of truth, aspiration for justice, generous human and civil sense, zeal for an intellectual and moral education, solicitude about liberty, the force behind and guarantee of every advancement. We look at the men of Risorgimento, those who acted, suffered, and died for Italy, and it seems to us that they are offended and concerned by the words and deeds of our adversaries, and admonish us to keep their flag flying. Our faith is not an artificial and abstract contrivance or excitement of the mind provoked by uncertain and badly understood theories but rather the possession of a tradition that has become a disposition of the sentiment, a mental and moral habit.

When Croce challenged the fascist intellectuals in the name of the religion of liberty, he had already developed a profound awareness of the contrast between an outward religiosity and true religion, which is a firm inner conviction. Only the latter opens the way to the modern world, and can free Italians from the false idols that have seduced and conquered their consciences. As Croce writes between 1924 and 1925 in *Storia della età barocca in Italia*, behind the concepts of Renaissance and Reformation,

> there are two fundamental ideal terms, that is "man and God," "individual and universe," "secular and religious spirit," and they are two terms that need one another. In modern times, in particular, prevalence is given, contrary to medieval times, to the harmony of the two forces, which therefore become both immanent. The ever-greater realization of this harmony in the general ideas and habits is the theme of the new history of mankind. This history is still ongoing, not yet finished; we all live within it, and we all suffer from a harmony that has not yet been reached or consolidated; we all feel the labor of the new

religion, which, even if it has appeared to those who can see it, is not yet safely placed in their hearts, and also the labor of the false idols— idols of luxury, intoxication, and violence—which often replace it.[2]

Whereas the terms "Renaissance" and "Reformation" express two principles that are both necessary for a full human life, the Counter-Reformation did not have a "human and eternal character," and hence should not be placed on the same level as the two other concepts. The Counter-Reformation was simply defending an institution, the Catholic Church, which is a great institution, but not an eternal spiritual and moral moment.[3] It was filled with austere men, heroic missionaries, and spotless and generous souls, but those virtuous men lacked moral inventiveness— the faculty of creating new and progressive forms of ethical life. The Jesuits' policy, unconsciously, ended up turning people against God—that is, against the moral laws established by God, which Jesuits skillfully knew how to undermine with their disreputable casuistry.[4] Notwithstanding the good temperament of Italians, their moral enthusiasm certainly withered away, and Italy declined compared to other countries. The Counter-Reformation, Jesuitism, pomposity, fetishism about titles, ceremonial excesses, dueling, bad taste, baroque style, empty virtuosity, and scientific hairsplitting all became characteristic of the Italian way of life—so much so that one could say that Italy was on vacation, that Italy "was amusing itself and was laughing, laughing at everything and everyone, and even at itself." In the midst of this, the Catholic Church taught a religiosity that pushed toward a civil decadence, for it kept itself closed to all attempts to lead souls back to that realm where they find themselves alone before God and humble before divine grace, which had been the best elements of the Reformation. The religiosity of the Counter-Reformation curbed bad passions, but did not constitute civil and ethical life; it was a legalistic and outward religiosity, which is the opposite of the religion of liberty.[5]

In the years in which he reflects on the corrupting effects of the Counter-Reformation in Italy, Croce elaborates on his conviction that fascist nationalism disowns not only the patriotism of the Risorgimento but also human and Christian ideals themselves. The work to be done is therefore to retrieve and renew those values.[6] The religion of fascism requires an irrational faith in *Il Duce*'s word. The religion of liberty teaches people to have faith in the moral principle, understood as the result of meditation and an inner search. Its goal is action, in man's world, and as such requires the harmony "of thinking with feeling and doing, as well as of feeling and doing with thinking, so that nothing exists that, once it has been thought, does not become a principle of action or does not change in some way one's action."[7]

Whereas the common herd thinks some things and longs for other things, or desires something and does something else, the wise man lives in harmony with the moral ideals in which he believes. In this sense the religion of liberty is an aristocratic ideal, but it instills neither haughtiness nor arrogance. It fully recognizes human weakness and also accepts the aid of grace as an unexpected gift that helps the living, as Croce observes:

> All the following wait for grace: the poet, who calls it inspiration; the philosopher, who calls it idea; the statesman, who calls it sure eyesight or firm hand; the man of war, who calls it boldness or impetus. Grace appears all of a sudden even to the humblest of men you can imagine, who is so much oppressed by tedium that he sometimes does not know how to get through it. It appears perhaps in the form of a sunray, or a landscape fresh with verdancy and dew, which infuses new joy and a love of life. Who, except for someone vain—and even this only in his empty words—could ever "do it alone" and renounce the assistance of grace?[8]

In these writings, Croce outlines a "human religion" that already has all the content of the religion of liberty that he will begin speaking about in the early 1930s. It is a human religion, which Croce considers a precious achievement of modern times because it is antimythological—that is, free from every naturalistic and utilitarian trace—and places God in the heart of man. It is not just a religion of mankind but also a human religion, a "religion of man." It is an achievement but above all a goal for the future:

> We are now witnessing the formative labor of this new religion, and are taking part in this labor. The old mythology has still, now and again, its vigorous revivals; the negative, nonreligious polemics that was necessary in the past comes back with its aridity, violence, prejudice, hasty rationalist, intellectualist, and utilitarian antireligions; but man will once more obtain the God that is suitable for him. For without religiosity—that is, without poetry, without heroism, without a conscience of the universal, without harmony, without aristocratic feeling—no society could ever live, and the human society wants to live, if only for this reason: that it cannot die.[9]

The religion of liberty was the kernel of the nineteenth-century movements of liberalism and national emancipation. Among these, for Croce, the Italian Risorgimento was prominent.[10] It was an age during which the "religion of the fatherland" or liberty triumphed over and dominated everyone, as Croce notes in *Storia d'Italia dal 1871 al 1915*, written in 1928 with a profound sorrow for the events of Italian politics.[11] Mazzini more than anyone else worked for the religious rebirth of Italy. He well understood that the problem for modern society, as for all societies, is the problem of moral education or reeducation, and hence also a problem of revived or renewed religiosity. He did not understand, though, that the religious reformation of a people "is the long and complex process of all the thought and all of history, which, in its richest and most elaborate forms, it was necessary to rejoin in order to bring it forward"; Mazzini instead persisted in preaching a generic religiosity to an imaginary *Popolo* (people). Consequently, the men of culture, who considered his ideas too vague, abandoned him, and workers preferred the socialist preaching inspired by the words of Marx, founder of the new religion of the people, just as Paul of Tarsus had been the founder of a new Christian religion.[12]

For Croce, however, the true enemy of the religion of liberty was not socialism but rather nationalism, "the turbid religion that was named after Nietzsche."[13] Owing to this poison, but above all because of his inability to keep the devotion to its ideals alive, liberalism had degenerated in Italy to a practice of power, and was no longer a lively and intimate faith, an inward and fervid enthusiasm, an object of solicitude and meditation, something sacred to be jealously defended from every threat.[14] The faith in liberty could experience a resurgence only through the work of new prophets who would challenge the grim religions of irrationality, might, and race. Croce was deeply persuaded that

> moral enthusiasm comes and goes. At times it is energetic and at other times it relaxes in leisure and forgetfulness. Therefore, in lay society as in the society of the church, it is necessary that from time to time apostles, martyrs, and saints intervene. Of course, these cannot be artificially created, and one needs to count on Providence, which, just as it has always sent them on earth, will continue to do so. Many thus think that the fundamental problem of our times is a religious one, and I am among them, with the following qualification: that the problem of all times is religious, and the point is not to invent a new religion for our time but rather to consolidate and deepen the existing one, what once used to be called the inherent or natural religion, and now could be called historical.[15]

To arrive at the conviction that the moral and religious conscience is a force that creates history, Croce departs from the narrow-minded realism that dominated his writings before and during the First World War. Evidence of this intellectual change can be seen in his remarks in *Elementi morali della vita politica*, and in particular *Stato e Chiesa in senso ideale e loro perpetua lotta nella storia*. In his opinion, the Catholic Church has earned the right to affirm moral lack in the face of a mere politics that claims to be the whole. It has the right to impose this theory, through its sturdy and pressing opposition, to correct its exaggerations and twisted logic, and return to what it was, while preserving the particular and original truth proper to it.[16] If one takes the church to mean a celestial and divine element, and the state the earthly and diabolical element,

> it is necessary to say that the sky cannot remain without the earth, nor God without the devil. In fact they are both human powers, which connect the process of human will and human deed; it's life that is elevated to morality and morality that is translated into life. There are times in which everything seems to be force and politics, utility and labor. They are times of poverty and privation, or else feverish mama's-boyism, tyranny, and servitude, in which certainly the moral and religious spirit, like the poetic and speculative spirit, breathe badly. And yet that spirit is never absent or inactive, and the empirical prevalence of the political element itself—the prevalence of the "state" over the "church"—is to be interpreted as the creation of something that the church, always triumphant, will subjugate and turn to its ends.[17]

Precisely in times of tyranny and servitude, such as those of Croce's day, moral conscience needs the help of the devotees of truth.[18] The state fulfills an essential historical function, but is not God, and can demand neither devotion nor veneration. In the 1928 preface to his *Pagine sulla guerra*, Croce clarifies his distance from the fascist religion of the state:

> In that controversy [over state power], I constantly rejected the concept of force understood in a materialistic way, and politics as separate and different from ethics, and instead maintained that politics was at once a specification of ethics and subject to it. For this reason I have always refused every sort of worship of the state, no matter whether it presents itself or represents itself as the "ethical idea of the state," and covers itself with the fitting rhetoric on the "state that is duty and that is God," and similar clumsiness. And here, too, I remain within the tradition of Christian thought, which gives Caesar what is Caesar's, but places above Caesar the religious

and moral conscience, which alone renders political action—each time—ethical, though acknowledging and respecting and utilizing the logic that is proper to it.[19]

Croce repudiates the concept of a state that becomes God, but emphasizes that liberty has a religious content. "Liberty," he writes, "is not the function of the bourgeoisie or any other economy but rather the human soul and its deep needs; it possesses qualities and origins that are not economic but instead moral and religious, and it is, in a word, the new form of Christianity. And Christianity (and here Hegel was right) must be considered the 'absolute religion,' which can be developed ever more, and continuously elaborated and reinvigorated through thinking, but can never be uprooted from man's heart."[20] To this conviction another one can be added that is equally important in the search for the religion of liberty: the most stringent duty of the learned man is to assist in the birth or, better yet, rebirth of a religious spirit that recovers both the teachings of the Rinascimento and the Reformation and the intellectual heritage of romanticism.

Croce considers the religious problem to be the most pressing demand of his time:

The real problem is of an ethical nature, and is a problem of all times and all conditions, and it musters all our intellectual and moral strengths. No one can predict what will happen, if not through arbitrary imaginations, but what counts is the present and specified duty, on which no doubt can be raised because it is dictated to us each time by our inner moral conscience. If one asked me what is the most general and fundamental problem of our times, I would say, as I have already said, that the formation or consolidation of the religious conception of modern times—a conception that cannot entail a return to the past but rather only a prosecution of that movement that, markedly commenced by the Rinascimento and Reformation, culminated in the great idealistic and historical philosophy of the end of the eighteenth and beginning of the nineteenth century. I believe that notwithstanding the different appearances, there still is a huge amount of religious spirit in the world, and that this hidden and disavowed treasure has enabled the people to bear the anguishes and horrors of war.[21]

Two years later, Croce returns to the theme of spiritual liberty as the lifeblood of history and elaborates on the concept of history as a history of liberty: "For the heart of human history is liberty, and everything that has been produced that is alive and sound is the product of free inventiveness—that is, is the creation of spiritual liberty. All the most splendid periods of the life of peoples confirm this simple truth…. The vital historical forms always arise in this way: as those which, in the given conditions of the times, represent the greatest liberty, the greatest possibility of welfare, development, and human dignity." During the same period, he adds that "liberalism has been the greatest revolutionary force of the nineteenth century; we owe to it our Risorgimento and our independence and unity. After it, no other revolutionary force has sprung up with an ethical and religious character."[22] At the International Conference of Philosophy in Oxford, Croce is even more explicit: liberalism is "the last religion for man, the last not in the sense of last remnants but rather in the sense that it's the highest one can draw from."[23]

The concept of the religion of liberty came to light toward the end of 1931 in a series of essays later collected in *Storia d'Europa nel secolo XIX*, published by Laterza at the beginning of 1932. Croce confirms in this work that the religion of liberty was the core of the liberal, democratic, and national movements that marked European history in the nineteenth century. That particular religion unified and harmonized the long history of liberty, and demonstrated its force with the examples of its "poets, theorists, orators, journalists, propagandists, apostles, and martyrs." It could penetrate into people's souls, driving them to action and sacrifice: "The heroic figure, who spoke to the hearts, was that of the poet-soldier, the intellectual who can fight and die for his idea; a figure who did not just remain in the raptures of imagination and educational paradigms but rather appeared in the flesh on the battlefields and on the barricades throughout Europe. The missionaries had crusaders of liberty as their fellows."[24]

The religion of liberty brought together various religious and philosophical aspirations: "Next to and above Socrates, it set the human and divine redeemer Jesus. And it felt that it had undergone all the experiences of paganism and Christianity, Catholicism, Augustinianism, Calvinism, and all the rest. It felt that it represented the highest demands, that it was the purifying, deepening, and power-giving agent of the religious life of mankind."[25] At the same time, it struggled against "rival and inimical religions," which gathered proselytes and represented robust historical forces. The Catholicism of the church of Rome, "the most direct and logical negation of the liberal ideal," was first among the religious faiths opposing the religion of liberty. Croce explains that the church of Rome

> can be considered the prototype or pure form of all the other oppositions, and at the same time the one that, with its undying hatred,

illuminates the religious character, the character of religious rivalry, of liberalism. To the liberal conception that the aim of life is in life itself, and duty lies in the increase and elevation of this life, and the method is free initiative and individual inventiveness, Catholicism answers that on the contrary, the aim lies in a life beyond this world, for which the life of this world is simply a preparation that must be made with heed to what a God who is in the heavens, by means of his vicar on earth and his church, bids us believe and do.[26]

The contrast with monarchies was of a tactical and not a religious nature. Croce notes how "there is no ideal that does not depend, in the last resort, on a conception of reality and therefore is religious; and that of the absolute monarchy implied the idea of kings as the shepherds of the peoples, and the peoples as sheep to be led to the pasture, mated and multiplied, protected against the weather and against wolves and other wild beasts." The contrast between liberalism and democracy was of a similar kind. Notwithstanding their similarities, democracy and liberalism "considered the individual, equality, sovereignty, and the nation in entirely different fashions." The first postulates "a religion of quantity, mechanics, calculating reason, or nature, like that of the eighteenth century"; the second "a religion of quality, activity, spirituality, such as that which had risen at the beginning of the nineteenth century: so that, even in this case, the conflict was of religious faiths."[27] Religion was finally also the opposite of communism (not socialism), because of the intrinsic materialistic character of that doctrine.

The liberal idea is a new religion because it is a conception of reality and has an ethics that conforms to it. It does not need "personifications, myths, legends, dogmas, rites, propitiations, expiations, classes of clergymen, pontifical robes, and the like." It condemns the literary man and the fainthearted and dreamy philosopher, the servile mentality and courtly flattery, and does not accept the idea that it is good to "separate man from citizen, the individual from the society that forms him and that he forms." It exhorts people to love their country; infuses a sense of duty; requires the search for truth; demands commitment in action or at least the desire for action; and teaches people to look at defeats as occasions to demonstrate and reaffirm the strength of liberty. The liberal idea is thus an incoercible force that no regime, not even the most despotic and totalitarian, can eradicate from human conscience: "So that when the question is raised whether liberty will enjoy what is known as the future, the answer must be that it has something better still: it has eternity. And today, too, notwithstanding the coldness and the contempt and scorn that liberty meets, it is in so many of our institutions and customs and our spiritual attitudes, and operates beneficently within them."[28]

This faith in liberty as an eternal principle allows Croce to formulate his extraordinary prophecy about European unity, meant to derive not from the dying out of the love of country but rather from its development:

> Meanwhile, in all parts of Europe we are watching the growth of a new consciousness, a new nationality (because, as we have already remarked, nations are not natural facts but rather historical states of consciousness and historical formations). And just as, seventy years ago, a Neapolitan of the kingdom or Piedmontese of the subalpine kingdom became an Italian without becoming false to his earlier nature but elevating it and resolving it into this new nature, so the French and the Germans and the Italians and all the others will raise themselves into Europeans, and their thoughts will be directed toward Europe and their hearts will beat for her as they once did for their smaller countries, not forgotten but loved all the better.[29]

The interpretation of religious faith as a devotion to the moral principle, and hence a faith that operates in history, also surfaces in some 1940s studies, such as the essay on the *Beneficio di Cristo*. Croce describes it as

> a little book written with the heart by a man who, having suffered the anguish of human misery and terror of perdition, and having finally found the road to salvation on which he now walks with spiritual joy, turned to the other men, his brethren, to draw them out of evil and despair, and communicate to them, too, the trust and joy that he enjoyed in the union of his soul with Christ. The little book, written by Benedetto da Mantova (1495–1556) between 1537 and 1540, expresses a faith that is a "moral renewal" strictly linked to deeds.[30]

Croce wanted to highlight the concept of the intimacy and force of moral conscience, as distinct from the aridity of law and order. This doctrine is expressed, first and foremost, in the highly contested concept that faith alone can justify anything: alone, as in without any cooperation of deeds; and faith, as in that which suffices unto itself, for it is in its own right a form of doing.

Croce remarks that in terms of modern ethics, one could say that intention is everything, for an earnest intention, insofar as it fills and moves the whole soul, is already action. If it is not action, it is not intention, as people used to and still tend to think, and as the disastrous casuists deemed it; rather, in this case faith is "fatuity, hypocrisy, and lie." Through the principle of salvation *sola fide*, Paul separated Christianity from Judaism, and raised it to a universal, human religion that was antilegalist. Yet the church of Rome, born from the preaching of Paul, had by then become even more legalistic than ancient Judaism. It had become a strong worldly structure. In the sixteenth century, the forces that most starkly opposed the degeneration of the church went back to Paul, and at the same time, as in any return, beyond him. Consequently, the very concept of church was profoundly transformed: "Once he had suppressed redemptive practices and intermediaries, man found himself in a direct relation with God."[31] Unfortunately, the demands for a religious reform did not find the same strength in Italy that they had found elsewhere, because of the "general enfeeblement of Italian life," both economic and civil, and could not be translated into effective action.

In another important essay, "Perché non possiamo non dirci 'cristiani' " (Why we cannot not call ourselves "Christians"), in 1942, Croce returns to the theme of moral conscience as an incoercible force that continually creates more history and new institutions of liberty. He concedes with no difficulties the great merit of Christianity in having revived and exalted moral conscience in its purest form—that is, as a merely inward voice that provides the individual with a law for living, and by making him work according to inward conscience alone, makes him free.[32] For this reason, Christianity "has been the greatest revolution that mankind has ever realized," and its work has been continued by many "workers in the vineyard," ultimately by liberalism and the advocates of the freedom of all nationalities, which the church never wanted to recognize because it was insensitive to the idea that there can be Christians outside its flock. The disciples of Christ outside the church were instead "all the more intensely Christian because they were free."[33]

This meant that the religion of liberty seemed heretical to the church, but was actually the most consistent elaboration of the Christian principle of a moral freedom founded on the sovereignty of conscience. Keeping in mind when they were written, the following words are among Croce's most moving ones:

> Keeping, inflaming again, and stirring up the Christian sentiment is our ever-recurring need, today more than ever sharp and tormenting, in between pain and hope. And the Christian God is still our God, and our refined philosophies call him the spirit, which always overcomes us and always remains in us. And if we no longer worship

him as mystery, the reason is that we know that it will always be a mystery to the eye of abstract and intellectualist logic, which undeservedly is considered and dignified as "human logic"; we know that the Christian God still is pellucid truth to the eye of concrete logic, which can well be called "divine," in the Christian sense of that toward which man unceasingly elevates himself, and which, by continuously joining him to God, renders him truly man.[34]

A few years later, in 1945, Einaudi, who was completely different from Croce in terms of his cultural education and style of thinking, states incisively that the origin of the liberal idea can be found in Christianity. "What is the source of the aura of untouchability surrounding certain principles? If one fixes one's eyes on the bottom of it, one gets to Christ, who announced to the world that all of them were equal before God and, by declaring them equal, proclaimed that the end of life was the betterment, the moral elevation of the human person. All that which degrades, oppresses the human person, all that which forces man to pretend he believes, thinks, and acts in a way that is contrary to his conscience, is evil; it is sin." He also emphasizes with equal firmness that liberty, precisely because it is a religious principle, must be lived coherently: "He errs who affirms that faith, the belief in a given vision of life, is just a private matter. No true believer is he who restricts faith to cult practices and does not conform to that faith all of his religious and civil life, economic and political life, the life of thought and the life of practice."[35] The two masters of Italian liberalism, who were divided on important theoretical and political questions, converged on the concept of the religious origin of modern liberty.

Bobbio writes that Croce's was too abstract a conception of liberty, and inattentive to specific juridical and institutional aspects.[36] In 1932, though, it was necessary to focus on the moral aspect of liberty, that inward aspect that fascism, as a totalitarian regime, aimed to conquer. To nurture some hope of resurrecting liberty, one could and must oppose another religion to the fascist one—the religion of liberty, understood as a spiritual force. This is precisely what Croce did. His work deserves admiration because it moved the conscience of the antifascists, and brought many young men and women into the antifascist struggle, and because his writings still speak to our moral conscience.

21

A RELIGION THAT INSTILLS HOPE

AFTER FINISHING *STORIA D'EUROPA*, on December 6, 1931, Croce wrote Thomas Mann, asking permission to dedicate his work to him:

> Now I ask you if you allow me to dedicate it to your name. I remember the converging thoughts of our Munich conversation, and I feel the natural desire to address it to one of the few (they are not many in Europe) who still cultivate certain ideals. You will see by reading the introduction what is the line of this history. I must tell you that there are unfavorable interpretations of Prussian, Bismarkian, Treitschkian, nationalistic history. But remember that I was educated on German books and thought, and that many of my critiques are critiques of myself, of my ideas of some time ago. And at this point we all *have examined and examine our conscience*.[1]

The ideas that Mann professes in his political writings are the same liberal notions that Croce advocates in *Storia d'Europa*. In his *Appeal to Reason*, in 1930, Mann denounces National Socialism as a movement born to fight against the principles of liberty, justice, culture, optimism, and faith in progress that liberalism had elaborated, and through which it had laboriously built modern civilization. Against the latter, National Socialism raises the banner of a religion of nature, inclined to orgiastic practices and unbridled thrill, far from the spirit of nineteenth-century nationalism, which had been rich in terms of "profound cosmopolitan and humanitarian veins." Following the teaching of Johann Wolfgang von Goethe, Mann invokes a faith in the good as a counterpoint to the barbarous religion of nationalism: "Of that courage, which sooner or later / triumphs against the opposition of the obtuse world, / of that daring faith that now soars higher and higher, / and now patient bows, / so that the good acts, grows, does good, / so that the magnanimous man is finally reached by the light."[2] Two years later, in his *Storia d'Europa*, Croce suggests that this same faith is the only way to achieve salvation from the vulgarity that threatens to suffocate the whole of liberal civilization.

From Mann's reply, on December 13, it is clear that the German writer well understood that the religion of liberty was an alternative to nationalism, which attacked the moral bases of European civilization:

> In your words, dear sir, speaks the faith in the idea, in *truth*, a disinterested passion for both, and that which holds together the spiritual society that I talk about is precisely your refusal to believe that the idea, the truth, and the passion for them can go out of date and become old-fashioned because of some revolution. Revolutions that are directed against the highest humanity are false and infamous revolutions, which are unworthy holders of their name just to confound the spirits. This is what separates me from a nationalism that lays claim to the appellation of young and new. What today, in a dark fashion, passes over Europe is a turbid incident, the end of which we will see, I am certain, if our vital impulse continues to resist. Karl Vossler, who also read your letter, told me that he had the impression that, with your history of the twentieth century [Mann's mistake], a work was born in which one could see the first glimmerings of a dawn. By accepting the dedication of your book, I fix my gaze on this first dawning sky, and I'd very much wish to be of help, with my weak forces, to realize it.[3]

Johan Huizinga, who was interned as a hostage by the German invaders of his country, the Netherlands, and died in Arnhem in 1945, interpreted the crisis of civilization as a religious crisis that demanded, as the only remedy, a religious catharsis. Huizinga entrusts his passionate message to *La crisi della civiltà* (The crisis of civilization), translated into Italian in 1937, which only partly rendered the meaning of the original title, *In the Shadow of Tomorrow*. His analysis is inspired by a Christianity lived, above all, as a faith in the moral message of Christ, Dutch republican civism, and the values of the rationalistic philosophical tradition.[4] From this idealistic and religious perspective, Huizinga remarks that civilization could be saved only through a change in the "spiritual *habitus* of man," a real catharsis—that is, the spiritual state of mind induced by the performance of tragedy, the stillness of heart in which compassion and fear have been dissolved, the purification of the soul that springs from having grasped a deeper meaning in things, creating a grave and new readiness for acts of duty and the acceptance of fate, shattering *hybris*, and leading the soul to peace.[5]

The redeeming purification was a rediscovery of the genuine Christian message intended as an imperative for living in the world:

> The new ascesis will not be one of self-domination, and tempered appraisal of power and pleasure. The exaltation of life will have to be toned down a little. One will have to remember how Plato once described the occupation of the wise man as a preparation for death. A steady orientation of the living consciousness on death heightens the proper use of life itself. The new ascesis will have to be a surrender to all that can be conceived as the highest. That can no more be nation or class than the individual existence of the self. Happy those for whom that principle can only bear the name of him who spoke: "I am the way, the truth, and the life."[6]

Although coming from a different philosophical perspective, Henri-Louis Bergson also felt the need during those same years to highlight the religious content of political liberty. Democracy, he observes in 1932, puts brotherhood above liberty and equality, and in this way reveals its "evangelical" essence. Such a religious root of democracy can be seen in Kant's Pietism, Rousseau's Protestantism, and the Catholicism with which both established contact. After all, the Declaration of Independence of 1776, which served as a model for the Declaration of the Rights of Man and Citizen of 1791, has clear Puritan roots. Whereas the motto of a democratic society should be "Ama, et fac quod vis" (Love and do what you will) that of a nondemocratic one should be "Authority, hierarchy, rigidity."[7] A few months earlier, in the *Discours à la nation européenne*, Julien Benda urged people to rediscover a universalistic religion to oppose the false religion of nationalism. He quotes the apostle, and notes that this does not mean that national differences no longer exist but instead that men should strive to feel that they belong to a human region to which all the nations attend.[8] The clergymen of all countries must reproach nations for always being evil, and if Plotinus blushed with shame because he had a body, modern intellectuals must blush because they have a nation.[9] Nationalism deifies the national character and therefore rails against Christianity, alleging that it is guilty of teaching indifference to the world.[10] Unlike Croce—who advocates a patriotism capable of elevating man to the ideal of Europe through the influence of a richer comprehension of its content, as well as its historical and ideal roots—Benda exhorts men to abandon any form of patriotism. Both, however, emphasize that European unity will result from the rediscovery of religious principles: God as the foundation of moral values for Benda; and the religion of liberty as the basis for Croce.

The *Storia d'Europa* appeared in a cultural context in which concern over the establishment of totalitarian religions stimulated free consciences to search for salvation in a renewed and rediscovered religious conception of life. It is no surprise that in terms of international public opinion, *Storia d'Europa* was enthusiastically received. *The New York Times Book Review* announced the forthcoming publication of *Storia d'Europa* with sincere admiration: "A new book by Benedetto Croce is always an event, but a history of Europe in the nineteenth century is epoch-making." Croce, stresses the reviewer, does not lose faith in liberalism, notwithstanding defeats, and his book, with its bold charge against raw materialism, petty egoism, blind tyranny, and mean prohibitions, will certainly be an inspiration for the spirit of liberalism in the world. "God knows how important such inspiration is."[11]

As could well have been foreseen, the doctrine of the religion of liberty encountered tough opposition from the church in Italy. The journal *Civiltà Cattolica* devoted four articles to the *Storia d'Europa* to demonstrate that it was an antiphilosophical and antireligious work that attacked "the Catholicism of the church of Rome."[12] Whereas liberalism holds that the end of life is in life itself, Catholicism states that man's goal is the afterlife. With his "system of irreligion palliated by 'religiosity,' " the great man "has infected a whole new generation of Italians in their head," and, to make matters worse, his philosophy is also known beyond Italy and is almost considered as "a representative of Italian culture, estranged from Catholic faith and morals."[13] In the *Storia d'Europa*, Croce elevates liberty "to an alleged religion, which he calls 'religion of the new era' and 'religion of liberty,' " and he stains himself with the serious crime of abusing religious language "in order to mask the most complete irreligiousness." Finally, and this is truly a capital sin, Croce dares to argue that the religion of liberty would restore the religious life of mankind, and that liberalism will be the religion of the new age.[14]

Giovanni Papini (1881–1956), too, who had become a fervent Catholic and a devout son of the Holy Mother Church, accuses Croce of posing as the prophet of a new religion that sought to destroy Catholicism. He remarks that the *Storia d'Europa* aspires to be "the apologetics of liberalism considered as the only valid and legitimate religion of the modern age." Croce shows himself to be "if not a radical adversary of religion—provided this is understood in his way—certainly not a friend of Christianity, and, above all, not a friend of that authentic and total Christianity that is the living substance of the church of Rome." Papini adds that for many years, "Croce has been talking about religiosity, and about religion too," with the aim of creating a double dissociation: at the theoretical level, separating "religion" from any transcendental philosophy; and, at the practical level, separating "religion" from any church—first and foremost from Catholicism. For Croce, "God does not exist, or exists only in man's heart"; that is, the supreme being is "man in his unceasing search for truth," while the churches are nothing but the remains of superseded and dead cultures, mere devotional and political machines. Christian religion thus must be replaced by the "human religion"; the spirit of man is God, and Croce is its prophet.[15]

For the devout Papini, "the religion of liberty" lacked the essential requisites of any true religion—first of all, "the incommensurable distance and difference between man and God," and the certainty that man is not God, and God is altogether other than man. Not to mention, Papini adds, that Croce's concepts are abstract and generic, by their nature incapable of inspiring that minimum of reverence and love indispensable in any form of religion, however simple. The religion of man or liberty "can give birth to a secular ethics that is scarcely effective in the mind of most people. It can perhaps inspire a philosophical and civic education that is without a doubt respectable. It cannot, however, provide that inner warmth and sublimation of the soul made possible by faith in a superhuman and supernatural presence that is proper to religions in the true and integral sense of the word. The religion of liberty is thus an incomplete or inferior religion, which cannot compete with Catholicism." Religion, Papini continues, is a collective fact, and therefore requires common prayer, public sacrifice, and ceremonials. Croce does not understand the beauty of the ritual of singing and symbols, and the necessity of a sacerdotal body. He does not appreciate the affective element of life, and of religious life in particular. Catholicism will perhaps not elicit an "intrinsic mental justification, but can offer love, the love of God for men, the love of men for God, and the love of all men for all men as sons of the same father, all redeemed by the same Son."[16]

Instead of establishing an alliance with the religion of liberty against the anti-Christian religion of fascism, the Catholic Church censored the *Storia d'Europa*. On July 13, 1932, it placed the work on the index of prohibited books: "Damnatur opus Benedicti Croce." The grave decision is well explained by an article published in the paper *La Stampa* on July 15, revealing the Vatican's perspective. Croce launched "a sort of program," "a new religion, the 'religion of liberty,' which was against 'the opposing religious faiths' and foremost against 'the Catholicism of the church of Rome.'"[17] This interpretation is confirmed by the assessment offered by Guglielmo Arendt of the Society of Jesus, who noted at a meeting of the council of the ecclesiastical court that

> *Storia d'Europa nel secolo XIX*, written by Benedetto Croce, requires a specified condemnation, for, more than heretical, it is of the highest impiety, as it perverts the foundations of the faith with the support of a *pantheistical evolution that routs God himself*. Thereby, it is offensive to the divinity and immutability of revealed dogma, to the church and the papacy. The university youth imbued with such a doctrine soon lose all faith, all morality, and becomes a victim of materialism. It is utterly to be deplored that one has to tolerate such hearths of nihilism in the universities of Catholic Italy.[18]

According to the fascists, Croce proposed a false concept of liberty. As Gentile himself explains in a brief note, in the "Giornale Critico della Filosofia Italiana," the concept that liberty is such only insofar as it is more universal and higher than the liberal conception of liberty: the former is not opposed to the state but rather contains and unifies the individual and the state. The straightforward conclusion is that there can be only a religion of the state, and not one of liberty; nay, the religion of the state is superior to the religion of the liberal liberty because it is a religion of a higher form of liberty.[19] As another fascist commentator proclaims in *La Stirpe*, the true religion of the time was not that of liberty but rather that of authority:

> Today, Italy dismally reads these words of Croce, for in them, more than a vivid hope in a new life, there is the echo of a foregone world. And if they are beautiful and even profound and allow one to think about everything with a serene mind, they die out before they translate into action. A new and ancient word has been repeated, after the great upheavals of the last years: a word that perhaps has not all the enchantment of the word *liberty*, but a severe and admonitory word that indicates the form of being of our time: the word *authority*. Today, the peoples hear this word and bow. Tomorrow, the historian will trace the history of this resurrected word, which will symbolize the new "religion" of the peoples that walk on the roads of civilization.[20]

Gerarchia (Hierarchy), the regime's official review that championed "fascist mysticism," remarks that the religion of liberty is yet another religion without God. Croce despises the Catholic Church, which vies with him for role of spiritual guide, but does not understand the "inner sense of our religious life, as he lacks any congeniality whatsoever with the Christian and Catholic soul; he does not have any idea of the communion of the saints, which is the lofty secret and intimate fragrance of the church of Christ."[21] What irritated the fascists so much that some "were itching to fight" was, besides its content, the success of Croce's book. "But go and see, for instance, Mondadori's shop-windows in the Gallery of Milan," one can read in *Libro e moschetto* (Book and musket), "and let us know if Croce is really treated as one who must be 'buried' as we mean it: volumes and photographs of Croce, photographs and volumes of Croce, of Croce, and Croce, all of it lit, even during the day, by lights that are so nice, so nice as those that are placed before Madonnas, the saints, and…the dead! But we do not believe that all of this aggrandizement has been done just because they consider Croce—as we do—buried. Quite the contrary!"[22]

When the *Storia d'Europa* got into antifascist hands, it inspired and moved. Leone Ginzburg, who died in prison on February 4, 1944, towing to Nazi torture, writes to Croce from Turin on March 22, 1932: "I don't need to tell you that the impression of the *Storia* when read all together and in one go is ten times superior to that which the single chapters already published produced. I am more and more convinced that we will reread this book of yours every year, for many years, and that every time we will draw new benefit from it."[23] Luigi Russo, in a letter of December 30, 1931, comments:

> I've read with great pleasure the last chapters of the *Storia d'Europa*, which are so fluent, so dense, so rich in faith and moral serenity. In the last chapters, it seems to me that Europe has especially become the natural center of your narration and meditations: apart from the introductory chapters, the others *Dal 1815 al 1848* [From 1815 to 1848] rise to the history of Europe starting from the Italian problem, and undoubtedly this point of departure was legitimate and necessary. But in the next two chapters, the historian is no longer just an Italian who becomes European, but is a European who speaks to his compatriots, with quiet strength, about the new common fatherland achieved. One passes from the history of a country to that of the others, without noticing: a truly unitary and circular history. Reading this book of yours, one can assess the enormous difference between the culture of the Risorgimento and our present culture—that is, the difference between a culture that produced great books, but national in scope, such as those of De Sanctis, and the current culture that produces books, like yours, so wide-ranging and positive. One needs

to go back to our Rinascimento, to Guicciardini and Machiavelli, for a more adequate comparison. I tell you that the last pages of the *Epilogo* cannot be read without a deep emotion; and forgive the confession but, be it because of the bitterness in my soul and the torment of the loneliness, in some passages I could not hold back my tears. This book of yours is quite Christian, which will give peace and faith to many tormented spirits. The rivals, too, should feel a clement objectivity in your grave historical assessment of the contemporary crisis. I would say that the tone is much quieter than in *Antistoricismo*, and that there are in it moving accents.[24]

Ernesto Rossi (1897–1967) was a harsh critic of Crocean historicism, which he considered too consolatory a conception. Nevertheless, on March 4, 1932, he writes from prison to his fiancée, Ada Rossi: "I also received by parcel post Croce's *Storia d'Europa*, and I couldn't have received a more welcome gift. I already knew the first three chapters, but now Manlio [Rossi Doria, his cellmate] read them aloud for us again and we proceed. I've always been biased against Croce because I could never digest any of his philosophical works.... But in this book, as previously in *Storia d'Italia*, I almost find no difficulties, and it seems to me that I recognize my very ideas elaborated and presented in the best way." And again from Piacenza, on March 11, 1932, he comments that *Storia d'Europa* has "truly wonderful pages. It is a book that represents an event of great importance in the history of Italian culture. I think of those who will become envious reading it, and of those others who will be overjoyed and will take deep breaths of a breathable air at last." Again, in a letter to his mother on December 11, 1936, he repeats that many pages of *Storia d'Europa* possess moving warmth.[25]

Ferruccio Parri himself, recalling at a conference the beginning of the Resistenza, remarks that the example and teaching of those "confessors" of liberty and democracy who came from other strands also contributed to the sudden awakening of the intimate and vital resources of the Italian people. "Croce is far from the Resistenza, but we cannot understand the Resistenza if we do not understand the masterly deeds and energy that he exerted in preparing those who will be the cadres of tomorrow."[26] In the memorandum in which he noted his thoughts, Alessandro Galante Garrone, a man who lived his long life always guided by "the religion of duty," writes on February 18, 1931: "The work, considered by many Croce's masterpiece, becomes something like a breviary for the little coterie of friends." He continues: "Read the first chapter, *The religion of liberty*. Wonderful. Perhaps these are Croce's pages that I've appreciated the most up to now. Great pages and everlasting." And on the next day, he adds: "Almost finished the booklet, which I lent to Garosci, titled *Fedi religiose opposte* [Opposing religious faiths]." As an eighty-year-old man recalling his reading of those pages, Galante Garrone cherishes the clear memory of the deep impression that *Storia d'Europa* provoked in him: "A young man of today would have difficulty in imagining that magic effect words like those could have on certain youths of that time, inciting them to disgust for any oppression and to the purpose—no matter whether it was generic and sentimental—of doing something in order to oppose it."[27]

Bobbio mentioned *Storia d'Europa*, together with *La storia del liberalismo europeo* by Guido De Ruggiero and *Il pensiero politico italiano dal Settecento al 1870* by Luigi Salvatorelli, as the books that formed "a whole generation of anti-Fascists." *Storia d'Europa* in particular was one of the books that "prevented us, during the raging of the war, from losing every hope for the future of European civilization."[28] Many years before, in 1955, Bobbio penned words that need no comment:

> Notwithstanding the many doubts that I feel I must raise about Benedetto Croce's theory of liberalism, I immediately say that I have no intention of downplaying the liberal function that his thought and his personality had in the years of the Fascist supremacy. Out of hatred for liberalism or out of hatred for Croce, some would like to refuse to recognize the merits and practical worth of the anti-Fascist position of the author of *Storia d'Europa*. Whoever has participated in the anxieties and hopes of those years—I mean intellectuals of course—cannot forget that the best way to convert to anti-Fascism the people who had doubts about the regime was to make them read and discuss Croce's books, and that those who were already anti-Fascists found solace in knowing that Croce, the highest and most eminent representative of Italian culture, did not surrender to the dictatorship. Every criticism of Croce's attitude during Fascism is just resentful and spiteful polemics. As such, it does not deserve to be discussed.[29]

It must be said that without Croce, Italian antifascism would not have acquired the moral value granted to it by the religion of liberty.

22

THE RELIGION OF DUTY

CROCE'S WORK was noteworthy not only because it indicated the moral and political contents, as well as historical references, of the religion of liberty but also because it collected and refined rich and varied reflections that searched for an effective alternative to the fascist religion. Among the protagonists of this search, though, first place goes to Carlo and Nello Rosselli, witnesses of a religion of duty that was different from Croce's philosophical premises and political conclusions, yet identical to it in the central role played by the principle of moral liberty. They had been led to the religion of duty by Gaetano Salvemini, their "uncle," as they fondly called him. Although Salvemini was a fierce enemy of clericalism, superstition, bigotry, and the authoritarianism and conservatism of the Vatican, he defined himself as a religious man. Concerning Donati's candidacy for the Chamber of Deputies in 1919, he writes: "I have not Donati's religious faith. Or rather, I have not the same form of religious faith. He is Christian..., Christian after the authentic Christianity of Jesus Christ: the Christianity of liberty for all, justice for the weak, charity for all men who are fellow sufferers in life. I belong to that Stoic religion that has no dogma and no hope in the afterlife, but shares with Christianity the respect for liberty, the need for justice, and the instinct for human charity."[1]

Christ's teaching was, for Salvemini, the foundation of the moral faith that guided his life.

When I have to explain what the bases of my moral faith are, I reply with no hesitation that I am a "Christian." And if the people ask me to explain better, I declare that I am Christian in that I unconditionally accept the moral teachings of Jesus Christ, and I try to practice them inasmuch as the weakness of human nature allows me to do so. As for the dogmas that over the centuries have been superimposed on these teachings, I do not care about them at all. I do not accept them, do not reject them, and do not discuss them: my faith in certain norms of moral conduct does not depend on believing that Christ was the son of God. There are scoundrels who acknowledge the divinity of Christ, and upright men who do not. I divide men depending on whether they are scoundrels or upright men, and not depending on whether they have dark or blue eyes, or depending on whether they acknowledge the divinity of Christ.[2]

Precisely because he fully agreed with the "Christianity of liberty," Salvemini reserves especially hard words for the Italians' supposed religiosity, which actually was truly irreligious. In his paper "La religione del popolo italiano" (The religion of the Italian people), in 1929, he remarks:

Exceedingly many Italians firmly believe in the Madonna. Indeed they constantly pray to her, and they equally constantly curse at her with a richness of imagination and vocabulary that is extraordinary. They know, and consequently pray to and curse, an endless number of saints as well. They also believe in purgatory, and accordingly pray for the poor souls that wait to be purged before they are admitted to paradise. But they never curse at them, for those souls represent in the afterlife more or less the proletariat in this world, and they feel for them a profound elective affinity, as they foresee that, if it goes well, 90 percent of the time they, too, will need to be prayed for, and not cursed. They care little about Jesus Christ. So little that they rather rarely curse at him. As for God, the Almighty Creator of all things, they find him in the creed together with Pontius Pilate: but who ever minds him or Pontius Pilate? This state of affairs predates the Gospels, and hence the Gospels are not responsible for it. And after all, how many people have ever read the Gospels in Italy, even if they can read?[3]

When Sturzo resigned from the office of secretary of the Popular Party in 1923—an event with negative consequences for the fight against fascism—Salvemini launched a severe indictment against the Catholic Church's role in morally corrupting the Italians. He admits that Sturzo is a man of robust intelligence and personal courage, yet argues that he cannot oppose the Vatican's politics because he is held back by filial devotion to the church:

This is the most dreadful aspect of the moral teaching imparted by the popes and the clergy: that it develops the vile sides of human nature, accustoming it to not feel its responsibilities but rather put them in the hands of the priesthood, which gives not the advice of a friend but instead the absolution or condemnation of a judge. After having lived in Protestant countries, I have fully understood what a moral disaster is for our country not so much abstract Catholicism, which comprises 6,666 forms of possible Catholicisms, among which are those of Saint Francis and Gasparone, Savonarola and Molina, Saint Catherine and Alexander VI, but rather that form of "moral education" that the Italian Catholic clergy provides to the Italian people, and that the popes wish always to be provided to the Italian people. The experience of the Protestant countries made of me not an anticlerical but instead an anti-Catholic: I would never vote for *anticlerical* laws (that is, laws that limit the political rights of the Catholic clergy or prohibit the Catholic apostolate); however, if I experience but one moment of life in an Italy freed by the Goths, I want to dedicate this last moment, as a free individual, to the struggle against the Catholic *faith*. If I die after having destroyed the faith in the Catholic Church in the heart of one Italian only, and if I have educated one Italian only to see in the Catholic Church the systematic corrupter of human dignity, I will not have lived in vain.[4]

For Carlo and Nello Rosselli, their mother, Amelia Pincherle Rosselli, was crucial to their moral and intellectual education. As Amelia recounts in her memoir, she was raised in Venice, in a Jewish environment, where the words "religion" and "fatherland" had a sacred aura:

Religion and fatherland were indissolubly linked to my heart as a child, for the same mystery by which they were enveloped and through which they were transmitted to me. Both were so high that never, when I saw a soldier or a priest, did I imagine that their work could be remunerated like that of any other official. Learning this one day, by chance, was one of the big wonders of my life as a thoughtful girl. Religion and fatherland: actually, religions both, and perhaps, nay certainly, the latter was more permeated with religious sense, in our family, than the former. If anyone had told me then that one day I, too, would suffer for the fatherland, and in the cruelest way; that this fatherland of mine, for which it seemed that they had done everything, would be threatened and oppressed in the very heart of that Veneto that had just been freed! And if anyone had told me that the day would come in which we, as Jews, would almost be denied—in words we were—the right to profess ourselves Italians!

Next to "religion" and "fatherland," the other fundamental word in Amelia's moral world was "duty": "*Duty*—the great mainspring that pushed her [Amelia's mother] generation and mine, obtaining great things from its release. A mainspring that today, maybe because it has been used too much, no longer works, is of no help. But from the sentiment of having fulfilled one's duty, an overflowing sweetness came to the heart, in its turn a source of joy and, I'd dare say, indescribable pleasures."[5]

The religion that surrounds Amelia in the house on the Grand Canal in Venice commands her to perform her duty, and leaves man alone before God and his law. It was

> such an elevated, transhumanized religion—notwithstanding the fetters of the forms through which it was anchored to the earth—that it did not bestow any consolation on its adepts, any help except for that which comes to them from the awareness of the strength of their own conscience. Man and God: no intermediary between them. Inexorable and eternal law that should not be infringed on: if man infringes on them, no one can talk to him about hope and forgiveness in the name of an angry Lord. The Jew drags with him for all his life, and beyond, the sad burden of his sins, for which nobody can atone on his behalf: he must contain within himself sin and atonement, reward and chastisement. He must be able to measure by himself the former and the latter: be every day the judge of himself; within his suffering heart, there must always be the tribunal that condemns. This awful face-to-face with God gives him that restless and tragic sense of life by which he unconsciously isolates himself, and by which one can distinguish him, without any doubt, among thousands.[6]

From their mother, Carlo and Nello embraced a religiosity of devotion to the moral principle lived inwardly, to be practiced with absolute intransigence. Amelia calls it "religious elements of a uniquely moral character." She recounts that Carlo had a religious crisis when he was about twelve years old. He went to the synagogue a few times and then stopped going. According to his mother, Carlo was no atheist. For him, religion was an eclipsed historical phenomenon. In his soul, however, he held a high and austere sense of life, which could be defined as religious—if religion means elevation, faith, and total dedication to one's own ideal.[7] A letter dated July 29, 1918, documents a revealing dialogue between Amelia and her sons on the religious problem. Amelia accepts Carlo's idea that "God is one's conscience," but she also invites him to reflect on the fact that a superior voice and law exist, and to recognize the historical and social importance of religion:

> I see that you engage in big discussions! As for your revolutionary ideas, as you call them, they do not frighten me too much. First of

all, you are wrong if you assume that I find you "witty" in your negations of the existence of God, or better, a harmonic force that rules the universes, a wonderful and exact law that oversees and regulates the atom and the immensity. For me, anyone who negates is never truly "daring." The very fact of negating something, the existence of which can be neither proved nor disproved, would be evidence, rather, of a somewhat retrograde mind, which limits the immensity of the unknown world to the exceedingly limited power of its discernment. Anyone who negates closes a door before him, with the pretext that no light comes to him through that door, and meanwhile he is annoyed by that open space through which, if he entered, something would penetrate his darkness: a ray of light, air, whatever. The fact of a brain that closes a door, instead of opening all doors, the greatest number of doors, will never convey to me the idea of a "daring," so to speak, mind. But it does not seem to me that you belong to this category of beings, certainly hardly enviable in that they are hardly rich inside.[8]

Amelia invites her children to reflect on the nobility of a religious conception of life that recognizes the existence of a superior law revealing itself in the moral conscience, but not confining itself to it:

You say that God is one's own conscience, and that for a fully developed man this must suffice. Of course it suffices. But what does God mean, and what conscience, and what religion, and what force, law, harmony? They all mean the same thing: the recognition, on our part, of a force—you name it—indeed universal and superior, whose voice we hear both within and outside us. I agree with you that the external form of this or that religion is a secondary thing, made for those who need a sort of model guide in order to behave rightly.... Socially speaking, anarchy does not lead to progress, for it represents a disorder; and hence spiritual anarchy does not lead to the elevation of mankind. After all, none of the great human spirits has ever been atheist. When you have read and above all lived more, you yourself will see that negation is always the privilege of spirits that I will not call base, as there are plenty of them who are utterly righteous and honest, but that do not elevate themselves above the average. As soon as one elevates himself, he understands the meanness of negating what he does not know.[9]

The two brothers probably reconsidered their assertions of atheism. In a speech at the Jewish Conference in Livorno on November 20, 1924,

Nello explicitly declared that he was not "atheist or irreligious." He exhorted those who possessed his sensitivity "to strive to identify this religiosity in their soul," so that all together they could try "to strengthen it, toughen it by contact with the air, fix it in order to ensure its endurance, so as to ensure it will not be lost to us—until it becomes for all a source of inspiration for daily life, safe refuge for the moments of downheartedness and disappointment, a constant elevation of our spirit so high that it may grant a balance to our life and *lead us serene to death*." His religiosity is Judaism as a "monotheistic conscience" that infuses a vivid sense of personal responsibility—that is, the idea that one's conscience is the sole judge—and repudiates any form of idolatry, however disguised. He sees himself as religious and Jewish for a number of reasons: he contemplates *"with Jewish severity the task of our earthly life, and with Jewish serenity the mystery of afterlife"*; he believes that one must love "all men as in Israel one is commanded to love, nay, as in Israel one cannot not love," that faith offers a "social conception that it seems to me to derive from our best traditions," and that one must hold to a "religious sense of family that, to those who watch us from outside, truly appears as a fundamental and unshakable characteristic of Jewish society."[10]

Carlo never publicly expressed his religious thoughts with the same clarity, but his letters reveal that he considered the notion of life after death to be a mystery in the face of which reflection stops. At times he talks about religion using a light tone, such as when, in London, he discovers and appreciates Protestant individualism, and declares himself ready to "pass to Luther." At other times he talks about it with great seriousness, such as when, marking the occasion of the birth of Nello's first daughter, he writes to his mother from his political confinement on Lipari, on July 14, 1928: "For us *not* skeptical, but certainly not convinced believers in the principle of immortality, begetting is the guarantee of a relative immortality. Perhaps also for this reason, that is, the lack of a faith in life after death, the Jews have such a powerful and profound sense of family life. Did you ever think about it?" In another letter, dated September 16, 1928, he confides to his mother that he feels the idea of an afterlife is more appealing than the materialistic idea that negates it:

> The more the years pass by and experiences accumulate and the time that one has yet to live shortens with respect to the time one has already lived, the more the narrowness of this earthly existence and the sentimental—rather than logical—necessity of another life becomes clear. My intimate nature is a little skeptical, and you know it.

But certainly I cannot consider as more positive the positivistic, nay the materialistic, hypothesis that negates any life after death. Indeed, I say that if with an act of faith I had to choose a creed on this matter, I would incline to the opposite faith…. But one would need a blind act of faith, to which I am not able to yield.[11]

His road to life after death is the religion of duty. This conviction emerges in a letter he writes to his mother on hearing of the death of his uncle on his mother's side, Gabriele Pincherle, who was like a father to him and Nello:

A whole part of life that painfully slides away. How much suffering! Now I am really close to him and I silently meditate on him and I pose again to myself the great mysterious questions. Can it be that everything is finished, concluded, cleared off, *forever*, as if nothing had been? Can it be? No, it cannot be. Human reason rebels against this even before sentiment. I cannot accept these vain phantoms in the world of the spirit, these brutal suppressions, these incomprehensible cancellations of long, laborious constructions. He, stoic, perhaps had faith amid the confusion, an immersion in the great all, the mystery of infinite nature. We do not know, do not believe; literally, we grope. But it seems to us, now that he no longer lives, that we perhaps possess more of him now that he is dead than when he was living. We desperately seek the essence, and reconstruct it through our memories, which surface from a thousand underground trickles, a thousand secret pools we did not even know we possessed. Perhaps thinking about him will be less frequent, but more intense and pure. His beautiful figure accompanies us and helps us discern, in the dark, truth from falsehood, good from evil, and gently admonishes us not to betray that religion of *duty* that saw him as its silent but perfect soldier in every hour of his life; his figure entreats us, finally, to take care of our mother, and his little sister, toward whom went much of his tenderness, which alas had for many years become anxious.[12]

The certainty that we can somehow live after death induced Carlo to completely commit himself to realizing the moral ideal: "And so, ever more intense and violent becomes my will to action and realization now, on this earth, in this that will be nothing but a single moment in the eternal time, in this that is nothing but a single point in the infinite space, but for me is all my time, all my space, all my world, all my reason for living." Carlo feels that the choice to dedicate his life to the struggle for liberty is a commitment of his own conscience. This is why he lives his choice serenely, in spite of the enormous sacrifices and suffering that it imposes. He is aware that he is following, in full liberty, the moral and religious education of his mother. "I confess," he writes to his mother on August 25, 1928, from Lipari,

> that despite everything, I love this life as it is unfolding before my mind's eyes. I could not choose a different one. And I also feel that you, Mother, have much cooperated in the fabrication of this thread, you who will never want to and never be able to fail to recognize the fruit of your labor. In substance, you have wanted us like this, even though you do not feel like following us in everything and everywhere—which after all is utterly human. In real life, as in the fictitious life of novels or dramatic characters, there always is—and it would be a problem if it were not so—a fatal separation between creator and creature. And the higher and nobler and purer was the creator's labor, the greater will be the autonomous capacity for life and original developments on the part of the creature. Indeed, one distinguishes the great artist by the fact that he has the rare privilege of being able to provide his creature with its own, intimate, unmistakable life, which allows it to evolve through roads different from those envisaged. Who knows how many times you, too, now meditate in the present and probable future on the life that once belonged entirely to you, and it will seem to you that it is growing away from the track you ideally assigned to it. But you will yield, I hope, considering as the proof of an ever more perfect individuation also those aspects of my thought and action that you do not feel like following entirely.[13]

The principle of life as a mission requires the strength to sacrifice oneself for an ideal. Carlo is perfectly aware of this, demonstrating his conviction to his mother with words that express all of his religiosity:

> You, too, soon will go up there [to the cemetery of Paluzza, where the remains of his elder brother Aldo, who died in World War I, where he fought as a volunteer, on March 27, 1916, were moved], perhaps alone, but accompanied by his two brothers, and will feel lost and daunted in that exceptional world. And your tragedy will be universalized by the awesomeness of the number, and it will happen that you will pose great questions to yourself also about earthly life. But whatever the conclusion you reach, you will feel that you have really created three nonvulgar lives, forces, souls, which no matter

how low, will not be vain numbers, will not leave the world as they have found it. *All three will perhaps burn, but for having tried to get too close to the light.*[14]

Living life as a path toward the light, even at the cost of burning out too early, is for Carlo the result of his moral persuasion. It is a command of conscience, he writes to his mother from Lipari on October 1, 1928.

But this is life, the fatality not just of our life but rather of what I would be tempted to call true life—that is, the life that wants to have and flatters itself that it can have a molding and determining power. Most people have only the aim of finding a little spot for themselves in the world as they found it when they were born. Few tend to modify it. One pays for such ambitions, and it is right and necessary that they are lavishly paid for. Perhaps you will achieve nothing with your effort! What does it matter? You will have in any case modified, improved, purified yourself—that is to say, your real world, which is not the external and material one but instead the inner, spiritual.

For Carlo, moral conscience and action in the world are strictly connected: "[My character] is my true *deus ex machina*. Doubts, uncertainties, bewilderments, spiritual complexity.... Then my character arrives and disentangles everything. Temperament is for me a formidable ally, my truest strength." As a political prisoner, thanks to this coherence between ideal and life, Carlo feels at peace within himself: "I have walked. But I am not tired. I will walk more. I will not lose myself. I see my road, I will arrive," he remarks on November 16, 1928. Then he adds:

This verb, "to arrive," is ugly; especially because, in a sense, truly it seems to me that I have almost arrived already. I say it without pride, as a mere ascertainment. I feel within myself such a flaming certainty and such a perfect correspondence between exterior life and the dictates of conscience that truly I could not know what more to desire today. Now the matter is to fix, to consolidate what I would like not to remain a short-lived stage; to mark that certainty on my deeds, be they small or large, and on the human matter that surrounds me.[15]

Carlo's was a religion of liberty in the purest sense of devotion to a moral ideal. He drew inner strength from it in order to resist fascism, at the cost of wearing himself out. What matters for Carlo is not being many or few but rather being at peace with one's conscience, even if one loses his liberty and family love. Whoever chooses the religion of liberty feels that he should set an example. When the lawyer Erizzo suggests that Carlo appeal to *Il Duce* for mercy, he replies from his prison cell in Como:

> Was not it possible to immediately say no through Uncle [Gaetano Salvemini]? The *no* is prejudicial, independently of the merits of the matter. Had they asked me to love my mother or wife, I would have shown the same demeanor. I do not want to adapt myself to recognize an attenuation of my rights. Of course, following such a rigid line of conduct today is not easy, and sometimes I ask myself whether perhaps we do not exaggerate, but the conclusion is always the same. No matter how our personal and collective adventure might end, I want to depart with my moral capital unsullied. I therefore refuse any form of guarantee, pawn, mortgage.[16]

A few days later, on May 2, he writes again to reject his lawyer's proposal that he promise the fascist regime that he will behave well in the future:

> When one accepts beginning a tacit transaction, one positions oneself on a terrible slippery slope; one never stops; all limits fall and everything becomes licit. I know that *almost everyone* in my place would have acted (and indeed *did act*) in a different way, even the best ones. I know that in these times every unilateral commitment is vitiated by the weakness of the obliger. I perhaps know even more: that the time might come in which I will almost regret this obstinacy. But the decision has been made, and it is useless to regret it. I repeat it: I feel on instinct that the example might be useful only insofar as it is pure, perfect, stainless, only insofar as it helps to demonstrate that there has been someone who, in spite of all, has been able to follow a line of morality, of absolute intransigence.[17]

Carlo's and Nello's opposition to fascism is absolute and intransigent because that regime offends the principles of their religious vision of life. In a letter to Nello on March 3, 1928, Carlo writes that Croce was right in judging fascism to be the expression "of a turbid state of mind, in between greed for pleasure, spirit of adventure and conquests, power-madness, restlessness, and at the same time disaffection and indifference, *typical of those who live out of focus, out of that focus that is for man the ethical and religious conscience.*" This is why, in *Socialismo liberale* (1928–29), Carlo points to the lack of inner liberty as the cause of fascism:

> It is a sad thing but true, that the education of man in Italy, the formation of the basic moral cell—that is, the individual—is in large

part still to be done. Most people lack the zealous and profound sense of autonomy and responsibility, because of misery, indifference, secular renunciation. Centuries of serfdom left the average Italian oscillating between servile habit and lawless revolt. He lacks the concept of life as struggle and mission, the notion of liberty as moral duty, the awareness of his own and the other's limits.[18]

This religious conception of life and the antifascist struggle led Carlo toward resolute polemics against the Catholic Church, guilty—in his judgment—of weakening the love of liberty. This is testified to by his correspondence with Sturzo, who was also an exile after he resigned from his post as secretary of the Popular Party. The resolution passed by the party in Turin in April 1933 demonstrates, Rosselli emphasizes,

that my thesis, that it was impossible for a militant Catholic to explicitly claim "freedom" without reservations and qualifications, was groundless. I assure you that never have I been gladder to acknowledge my mistake! What instead remains still open is the other problem, that of the interference that the Vatican exerts, in fact and law, especially in Italy, on a Catholic political movement. That this interference has been present in the past, and in a way that was not conducive to liberal positions, is evident to me. And it seems to me probable that it will happen in the future as well. I believe you agree with me that any big social problem, even of an economic nature, is a political and *moral* problem in its final consequences, just because it is a human problem. Now if the church can be indifferent to technical and political aspects, by definition it cannot be indifferent to the moral one, on which from a Catholic perspective it has an *absolute* normative power. It follows that in times of crisis, or in the face of extremely important issues, the church has the right and duty to inform the believers about what it thinks about them, and the believers have the obligation to follow its judgment. I do not contest the right of a fraction of the community to conform its practical attitude to the dictates of a religion or church. What I maintain is that the alienation of one's own autonomy of thought in such a decisive sphere as morality, the a priori recognition of a relationship of subjection and a realm of infallibility, is the very antithesis of the liberal *forma mentis* [mind-set]. I do not deny that Catholic individuals can be liberals, exceedingly more genuine and consistent than many pseudo-liberals; but I dispute that an organization of truly *believing and obedient* Catholics can educate liberally.[19]

In response to the allegation put forth in *Osservatore Romano* that GL (Giustizia e Libertà [Justice and liberty]) was affiliated with Freemasonry, Carlo states that "we are adversaries of the Catholic Church; nay, we are the only antifascist movement that tightly and openly links the antifascist struggle with the fight against Catholic morality, politics, and hierarchy; however, we feel no sympathy whatsoever for that moribund remnant of the bourgeois Enlightenment called Freemasonry."[20] In a subsequent statement, he explicitly declares that for three centuries at least, "Christianity and the good Lord himself are in the state of an unburied corpse," and that justice and liberty are inspired by a religion that is "atheistic, immanentistic, humanistic: anti-Catholic, anti-Christian, antitheistic."[21]

Carlo was well aware of the anti-Christian character of Nazism and hoped for a "more Christian European conscience," which would take moral values more to heart and, in the name of that conscience, isolate and firmly condemn Adolf Hitler. Like Croce, he believed that the crisis of the contemporary world was a religious crisis, and that the religion of those who fought against fascism and Nazism was Christianity's heir. For him the old God died in Spain, because of the church. The defeat of the antifascists was the defeat of the last religious men, those men who believed that "in order to live one needs reasons to live for. They are the last who believe in a God, the last who evidently testify that man is not an animal to be preyed upon or slaughtered." The answer to the religious crisis brought about by the victory of fascism and Nazism, and the death of the old God, could only be the new religion that had inspired the antifascist and anti-Nazi struggle. Our religion, Carlo observes, "is precisely the embodiment of that enthusiasm, the popular and social organization (in Greek, the ecclesiastical organization) of what has sent the heart of so many thinkers and martyrs throbbing since the origins of the modern world..., and what has flashed through us in an unforgettable moment of our youth as the sole beauty for which it is worth living and dying."[22]

From this premise, Carlo drew the conviction that the victory over fascism would be possible and complete only when Italians achieved inner liberty, before and above civil and political liberty:

The Italian problem is essentially a problem of liberty. A problem of liberty in its comprehensive meaning: at the individual level, it is a problem of spiritual autonomy, emancipation of conscience; at the social level—that is, at the level of the construction of the state and the relationships between groups and classes—it is a problem of the organization of liberty. Without free men, there can be no free state. Without emancipated consciences, there can be no emancipation of classes. The circle is not vicious. Liberty begins with the education of man and ends with the triumph of a state of free citizens, with equal rights and duties—that is, a state in which the liberty of each is the condition and limit of the liberty of all.[23]

Fascist hired killers assassinated the Rosselli brothers on June 9, 1937. That same year, on April 27, Antonio Gramsci died in prison in Rome. In prison, Gramsci, too, reflected on moral and religious reformation. He defines Croce as "a religious reformer" capable of maintaining a detachment between intellectuals and Catholicism, and remarks that "*Storia d'Europa* is Croce's first book in which his antireligious opinions took on the force of active politics and had an unprecedented circulation."[24] Gramsci also acknowledges that he himself and many people of his generation "participated in all or in part in the movement of moral and intellectual reform promoted in Italy by Benedetto Croce." The fundamental principle of that reform was the concept that "modern man can and must live without religion, meaning without a revealed or positive or mythological religion, or however else one terms it." For Gramsci, "the greatest contribution that modern Italian intellectuals have given to world culture" resides in this idea—a precious "civil conquest" that must be defended.

Gramsci interprets the Crocean religion of liberty as a simple faith in modern civilization, which needs no transcendence and no revelation, but contains its own rationality and origin within itself. This religion is therefore antimystical, but one should not forget that for Croce, "every conception of the world, every philosophy, insofar as it becomes a norm of life, is a religion."[25] In spite of its historical and moral value, Croce's reform failed because he more closely resembled Erasmus than Luther: he was more a man of the Rinascimento than of the Reformation. Gramsci thus meant to stress that Croce did not understand that a great movement of moral and intellectual rebirth sustained by large popular masses—as happened with Lutheranism—necessarily took on rough and superstitious forms.[26] Instead of condemning the immaturity and superstition of the people, Croce should have committed himself to elevating the people, as Luther did. For Gramsci, the need for a religious and moral reform remained valid, and could not be postponed; but the methods had to be different, and the protagonist had to be different as well.

The preacher of the reform had to be a new prince similar to that idealized by Machiavelli, and the subject had to be the proletariat. Gramsci interprets *The Prince* as the work in which Machiavelli first explains how a political chief must be capable of leading a dispersed and downtrodden people to found a new state by exciting and organizing its "collective will"; from there, the chief calls men to action with the passionate cry of the "Exhortation." Gramsci sees in Machiavelli the elements of an "intellectual and moral revolution" understood as a "question of religion or a conception of the world." From these elements, Gramsci elaborates on the conviction that the modern prince—the Communist Party—"must be and cannot avoid being the propagandist and organizer of reform both moral and intellectual," capable of developing "the national, popular collective will toward the achievement of a superior form of modern civilization." One of the elements of the conception of the world, or religion, that must be drawn from Machiavelli is the principle of "losing one's soul to save the fatherland or state"—"an element of absolute laicism" against the dominant religion or dominant conception. Gramsci writes that the prince "takes the place of the divinity or the categorical imperative in the consciences, and becomes the basis of a modern laicism and a complete secularization of all life and all customary relations."[27] Like Gobetti, Croce, and Carlo Rosselli, Gramsci understands that liberation from fascism could not be merely political but should also involve the conscience, and hence needed to be religious. In contrast to them, however, Gramsci posits a collective entity and not the individual's moral conscience as the principle of the new religion. For this reason, his idea of a religious and moral reform was not the true alternative to fascism and its religion of state.

23

AS IF GOD EXISTED

It was Ernesto Rossi who instead recognized the absolute authority of moral conscience and posited it as the foundation of his religious conception of life. Sentenced to twenty years in prison for his participation in the conspiratorial activity of GL, he wrote to his mother, Elide Rossi, from the penitentiary in Piacenza, on January 20, 1933, that he was happy she no longer had any tie with the Catholic religion:

Usually, when they grow old, women become bigoted: you, instead, have moved further and further away not only from the Catholic religion but also, more important, from any revealed religion. And you, too, really could have needed a "crutch" on which to lean, after all the blows you have received in life. The fact is that whereas other women grow senile when they get older, your mind has become ever more lucid, and your desire for sincerity, even toward yourself, has prevented you from accepting religion as a "crutch," once it has no longer pleased your reason. I believe that the first foundation of human dignity lies in the conviction that we have to give account of our actions to ourselves and *anyone else*. Since the time I started to reason for myself, I have freed myself from every theological construction, and I no longer felt the need for it. You remember: I was still a baby and did not want to take Holy Communion, and you had the intelligence to not impose it on me, and left me free to form my convictions as I wished. Over the years, the religious problem has become for me a historical problem, and I could therefore appreciate the relative and contingent character of any religious conception, and I abandoned the anthropomorphic conception of the universe, ceasing to look for an end beyond the field of human will, and to pose to myself questions in terms that cannot be comprehended by our mind. In this way I became not irreligious, as I would never feel like scoffing at or resisting the religious sentiment of others, but I rather became completely a-religious, if one means by religious what one commonly means by it: the revealed religion.[1]

Elide was a woman who lived her Christian faith with sincerity. Shortly after her son's arrest, she says to him: "For the time being, let us repose all our trust in this hope, and 'the one who vexes and gives rest to us' will finally have mercy on our suffering." She goes so far as to write to her son in prison that he should feel like "one of God's favorites," and should believe that "he will not abandon you." When she receives the terrible news of the suicide of Umberto Ceva—whose story will be discussed below—she restates the fundamental principle of her faith: "Of course one needs to believe in the afterlife, otherwise the cruelty of separating good creatures who adore each other, and the cruelty of tolerating the existence of beings who can conceive only of evil and their own filthy interest, would be incomprehensible."[2] But sorrow and pain over her son's suffering in prison weakens her faith in a good and just God, and perhaps even suffocates it. The strength to go on thus comes from her moral conscience. She writes to Ernesto on September 10, 1931:

> I even went to church—where I never go—to seek in prayer that solace that the good mother of Mazzini, so full of faith in God, used to find: but unfortunately I little resemble her with regard to religion. I, too, speak of a supreme being who should personify justice and goodness, but I feel it so distant that I am not able to establish even the tiniest stream of understanding and love, and therefore I turn again to my dear dead, whom I feel always alive, and from whom alone I draw serenity and solace. I must thank fate, though, for having endowed me with some moral strength and willpower, which help me endure with relative tranquillity the crises of despondency. When I particularly grieve at your life of sacrifice, I think that voluntarily you have burdened yourself with this heavy cross for the triumph of a holy ideal. If I compare your life to the despicable one of those who live only for themselves and defend their mean interest, then I do not cry anymore, and I feel infinitely proud of being your mother.

How different are the religious sensibilities of mother and son becomes clear when one compares the ways in which they reflect on the terrible experience of the nearly fatal wound that Ernesto suffered during the war. Elide reveals that she was supported by the faith that God had saved her son "to do good," that he would fight for the triumph of justice, achieving for troubled humanity those rights that they had been deprived of, and teaching them love, disinterestedness, and loyalty.[3] Ernesto, too, in prison, remembers that experience, but God is absent from his narration:

> Even when I was on the brink of death, at Quisca's little hospital, I did not at all feel the need for religious illusion. I remember that next to my bed, there was a lieutenant who was also seriously wounded, and was moaning all the time because he did not want to die. The chaplain came, comforted him, and convinced him to receive the sacraments. Then he asked me if I wanted to receive them as well. I thanked him and said I did not need them. My fellow died during the night, after having regained serenity in hope, and certainly that was a great gift for him. But that hope was not necessary for me: I felt I was departing slowly, slowly, without any worry about what would have happened next. Dying is a consoling thought, when one knows what life is, and keeping this thought always in mind suffices for nurturing less mean values in life.[4]

Ernesto sincerely admired those men who knew how to live with moral dignity, like the anarchic streetcar driver Papini, his fellow prisoner. Papini was born in Treviglio in 1881 and had been sentenced in 1928, by a special tribunal, for having reorganized the Confederazione Generale del Lavoro (General Confederation of Labor) in Milan. Rossi describes him as "pure of heart," one of those men whom one needs the good fortune to meet sometime "so as not to despair completely of mankind."[5] "I never experienced anyone else," Rossi writes, "who had such a benevolent indulgence toward human weaknesses, which he always tried to understand rather than condemn." He used to say: "'It is not enough to ask our Lord the Almighty to give us this day our daily bread. One needs to ask: give us our daily bread, *but without infamy.*' And he was right." Papini felt morally close to Captain Cambini, about whom Omodeo had written in *Momenti della vita di guerra*, for he "is one of the very few who stood firm by himself, without the support of any religious faith (I use the word religion in the narrow sense of 'revelation')," and he also "imagined that, if God had heard one of his awful curses, he would have said, 'You see, if this boy did not curse it would be better, but come on, poor guy, such things happen to him that, if I were in his shoes, I, too, would curse.'"[6]

Rossi's harshest criticisms were aimed at the incoherence of Christian theology and at Catholic hypocrisy. On November 13, 1936, he explains to his mother that

> the theologians—just like their brothers the philosophers—appear to drive their hooks, to which they can then hang the chain of their syllogisms, into clouds of smoke, as deep as they can, so that from afar the last links disappear in the haze. Considering the sturdiness of the links and paucity of their own strengths, many people do not dare pull the chains, in awe. But the chains hold just because they are not pulled, for it is impossible to drive hooks into the clouds. Meanwhile, life goes on, and uses the same theories to justify opposing activities. On a Gospel that preaches the abandonment of earthly goods, brotherly love among men, and a religion that is all inward, one builds the church with its mundane magnificence, with a completely outward religiosity that preserves the privileges of the masters over the slaves and the rich over the poor, with its holy Inquisition, indulgences, worship of images and relics, blessing of cannons and battleships, and so on and on.[7]

What offends him especially is the striking contrast between the morality of the Gospel, the Sermon on the Mount in particular, and the behavior of the priests. Christ said:

> "*When thou prayest, enter into thine inner chamber, and having shut thy door, pray to thy Father who is in secret.*" And the crowds of believers go to pray in famous sanctuaries, particular places, convinced that there better than anywhere else their prayers might be heard. "*And when ye pray, use not vain repetitions, as the heathen do: for they think that they shall be heard for their much speaking.*" And the worshippers repeat dozens of time the same *Hail Mary*, counting the rosary beads to be sure that they have arrived at the right number. "*Do not swear at all.... And do not swear by your head, for you cannot make even one hair white or black. Simply let your 'Yes' be 'Yes,' and your 'No,' 'No'; anything beyond this comes from the evil one.*" And all the Christians swear, and the priests themselves make people swear on the book of the Gospel that contains this prohibition. "*Do not store up for yourselves treasures on earth.... You cannot serve both God and Money.*" And when the liberal revolutions have come to confiscate the treasures of the clergy, the latter possessed all over the earth the majority of the best lands and the safest revenues; and

today it still reconciles, with the utmost impudence, service to God and money." *"You have heard that it was said to the people long ago, Do not murder.... But I tell you that anyone who is angry with his brother will be subject to judgment." "You have heard that it was said: Eye for eye, and tooth for tooth. But I tell you: Do not resist an evil person: If someone strikes you on the right cheek, turn to him the other also." "You have heard that it was said: Love your neighbor and hate your enemy. But I tell you: Love your enemies and pray for those who persecute you."* And in the name of the Gospel, in support and defense of this word of brotherhood and peace among men, baptism has been imposed on entire peoples by laying waste their countries, the heretics have been exterminated, countless and most atrocious wars have been waged; and still today military chaplains celebrate Mass with the Gospel on the altar, amid cannons, and all the priests of the various countries at war pray the Lord for the victory of their arms.[8]

Catholicism is, for Rossi, at most an inferior conception of life compared to philosophical knowledge. Rossi prefers a soft religion—soft and yet capable of guiding one's action—to a revealed or bad religion. But the true guide of his choices is a sense of duty, which he lives by religiously, not as an abstract principle to which one must bend but rather as an inner voice to be heard and followed simply because it is our own voice:

I cannot ask myself if it were not "better to think about ourselves without caring for anything," for I cannot "think about myself" without caring for all those matters in which it seems to me that I have something to say, and that it is my duty to say it. I have never kept the prime mover of my actions outside myself. Indeed, it even seems inconceivable to me that anybody does anything "for the others." What I do, I do for me, in order to be at peace with my conscience. If I wish to relieve other people's suffering, or give others a greater dignity of life, the reason is that I grieve at their sufferings, I feel them as if they were mine, and their despicableness, their brutishness offend me: in them, I feel my own humanity offended. Until I am like this, I will not be able to act as if I were different: I could not, for instance, just think of stuffing my belly, keeping it well-covered, warm, and rubbing it against another belly so as to leave someone who could continue the same sort of trick after my death. Would it be worth it? Why should I consider such a life better than that which I can otherwise live?[9]

A sense of duty makes any consoling conception of history superfluous. With all his skepticism, Rossi writes, "I have never had sympathy for the intellectuals who hide their moral sluggishness by taking the place of the Lord Almighty and thereby justifying every reality, which, as such, 'is always rational.'" At most, Rossi admits a God conceived as a superior moral principle, but not as the necessary foundation of moral behavior.

> The Jansenists said: "Believe in God, but act as if he did not exist." Their maxim had a high significance against Jesuitical morals, which were based on the fear of hell and expectation of reward. I would rather say: "Do not believe in God, but act as if he did exist." As if a God existed—mind you—not in the Catholic sense but instead in the sense of an explanation about what we see in the world that is superior to our intelligence. It is for us, men, to do the best we can with our lot as men. As for the rest…to the rest "God provides, God who is saint enough."[10]

His meek reason and consciousness of duty spurred him to become an example of intransigence in a country of spineless men, as well as a witness to the religion of liberty.

> Whatever the political situation to come, we are doomed to be defeated until we live. It is an easy prophecy…. I know Italians and their history to well to have illusions. Cavour was an Englishman, born by chance in a Balkan country. One does not change in two or three generations the characteristics of a people accustomed for centuries to rid itself through the confessional of any worry about the evaluation of moral problems, and to cede any dignity of social life into the hands of foreign rulers. But this matters little. There are people whose function it is to sign decrees, and others whose function it is to die in the trench or rot in prison. This, too, is a division of labor. And one can prefer the latter over the former function when one believes in affirming thereby values that constitute the very reason of our life. Force can beat us individually, but remaining faithful to ourselves means passing on to the generations to come, by one's example, which counts more than the word, what we hold to be the brightest of the thoughts inherited from past generations—that is what makes man truly a man: liberty.[11]

Massimo Mila, too—who graduated in Turin in 1931, at the age of twenty-one, having completed a thesis on Verdi's music, and who was imprisoned in 1935 because he also belonged to the Justice and Liberty movement—believed not in the Christian religion but rather in a profound secular religion, based on the supreme value of the intrinsic intention of the one who acts and the conviction that one's faith is solely the "purity of the moral intention." He writes from prison in 1938 that he who does good "cannot despair, independently of the fact that this good is or is not rewarded, as in the tales for kids." He defines himself as a nonbeliever who does not at all envy the believer, "for the good reason that I, too, have my faith." He respects traditional religiosity, even when it is a little bigoted, like that of his grandmother, but his own faith is of a different nature.[12]

He does not believe in the God of revelation, because he does not need to in order to live and die well. If by any chance God decides to offer him a surprise, all the better:

> I confess that, if I am able to live my way, should I live to be eighty years old, the remaining time will have not only seemed but also have been long. Until when, as I will have no more purposes, no duties, no desires, I will quietly "consent"—as Goethe used to say—to die. And this without "artificial means," as one says in the alpine jargon—that is to say, without the need of eternal fathers, heavens, and other lives, but just with the simple means of this life, which, after all, remains our only certain heritage. I would be very sorry to have wasted this life in the contemplation of another one, which is uncertain. At most, I can keep in the bottom of my heart, in a closet, consequence-free hope that—as [Heinrich] Heine used to say—once we are dead, the good God will want to give us a nice surprise.[13]

Mila's discreet religiosity makes him abhor the pride of the "saints," who proclaim their own virtue, and think they can go to heaven strutting and holding their head high. With equal intensity he loathes the hypocrisy of the Catholic Church, which "mobilizes millions of men…and dollars in order to create a movement that aims to make the skirts of Hollywood actresses fifty centimeters longer and prescribes the maximum length of kisses in the movies, whereas the very same church approves and blesses the infinite swindles of the great bankers, frauds of kings of oil, usurpations of authority, and so on and so forth." He instead admires and respects the true Christian ethic when it becomes a way of life, not a sterile declamation. Subjection before the wretched, and feeling responsible, if indirectly, for their miserable condition, and shame for one's own relative wealth—all these sentiments, he writes to his mother, "*ought* to be in every upright man's heart for the past two thousand years, I mean since the time the Gospel was preached."[14]

Among the many books that Mila reads, *Robinson Crusoe* strikes him in particular, for the character "amounts to a symbol of mankind." Poor Robinson, Mila observes, alone in his hut in the evening, before the Bible, is the man who turns to himself in search of the truth of things and himself. In solitude, face-to-face with himself, the old blasphemous sailor—a man enslaved to matter—finds God, who is spirit. The first thing Robinson discovers is the immense value of life: "even when abandoned on the desert island, he appreciates its value through the rough comparison between his lot and that of his fellows who lie on the sea floor." He then discovers the essence of morality, which is liberty and responsibility—that is, "self-discipline and obedience to one's own law, and not the exterior formalism of licit and prohibited actions." Finally, in his relationship with Friday, he becomes "conscious of the equal dignity of all human creatures, whatever their color, thanks to the equality of the divine gifts of the spirit, which are bestowed on all."[15]

In his religious views, which identify God with a moral principle, Mila feels close to the Protestant conception of salvation through faith as well as to Christ who condemns hypocrisy and exterior formality:

> The pride of the good people who think they are good is stupid, and stupid are those judgments that one necessarily pronounces considering the people's actions. Or else, rather than stupid, they are useful, and as such they are neither true nor false. Jesus taught this when he reproved the hypocritical exteriority of the Pharisaic religion, when he promised to the repentant thief who was dying on the cross next to him: this evening you will be with me in paradise. This is the meaning of certain parables that so violently shock the common sense, for they treat under the material species spiritual values, and thereby affect their character with revolutionary and demolishing power.

According to Mila, one should always give some credit to the publican and the sinner, and never believe in the inalterable absolute perfection of the alleged saints: "He who does not do so errs, and commits a sin against the spirit, which is the gravest sin, or rather *the* sin, as I do not know any other sins."[16]

While in prison, Mila often reflects on the Reformation. His search originates from the need for an inward religiosity. He reads many books on the topic and summarizes his remarks in a long document, which he shares with his mother. He feels the need to examine "the Christian concept of liberty" in depth, and therefore he wants to reread the New

Testament, the church fathers, the *Summa*, and in general the Scholastics prior to Dante. His secular religiosity provides him with all the necessary strength to withstand the loss of liberty, and resist the seductions of glory and fame. "Not even the chains of seven years in prison will fetter my freedom of thought: nor will they be able to alter or touch the perfect serenity of my spirit. I live high above these trifles, and I even feel I am with you, next to you, always."[17]

His God is conscience, which forces him to operate in the world. In the name of this religion, he condemns the idea of a quiet life, the true foundation of fascism:

> Indeed, without resorting to Dante's lightning toward the scoundrels who never were really alive, these allegedly cunning fellows who preach absenteeism, disinterestedness, and a renunciation of living the history of one's own time, are disproved by reality on their own terrain: that of interest. Can one believe, today, that by taking no interest in the things of the world one can live quietly, when the things of the world chase you, haunt you, drive you out of your last shelters, disguised as wars, laws, taxes, and so on? This is the tactic of the ostrich, who buries his head in the sand to avoid seeing the danger. If today, for instance, Sweden and Norway refused to support the good Finns and let them yield to the enemy because, they say, they do not want troubles, who can doubt that they would be next, and their present neutrality would be useless?[18]

Our duty as men is not to observe the vicissitudes of the world but instead "to realize in the world the word of the God of conscience regardless of the meagerness of our forces and without finding an excuse that lets us just do as we like. Heaven help us if all the good people disdainfully withdrew and left the world to the rascals!"[19]

In the name of this religious conception of life, Mila rejects Catholicism and extols Mazzini's teaching:

> Again, the usual soporific effect of the Catholic idea explicitly wants to divert man from this world. Mazzini wrote to his mother: "Man cannot save himself but through this world, by transforming the world." And mind you, I am not saying that we all must bustle and demonstrate and struggle and fight and conspire—all things for which I myself am so little cut out. But at least we should try to understand: we, who in scorn are called intellectuals, have just this particular duty of ours: to understand the things of this world,

approach it with intelligent sympathy, and bring to it the order of reason. The Catholics instead glance at it with horror and exclaim, "Oh my God, what a mess! What a chaos, what a confusion, what a disorder!" and then withdraw and go about their own business, prayers, masses, confessions, and so on—all practices aimed at saving *his own* individual little soul. Whether men massacre each other or sacrifice themselves, and whether they do something heroic or shameful, these are all things that do not interest him, and confound and distract him instead; he does not even want to make the minor effort of understanding them. Of course, not all Catholics are like this.... But I am afraid that inasmuch as they are Catholics they are like this, and inasmuch as they are different they are not properly Catholics.[20]

Not even Croce's religious conception satisfies him. It involves too much consolation, since Croce's idea of history is similar to that of divine Providence, which governs the world's rationality and organizes the individual wills, inspired by moral conscience or egoism. He completely agrees with Croce, though, on the fact that theirs is a time "of grand upheavals and struggle that are, in their substance, religious." In order to be worthy of the era in which they happen to live, to master the difficulties and not be crushed by them, Mila observes that one needs a faith that teaches people the "full devotion of the soul to what reason determines to be our duty."

24

ONLY A GOD CAN EXPEL A GOD

IN THOSE SAME YEARS, Calamandrei, a Florentine who was a nonbeliever and a nonpracticing Christian as well as a distinguished lawyer, reached the conclusion that in order to save human and Christian civilization from Nazism and fascism, men needed to rediscover faith in God. We can follow his reflections in the pages of his diary, which he kept from 1939 to 1945, putting both himself and his relatives at risk, so that some person of goodwill, a few centuries later, could understand how and why a whole civilization had died out. The anguish that filled him during the war years, however, was rooted in an older melancholy, which remained firmly tied to his soul even after the liberation. As Galante Garrone eloquently notes, Calamandrei

> had been carrying along with him for many years this underlying sadness, which his scintillating wit and easygoing manner could not dissimulate. He had always had it, as it was ingrained in his very way of life. As the years went by, he more and more considered life to be "a quick, mysterious flight into death." In 1950, after the death of a friend, he wrote: "I am consoling myself by thinking that we are all sentenced to death, *we all are already dead. One's birth is a death sentence.*"

After Livio Bianco's death in the mountains, Calamandrei writes to Galante Garrone on August 21, 1953: "And then, and then, dear Sandro, this sense of ever-quicker flight from this world, which recedes behind our shoulders, with all the happiness that was.... And yet...*il faut tenter de vivre!*" On January 30, 1955, commemorating his friend Giorgio Querci, he affirms: "We ever more feel, as the years pass by, like the rear guard of an already-emigrated tribe, here on the dock, waiting for the boat that will come to get us too, and we already see it on the horizon, with its dark sail."[1]

Calamandrei's melancholy reached its height in *Inventario della casa di campagna*, written in Poveromo between August 1939 and August 1941. He describes his desperate search for the happy world of childhood, watched over by his father and mother, and the continuity between the boy at that time and the grown-up man, and the passing of years, increasingly wrinkled faces, and the brevity of mortal life, as in his depiction of a visit to the Etruscan ruins of Cosa: "Among these walls, at sunset, creatures as ephemeral as we are tried to suffocate in sleep this anguish of farewell, by which every minute of our life, now as back then, is made." One finds in Calamandrei a tormenting perception of the swift passage of life without anyone's being able to stop it; a life lived with regret for an irremediably vanished happy age.[2]

Calamandrei does not believe in the God of revelation; he instead regulated his actions as if God did exist and were a severe God.[3] He holds to a "Mazzinian and Christian faith" according to which "a wrong committed against my fellow man is a wrong committed against myself, and love of country is love of all countries and every liberty."[4] Calamandrei warns that philosophy, especially a Crocean philosophy, cannot be a guide or an inspiration to act in times like his: "Every philosophy needs a religion that affirms the moral dogma." The pure critic, he writes on September 10, 1940,

> is a little like the pure man of letters: he is out of the world, and lets the world collapse to understand the reason for the collapse or to describe it. But we are sick of these pure critics and men of letters; they led us to this situation. And how does one reconcile this historicism…with the necessity of a moral creed from which to start with certainty to build the future? And can this historicism be sufficient to constitute the moral creed? Is it enough to say that this is history to be able to leave with clarity for the future? In his last books, Croce tries to resolve this dispute: he tries to reconcile free criticism with the existence of a moral dogma, a sentiment about which one cannot quarrel, and that one can take as given. But this is the central point in which every philosophy results: the point where it seems that every philosophy needs a religion whose dogmas cannot be questioned by criticism.[5]

He feels the strength of a Christ who immolates himself for men, but is annoyed by a religion that reduces itself to mere external appearance. He expresses these feelings in his writings, composed around

1925, on Benvenuto Cellini. Describing Cellini's representation of Christ, he notes that

> if one looks with attention, one notices that this sweetness is too sweet, that this beauty is too beautiful. The customary pet name given by the author to this statue assumes the value of a psychological revelation; "il mio bel Cristo" [my beautiful Christ], beautiful, only beautiful: neither [Filippo] Brunelleschi nor Donatello could have ever thought of calling thus the suffering image of the savior. To be sure, this head is pretty, but what a sad and manly acceptance shines in Brunelleschi's Christ, which recalls Masaccio and perhaps the great Trecentists! Here, in "my beautiful Christ," the sensual mouth, the too-small and almost-womanish nose, the sinuosity of the half-closed eyelids, and then that smooth skin, without a wrinkle, without a contraction; if it did not have a beard, it would be the face of a sleeping ephebus. And the hair and beard, too, though treated with great mastery, seem so neatly detached from the glabrous flesh as they are, the arranged curls of an exceedingly beautiful makeup; by contrast, in the squalid hair of Donatello's and Brunelleschi's crucifixes, one sees the set sweat of agony.... Maybe there is in this curly head some pagan reminiscence of the "antiques" dear to Benvenuto; certainly transferred to the marble is his meticulous goldsmith's skill; but Christian passion is not there. The same mannered sweetness of this beautiful face seems to approximate the threshold beyond which Guido Reni will come, and the conventional mawkishness of the small holy pictures: superstition, not religion.[6]

Calamandrei acknowledges that the Christian religion promises an absolute foundation for morals, and hence can console, but he is also aware that it does not keep its promise, and hence disappoints and leaves people defenseless. The only way to supply an absolute foundation for moral principles "is to believe in a revealed religion on which morals are based, but such a foundation is illusory, for the adversary, just as he negates your morals, can negate your religion." As Calamandrei writes in October 1940, "[We antifascists] start from moral premises of a clearly religious character, which are superior to the state, and starting from them, one necessarily arrives at conclusions that are conducive—let us say so—to 'free thought.' " If one lacks these premises, however, or starts from utilitarian and materialistic premises, the conclusions one reaches are those of the fascists—that is, that philosophy must serve the regime.

Liberalism, too, needs a religious foundation: "If one believes in eternal, unquestionable, religious principles, superior to any historical contingencies, one can build liberal thought on them; but if one lacks this religion, historicism leads one naturally to assert that philosophy, too, must bend before the fait accompli, and that philosophers, too, must immerse themselves in this reality, even if this reality is a sea of mud."[7]

In Calamandrei's view, liberty itself is based on religious premises, or, more precisely, Christian premises, and these premises serve to ensure that people "consider liberty the most venerable good, even more than life itself." Liberty draws the strength to combat its deadly enemies from its Christian premises. Only England, Calamandrei contends in October 1940, persists in making plans for war that have as their premise "the goodness of certain Christian principles" and the illusion that all peoples necessarily must, perhaps just in the bottom of their heart, deem them the best." Calamandrei dejectedly remarks that the world watches "with compassion the boldness with which England defends its Christian morals," ready to bow before Hitler, who "has affirmed opposing morals that preach and exalt force, and disdain and deride the sacred principles."[8]

The tragedy of Italy and Europe is, for Calamandrei, the consequence of the decline of a faith in liberty. On one of the first pages of his diary, he notes: "Young people no longer believe in liberty. They no longer realize that the only order one can serve with dignity is an order freely accepted in a state where everyone can still make his opinion heard." On September 9, 1939, his analysis becomes even more precise: "This incapacity to believe in life's seriousness, this lack of faith, and this lack of faith in faith, made fascism possible in Italy." He then narrates a trivial event that nonetheless proves the contrast, in fascist Italy, between those who live the religion of liberty and those who have no spiritual life left: "During the faculty meeting, La Pira rightly pointed out the Christian character of the war: at that moment, C., who spiritually is as dried-up as a cicada's castoff shell, said: 'Christianity is already dead; no one can die anymore.' I reminded him that this could be said before France and England declared war; not now that two great peoples die just for defending Christian civilization."[9]

With the declaration of war against Germany, France and England demonstrated, according to Calamandrei, that "democracies" will not give up without a fight—a demonstration that within those who defend liberty and Christian liberty, "there still is the strength to sacrifice oneself for this ideal." Precisely because they were Christians, these people could fight and sacrifice themselves for liberty. Without a faith in the Christian God, it is impossible to fight against the Nazi and fascist God. Beginning in spring 1940, Calamandrei reflects with increasing intensity and anguish on this problem, and discusses it with his most trustworthy friends. "I talked to Calogero for a long time about the ideals to be opposed to Hitler's ideals," he writes on May 7. "In order to resist the overwhelming deviationism of that call to the basest bestial appetites, such as those of conquest and violence, one would need a heroic Christianity, with martyrdoms and tortures. One must implant a human ideal that can be communicated to the masses, for no *rational* reasons exist to usefully fight among the people Nazism's elementary and barbaric creed."[10]

He returns to the topic a few days later, in a heated debate with his friend Piero Pancrazi, journalist and writer (1893–1952)—a dispute that reveals Calamandrei's soul.

> Personally, I am not a believer or a practicing Christian, but I have morals that are the remains of Christian religion. How can I defend a civilization that is based on these remains, if not by doing my best to prevent the source of these remains from drying up among that people? What other faith can we oppose to the savage faith of the Germans bewitched by Hitler (a faith capable of leading men to death and resistance against those savages), if not the Christian faith based on the certainty of the afterlife? If one does not want to abdicate to the invaders by refusing to fight, if one does not want to foment in all people the savage fury of nationalism in order to respond to the other nationalisms, one cannot but cultivate in the people a belief in the afterlife that makes us defend here goodness, charity, and liberty, and that gives us the strength to die for these ideals.

Calamandrei's thoughts turn to the Italian people, and above all to the possibility that Italians may also find the strength and courage to go to war against fascism and Nazism, but in whose name?

> Suppose we know that in ten years the Italian people will have to face a deadly conflict with the Germans, and that we want to prepare for it spiritually with a mysticism that allows Italy to enter the fray with the same spirit of sacrifice, the same "dynamics," through which Hitler's savage ideal leads those raving madmen. What will we teach the Italian people? Not the liberal ideals, which have a grip only over us learned people and not over the masses; not an

opposing nationalism; in order to teach them the Christian ideal, one cannot but revive within them the early martyrs' Christian faith. Only religion enables the defense of the morals that are its remains.[11]

To Pancrazi, who objects that religion becomes thus *instrumentum regni*, Calamandrei rejoins that there is nothing wrong with making the Christian religion serve liberty, and that, first, fascism's victory and, second, the Italians' submissiveness were the consequence of a lack of true religiosity:

> Why could not [the Christian faith] serve tomorrow as the ferment to guide those social claims toward which the future is heading? What is happening in Italy today, this absolute passivity in the face of injustice, is the result not only of M[ussolini]'s and fascism's own work but also of the entire work of anticlerical materialism that was foolishly pursued in Italy in previous decades. How could the Mazzinian ideal, too, become effective and comprehensible by the masses if it were not accompanied by a belief in the afterlife? [In order to provide] men with a weapon to free themselves from slavery to the returned Barbarians, I do not see any other means than the Christian faith.

Otherwise, Calamandrei continues, Italians should abase themselves beneath the Huns' heel and wait for liberation through death, which will annihilate everyone, "oppressors and oppressed."[12]

Faith is the last resource against the tragedy of Nazism's triumph. As the fall of France looms near, Calamandrei is ready to pray together with his Christian friend: "Yesterday, La Pira told me that the Germans cannot win because millions of believers, millions of the religious, monks, innocent creatures pray in the monasteries for France.…Good La Pira: and yet, who knows whether in this intensity of thought and faith that rises from all over the world toward France, there is not some mysterious counterweight against the Germans' savage mysticism. If I could pray, today I would pray on my knees for France." While the Italian troops move toward the French border to deal a stab in the back to the defeated France, Calamandrei focuses on the following alternative: either the Christian faith, or the dominion of force. "The imbeciles and the wicked are always right. When one says that justice prevails in the end, one utters a perfectly nonsensical sentence. The fact is that we reasoning men in the end find a way to demonstrate that justice is on the side of those who have triumphed. If there is no God, in the world nothing counts but force. Without God, morals are an illusion, a deception. Whoever believes in justice without believing in the afterlife is a vile hypocrite who refuses to look clearly at reality."[13]

When injustice triumphs in the world without any shame or restraint, the moral strength to resist can come only from Christian religion. "Last night at Mass," he writes on January 25, 1945,

> I heard the last trump blaring: *Nihil inultum remanebit*. This is the great solace of faith: religion is a faith in justice more than a faith in joy and personal eternity. Christian religion makes the centuries end in a great judgment: in order to tolerate the suffering of life, one cannot but hope that all infamous acts come to an end and to a judgment. I was thinking this last night. The theory according to which politics has nothing to do with morals is irreligious. The last day's justice will not distinguish politicians from "private citizens."[14]

It was the Risorgimento's lesson, as we have seen:

> I also read Settembrini's *Ricordanze*: Settembrini is a naive man and not of great stature, but what a character! Today there are no longer men of that temperament: coherent and courageous, capable of facing death or a life sentence just to avoid saying a less than dignified word, just to reject even the smallest compromise with their conscience. Among us, even among the best ones, at least among those of the circle I know, such men no longer exist: even the honest men are more skillful, but less fierce. How could one of us (I am thinking of myself, Pancrazi, Russo) face with serenity what Settembrini endured twice? Perhaps the difference is the following: that he firmly believed in God, in the afterlife, and we do not. Ours are noble spirits, but limp and disheartened: we feel our country's tragedy, but this gives us more sadness and discouragement than active indignation.[15]

His religiosity made him feel that the people who fought for liberty were his compatriots. Their fatherland became his fatherland. The English, French, and Norwegians who defend liberty, he comments on April 11, 1940, "are now my country." His idea of country was that of Mazzini—the country that respects all peoples. For this reason, Calamandrei saw the fall of fascism as the fatherland's redemption. On August 1, 1943, he writes in his diary that

> truly, the sensation that one has felt in these days can be summed up, without rhetoric, in the following sentence: one has recovered the

fatherland—the fatherland as the sense of friendliness and human understanding that exists among people born in the same country, who understand each other with a glance, a smile, a hint; the country, this sense of vicinity and intimacy that, in certain moments, allows familiarity and a tone of friendship between persons who do not know each other, of different education and professions, and who nevertheless recognize in each other something deeper that they have in common and stand solidly behind. What a breath! One can talk to one another, one can speak one's mind clearly, on the road, on the trains, to the peasant who works in the field, to the worker who passes by on his bike; one can express indignation, reproof, or just a joke (which often enthralls more than an invective) without fear of a denunciation. We all can repeat over and over again the same banal phrases, which bring us together and unite us like a password, like a sacred symbol among believers of the same religion: "At last! These assassins! This coward! This buffoon!" Underneath this kind of speech, uttered more with excited, joyful trembling than with rage, there lies a quivering tenderness. We have met again.... Killing the sense of the fatherland was one of fascism's gravest misdeeds. For twenty years, this word—fatherland—has been disgusting. This haughty self-conceit that could not speak about Italy without adding that all the world looked to Rome, this puppet-theater tone of intimidating authoritarianism, which, drawn from *Il Duce*'s [Mussolini's] speeches, influenced even the radio speakers, rendered any reference to patriotism unbearable to all properly constituted stomachs. One had the impression of being occupied by foreigners: the fascist Italians who encamped on our soil were foreigners; if they were Italians, we were not. A country occupied by a tribe of savages—for twenty years we lived under this heel. Therefore, in this first week, a shiver has run through Italy similar to that of the Risorgimento, when the foreign kings were leaving, and the people demonstrated, and everyone sang and embraced each other.[16]

With the fall of fascism, Calamandrei again discovered a love of country, as many other Italians did, but not a love of God, even though he felt the need for him and searched for God during the war. He had the religion of liberty based on a moral sense but probably believed that his faith lacked something:

The intense work never prevented me from thinking about what counts more in life—that is, love first, and now death. But I have never found God and do not find him yet; I only find a great sense of neglect, weak resignation to this flowing of events that overwhelms us. This faith in honesty and justice, this conviction that I am serving a just cause, this moral sense that—according to my friends—is a limit to my intelligence, accompany me without my doing anything to cultivate them. I, too, when I try to analyze them, find them naive and puerile: as naive and puerile as the faith of these humble Colcellese women, who go to receive Holy Communion from Don Mentore and thereby believe they can set their conscience at rest.[17]

La Pira, commemorating Calamandrei in the Palazzo Vecchio on his death, since he knew him well, says that he "was a man of inner spirituality.…[W]ithin the limits set by his Kantian-like moral and spiritual education—moral law within myself, and the starry sky above myself—he was able to understand the graceful mystery of redemption and peace that is concealed within a life of silence and prayer." Calamandrei revealed his inward religiosity with reserve, and perhaps only to his closest friends, like Pancrazi, with whom he used to visit Camaldoli's and Certosa's cells. La Pira speaks of the "mystery of adoration and prayer" that Calamandrei carried in the bottom of his soul.[18] It's a good description, yet for a profound religion of liberty, where God is absent, such mystery is only a backdrop. But truly, it was as if God existed.

25

LEAVING LIFE

CALAMANDREI EXPRESSED the religion of liberty by throwing himself into work, teaching, and writing, and tirelessly defending the Resistenza's moral and political legacy. Others gave their life for that same religion. Umberto Ceva is one example, among many others. Born in Pavia in 1900, he was a chemist and manager. As early as 1929, he joined Giustizia e Libertà. He was arrested in 1930 together with Ernesto Rossi and Riccardo Bauer (betrayed by the Friulan lawyer Carlo Del Re). Fearful of breaking down under torture and jeopardizing his fellows, he committed suicide in the Regina Coeli prison. His sister Bianca told his tragic story in *1930: retroscena di un dramma*, released in 1955 by a small Milanese publishing house. His sister recalls that Umberto, "talking to his family and friends, had several times declared sorrowfully that in that atmosphere, created by the violence of a few on one side, and the inert conformism and vile mediocrity on the other, he could have not educated his children." By educating he meant elevating the youths' souls to that sphere of spiritual liberty that alone can sustain civil and human ideals.[1]

These words about the impossibility of teaching his children about spiritual liberty in a totalitarian regime supply a sufficient understanding of the religious sense of liberty that lived in Ceva's soul. But the most telling document, so telling that it needs no comment at all, about the religious faith that inspired his antifascism is a letter he writes to his wife—one day before he commits suicide:

> Now listen to me, Elena. My words are not vain. Listen, my angel. You must not think of me as a victim of discouragement, desperate, anguished. During a long month of solitude, with the friendly company of books, I reflected at length, looking to the bottom of my soul, and I have found that faith that instinctively I always searched for. I am not dying, Elena. In a short while, my soul will be among

all of you, my dear beloved, and will lightly touch you with a divine kiss. Always next to you, next to my father, my sweet mother, my good sisters, my babies. How many kisses will skim over their blond little heads! I am not dying, Elena. I am simply going where all of us have to go, and I would go there with joy if I were not clouded by the thought of your pain. But you will understand me. Once the anguish has been calmed down, you will feel rise within you the harmony that I am feeling. And holding to our young hopes, you will wait with firm faith for the day that will unite us in the true life. The soul is immortal, Elena. See you, my angel, see you again in a day that I hope will be far away for all of you, but certain. We will meet again, aware of what we truly are. Free from any earthly dross, you will find me waiting for you, as at a tryst.[2]

During those same years, Lauro de Bosis, one of the first to use the phrase "religion of liberty," offered another important testimony. Born in Rome in 1901, the child of Adolfo and Lilian Vernon, de Bosis grew up in an environment rich with fervid intellectual and cultural interests. His father directed the journal *Il Convito*, which came out from January 1895 to December 1907. Carducci published his *Canzone di Legnano* in it, and Pascoli published a few of his best *Poemi conviviali*. A liberal and a monarchist, de Bosis became an antifascist starting with the march on Rome. In 1924, the Italian American society of New York invited him to the United States to give history, literature, and philosophy lectures, and in 1926 he lectured at Harvard. He published in an abridged version the already-famous work *The Golden Bough* by James George Frazer, translations of *The Private Life of Helen of Troy* by John Erskine, and *The Bridge of San Luis Rey* by Thornton Wilder. De Bosis alternated between translating English works and—with equal skillfulness—the classics. In 1927, he translated Sophocles's *Antigone* and wrote *Icaro*, his only poetic work, which came out in 1930, in Milan, published by Edizioni Alpes, in a modest edition whose title page features a leafless tree, on whose branches perch three little birds.

Icaro is the dramatic prophecy of the author's death, which occurred on October 3, 1931, after he had flown to Rome to cover the city with antifascist broadsheets. In de Bosis's story, Icarus has been educated by his father, Daedalus—a prisoner in the tyrant Minos's palace—to believe in a God who is "the One, the Becoming, the Word," and "comprises everything in himself" and "dominates even Fate." Whereas his father does not want to hear anything about "tyrants and liberty," for he thinks that both pass away, and believes only in science, Icarus dreams of true glory: "The triumph of the free men and the wise / over what oppresses the world / dark and prone and unrighteous; the rising of a time / new and fertile and meant for victories / of the human spirit against the dead / matter and against torpid ignorance! / Winds foreboding a new dawn, Phaedra, / already graze our face." To Phaedra, who asks him who will be "the peoples without King, the numina on earth who with announcements impose God's will," Icarus replies: "They are / poets and saints and creators and all those who / are bitten by the sharp fever of the unknown!"; men animated by a "faith not unarmed" but rather "armed with wings and strength—a militant dream."[3] For this faith Icarus sets about flying, conscious that if he falls, "the flow of his blood will be stemmed in time, and will sparkle again throughout the ages."[4]

The night before the fatal flight, de Bosis wrote *Storia della mia morte* (The story of my death), convinced that "fascism will not fall if one can first find about twenty young men who will sacrifice their lives to spur Italians' soul. Whereas during the Risorgimento there had been thousands of young men ready to give their life, there are few today. It is necessary to die." An image of Icarus falling appears on the book's cover, and the book contains a chapter titled "The Religion of Liberty." De Bosis explains that "a religion, in the broadest sense of the word, is nothing but a philosophy"—a philosophy that "by becoming action, stops at a certain stage of its development, crystallizes in a definitive system, and surrounds itself with an aura of holiness that, while protecting it from further developments, entrusts it to the people's acceptance." The religion of liberty is therefore a particular philosophy, based on the conviction, backed by the history of Europe, that the development of liberal institutions is continuous, and moments of arrest and reaction are just "separate, static black spots that serve to stress the light by contrast, but that have neither a light nor a historical significance of their own."[5]

Just like any other religion, the religion of liberty, too, has its martyrs, like Jan Hus and Giordano Bruno along with those who fell in battles for national independence or political liberty. It can even boast of having martyrs for Christianity, whereas Christianity cannot boast of having martyrs for the religion of liberty, because when Christianity became orthodoxy, the religion of liberty separated from it and left it behind. For de Bosis, too, the religion of liberty is liberalism, which, precisely because it is a religion, cannot impose itself by force. If it tried to do that, it would become one of the many religions of the past. With his flight of October 3, 1931, de Bosis wanted to demonstrate that like his dear Icarus, the religion of liberty belonged not to the past but rather to the future; indeed, as Croce noted a few months after de Bosis's death, to eternity.

If de Bosis had gotten to know Willy Jervis, he would certainly have thought that the religion of liberty had been resurrected. Jervis's son Giovanni writes of his father that "he was not religious and even less so a devotee, although he considered himself a believer and a Waldensian." The theologian Giovanni Miegge, more perceptively, observes instead: "Had not the word been devalued by twenty years of inauspicious exaltation as pure action, one should say that he was a man of action. In the sense, though, that he was a man of the unavoidable action, the man who, in the presence of a clear duty indicated by circumstances, did not hesitate and acted. He did it without reservations, with a consciousness of the absolute that was the fruit of his Christian faith."[6] Consciousness of one's duty and Christian faith lived together within Jervis: the faith revealed to him the moral duty as a duty toward God; the duty found in his faith was a support and consolation.

In addition to the Waldensian environment and his wife, Bianca (daughter of Luigi Rochat, an antifascist doctor in Florence, and nephew of Giovanni Rochat, a Waldensian pastor, she graduated in English literature with a thesis on John Bunyan's *The Pilgrim's Progress*), the cultural and political education he absorbed at Camillo and Adriano Olivetti's factory, where Jervis worked as an engineer, was significant. Jervis came into contact with a serious, profound antifascist environment, in which liberty was considered the daughter of Christian faith, and antifascism was a religious principle. In a manuscript titled "Il pensiero socialista, quello liberale e quello comunista," which was not published and can be found in the Fondo Camillo Olivetti at the Associazione Archivio Storico Olivetti of Ivrea, one reads: "The concepts of order and liberty are inborn in the teachings of the Old and New Testaments, and should therefore be readily accepted by all those who, no matter the religion or race they belong to, host in their soul Christian sentiments."[7] In his Olivetti department, from which twenty-four employees fell in the fight for liberation, Jervis's faith was reinforced. His Anglo-Saxon origins as well as his Protestant and Waldensian education translated into a great intransigence and moral austerity on his part, especially toward himself. He allowed himself no weakness, yielding, nor compromise; in his behavior toward his employees and pupils, he did not engage in acts of placation, helpfulness, or superficial favors. He was not indulgent toward others because he was not indulgent toward himself, and expected that everyone could and must do his utmost, as he did.[8]

Karl Barth's theological reflection, which circulated widely among the Waldensians (in particular in the pages of their journal *Gioventù cristiana* [Christian youth], where Jervis served as administrator), had an influence on Jervis's religiosity as well. A central topic of Barth's writings in the 1930s was the concept of bearing witness. If God needs witnesses, it means that a trial is taking place between God and men. In this trial, "God calls witnesses against the men who have departed from him, the men who have obstinately rebelled against him."[9] Serving as witnesses because God needs it, means fighting with all one's strength against those who, destroying liberty and human dignity, have offended God. The fight for liberty is the witness that God demands from the believer. Witnessing, however, does not mean being a bystander or a narrator; it entails completely throwing oneself into the struggle.[10]

To witness God's word in history means to freely assume responsibility and duty. Precisely because duty is freely assumed in order to help God, no force can bend it: "One must have the courage to stand alone, and also the humility to be a private soldier next to many others in the ranks of the work and struggle; one must be ready for both silent waiting and the most intense action; one must be both a man of peace and, if necessary, a man of war."[11] The Barthians who gathered around *Gioventù cristiana* conjoined theological reflection and political commitment, fully coherent with the theory that at times of great crisis in the world, when some men openly rebel against God's law, God calls witnesses. The Christian has the religious duty to become a witness of God's law, and hence resist: "If we must obey the authorities when by so doing we fulfill God's will, we cannot but rebel against them when they command something that goes against the Lord's will…. So long as one is asked to put aside one's own interests, goods, families, pride, and life, the Christian does not find reasons to rebel; but when the law offends God's cult and majesty, then what holds is the other apostolic teaching: 'It is better to obey God than men.'"[12]

As the war drew closer, Barth explicitly called for resistance. About ten days before the shameful Munich treaty that handed the Sudetes over to Germany, Barth writes: "Every Czech soldier who fights and suffers, will be doing it also for us, and I say this today without reserve, will be doing it also for the Church of Jesus Christ, which in the atmosphere of the Hitlers and Mussolinis, can be overcome only by ridicule and extermination. What peculiar times are those in which a reasonable man can say only this: that faith orders us resolutely to drive back the fear of violence and love of peace, and resolutely to put the fear of injustice and love of liberty first." The Christian community does not have a right to be disinterested in peace and war, tyranny and liberty. Barth complains that

> too often it yielded to intimidations and remained silent, when it should have spoken.... The duty of the church is not to take part in politics and govern. It can and must bear witness, however, before peoples and governments, that politics is a service rendered to God, and that justice and liberty are God's gifts. It frankly and charitably can and must question, call, exhort, and admonish the state whenever the state tends to withdraw or, on the contrary, impose itself too much; whenever it tends to offend justice and liberty; whenever it tries to overthrow God's sovereignty, or man's rights, or both. In this sense, the Christian community is responsible for what the state does and does not do.

For the Barthians, the war against Hitler and Mussolini thus was not only tolerated but also desired by God—that is, "imposed by the faith in Christ."[13]

It was for this faith that Jervis chose to become a witness and abandon his family, whom he loved with all his heart, to join the Resistenza. With that faith, he faced imprisonment and death. The little notes he managed to send to his wife from prison on April 19, 1944, are evidence of this:

> The faith in God supported me. The faith in God consoled me.... I pray God to survive and return to my dear family. God will give me the strength to endure everything.... [M]y body resists well, thanks be to God.... [T]hinking of you, I feel anguished, but I trust in God.... I trust in God's benignity.... [F]aith will not abandon me.... [M]y trust in God always increases and allows me to think of the future calmly.... [I]t was destined by God that we had this trial.... [T]he faith in the afterlife in a great thing, though.

He finds great solace in reading the Bible: "On this tragic eve, books would not help. The Bible is precious instead. The Bible gives me solace.... I pray, sing hymns, and read the Bible.... [T]he Bible keeps me company." Conscious that his end was imminent, on August 4, 1944, he writes these words on the cover of the Bible that was found next to his dead body: "God bless you and preserve you. We will meet again up above.... God's will be done. I will have faith until the end and keep hoping. I am serene; God comforts me. I am sure you, too, will find consolation in God, I will always think of you."[14] In that "We will meet again up above" one finds all the meaning of his faith and his witness to a religion that simply commands—but it is an absolute command—that one side with the just, with those who are morally right, even if this demands the sacrifice of one's life.

26

TWILIGHT

How many people lived by the religion of liberty? Certainly more than the few whose stories I have tried to recount. I hope that other scholars will relay other stories. But numbers count little. From a historical and moral point of view, what counts is that there were men and women who opposed fascism and Nazism in the name of the religion of liberty. This is a historical fact. Intellectual honesty requires that we rediscover and recognize that fact. The religion of liberty gave the Resistenza a religious character. The first who understood this was, I believe, Raffaele Pettazzoni, a valiant historian of religions. In his *Italia religiosa*, published in 1952, he emphasizes that "the movement of the Resistenza must be recorded in Italy's religious history. The Risorgimento's religious spirit revives in it. The letters of those who were sentenced to death during the Italian Resistenza are documents of a religiously professed faith, which the writers shared with many others who died without writing anything, and with the very many who suffered without dying."[1] Many of those who died were practicing Catholics, but the Catholic faith was not the issue. They did not die for that. The others, the secular people, all died for another idea, which, too, was religiously felt, witnessed, and suffered for to the point of utmost sacrifice: the idea of liberty, justice, or socialism, or communism, and above all, the notion of fatherland, a free Italy, honored and glorious. Among believers, this secular faith did not interfere with traditional religion; among nonbelievers, it was the only religion. Those who were Christian and died for liberty believed in salvation and eternal life; those who died for liberty but were not Christian expected neither salvation nor a reward in another life. Yet all were religious, and for all of them the Resistenza was a religion.[2]

Calamandrei, too, understood this well. Almost ten years after the end of the Resistenza, he writes that "some talked of 'collective soul,' others of 'providence'; perhaps one should talk of God—this unknown God who is inside each of us." The Resistenza had a "religious character" because religion means the "seriousness of life, commitment to moral values, coherence between thought and action."[3] How and why a people, or at least its best men, could resurrect itself from the moral death of servile life appeared to Calamandrei and others as a "miraculous and mysterious" event. It was miraculous and mysterious indeed, but if we interpret it as the rebirth of the religion of liberty that germinated and spread in Italy at the end of the Middle Ages, and lived its highest moments during the Risorgimento, the second Risorgimento also—that is, the Resistenza—becomes more understandable and reveals its value. Religion was not an external ornament but rather an essential component of the Resistenza. Against the fascist religion, only a contrary religion could fight and win, and this was the religion of liberty, or, as Ralph Waldo Emerson observes, only a God can expel another God.[4] Only a faith can motivate the choice to fight against a totalitarian regime and a foreign invader, at the risk, and at times certainty, of exile, imprisonment, torture, and death. If Carlo and Nello Rosselli, Jervis, or Ceva, to mention just a few among many possible others, had listened to the voice of their interest, they would have looked to their own well-being, and continued to enjoy their families, studies, and friends. The religion of liberty was necessary inasmuch as it emancipated man's inner conscience—that conscience that fascism knew how to fascinate and conquer. If political liberty was to be attained, it was necessary that at least a few people listen to the God who speaks through conscience. That God could be the deity of the Jews or of the Christians, as long as God lived in one's personal conscience.

Once the Resistenza was over, Italians, with few exceptions, regarded the religion of liberty as a useless idea. Such a sentiment is echoed in a few high moments of the Constituent Assembly debates, starting with the salutation that Vittorio Emanuele Orlando pronounces on June 25, 1946:

> From the past, good wishes to you, to whom our fatherland's future is entrusted in this tragic hour of her, of this Italy that, even though among errors and faults, we have loved with boundless love, and served with absolute devotion.... Italy has not yet finished being Italy, and as Italians we still have some tasks assigned to us by the history of the world. [A burst of applause.] We will wait for our revenge, not in the form of a war, which we fervently condemn in the name of the civilization in peril; however, since there are those who

wish to destroy us, our revenge will consist in our resurrection, in which we have the firmest faith.

Echoes of the religion of liberty resound in the report that Meuccio Ruini, president of the commission charged to write the Constitution's draft, presented to the assembly on February 16, 1947. Ruini not only recalled that liberalism is an orientation that "invokes the 'religion of liberty'" but also remarks how "a lucid spirit, Stendhal, said that approaching a Constitution one experiences an almost religious feeling," and concluded by speaking of a "shared devotion to the fatherland and the ideals of liberty and justice that should inspire us." Ruini, a secular person, also spoke of the sacred character of the Constitution in his speech at the morning session of December 22, when he presented the results of the coordination work on the draft's approved articles: "So far, we have split, quarreled, and torn in the discussion of the constitutional text. But there has always been an effort to reach an agreement and unity. And now I am positive that on the final passage we will get a consensus; beneath our clashes, there is only one Italian soul. Italy will have a Constitution, which will be *sacred* for all Italians, united in their acclaim for the Republic and the Constitution."

At the end of his address of March 11, 1947—in which he recalled his famous other speech of May 24, 1929, against the Lateran Treaty— Croce expressed his profound religious sentiment: "If my Christian Democrat friends (whose roles I do not want to usurp) will allow me, I wish to conclude this address by inviting all those present to intone the sublime hymn's words":

> *Veni, creator spiritus,*
> *Mentes tuorum visita;*
> *Accende lumen sensibus,*
> *Infunde amorem cordibus.*

The Constituent Assembly had the opportunity to establish an explicit religious foundation for the Constitution when it discussed La Pira's proposal to insert a preamble containing the Universal Declaration of Human Rights and an invocation to God. La Pira explains how— through the principle "not the state for the individual but rather the individual for the state"—the fascist state annulled the fundamental juridical and political achievement of Christian civilization. For this reason, "the totalitarian state was essentially a radical denial of the human person's value as it had been elaborated throughout the whole history of Christian civilization on the basis of the Gospel and the highest human reflections."

In order to provide a solid foundation asserting the priority of the person over the state, the Constitution should comprise a metajuridical statement: that man transcends the state, "because man's nature is spiritual and thus transcends all temporal values." According to La Pira, such a philosophical foundation was absolutely necessary: "This spiritual and religious root of man is the only ground on which it is possible to firmly construct the building of natural rights—sacred and imprescriptible."

In opposition to the fascist religion, La Pira wanted to assert the principle of man's natural rights proclaimed not only before mankind but also before God. The proposed preamble read:

> Having experienced through the painful tyranny of the totalitarian fascist state how the disregard and defiance of man's and the fundamental human communities' natural rights truly are the biggest causes of public tragedies, the Italian people decide to list these sacred and indefeasible rights in a solemn declaration as the preliminary act of their new democratic and republican life. Aware of the great problems of renewal that present times raise, we aim, with this declaration and the Constitution that accompanies it, to create a social and political order that conforms to the high dignity of the human person and human brotherly solidarity, and that thereby guarantees everybody his place and function in the well-ordered national community. We thus regain our place within Christian civilization—ferment and essence of our history and culture—and within the community of peoples who love liberty, labor, justice, and peace. We consequently proclaim, in the sight of God and the human community, the following declaration of the rights of man.

La Pira further clarified the religious significance of the Constitution in his speech at the meeting of the first committee on September 9, 1946: "I believe that it is essential—in building our new state—to proclaim in the Constitution's opening declaration the spiritual nature of the person, through which his imprescriptible natural rights are legitimated." La Pira had in mind a state that affirmed the rights of man before God because only a state with these characteristics could be an alternative to the fascist state that was born and lived to affirm on earth a religion contrary to the Christian one. Concetto Marchesi (a Marxist and eminent Latinist) remarked that in Italy, there was a dominant religion, and it was the Catholic one. Affirming the religious nature of the democratic state would have implied affirming an absurd and disrespectful principle.

The Constituent Assembly discussed at length the old problem of how one can provide the republican state with a religion that sustains the spirit of liberty in a country where the Catholic religion was dominant. How could the church tolerate another religion in Italy? As Marchesi suggested, one should "not take the name of the Lord in vain." Whereas Palmiro Togliatti, the general secretary of the Communist Party, intervened to shift the discussion from philosophical and theological questions to political ones, the Socialist Giovanni Lombardi asserted that besides the Christian faith, another, secular faith existed, and that the Constitution should recognize only the former to the detriment of the latter. At the next day's meeting, on September 10, 1946, President Tupini acknowledged La Pira's idea that human rights originated from class struggles, wars, and revolutions, and among these "the great Christian revolution, by which for the first time the rights of liberty were affirmed." The discussion was delayed until the conclusion of the Constituent Assembly's proceedings, once the Constitution draft had been completed.

The conversation over La Pira's proposal was resumed on December 22, 1947, during the morning session. When the debate was moving to a close, La Pira took the floor to address the issue of the preamble with the invocation of God, which he had raised at the beginning of the Constituent Assembly's proceedings: "As my colleagues already know, last night I presented to the presidency the proposal that the constitutional text be preceded by a short phrase of a spiritual nature, which said: 'In the name of God, we, the Italian people, adopt the present Constitution.'" The phrase proposed, La Pira explained,

> is not a specific profession of faith, hence everyone could agree on it: the Mazzinians, with their phrase "God and People"; the liberals, because there also exists a neoliberalism that accepts this point; and also among Marxists there is a considerable tendency to separate the dialectical materialism from the historical one. In substance, I want to say that there is a point of contact for all creatures and there always is a superior reality. Therefore, if, above any political points, we all could unanimously cleave to this phrase, it would really be a triumph of faith.

President Umberto Terracini informed the assembly that the issue had been debated several times and had been referred to the Drafting Committee. He advised La Pira to pose the problem again at the end of the proceedings, remarking that such a preamble required the support of a large majority, which, judging from his contacts, did not exist. He then opened the discussion, with the plea that speakers choose words adequate to the theme's delicacy. Togliatti was the first to speak. He stressed the need to preserve the unity they had arrived at, and since voting on the preamble would divide the assembly, he asked La Pira to withdraw the proposal, and added a harsh reference to the predictable opposition from the Vatican and Catholic hierarchy: "I do not even know whether a position that makes faith something collective and not just personal would be accepted by all the Catholics. I understand how Hon. La Pira arrived at it, starting from certain doctrines, but I cannot forget that also recently and at very elevated venues these doctrines have been closely examined and have evoked quite nervous criticisms. Even in his own field, therefore, Hon. La Pira could find not all the consent he wishes. What is certain is that he would not find all the consent of the Assembly." Marchesi sided with Togliatti:

> Within my conscience, I have always rejected the atheistic hypothesis that God is a class ideology. God is in the mystery of the world and the human soul. For those who believe, he lies in the light of revelation; in the unknowable and the unknown, for those who have not been touched by that ray of grace. I have just said to my colleague La Pira that this mystery, this supreme mystery of the universe, cannot be solved in an article of the Constitution, in any article of the Constitution that concerns all the citizens—those who believe, those who do not believe, those who will believe.

He seconded Togliatti's request that La Pira withdraw his proposal. Calamandrei then took the floor to say that it was not the case that carrying on a discussion would surely divide the assembly. He added that had it not been so late, he would have suggested that the Constitution should have a preamble with these words: "We, the Italian people, to the memory of the brothers who fell to restore Italy's liberty and honor, consecrate the present Constitution."

In his short reply, La Pira defined Togliatti's words as noble, warm, and insightful, like those of his friends Calamandrei and Marchesi. He suggested to combine his proposal with Calamandrei's one. What is important, he emphasized, is to avoid a specific declaration of faith as in the Irish Constitution; "but why should we refuse to say 'In the name of God'?" Francesco Saverio Nitti's speech marked the turning point in the discussion. He argued that God is too high a principle to be put to the vote, and no tradition exists in Italy of solemnizing the Parliament's activity with religious rites. The question at issue is spiritual and not political. "God is too great. God is above all things, and all believers must commit to serve him in the common desire for mankind's good. Therefore, I do not find the proposal strange, but a vote now would cause a deep division. Why should we divide about God's name? God's name is too great, and our disputes too little."

La Pira replied with words that revealed his high moral and civil principles: "I wanted to be a bearer of peace and unity. But if peace and unity cannot be reached, what should I say?" After an interruption, he goes on: "Frankly, if all of this is doomed to cause a split in the assembly, I can say only this: in accordance with my conscience, I have fulfilled the act I had to fulfill." If the Constituent Assembly had accepted La Pira's preamble, however, supplemented with that of Calamandrei, it would have solemnly recognized an origin of the republic in the religion of liberty, and would have continued to teach the Italians that defending liberty is a duty before God.

Even without the preamble, the Constitution shows the traces of a long religious history. Alcide De Gasperi, who took the floor as president of the Council of Ministers during the afternoon session of December 22—that is, after the final vote—understood this well when he declared, "May the breath of the spirit that animated our history and Christian civilization inspire this hard work of ours, which is weak, for it is human, but is great in its ideal aspirations. May it consecrate in the people's heart this fundamental law of fraternity and justice, so that Europe and the world may recognize in the new Italy, in the new republic grounded on liberty and democracy, the worthy heir and follower of its millenary and universal civilization." The old liberal Vittorio Emanuele Orlando, finally, declared that the Constitution had received, with the solemn assembly's vote, a "secular consecration."

After the Constituent Assembly, the religion of liberty was soon forgotten.[5] A late ray could be seen in serious but minimally influential writings such as *La filosofia del dialogo* (*The Philosophy of Dialogue*), written by Guido Calogero in 1962.[6] But it was just the reverberation of an ideal, at its sunset, rather than a little flame destined to become brighter and warmer. Italy had moved too far away from the religion of liberty. Yet, without the moral nourishment of the religion of liberty, the liberal and democratic institutions that were birthed by it were doomed to become corrupt, empty forms masking the dominion of arrogant and cunning men, in a context of depressing banality and poverty of ideals.

The tragedy of fascism and Nazism should have taught us that totalitarianism establishes itself through banal men, and that the true antidote is a religion that prevents one from adoring men who pretend to be gods, for it teaches us to love instead the inner God of moral conscience, and to defend liberty with absolute devotion. It's a lesson of history to be pondered. Carlo Rosselli understood and expressed this well when he wrote: "Without free men, there is no possibility of having a free state." This book, having narrated a few moments of the history of the religion of liberty in Italy, will certainly not help bring it back to life, even though it is desperately needed; but it will at least help us preserve the memory of the men and women who lived for it.

NOTES

<hr>

PREFACE TO THE ENGLISH EDITION

1. Maurizio Viroli, *The Liberty of Servants: Berlusconi's Italy* (Princeton, NJ: Princeton University Press, 2011).

2. Eric Nelson, to cite only the most recent example, has claimed that

Renaissance humanism, structured as it was by the pagan inheritance of Greek and Roman antiquity, generated an approach to politics that was remarkably secular in character. The political science of the humanists did not rely on appeals to Revelation, but rather on the sort of prudential knowledge to be found in the study of history and in the writings of the wise. It was, rather, in the seventeenth century, in the full fervor of the Reformation, that political theology reentered the mainstream of European intellectual life. The Protestant summons to return to the biblical text brought with it incessant appeals to God's constitutional preferences as embodied in Scripture. To use a crude but revealing measure: if one compares the average number of biblical citations in the political works of Petrarch, Bruni, Machiavelli, More, and Guicciardini with the number in the political works of Grotius, Selden, Milton, Pufendorf, and Locke, one can be in no doubt about the direction in which the discourse is moving.

Eric Nelson, *The Hebrew Republic: Jewish Sources and the Transformation of European Political Thought* (Cambridge, MA: Harvard University Press, 2010), 2.

3. Quentin Skinner, "Machiavelli's *Discorsi* and the Pre-humanist Origins of Republican Ideas," in *Machiavelli and Republicanism*, ed. Gisela Bock, Quentin Skinner, and Maurizio Viroli (Cambridge: Cambridge University Press, 1990), 121–41.

4. Brunetto Latini, *Tresor*, ed. Pietro G. Beltrami, Paolo Squillaccioti, Plinio Torri, and Sergio Vatteroni (Turin: Einaudi, 2007), 3.73:791.

5. Ibid., 3.74:793.

6. Nicolai Rubinstein, *The Palazzo Vecchio, 1298–1532: Government, Architecture, and Imagery in the Civic Palace of the Florentine Republic* (Oxford: Clarendon Press, 1995), 73.

7. Patricia Fortini Brown, *Art and Life in Renaissance Venice* (New York: Harry N. Abrams, 1997), 67.

8. Nelson, *The Hebrew Republic*, 2.

9. Konrad Burdach, *Riforma Rinascimento Umanesimo: Due dissertazioni sui fondamenti della cultura e dell'arte della parola moderne*, trans. Delio Cantimori (Florence: Sansoni, 1935), 92–93, 95.

10. Francesco Petrarca, *Prose*, ed. Guido Martellotti (Milan: Ricciardi, 1955), 981–87.

11. Paolo Viti, ed., *Opere letterarie e politiche di Leonardo Bruni* (Turin, UTET, 1996), 568–69, 646–47, 48–49.

12. See Eugenio Garin, "I cancellieri umanisti della Repubblica Fiorentina da Coluccio Salutati a Bartolomeo Scala," in *La cultura filosofica del Rinascimento italiano* (Florence: Sansoni, 1961).

13. Michael Allen Gillespie, *The Theological Origins of Modernity* (Chicago: University of Chicago Press, 2008), 69–100.

14. On the influence of Machiavelli's ideas on later English and US conceptions of civic religion, see Mark Goldie, "The Civil Religion of James Harrington," in *The Languages of Political Theory in Early-Modern Europe*, ed. Anthony Pagden (Cambridge: Cambridge University Press, 1987), 197–222.

15. Alberto Mario Banti and Paul Ginsborg, "Per una nuova storia del Risorgimento," in *Storia d'Italia, Annali 22, Il Risorgimento*, ed. Alberto Mario Banti and Paul Ginsborg (Turin: Einaudi, 2007), xviii–xxxiv; see also Alberto Mario Banti, *La nazione del Risorgimento. Parentela, sanità e onore alle origini dell'Italia unita* (Turin: Einaudi, 2000).

16. This basic distinction has been stressed in Paul Ginsborg, *Salviamo l'Italia* (Turin: Einaudi, 2010), 34–41); see also Lucy Riall, *Il Risorgimento: Storia e interpretazioni* (Rome: Donzelli, 2007).

17. This distinction escapes Simon Levi Sullam, who grants Mazzini the distinction of having produced one of the highest expressions of political religion within European nationalism of the early nineteenth century, "'Dio e il Popolo': la rivoluzione religiosa di Giuseppe Mazzini," in *Storia d'Italia, Annali 22, Il Risorgimento*, ed. Alberto Mario Banti and Paul Ginsborg (Turin: Einaudi, 2007), 401–22; Simon Levi Sullam, "Nazione, religione, rivoluzione: Risorgimento italiano e religioni politiche," *Società e Storia* 17 (2004): 681–86; Simon Levi Sullam, "'Fate della rivoluzione una religione.' Aspetti del nazionalismo mazziniano come religione politica (1831–1835)," *Società e Storia* 17 (2004): 705–30. How can such a title be bestowed on a thinker who considered the nation a medium to attain the principle of humanity and the brotherhood of nations; drafted a constitution (for the Roman Republic of 1849) asserting that "the republic regards all peoples as brothers, respects all nationalities; promotes the Italian one" ("La Repubblica riguarda tutti i popoli come fratelli: rispetta ogni nazionalità: propugna l'italiana"); and declares freedom of thought and teaching an inviolable right (in Mazzini's *Of the Rights and Duties of Citizens*). Stefano Recchia and Nadia Urbinati correctly call Mazzini's position "a cosmopolitanism of nations" (*A Cosmopolitanism of Nations: Giuseppe Mazzini's Writings on Democracy, Nation Building, and International Relations*, ed. and intro. Stefano Recchia and Nadia Urbinati [Princeton, NJ: Princeton University Press, 2009]). I stress the profound difference between Mazzini's patriotism and nineteenth-century nationalism in my *For Love of Country: An Essay on Patriotism and Nationalism* (Oxford: Oxford University Press, 1995), 144–53.

18. "Protesta contro il manifesto degli intellettuali fascisti," *Il Giornale d'Italia*, May 1, 1925.

19. See Giovanni Pugliese Carratelli's splendid preface to Adolfo Omodeo, *L'Età del Risorgimento Italiano*, rev. 4th ed. (Naples: Vivarium, 1996), 7–11.

20. (Religious people can be slaves, but no irreligious people ever remained free.) See Benjamin Constant, *De la religion considérée dans sa source, ses formes et ses développements*, ed. Pierre Deguise (Lausanne: Bibliothèque romande, 1971), 85–87.

21. On this subject, see Robert Putnam, *American Grace: How Religion Divides and Unites Us* (New York: Simon and Schuster, 2010).

INTRODUCTION

1. Jacob Burckhardt, *Die Kultur der Renaissance in Italien* (Leipzig: Seeman, 1877–78). Translated by S.G.C. Middlemore as *The Civilization of the Renaissance in Italy* (New York: Macmillan, 1890), 542.

2. Hans Baron, *The Crisis of Early Italian Renaissance* (Princeton, NJ: Princeton University Press, 1966). A critical correction to Baron's interpretation can be found in Donald Weinstein's work. His *Savonarola and Florence: Prophecy and Patriotism in the Renaissance* (Princeton, NJ: Princeton University Press, 1970) is a precise reconstruction of the role of religious prophecy in the birth of the Republic of Florence in 1494 as well as the formation of the ideas concerning republican liberty. Weinstein explains that Savonarola's movement was not at all a medieval aberration in the life of a modern city but rather exemplary of an adaptation of Christian doctrine to the ends and hopes of a society that lived republican patriotism in a profound way. That being said, Weinstein insists too much on an allegedly uniquely Florentine compenetration between Christianity and the republican spirit. Savonarola's interpretation was undoubtedly unique; but the compenetration also existed in other republican cities.

3. John Greville Agard Pocock, *The Machiavellian Moment: Florentine Political Thought and the Atlantic Republican Tradition* (Princeton, NJ: Princeton University Press, 1975), 462.

4. Ibid., 193–94, 213–14.

5. Quentin Skinner, *The Foundations of Modern Political Thought* (Cambridge: Cambridge University Press, 1978), 1:19ff.

6. Ibid., 1:34, 77–78.

7. Ibid., 1:100–101.

8. Ibid., 1:167–68.

9. Niccolò Machiavelli, *Discorsi sopra la prima deca di Tito Livio*, 3:40, in vol. 1, *Opere*, ed. Corrado Vivanti (Turin: Einaudi-Gallimard, 1997). Translated by Harvey C. Mansfield and Nathan Tarcov as *Discourses on Livy* (Chicago: University of Chicago Press, 1998).

10. Alexis de Tocqueville, *De la Démocratie en Amérique*, ed. Eduardo Nolla (Paris: Vrin, 1990), 1:35–36. Translated by George Lawrence and edited by J. P. Mayer as *Democracy in America* (New York: Harper and Row, 2000), 47.

11. Ferruccio Parri, "Le speranze della Resistenza," in *Il nostro Parri*, ed. Sandro Pertini et al. (Vicenza: Neri Pozza, 1983), 88.

12. On this point, see Walter Barberis, *Il bisogno di patria* (Turin: Einaudi, 2004), 4–7.

13. Niccolò Machiavelli, *Dell'arte della guerra*, in *Opere*, ed. Corrado Vivanti (Turin: Einaudi-Gallimard, 1997), 689.

CHAPTER 1: REPUBLICS PROTECTED BY GOD

1. Augustine Thompson, O.P., *Cities of God: The Religion of the Italian Communes, 1125–1325* (University Park: Pennsylvania State University Press, 2005), 103–40.

2. *Oculus pastoralis*, 1:1–11. I am quoting from Dora Franceschi, ed., *Oculus Pastoralis*, cited in *Memorie dell'Accademia delle Scienze di Torino* 11 (1966): 1–75.

3. Ibid., 3:58–61, 4:81–89.

4. Ibid., 2:1–15, 3:59–68.

5. Ibid., 2:45–56, 2:125–30.

6. Ibid., 4:43–45, 80–96.

7. Ibid., 5:205–10.

8. Ibid., 6:265–75.

9. Orfino da Lodi, *De regimine et sapientia potestatis*, ed. Sandra Pozzi (Lodi: Archivio Storico Lodigiano, 1998), verses 310–15, 410–15, 465, 822–23.

10. Brunetto Latini, *Livres dou Tresor*, ed. Pietro G. Beltrami, Paolo Squillaccioti, Plinio Torri, and Sergio Vatteroni (Turin: Einaudi, 2007), 3.73:791.

11. Ibid., 3.74:793.

12. Ibid., 2.126:625, 2.128:627, 2.127:625.

13. Ibid., 3.75:797, 3.79:808–9, 3.84:823, 3.97:844–45.

CHAPTER 2: IMAGES OF THE CIVIL RELIGION

1. "Li angelichi fiorecti, rose e gigli, / onde s'adorna lo celeste prato, / non mi dilettan più che i buon' consigli. / Ma talor veggio chi per proprio stato / disprezza me e la mia ter[r]a inganna, / e quando parla peggio è più lodato. / Guardi ciascun cui questo dir conda[n]na."

2. "Diletti miei, ponete nelle menti / che li devoti vostri preghi onesti / come vorrete voi farò contenti. / Ma se i potenti a' debil' fien molesti, / gravando loro con vergogne o danni, / le vostre orazion non son per questi / né per chiunque la mia terra inganni."

3. Nicolai Rubinstein, "Political Ideas in Sienese Art: The Frescoes by Ambrogio Lorenzetti and Taddeo di Bartolo in the Palazzo Pubblico," *Journal of the Warburg and Courtauld Institutes* 21 (1958): 179–207. On this theme, see Maria Monica Donato's excellent study, "Ancora sulle 'fonti' nel Buon Governo di Ambrogio Lorenzetti: Dubbi, precisazioni, anticipazioni," in *Politica e cultura nelle repubbliche italiane dal medioevo all'età moderna*, ed. Simonetta Adorni Braccesi and Mario Ascheri (Rome: Istituto Storico Italiano per l'Età Moderna e Contemporanea, 2001), 43–79.

4. "QUESTA SANTA VIRTU [la Giustizia] LADDOVE REGGE INDUCE ADUNITA LIANIMI MOLTI. EQUESTI ACCIO RICCOLTI UN BEN COMUN PERLOR SIGROR SIFANNO."

5. Quentin Skinner, *Visions of Politics*, vol. II, *Renaissance Virtues* (Cambridge: Cambridge University Press, 2002), 99.

6. "LADOUE STA LEGATA LA IUSTITIA. NESUN ALBE(N) COMUNE GIAMAY / SACORDA. NE TIRA ADRITTA CORDA. P(ER)O CONVIE(N) CHE TIRANNIA / SORMONTI."

7. See also Thomas Aquinas, *Summa Theologiae*, Pars Prima Secundae, question 97, art. 4.

8. "Caritas non quaerit quae sua sunt, quod hoc sit est intelligendum, quia caritas communia propriis anteponit"; Remigio de' Girolami, *De bono pacis*, in

La "teologia politica comunale" di Remigio de' Girolami, ed. Maria Consiglia De Matteis (Bologna: Patron Editore, 1977), 56–57. See also Charles T. Davis, "An Early Florentine Political Theorist: Fra Remigio de' Girolami," *Proceedings of the American Philosophical Society* 54 (1960): 662–76. On the relationship between civic conscience and charity of country, see A. Bosisio, "Milano e la sua coscienza cittadina nel Duecento," in *Atti dei Convegni del Centro Studi sulla Spiritualità medievale* (Todi, 1972), 47–93.

9. Remigio de' Girolami, *De bono communi*, in *La "teologia politica comunale" di Remigio de' Girolami*, ed. Maria Consiglia De Matteis (Bologna: Patron Editore, 1977), 43. See also Charles T. Davis, "Remigio de' Girolami and Dante: A Comparison of Their Conceptions of Peace," *Studi Danteschi* 36 (1959): 105–36, and "An Early Florentine Political Theorist."

10. "Amor patriae in radice charitatis fundatur, quae communia propriis, non propria communibus anteponit"; Tolomeo da Lucca, *De regimine principum*, in *Divi Thomae Aquinatis Opuscula Philosophice*, ed. Raimondo Spiazzi (Turin: Marietti, 1954), 299. Augustine disappoves of the ancients' love of country in *De civitate Dei*, 5:12; see also Charles T. Davis, "Ptolemy of Lucca, and the Roman Republic," *Proceedings of the American Philosophical Society* 118 (1974): 30–50.

11. Dante Alighieri, *Opere minori*, vol. 1, part 2, ed. Cesare Vasoli and Domenico De Robertis (Milan: Riccardo Ricciardi Editore, 1979), 571–73. Petrarch instead considers the ancients' love (charity) of country to be an imperfect love, and does not accept the idea of a specifically Christian patriotism. See Charles Trinkaus, *In Our Image and Likeness: Humanity and Divinity in Italian Humanist Thought* (London: Constable, 1970), 1:37–38. In *De vita solitaria*, however, Petrarch maintains that nothing is more suitable for man, and nothing renders him more similar to God, than working toward the common good: "quid aut homine dignius aut similius Deo est, quam servare et adiuvare quam plurimos?" (cited in Guido Martellotti, ed., *Prose* [Milan: Ricciardi, 1955], 322, 328).

12. Robert Freyan, "The Evolution of the Caritas Figures in the Thirteenth and Fourteenth Centuries," *Journal of the Warburg and Courtauld Institutes* 11 (1948): 68–82.

13. Rodolfo Funari, ed., *Un ciclo di tradizione repubblicana nel Palazzo Pubblico di Siena: Le iscrizioni degli affreschi di Taddeo di Bartolo (1413–1414)* (Siena: Accademia Senese degli Intronati, 2002), 5.

14. Ibid., 25, 31.

15. To ensure his political and religious lesson was clear, Taddeo di Bartolo places a long inscription, in the vernacular, on the main wall:

> You who rule, mirror yourselves in these men / If you want to rule for thousands of years, / Pursue the common good and do not be led astray / If you have any passion within you / The more you remain united the more you will be powerful / And will rise to the sky full of glory / As the great followers of Mars did, / a people that had won the whole world, / but then, as they had factions / Lost liberty everywhere" (Specchiatevi in costoro voi che reggete / Se volete regnare mille et mille anni, / Seguite il ben comune et non v'inganni / Se alcuna passione in voi avete / Dritti consegli come quei rendete, / Che qui di sotto sono con longhi panni / Giusti co' l'arme ne' comuni affanni, / Come questi altri che qua giù vedete. / Sempre magiori sarete

insieme uniti / Et saglirete al cielo pieno d'ogni gloria / Si come fecie il gran popolo di marte, / El quale avendo del mondo victoria, / Perché infra loro si furo dentro partiti / Perdé la libertade in ogni parte).

16. See Horst W. Janson, *The Sculpture of Donatello* (Princeton, NJ: Princeton University Press, 1963), 3–7. See also Nicolai Rubinstein, *The Palazzo Vecchio, 1298–1532: Government, Architecture, and Imagery in the Civic Palace of the Florentine Republic* (Oxford: Clarendon Press, 1995), 55–56; Donato, "Ancora sulle 'fonti' nel Buon Governo di Ambrogio Lorenzetti."

17. See Rubinstein, *The Palazzo Vecchio*, 52–53; A. Teresa Hankey, "Salutati's Epigrams for the Palazzo Vecchio at Florence," *Journal of the Warburg and Courtauld Institutes* 22 (1959): 363–65.

18. See Rubinstein, *The Palazzo Vecchio*, 64.

19. See ibid., 73.

Chapter 3: Republican and Monarchical Religion

1. The best study on sacred kingship is still that of the late Clifford Geertz, "Centers, Kings, and Charisma: Reflections on the Symbolics of Power," in *Culture and Its Creators: Essays in Honor of Edward Shils*, ed. Joseph Ben-David and Terry Nichols Clark (Chicago: University of Chicago Press, 1977), 150–71.

2. Ernst H. Kantorowicz, *The King's Two Bodies: A Study in Mediaeval Political Theology, with a New Preface by William Chester Jordan* (Princeton, NJ: Princeton University Press, 1997), 209–10.

3. Ibid., 216–23.

4. Marc Bloch, *Les rois thaumaturges* (Strasbourg: Librairie Istra, 1924), 69–70.

5. Ibid., 186.

6. Ibid., 194.

7. "Quant le roy se despoille, c'est signifiance qu'il relenquist l'estat mondain de par devant pour prendre celui de la religion royale; et s'il le prent en tele devocion comme il doit, je tieng qu'il est telement nettoié de ses pechiez comme celui qui entre nouvellement en religion esprouvée: de quoy dit saint Bernart ou livre *de precepto et dispensacione* vers la fin: que aussi comme ou baptesme les pechiez sont pardonnez, aussi à l'entrée de la religion" (ibid., 483).

8. Ibid., 201.

9. Ibid., 211. Jean Gerson, one of the principals of Christian mysticism, utters the following words when preaching before Charles VI: "Roy tres crestien, roy par miracle consacré, roy espirituel et sacerdotal" (ibid., 213).

10. Ibid., 10.

11. Gina Fasoli, "Liturgia e cerimonia ducale," in *Venezia e il Levante fino al secolo XV*, ed. Agostino Pertusi (Florence: Leo S. Olschki, 1973), 261–95.

12. Ibid., 278.

13. "Ut populum Venecie regas et protegas"; Fasoli, "Liturgia e cerimonia ducale," 276.

14. Edward Muir, *Il rituale civico a Venezia nel Rinascimento* (Rome: Il Veltro Editrice, 1984), 218–19.

15. Matteo Casini, *I gesti del principe: La festa politica a Firenze e Venezia in età rinascimentale* (Venice: Marsilio, 1996).

16. Ibid., 230.

17. Cited in ibid., 234–36.

Chapter 4: A Religion That Instills Virtue

1. Francesco Novati, ed., *Epistolario di Coluccio Salutati* (Rome: Istituto Storico Italiano, 1891–1911), 1:21, 2:87, 3:638.

2. Ibid., 1:253–54, 318.

3. Ibid., 4:20.

4. Ibid., 3:285–308.

5. Eugenio Garin, "I trattati morali di Coluccio Salutati," in *Atti e memorie dell'Accademia fiorentina di scienze morali la Colombaria* (Florence: Felice Le Monnier, 1947), 1:62. See also Eugenio Garin, "I cancellieri umanisti della Repubblica Fiorentina da Coluccio Salutati a Bartolomeo Scala," in *La cultura filosofica del Rinascimento italiano* (Florence: Sansoni, 1961), 11.

6. Eugenio Garin, *La cultura filosofica del Rinascimento italiano* (Florence: Sansoni, 1961), 128. On the evolution of Salutati's thought from Stoicism to Christianity, see Ronald G. Witt, *Hercules at the Crossroads: The Life, Works, and Thought of Coluccio Salutati* (Durham, NC: Duke University Press, 1983), 355–67.

7. Coluccio Salutati, *De nobilitate legum et medicinae*, ed. Eugenio Garin (Florence: Vallecchi, 1947), 98, 166.

8. To clarify this essential aspect of his Christian conception of the law and the Christian citizen's ideal, Salutati quotes the Book of Proverbs (29:18), "Happy is he who keeps the law," and comments that he is "truly happy when he has lived according to the law" (ibid., 166–67).

9. Witt, *Hercules at the Crossroads*, 342–43.

10. "Loquetur ad eum Deus facie ad faciem, sicut home ad amicum suum"; Salutati, *De nobilitate legum et medicinae*, 55.

11. See Vespasiano da Bisticci, *Vite di uomini illustri del secolo XV* (Florence: Rinascimento del libro, 1938), 456.

12. Leon Battista Alberti, "I libri della famiglia," in *Opere volgari*, ed. Cecil Grayson (Bari: Laterza, 1960), 182–84.

13. Matteo Palmieri, *Della vita civile*, ed. Felice Battaglia (Bologna: Zanichelli, 1944), 45.

Resta dunque che in terra non si faccia niuna cosa più cara nè più accetta a Dio, che con iustizia reggere e governare le congregazioni e moltitudini d'uomini, unitamente con iustizia ragunati: per questo promette Iddio a' giusti governatori delle città, e conservatori della patria, in cielo determinato luogo, nel quale eternalmente beati vivono co' suoi santi [Nothing is therefore dearer to or more well accepted by God than justly ruling and governing the congregations and multitudes of men who are justly assembled in unity: hence does God promise to the just governors of the cities and the preservers of the fatherland an assured place in heaven, where they forever happy will live together with the saints].

14. Ibid., 168.

15. Giannozzo Manetti, "De dignitate et excellentia hominis," in *Prosatori latini del Quattrocento*, ed. Eugenio Garin (Milan: Ricciardi, 1952), 459, 485–87.

16. Lorenzo Valla, *Scritti filosofici e religiosi*, ed. Giorgio Radetti (Florence: Sansoni, 1953), 195.

17. Lorenzo Valla, *Collatio Novi Testamenti*, ed. Alessandro Perosa (Florence: Sansoni, 1970). The first printed edition of this work, written between 1442 and 1444, came out in Paris in 1505, thanks to the initiative of Desiderius Erasmus.

18. Compare Charles Trinkaus, *In Our Image and Likeness: Humanity and Divinity in Italian Humanist Thought* (London: Constable, 1970), 385.

19. Bartolomeo Sacchi (Platina), *De optimo cive*, ed. Felice Battaglia (Bologna: Zanichelli, 1944), 206.

20. On Ficino's religiosity, meant as "Paul's doctrine and practice of *caritas*, i.e., a faith in and experience of divine love, beyond any motive of separation and discord," compare Cesare Vasoli, "Dalla pace religiosa alla 'prisca theologia,' " in *Firenze e il Concilio del 1439: Convegno di Studi*, ed. Paolo Viti (Florence: Leo S. Olschki, 1994), 1:3–25.

21. Marsilio Ficino, *Libro di Marsilio Ficino Florentino Della Cristiana Religione ad Bernardo del Nero Clarissimo Cittadino Fiorentino* (n.p.: Proemio, n.d.).

22. Ibid., chapter 8.

23. Cesare Vasoli, "Giovanni Nesi tra Donato Acciaiuoli e Girolamo Savonarola: Testi editi e inediti," *Memorie Domenicane* NS 4 (1973), 103–79, 110.

24. Ibid., 150.

25. Ibid., 151.

26. Giovanni Pico della Mirandola, *De hominis dignitate*, ed. Eugenio Garin (Florence: Vallecchi, 1942), 106–7.

Chapter 5: Sacred Laws and Sacred Republics

1. Coluccio Salutati, *De nobilitate legum et medicinae*, ed. Eugenio Garin (Florence: Vallecchi, 1947), chapter 5; Eugenio Garin, "I cancellieri umanisti della Repubblica Fiorentina da Coluccio Salutati a Bartolomeo Scala," in *La cultura filosofica del Rinascimento italiano* (Florence: Sansoni, 1961), 10–11, 14–15; Matteo Palmieri, *Della vita civile*, ed. Felice Battaglia (Bologna: Zanichelli, 1944), 93.

2. Palmieri, *Della vita civile*, 93.

3. Matteo Palmieri, "Libro del Poema chiamato Città di vita composto da Matteo Palmieri Fiorentino," in *Smith College Studies in Modern Languages*, ed. Margaret Rooke (1927–28), 8:vii–ix.

4. Ibid., 3:22, vv. 26–35.

5. "Qui saper basti insino al cielo trovoro / esser saliti que che vixon giusti / and con giustitia in terra governoro" (It suffices to know here that to heaven / have risen those who lived upright / and with justice ruled on earth) (ibid., vv. 49–50).

6. Ibid., vv. 6–10.

7. Bartolomeo Sacchi (Platina), *De optimo cive*, ed. Felice Battaglia (Bologna: Zanichelli, 1944), 185.

8. Ibid., 186–87.

9. Ibid., 187–88.

10. Ibid., 189–90.

11. Girolamo Savonarola, *Prediche sopra Aggeo con il Trattato circa el reggimento e governo della città di Firenze*, ed. Luigi Firpo (Rome: Angelo Belardetti Editore, 1965), 422–23.

12. As Savonarola (ibid., 436) explains,

I have preached for many years by God's will in this city, and have pursued four topics: proving, through the efforts of all my intellectual abilities, that faith is true; demonstrating that the Christian life's simplicity is the highest wisdom; foretelling future events, some of which have already occurred and some others are soon approaching; and, finally, the new government of this city of yours. And since I have written about the first three (but the third book, titled *Della verità profetica*, remains to be published), I still ought to write about the fourth topic, so that the whole world can see that we preach a healthy science, and in agreement with natural reason and the doctrine of the Church.

13. Ibid., 456–66.

14. See Donald Weinstein, *Savonarola and Florence: Prophecy and Patriotism in the Renaissance* (Princeton, NJ: Princeton University Press, 1970), 289–316.

15. Savonarola, *Prediche sopra Aggeo*, 467–68.

16. Ibid., 469–70.

17. Ibid., 476–77.

18. Ibid., 487.

19. Weinstein, *Savonarola and Florence*, 324–33. Weinstein ("Critical Issues in the Study of Civic Religion in Renaissance Florence," in *The Pursuit of Holiness in Late Medieval and Renaissance Religion*, ed. Charles Trinkaus and Heiko Oberman [Leiden: E. J. Brill, 1974], 265) emphasizes the presence of "a characteristically *civic* set of religious modalities arising out of the special experience of Italian communal life." See also David S. Peterson, "Religion, Politics, and the Church in Fifteenth-Century Florence," in *Girolamo Savonarola: Piety, Prophecy, and Politics in Renaissance Florence*, ed. Donald Weinstein and Valerie R. Hotchkiss (Dallas: Bridwell Library, 1994), 75–83; Timothy Verdon and John Henderson, eds., *Christianity and the Renaissance: Image and Religious Imagination in the Quattrocento* (Syracuse, NY: Syracuse University Press, 1990).

20. Savonarola, *Prediche sopra Aggeo*, 51, 102, 245. On the last point, see Lorenzo Polizzotto, *The Elect Nation: The Savonarolan Movement in Florence (1494–1545)* (Oxford: Clarendon Press, 1994); Guidubaldo Guidi, *Lotte, pensiero e istituzioni politiche nella repubblica fiorentina dal 1492 al 1512*, 3 vols. (Florence: Olsckhi, 1992). On the Florentines' "civil" religiosity and charity, see Arnaldo D'Addario, *Aspetti della Controriforma a Firenze* (Rome: Pubblicazioni degli Archivi di Stato, 1972), 3.

21. Savonarola, *Prediche sopra Aggeo*, 274, 111–12, 205–6.

22. Ibid., 483.

23. Ibid., 484.

24. Ibid., 336–37. See also Pasquale Villari, *La storia di Girolamo Savonarola e de' suoi tempi*, vol. 1, *La storia di Girolamo Savonarola e de' suoi tempi* (Florence: Le Monnier, 1887–88), where Savonarola writes: "Lex est ordinatio rationis ad bonum comune, ab eo qui curam comunitatis habet promulgata" (23), and "idest a Deo, qui universa gubernat ad bonum comune, id est ad se ipsum qui est omne bonum, iuxta Ex., 333 *Ostendat tibi omne bonum*" (24). Savonarola maintains that Florence's political and religious reform would have been a return to the ancient way of life. See Felix Gilbert, "Florentine Political Assumptions in the Period of Savonarola and Soderini," *Journal of the Warburg and Courtauld Institutes* 20 (1957): 211.

25. Savonarola, *Prediche sopra Aggeo*, 469–70, 466–69, 481–87.

26. Ibid., 134–35.

27. Girolamo Savonarola, *Prediche italiane ai Fiorentini* (Perugia: La Nuova Italia, 1930), 2:390.

28. See Felix Gilbert, "Florentine Political Assumptions in the Period of Savonarola and Soderini," *Journal of the Warburg and Courtauld Institutes* 20 (1957): 207.

29. Ibid.

30. Ibid.

31. "Referendovi sempre piutosto al consiglio christiano che philosophico perché è più secondo Iddio" (referring always to Christian reasoning rather than philosophical reasoning, for the former is more in accordance with God), July 17, 1512; ibid., 6:208.

32. Ibid., 6:210.

33. Ibid.

34. Lamberto del Nero Cambi, in Benedetto Varchi, *Storia fiorentina* (Florence: Salani, 1963), 1:10.6, pp. 627–28.

35. Ibid.

36. Ibid.

37. Varchi, *Storia fiorentina*, 3:10.9.

38. Cambi, in Varchi, *Storia fiorentina*, 1:10.6, pp. 628, 633–34.

Chapter 6: Republican Religion and Religious Reform

1. In "Desideri di riforma nell'oratoria del Cinquecento" (in *Contributi alla storia del Concilio di Trento e della Controriforma* [Florence: Vallecchi editore, 1948], 1–11), Eugenio Garin writes that the need for a moral reform of the church and the Christian community expressed itself in a

controversy, sometimes harsh and enraged, against the clergy's mundanity, the Curia's temporal claims and corruption. It also resulted in an invective against the hypocrisy and the moral failure of the religious orders, especially of the mendicant ones. And finally, it uttered a call for an inner life where religion and morality can be reconciled. At the same time, this was to be a renewed appraisal of the individual who is active in civil solidarity, where inner faith and fruitful work converge. These are the themes that permeate the whole pre-Reformation moralistic literature, together with a faithful awaiting of a new Christian spring, which witnesses the conversion of a humanity renewed under the sign of Christ's religion, taken as a true religion of man.

Compare also Delio Cantimori, *Umanesimo e religione nel Rinascimento* (Turin: Einaudi, 1975), especially 142–57, 256–58; Cesare Vasoli, *Civitas mundi: Studi sulla cultura del Cinquecento* (Rome: Edizioni di Storia e Letteratura, 1996), and *Le filosofie del Rinascimento*, ed. Paolo Costantino Pissavino (Milan: Bruno Mondadori, 2002), 154–74.

2. For the biblical sources, see, for instance, "Et dabo eis cor aliud et spiritum novum tribuam in visceribus eorum" (Ezek. 11:19); "Et dabo vobis cor novum et spiritum novum ponam in medio vestri" (Ezek. 36:26).

3. Ovid, *Metamorphoses*, 9.399.

4. Ibid., 15:165, 184, 215, 270, 274, 391–402.

5. "Reformatur qualis fuit ante figura"; Lactantius, *De ave Phoenice*, 5.105.

6. Compare Konrad Burdach, *Riforma Rinascimento Umanesimo: Due dissertazioni sui fondamenti della cultura e dell'arte della parola moderne*, Italian trans. Delio Cantimori (Florence: Sansoni,1935), 23–26.

7. "Renovamini autem spiritu mentis vestrae et induite novum hominem" (Eph. 4:22); "induentes novum [hominem] eum, qui renovatur…secundum imaginem eius, qui creavit illum" (Col. 3:10).

8. See Luigi Salvatorelli, *Vita di San Francesco d'Assisi* (Bari: Laterza, 1926), 25–26.

9. Dante, *Convivio* 4.12, 14.

10. Virgil, *Eclogues*, 4.5.

11. Dante, *Purgatorio*, 33.143–45.

12. Burdach, *Riforma Rinascimento Umanesimo*, 16.

13. Ibid., 16, 21–22. See also ibid., 17.

14. Ibid., 19.

15. On Petrarch's religion, see Ugo Dotti, *La città dell'uomo* (Rome: Editori Riuniti, 1992); Giuseppe Billanovich, "Nella biblioteca del Petrarca, I; il Petrarca, il Boccaccio e le *Enarrationes in Psalmos* di S.Agostino," *Italia medioevale e umanistica* 3 (1960): 1–27.

16. Burdach, *Riforma Rinascimento Umanesimo*, 92–93, 95.

17. Raffaello Morghen (*Civiltà medievale al tramonto* [Bari: Laterza, 1971]) writes that such "ancient deeds" are not the heroic deeds of the saints and martyrs but rather "the great deeds of the forefathers, the 'virtuous Romans.'" The ancient deeds that will generate the new golden age "must undoubtedly be searched [for] in the examples of 'virtue' and 'glory' transmitted to us by the tradition of our fathers, and the rebirth of the ancient virtues, together with the cult of Christ, will bring us to the final victory over the *Ecclesia carnalis*, thereby constituting the fundamental elements of that *docta pietas* which will be the most lively ideal of Christian humanism."

18. Eugenio Garin, "I cancellieri umanisti della Repubblica Fiorentina da Coluccio Salutati a Bartolomeo Scala," in *La cultura filosofica del Rinascimento italiano* (Florence: Sansoni, 1961), 11.

19. Leonardo Bruni, *Istoria Fiorentina di Leonardo Aretino, tradotta in volgare da Donato Acciajuoli* (Florence: Le Monnier, 1861), 24–25. See also Vasoli, *Civitas mundi*, 217–18; Riccardo Fubini, "Cultura umanistica e tradizione cittadina nella storiografia fiorentina del '400," *Atti e Memorie dell'Accademia Toscana di scienze e lettere "La Colombaria"* 56 (1991): 65–102; Paolo Viti, *Leonardo Bruni cancelliere della Repubblica di Firenze: Convegno di studi (Firenze, 27–29 ottobre 1987)* (Florence: Olshki, 1990).

20. Eugenio Garin, *L'età nuova. Ricerche di storia della cultura dal XII al XVI secolo* (Naples: Morano, 1969), 96–97. The need for spiritual renewal and a revolt against the corruption of the clergy was also strong in such highly religious men as Galateo (Antonio de Ferrariis, 1444–1517), who wrote invectives against the hypocrisy of the monks. He denounces them not only for being evil—for instance, when they protect "usurers, the unjust, those who steal the property of others, and those who batten off the people"—but also for making "God an accomplice to their rapines," and thus, through fraud, establishing a religion that "does not remove vices but conceals them." See Antonio de Ferrariis (Galateo), *Esposizione del Pater noster* (Lecce: Collana di scrittori di Terra d'Otranto, 1868, 1871), 4:145–238, 18:5–104, *L'Heremita* (Lecce: Collana di scrittori di Terra d'Otranto, 1875), 12:3–134. Even a pious and melancholy humanist such as Lapo da Castiglionchio, who died in 1438 in Ferrara while attending the council as a secretary to the Roman Curia, perceived with sincere mortification how grievous the church's corruption had become; Lapo da Castiglionchio, "Dialogus de curiae commodis," in *Prosatori latini del Quattrocento*, ed. Eugenio Garin (Milan: Ricciardi, 1952), 171.

21. Poggio Bracciolini, "Epistole," in *Prosatori latini del Quattrocento*, ed. Eugenio Garin (Milan: Ricciardi, 1952), 220–29.

22. Ibid., 229–41.

23. Francesco Vettori, *Viaggio in Alamagna*, in *Scritti storici e politici*, ed. Enrico Nicolini (Bari: Laterza, 1972), 42, 25.

24. Francesco Vettori, *Sommario della istoria d'Italia*, in *Scritti storici e politici*, ed. Enrico Nicolini (Bari: Laterza, 1972), 157.

25. Vettori, *Viaggio in Alamagna*, 32.

26. Ibid., 20–21. On Bernardo (or Bernardino), see the entry edited by Giampaolo P. Tognetti in *Dizionario Biografico degli Italiani*, vol. 9 (Rome: Istituto della Enciclopedia Italiana, 1967). See also Ottavia Niccoli, *Profeti e popolo nell'Italia del Cinquecento* (Bari: Laterza, 1987).

27. The reference is to Matthew 22:37.

28. Vettori, *Viaggio in Alamagna*, 40–41.

29. Niccolò Machiavelli, "Legazioni e commissarie," in *Opere*, ed. Corrado Vivanti (Turin: Einaudi, 1999), 2:1370–71.

30. Bartolomeo Cerretani, *Dialogo della mutatione di Firenze*, ed. Raul Mordenti (Rome: Edizioni di Storia e Letteratura, 1990), 18–19.

31. Ibid., 4–5. On this point, see Paolo Simoncelli's excellent study "Preludi e primi echi di Lutero a Firenze," *Storia e politica* 22 (1983): 674–744, especially 699–702.

32. Girolamo Savonarola, *Prediche sopra Aggeo con il Trattato circa el reggimento e governo della città di Firenze*, ed. Luigi Firpo (Rome: Angelo Belardetti Editore, 1965), 239. On this point, see Cesare Vasoli's remarks in Vasoli, *Civitas mundi*, 8, 51–52.

33. Savonarola, *Prediche sopra Aggeo*, 243.

34. Ibid., 205.

35. Giovanni Pico della Mirandola, *De hominis dignitate*, ed. Eugenio Garin (Florence: Vallecchi editore, 1942), 106–7.

Chapter 7: A Religion to Live Free

1. Niccolò Machiavelli, *Dell'arte della guerra*, in *Opere di Niccolò Machiavelli*, ed. Corrado Vivanti (Turin: Einaudi-Gallimard, 1997), 1:689.

2. Niccolò Machiavelli, *Canto degli spiriti beati*, in *Opere di Niccolò Machiavelli*, ed. Corrado Vivanti (Turin: Einaudi, 2005), 3:28.

3. Niccolò Machiavelli, *Discorsi sopra la prima deca di Tito Livio*, in *Opere di Niccolò Machiavelli*, ed. Corrado Vivanti (Turin: Einaudi-Gallimard, 1997), 1:1:12, 233.

4. Ibid., 1:2:2, 333.

5. Ibid., 1:2:2, 334. Savonarola praises humility and charity in his *Trattato dell'umiltà*, written in 1492: "Humility and charity are two virtues at the extremities of the spiritual edifice; for humility provides its foundation, and charity the perfection and consummation of the whole"; cited in Pasquale Villari, *La storia di Girolamo Savonarola e de' suoi tempi* (Florence: Le Monnier, 1887–88), 1:116.

6. See, above all, Isaiah Berlin, "The Originality of Machiavelli," in *Studies on Machiavelli*, ed. Myron P. Gilmore (Florence: Sansoni, 1970), 168–70, 172–74, 198. See also Friedrick Mainecke, *L'idea della ragion di stato nella storia moderna* (Florence: Vallecchi, 1942), 1:47–48. See also Maurizio Viroli, *From Politics to Reason of State: The Acquisition and Transformation of the Language of Politics (1250–1600)* (Cambridge: Cambridge University Press, 1993).

7. On religion in Machiavelli, see, among the most recent works, Corrado Vivanti, *Niccolò Machiavelli: I tempi della politica* (Rome: Donzelli, 2008); Francesco Bausi, *Machiavelli* (Rome: Salerno Editrice, 2005). See also Maurizio Viroli, *Il Dio di Machiavelli e il problema morale dell'Italia* (Rome: Laterza, 2005); translated as *Machiavelli's God* (Princeton, NJ: Princeton University Press, 2010).

8. Machiavelli, *Discorsi*, 2:2.

9. Niccolò Machiavelli, *Discorsi*, 3:1.

10. Niccolò Machiavelli, *Lettere: Francesco Vettori a Niccolò Machiavelli (5 agosto 1526)*, in *Opere di Niccolò Machiavelli*, ed. Corrado Vivanti (Turin: Einaudi, 1999), 2:435–37. In a letter to Machiavelli dated August 5, 1526, Vettori mentions the "Lutherans" without feeling any need to provide his friend with further explanations; cited in Montevecchi, *Opere di Niccolò Machiavelli*, 3:601. See also Paolo Simoncelli, "Preludi e primi echi di Lutero a Firenze," *Storia e politica* 22 (1983): 674–744; Silvana Seidel Menchi, "Le traduzioni italiane di Lutero nella prima metà del Cinquecento," *Rinascimento* 17 (1977): 31–108.

11. Machiavelli, *Discorsi*, 1:11.

12. Machiavelli, *Discorsi*, 1:1:11, 231.

13. Livy, *Ab urbe condita*, 1:21.

14. Machiavelli, *Discorsi*, 1:1:2, 202–3.

15. Ibid., 1:1:18, 245.

16. Ibid., 1:1:3, 207.

17. Ibid., 1:11.

18. Ibid., 1:1:58, 318.

19. Ibid., 1:1:11, 230.

20. Ibid. Besides Livy, Machiavelli's source on the Romans' religion was Polybius (*Historiae*, 6:56).

> In my opinion, the Roman government is especially noteworthy for its conception of the gods. I believe that, indeed, that which other peoples blamed— that is, superstition—appears to be the very thing by which this republic was chiefly kept united. This element was introduced among the Romans, both in the private sphere and in the public affairs of the city, in a degree that can hardly be exceeded. This may appear astonishing to many, but I believe they did this for the sake of the multitude. Indeed, were it possible to create a state composed of wise men only, probably there would be no need of any such measure; but since any multitude of people is inconstant and prey to lawless desires, irrational wrath, and violent passions, there is no way left to restrain them but by obscure fear, and by all this fiction. I argue, therefore, that not randomly nor rashly did the ancients spread among the multitude notions concerning the gods, and the belief in infernal punishments. Rather, those of the present age act randomly and rashly when they eliminate these things. For example, whereas in Greece, when just one single talent is entrusted to those who rule the commonwealth, and ten auditors are assigned and as many seals and twice as many witnesses, they are unable to discharge the trusts reposed in them with integrity, in Rome, on the other hand, those who, as magistrates and legates, handle the greatest sums of money, perform their duty with utmost honesty simply by virtue of the word given in an oath. Whereas, among other peoples, a man is rarely found who refrains from touching public money and who is hence pure in this respect, it is rare among the Romans to discover one that is tainted with such a crime.

21. Machiavelli, *Discorsi*, 1:2, 2:4. Bruni, too, had stressed the religiosity of the Etruscans (*religiosità degli Etruschi*); see Leonardo Bruni, *Historia fiorentina*, trans. Donato Acciaioli (Florence, 1476), book 1.

22. Machiavelli, *Discorsi*, 1:15.

23. Machiavelli, *Discorsi*, 1:55.

24. Ibid., 1:12.

25. Ibid.

26. Niccolò Machiavelli, *L'Asino*, in *Opere di Niccolò Machiavelli*, ed. Corrado Vivanti (Turin: Einaudi, 2005), 3:49–78. Evidence of the deep roots of the religion of idleness that Machiavelli (*Lettere*, 2:435–37) combats so strenuously can be found in the letter Vettori writes to Machiavelli on August 5, 1526: "We are having very poor harvests here [in Rome], and we hear that they are worse elsewhere;

so we judge that the year is going to be very bad, because of war, plague, and famine; and since in times of tribulation one turns toward God, still remembering that the saints have interceded in response to prayers and processions, we have tried to obtain from Our Lord a Jubilee for the middle of August, to be taken without money, and fasts, confessions, and prayers will suffice to take it."

27. Machiavelli, *Discorsi*, 1:55.

28. Ibid., 1:1:55, 310.

29. Ibid., 1:12.

30. Ibid., 2:5.

31. Ibid., 1:12.

32. Niccolò Machiavelli, *Istorie fiorentine*, in *Opere di Niccolò Machiavelli*, ed. Corrado Vivanti (Turin: Einaudi, 2005), 3:1:9, 324.

33. Ibid., 3:1:9, 325.

34. Ibid., 3:6:29, 613–14.

35. Machiavelli, *Discorsi*, 1:27. Francesco Guicciardini is even harsher than Machiavelli in his condemnation of the temporal power and corruption of the church. See Francesco Guicciardini, *Storia d'Italia*, in *Opere di Francesco Guicciardini*, ed. Emanuella Lugnani Scarano (Turin: UTET, 1981), 2:471–72.

36. "Conditions that were all accepted by Henry, and such a king did submit himself to a judgment to which today a private man would be ashamed to submit himself"; *Istorie fiorentine*, 1:19.

37. Machiavelli, *Discorsi*, 1:12.

38. "And when malice has greatness in itself or is generous in some part, they do not know how to enter into it"; ibid., 1:27.

CHAPTER 8: WITHIN THE SOUL

1. Niccolò Machiavelli, *Il Principe*, in *Opere di Niccolò Machiavelli*, ed. Corrado Vivanti (Turin: Einaudi-Gallimard, 1997), 1:26.

2. Niccolò Machiavelli, *Istorie fiorentine*, in *Opere di Niccolò Machiavelli*, ed. Corrado Vivanti (Turin: Einaudi, 2005), 3:1:5.

3. Flavio Biondo, *Le decadi*, trans. Achille Crespi (Comune di Forlì, 1963), 50.2.

4. See Giuliano Procacci, "Frate Andrea Alamanni confessore del Machiavelli?" in *Machiavelli nella cultura europea dell'età moderna* (Rome: Laterza, 1995), 423–31.

5. Niccolò Machiavelli, *Lettere: Niccolò Machiavelli a Giovanni Vernacci (26 giugno 1513)*, in *Opere di Niccolò Machiavelli*, ed. Corrado Vivanti (Turin: Einaudi, 1999), 2:264. See also the letters dated August 18, 1515, November 19, 1515, and February 15, 1516.

6. Niccolò Machiavelli, *Lettere: Niccolò Machiavelli a Francesco Guicciardini (17 maggio 1526)*, in *Opere di Niccolò Machiavelli*, ed. Corrado Vivanti (Turin: Einaudi, 1999), 2:426.

7. Niccolò Machiavelli, *Lettere*, in *Opere di Niccolò Machiavelli*, ed. Corrado Vivanti (Turin: Einaudi, 1999), 2:357 (*5 Gennaio 1518*), 2:387 (*31 Agosto 1523*), 2:455 (*2 Aprile 1527*).

8. Niccolò Machiavelli, *Decennale primo*, in *Opere di Niccolò Machiavelli*, ed. Corrado Vivanti (Turin: Einaudi-Gallimard, 1997), 1:94.

9. Ibid., 1:106.

10. Niccolò Machiavelli, *Clizia*, act 3, scene 6, in *Opere di Niccolò Machiavelli*, ed. Corrado Vivanti (Turin: Einaudi, 2005), 3:216–17.

11. Niccolò Machiavelli, *Discorsi sopra la prima deca di Tito Livio*, in *Opere di Niccolò Machiavelli*, ed. Corrado Vivanti (Turin: Einaudi-Gallimard, 1997), 1:1:12, 2:2.

12. Niccolò Machiavelli, *Discursus florentinarum rerum post mortem iunioris Laurentii medices*, in *Opere di Niccolò Machiavelli*, ed. Corrado Vivanti (Turin: Einaudi-Gallimard, 1997), 1:744. Machiavelli's God is first of all the God of captains, princes, lawgivers, and the strong in general. Castruccio Castracani frequently said, and Machiavelli agreed, that men "ought to try everything, be afraid of nothing; God loves strong men, which can be seen by how He always punishes the powerless by means of the powerful"; Niccolò Machiavelli, *La vita di Castruccio Castracani*, in *Opere di Niccolò Machiavelli*, ed. Corrado Vivanti (Turin: Einaudi, 2005), 3:295.

13. Niccolò Machiavelli, *Mandragola*, act 4, scene I, in *Opere di Niccolò Machiavelli*, ed. Corrado Vivanti (Turin: Einaudi, 2005), 3:169–70.

14. See Gennaro Sasso, *Il "celebrato sogno" di Machiavelli*, in *Machiavelli e gli antichi e altri saggi* (Milan: Ricciardi, 1988), 3:211–94, and *Paralipomeni al "sogno" di Machiavelli* (Milan: Ricciardi, 1988), 325–60.

15. Machiavelli, *Mandragola*, act 3, scene 3, 3:160–61.

16. Ibid., act 2, scene 6, 3:155–58.

17. Machiavelli, *Clizia*, act 2, scene 3, 3:204–7.

18. Niccolò Machiavelli, *Capitoli per una compagnia di piacere*, in *Opere di Niccolò Machiavelli*, ed. Corrado Vivanti (Turin: Einaudi, 2005), 3:244–45.

19. Machiavelli, *L'Asino*, in *Opere di Niccolò Machiavelli*, ed. Corrado Vivanti (Turin: Einaudi, 2005), 3:60, 67. Free will is, in Dante's view (*Paradiso*, 5:19–24), the greatest gift that God gave to mankind: "The greatest gift that God in His largess / made while creating, and to His own goodness / most akin, and that which He most highly prizes / was the freedom of the will; / wherewith all creatures made intelligent, / they all, they only, have been endowed with will."

20. Machiavelli, *Decennale primo*, 1:94.

21. Ibid., 4:292.

22. Machiavelli, *L'Asino*, 3:60–61.

23. "Yet it could be that since this air, as some philosopher would have it, is full of spirits which, by means of natural virtues, foresee future things and have compassion for men, such spirits warn men with like signs so that they can prepare themselves for defense"; Machiavelli, *Discorsi sopra la prima deca di Tito Livio*, 1:56.

24. Ibid.

25. Niccolò Machiavelli, *Lettere: Lattanzio Tedaldi a Niccolò Machiavelli (5 giugno 1509)*, in *Opere di Niccolò Machiavelli*, ed. Corrado Vivanti (Turin: Einaudi, 1999), 2:187.

26. Machiavelli, *Lettere: Niccolò Machiavelli a Francesco Guicciardini*, 2:452.

27. Niccolò Machiavelli, *Lettere: Niccolò Machiavelli a Bartolomeo Cavalcanti (6 Ottobre 1526)*, in *Opere di Niccolò Machiavelli*, ed. Corrado Vivanti (Turin: Einaudi, 1999), 2:447.

28. Anthony Parel, *The Machiavellian Cosmos* (New Haven, CT: Yale University Press, 1992), 63–67.

29. Niccolò Machiavelli, *Di fortuna*, in *Opere di Niccolò Machiavelli*, ed. Corrado Vivanti (Turin: Einaudi, 2005), 3:33–37.

30. Niccolò Machiavelli, *Decennale secondo*, in *Opere di Niccolò Machiavelli*, ed. Corrado Vivanti (Turin: Einaudi, 2005), 3:107–12.

31. Niccolò Machiavelli, *Lettere: Niccolò Machiavelli a Giovan Battista Soderini (13–21 settembre 1506)*, in *Opere di Niccolò Machiavelli*, ed. Corrado Vivanti (Turin: Einaudi, 1999), 2:135.

32. Machiavelli, *Discorsi sopra la prima deca di Tito Livio*, 2:29.

33. Ibid., 2:5. On this point, see Gennaro Sasso, *Machiavelli e gli antichi e altri saggi* (Milan: Ricciardi, 1988), 1:167–376.

34. Niccolò Machiavelli, *Dell' ambizione*, in *Opere di Niccolò Machiavelli*, ed. Corrado Vivanti (Turin: Einaudi, 2005), 3:43–47.

35. See Parel, *The Machiavellian Cosmos*, 54–59.

36. Machiavelli, *Istorie fiorentine*, 3:8:19, 707.

37. Gaeta, *Opere di Niccolò Machiavelli*, 3:518–19. Guicciardini's irony was well founded, even though finding good preachers for Lent was a serious matter for both townships and guilds. See Francesco Bruni, *La città divisa: Le parti e il bene comune da Dante a Guicciardini* (Bologna: Il Mulino, 2003).

38. Niccolò Machiavelli, *Dialogo intorno alla nostra lingua*, in *Opere di Niccolò Machiavelli*, ed. Corrado Vivanti (Turin: Einaudi, 2005), 3:261. Machiavelli expresses his love of country as well in the opening to his *Discorso o dialogo intorno alla nostra lingua*:

> Whenever I have had an opportunity of honoring my country, even when this was burdensome and dangerous, I have done it willingly: for man in his life is under no greater obligation than to his country, as we owe it our very being, and later, all the benefits that nature and fortune have offered us; and the nobler one's country, the greater one's obligation. Truly, he who by thought or deed shows himself an enemy of his country deserves the name of parricide, even if by his country he had been offended.

39. Cited in Gaeta, *Opere di Niccolò Machiavelli*, 3:422.

40. Niccolò Machiavelli, *Lettere: Niccolò Machiavelli a Francesco Guicciardini (19 Maggio 1521)*, in *Opere di Niccolò Machiavelli*, ed. Corrado Vivanti (Turin: Einaudi, 1999), 2:378.

41. Ibid., Gaeta, 3: 423–28. See also Christian Bec, *Cultura e società a Firenze nell'età della rinascenza* (Rome: Salerno Editrice, 1981), 228–44.

42. "From the house one enters directly into church, which—religious as you know I am—comes most to the purpose"; cited in Gaeta, *Opere di Niccolò Machiavelli*, 3:420.

43. Marsilio Ficino, *Platonis opera, Marsilio Ficino interprete* (Venice, 1517), clxxvi.

44. Marsilio Ficino, *Commento di Marsilio Ficini Fiorentino sopra'l Convitto di Platone* (Florence: Filippo Giunti, 1594), 37–38. See also Marsilio Ficino, *El libro dell'amore*, ed. Sandra Niccoli (Florence: Leo S. Olschki editore, 1987), 34–35. On Ficino, see also the entry edited by Cesare Vasoli in *Dizionario biografico degli italiani* (Rome: Istituto della Enciclopedia Italiana, 1997), 47:378–95.

45. Ficino, *Platonis opera*, 208c–e.

46. Ibid., 209a–e.

47. In Ficino's view, love is a source of justice, for where true love resides, there one finds "scambievole benivolenza [reciprocal benevolence]," which is charity, so powerful that it alone can preserve mankind and its tranquillity and peace. See Ficino, *Commento di Marsilio*, 112–13.

48. Machiavelli, *Istorie fiorentine*, 3:3:7. In his translation into the vernacular of the *Istoria* by Poggio Bracciolini, Iacopo Bracciolini explains that when the Florentines stood up to Pope Gregory XI, they had to choose between "the love of the fatherland" and "the fear of religion," and "as it was right to do inasmuch as they were good citizens and good Christians, they placed the love of the fatherland above any other obligation, tie, or consideration"; Iacopo Bracciolini, *Istoria di M. Poggio Fiorentino: Tradotta di latino in volgare da Iacopo suo figliuolo* (Florence: Filippo Giunti, 1598), 35.

49. Niccolò Machiavelli, *Lettere a Francesco Vettori e a Francesco Guicciardini*, ed. Giorgio Inglese (Milan: Rizzoli, 1989), 384n9.

50. On this theme, see Hannah Arendt, *On Revolution* (New York: Viking Press, 1963), 290.

51. Machiavelli, *Istorie fiorentine*, 3:3:7.

52. Niccolò Machiavelli, *Dell'arte della guerra*, in *Opere di Niccolò Machiavelli*, ed. Corrado Vivanti (Turin: Einaudi-Gallimard, 1997), 1:532.

CHAPTER 9: THE TWILIGHT OF REPUBLICAN RELIGION

1. Francesco Guicciardini, *Le cose fiorentine*, ed. Roberto Ridolfi (Florence: Olschki, 1945), 124.

2. Francesco Guicciardini, "Ragioni che consigliano la Signoria di Firenze ad accordarsi con Clemente VII," in *Scritti politici*, ed. Roberto Palmarocchi (Bari: Laterza, 1933), 218–19.

3. Francesco Guicciardini, *Ricordi*, in *Opere di Francesco Guicciardini*, ed. Emanuella Lugnani Scarano (Turin, UTET, 1981), 1:C147.

4. Ibid., 1:C92; see also ibid., 1:C 33 (A40–B65).

5. Francesco Guicciardini, *Dialogo del reggimento di Firenze*, in *Opere di Francesco Guicciardini*, ed. Emanuella Lugnani Scarano (Turin: UTET, 1983), 1:464.

6. Ibid., 1:465.

7. Luigi Lazzerini, *Nessuno è innocente: Le tre morti di Pietro Pagolo Boscoli* (Florence: Olschki, 2002), 4–6. For the text, see Luca Della Robbia, *La morte di Pietro Paolo Boscoli*, ed. Riccardo Bacchelli (Florence: Le Monnier, 1943), 71.

8. Ibid., 80, 261.

9. Ibid., 89–90.

10. Ibid., 121.

11. Ibid., 143.

12. Ibid., 147–48.

13. Antonio Brucioli, *Dialogi*, ed. Aldo Landi (Naples: Prismi Editrice, 1982).

14. Commentary to Antonio Brucioli's *Dialogi*, in ibid., 553–58.

15. See the excellent analysis in Lazzerini, *Nessuno è innocente*, 39–49.

16. Ibid., 131, 178–79, 504.

17. Ibid., 201–2. See also Giorgio Spini, *Tra Rinascimento e Riforma: Antonio Brucioli* (Florence: La Nuova Italia, 1940), 141. See also Carlo Dionisotti, "La testimonianza del Brucioli," in *Rivista Storica Italiana* 91 (1979): 26–51; now in *Machiavellerie: Storia e fortuna di Machiavelli* (Turin: Einaudi, 1980).

18. Rudolf von Albertini, *Firenze dalla repubblica al principato: Storia e coscienza politica*, preface Federico Chabod (Turin: Einaudi, 1970), 104–78.

19. Bedetto Varchi, *Storia fiorentina*, ed. Gaetano Milanesi (Florence: Le Monnier, 1857), 11:24.

20. Cecil Roth, *The Last Florentine Republic* (New York: Russell and Russell, 1968), 203–4.

21. John N. Stephens, *The Fall of the Florentine Republic, 1512–1530* (Oxford: Clarendon Press, 1983), 216–19.

22. Ibid. See also the splendid book by Michael Walzer, *The Revolution of the Saints: A Study on the Origins of Radical Politics* (Cambridge, MA: Harvard University Press, 1965).

23. Varchi, *Storia fiorentina*, 8:26.

24. Piero Vettori, "Oratione di Piero Vettori, fatta alla militare ordinanza fiorentina l'anno M.D.XXIX il dì 5 febbraio," cited in Albertini, *Firenze dalla repubblica al principato*, 418–24.

25. As Bartolomeo Cavalcanti (*Orazioni politiche del Cinquecento*, ed. Manlio Fancelli [Bologna, 1941], 18) explains,

> But can you not see how those ancient sages who established kingdoms and republics determined that their armies should be guided and governed by religion? Consider Numa, who, as soon as he took over the kingdom of Rome, thought of nothing other than to fill with religion the too-savage souls of that bellicose people, since he clearly understood that that ferocious army devoid of religion could not provide safety to that city nor lead it to happiness. You know that from then on, in all public affairs and especially in military matters, that city was such a diligent observer of religion that it sternly punished those who scorned the augurs, the sacred laws of war, and other ceremonies; such actions were reproached however good their outcomes. Consider that the Romans judged the observance of religion to be of greater importance to the safety of the city than defeating the enemies.

26. Ibid., 17–18. In this connection, see Paolo Simoncelli, "Preludi e primi echi di Lutero a Firenze," *Storia e politica* 22 (1983): 727–30.

27. Cavalcanti, *Orazioni politiche del Cinquecento*, 18. See also the observations of Donato Giannotti (1492–1573) on this subject. He, too, invokes the religion of virtue that teaches that God helps only those peoples who are able to fight to defend their liberty. In the name of this same religion, and the necessity

to protect the republican government, Giannotti denounces the bad customs of youths along with the hypocrisy and corruption of friars. In order to perfect the Florentine Republic, he writes, it is necessary that youths be "tempered, sober, reverent of the elderly, lovers of the good, enemies of the wicked, concentrated on the public good, observers of the law, pious, and in every action of theirs merry and joyful"; Donato Giannotti, "Della Repubblica Fiorentina," in *Opere politiche e letterarie di Donato Giannotti*, ed. F. L. Polidori (Florence: Le Monnier, 1850), 1:229.

28. See Guicciardini, *Ricordi*, 725–26, 767.

29. Luigi Guicciardini, "Dialogo," cited in Albertini, *Firenze dalla repubblica al principato*, 428–32.

30. See Delio Cantimori, "Atteggiamenti della vita culturale italiana nel secolo XVI di fronte alla Riforma," *Rivista Storica Italiana* 53 (1936): 83–110; Elisabeth G. Gleason, "Sixteenth Century Italian Interpretations of Luther," *Archiv für Reformationsgeschichte* 60 (1969): 160–73.

31. Rudolf von Albertini, *Firenze dalla repubblica al principato*, 384–85; see also Rita Belladonna, "Aristotle, Machiavelli, and Religious Dissimulation: Bartolomeo Carli Piccolomini's *Trattati nove della prudenza*," in *Peter Martyr Vermigli and Italian Reform*, ed. Joseph C. McClelland (Waterloo: Wilfred Laurier University Press, 1980), 29–41.

32. Rita Belladonna, "Pontanus, Machiavelli and a Case of Religious Simulation in Early Sixteenth-Century Siena (Carli's *Trattati nove della prudenza*)," *Bibliothèque d'Humanisme et Renaissance* 37 (1975): 384–85.

33. See Silvana Seidel Menchi, "Passione civile e ancliti erasmiani di riforma nel patriziato genovese del primo Cinquecento: Ludovico Spinola," *Rinascimento* 18 (1978): 87–121, especially 96–100.

34. Ibid., 106.

35. Ibid., 101–2.

36. Ibid., 106–7.

37. Ibid., 105–6.

38. Ibid., 111.

39. Agostino Giustiniani, *Annali della Repubblica di Genova* (Genoa: libraio Canepa, 1854), 1:7–8.

40. Innocenzo Cervelli, "Storiografia e problemi intorno alla vita religiosa e spirituale a Venezia nella prima metà del '500," *Studi Veneziani* 8 (1966): 447–48.

41. Germano Rosa, "La 'religione politica': Repubblica di Venezia e corte di Roma nei Pensieri di Fulgenzio Micanzio," *Annali dell'Istituto Italiano per gli Studi Storici* 14 (1997): 309–43.

42. Fulgenzio Micanzio, "Annotazioni e pensieri," in *Storici e politici veneti del Cinquecento e del Seicento*, ed. Gino Benzoni and Tiziano Zanato (Milan: Ricciardi, 1982), 860; see also William J. Bouwsma, *Venice and the Defense of Republican Liberty: Renaissance Values in the Age of the Counter Reformation* (Berkeley: University of California Press, 1984), 497–500, 528–29, 595–96.

43. Fulgenzio Micanzio, "Vita del padre Paolo," in *Istoria del Concilio Tridentino*, by Paolo Sarpi, ed. Corrado Vivanti (Turin: Einaudi, 1974), 2:1389.

44. Ibid., 2:1329.

45. Cited in Lazzerini, *Nessuno è innocente*, 164.

46. Ibid., 165.

CHAPTER 10: WITHOUT GOD

1. Raised in the republican milieu of Geneva, where Machiavelli's intellectual legacy was strong, Rousseau sincerely admired the political thought of the Florentine secretary. In a notation added to the 1782 edition of *Du Contrat Social* (in *Œuvres complètes*, ed. Bernard Gagnebin and Marcel Raymond [Paris: Gallimard, 1964], 3:1480), he writes:

> Machiavel étoit un honnête homme et un bon citoyen: mais attaché à la maison de Medicis il étoit forcé dans l'oppression de sa patrie de déguiser son amour pour la liberté. Le choix seul de son éxécrable Heros manifeste asses son intention secrette et l'opposition des maximes de son Livre du Prince à celles de ses discours sur Tite-Live et de son histoire de Florence demontre que ce profond politique n'a eu jusqu'ici que des Lecteurs superficiels ou corrompus. La Cour de Rome a sévérement défendu son livre, je le crois bien; c'est elle qu'il dépeint le plus clairement.

2. Ibid., 465–66.

3. Girolamo Bocalosi, "Dell'educazione democratica da darsi al popolo italiano," in *Giacobini italiani*, ed. Delio Cantimori and Renzo De Felice (Bari: Laterza, 1964), 2:144–45, 147.

4. Enrico Michele L'Aurora, "All'Italia nelle tenebre l'aurora porta la luce," in *Giacobini italiani*, ed. Delio Cantimori and Renzo De Felice (Bari: Laterza, 1964), 1:173.

5. Ibid., 176–77.

6. Matteo Galdi, "Saggio d'istruzione pubblica rivoluzionaria," in *Giacobini italiani*, ed. Delio Cantimori and Renzo De Felice (Bari: Laterza, 1964), 1:242–43.

7. Ibid., 242.

8. Vincenzio Russo, "Pensieri politici," in *Giacobini italiani*, ed. Delio Cantimori and Renzo De Felice (Bari: Laterza, 1964), 1:321–22, 371, 372, 373.

9. Giovanni Antonio Ranza, "Della vera chiesa istituita da Gesù Cristo," in *Giacobini italiani*, ed. Delio Cantimori and Renzo De Felice (Bari: Laterza, 1964), 1:218.

10. Gaetano Filangieri, *Scienza della legislazione*, cited in Vincenzo Ferrone, *La società giusta ed equa: Repubblicanesimo e diritti dell'uomo in Gaetano Filangieri* (Bari: Laterza, 2003), 154, 153.

11. Ibid., 153. See also Luigi Salvatorelli, "Il problema religioso nel Risorgimento," in *Atti del XXXIII Congresso di Storia del Risorgimento Italiano* (Messina, September 1–4, 1954) (Rome: Istituto per la storia del Risorgimento italiano, 1958), 9.

12. *La Religion cattolica amica della democrazia: Instruzione d'un teologo al clero e al popolo romano* (Perugia: Carlo Baduel e Figli stampatori nazionali, 1798), cited in Vittorio E. Giuntella, *La Religione amica della Democrazia: I cattolici democratici del Triennio rivoluzionario (1796-1799)* (Rome: Studium, 1990), 166, 167.

13. Ibid., 169, 172–74, 175.

14. Ibid., 176–78.

15. Ibid., 179–81, 182–83.

16. Riccardo Bartoli, *I Diritti dell'uomo: Catechismo Cattolico-democratico del cittadino* (Reggio: Davolio, 1797), cited in Vittorio E. Giuntella, *La Religione amica della Democrazia: I cattolici democratici del Triennio rivoluzionario (1796–1799)* (Rome: Studium, 1990), 209. See the corresponding entry edited by Fernando Manzotti in *Dizionario Biografico degli Italiani* (Rome: Istituto della Enciclopedia Italiana, 1964), 11:588–90.

17. Bartoli, *I Diritti dell'uomo*, 217–19.

18. Vincenzo Palmieri (Niceta Tirio), *La libertà e la legge considerate nella libertà delle opinioni e nella tolleranza de' culti religiosi* (Genoa: Olzati, 1798), cited in Vittorio E. Giuntella, *La Religione amica della Democrazia: I cattolici democratici del Triennio rivoluzionario (1796–1799)* (Rome: Studium, 1990), 255–56.

19. Gregorio Luigi Barnaba Chiaramonti, *Omelia del cittadino cardinal Chiaramonti vescovo d'Imola diretta al popolo della sua diocesi nella Repubblica cisalpina nel giorno del santissimo Natale l'anno MDCCXCVII* (Imola: nella stamperia della Nazione, l'anno VI della libertà, 1797), cited in Vittorio E. Giuntella, *La Religione amica della Democrazia: I cattolici democratici del Triennio rivoluzionario (1796–1799)* (Rome: Studium, 1990), 274–75.

20. Ibid., 217–19.

21. Ibid., 287.

22. Ibid., 289.

23. Giuseppe Maria Capece Zurlo, *Lettera pastorale dell'arcivescovo di Napoli card* (Naples, February 12, 1799), cited in Vittorio E. Giuntella, *La Religione amica della Democrazia: I cattolici democratici del Triennio rivoluzionario (1796–1799)* (Rome: Studium, 1990), 293–94.

24. For more on Conforti, see the entry edited by Pasquale Villani in *Dizionario Biografico degli Italiani* (Rome: Istituto della Enciclopedia Italiana, 1982), 27:793–802.

25. Vincenzo Cuoco, *Saggio storico sulla rivoluzione napoletana edl 1799*, ed. Fausto Nicolini (Bari: Laterza, 1913), 130.

26. Giorgio Spini, *Una "testimone della verità": Eleonora de Fonseca Pimentel tra impegno civile e riflessione etico-religiosa* (Naples: La città del sole, 2007), 30–31. See also Benedetto Croce, *La rivoluzione napoletana del 1799: Biografie, racconti, ricerche* (Bari: Laterza, 1948).

27. Spini, *Una "testimone della verità,"* 42–44.

28. Ibid., 45–46.

29. Ibid., 63.

30. Ibid., 73–74.

31. Ibid., 68–69.

32. Ibid., 86.

33. Niccolò Rodolico, *Il popolo agli inizi del Risorgimento nell'Italia meridionale, 1798–1801* (Florence: Le Monnier, 1926), 138–39.

34. Cuoco, *Saggio storico sulla rivoluzione napoletana del 1799*, 144–45.

35. Ibid.

36. Ibid., 103.

37. Ibid., 129.

CHAPTER 11: AFTER THE REVOLUTION

1. Vincenzo Cuoco, *Scritti vari*, ed. Nino Cortese and Fausto Nicolini (Bari: Laterza, 1924), 315–16. Compare Antonino De Francesco, *Vincenzo Cuoco: Una vita politica* (Bari: Laterza, 1997).

2. Ibid., 7, 58, 59.

3. Ugo Foscolo, *Sepolcri* (1807), vv. 198–201.

4. Ugo Foscolo, "Della religione di Lucrezio," in *Edizione Nazionale delle Opere di Ugo Foscolo* (Florence: Le Monnier, 1933), 8:360.

5. Ugo Foscolo, "*Della servitù dell'Italia*," in *Edizione Nazionale delle Opere di Ugo Foscolo* (Florence: Le Monnier, 1933), 8:227–28.

6. Ibid., 8:224.

7. Benjamin Constant, *De la religion considérée dans sa source, ses formes et ses développements*, ed. Pierre Deguise (Lausanne: Bibliothèque romande, 1971), 1.4:84–85.

8. Ibid., 1.6:107.

9. Ibid., 1.4:85–87.

10. Ibid., 17–19.

11. Ibid., 182.

12. Saint-Simon, *Le Nouveaux Christianisme* (Paris: Au bureau du Globe, 1832), 10–11.

13. Ibid., 34.

14. Ibid., 99–100.

15. Ibid., 341–34.

16. François M. Guizot, *Cours d'histoire moderne* (Paris: Pichon et Didier Éditeurs, 1829), vol. 1, passim.

17. Thèodore Jouffroy, *Mèlanges philosophiques* (Paris: Librairie de l'Adrange, 1838), 3–27.

18. Hugues-Félicité-Robert de Lamennais, "Du Catholicisme dans ses rapports avec la société politique," in *Oeuvres Complètes de Lamennais* (Paris: Pagnerre Editeur, 1844), 7:38–39.

19. Ibid., 6:56.

20. Hugues-Félicité-Robert de Lamennais, "De l'absolutisme et de la libertè," in *Oeuvres Complètes de Lamennais* (Paris: Pagnerre Editeur, 1844), 7:281.

21. Ibid., 7:283.

22. "Aussi seroit-il impossibile de dire—scrive—à quel degré une fausse instruction religieuse a été funeste à la morale en Italie. Il n'y a pas en Europe un peuple qui soit plus constamment occupé de ses pratiques religieuses, qui soit plus universellement fidèle. Il n'y en a pas un qui observe moins les devoirs et les vertus que prescrit ce christianisme auquel il paroît si attaché"; Jean Charles Leonard Simonde de Sismondi, *Histoire des républiques italiennes du Moyen Age* (Paris: chez Treuttel et Würtz libraires, 1826), 422–23.

23. "Chacun y a appris, non point à obéir à sa conscience, mais à ruser avec elle; chacun met ses passions à leur aise, par le bénéfice des indulgences, par les restrictions mentales, par le projet d'une pénitence, et l'espérance d'une prochaine absolution; et loin que la plus grande ferveur religieuse y soit una

garantie de la probité, plus on y voit un homme scrupuleux dans ses pratiques de dévotion, plus on peut à bon droit concevoir contre lui de défiance"; ibid. Against Simonde de Sismondi's thesis, Alessandro Manzoni remarks that Catholic morality was not at all the cause of Italy's moral corruption. See Alessandro Manzoni, *Osservazioni sulla morale cattolica*, ed. Franco Mollia (Milan: Garzanti, 1985), 3.

24. Alexis de Tocqueville, *Democracy in America*, trans. George Lawrence, ed. J. P. Mayer (New York: Harper and Row, 2000), 291.

25. Ibid., 46.

26. Ibid., 288.

27. Ibid., 288–90.

28. Ibid., 292.

29. Ibid., 294.

30. Ibid., 444.

31. Edgar Quinet, *Les révolutions d'Italie*, in *Oeuvres d'Edgar Quinet* (Paris: Hachette, 1895), 2:3–4. On this point, see the excellent essay of Gennaro Maria Barbuto, *Ambivalenze del moderno: De Sanctis e le tradizioni politiche italiane* (Naples: Liguori, 2000), in particular 21–27.

32. Barbuto, *Ambivalenze del moderno*, 6–8.

33. Ibid., 55, 57.

34. Ibid., xi.

35. Edgar Quinet, *La Révolution* (Paris: Librairie Internationale, 1869), 1:151–56. In his introduction to the Italian edition (Quinet Edgar, *La Rivoluzione*, ed. Alessandro Galante Garrone [Turin: Einaudi, 1974], 102), Garrone writes that "he [Quinet] was the first one, if I am not mistaken, who talked about a 'religion of liberty.'" During those years, Jules Michelet (*Renaissance et Réforme: Histoire de France au XVI siècle* [1855; repr., Paris: R. Laffont, 1982], 92) put forth a similar thesis concerning the problem of religious and political reform in Italy:

> The prophet of the rebirth of Italy through a religion was Savonarola. Savonarola's defeat, however, was proof that reforming the Catholic Church by reducing it to its first principles was an impossible task, and that democracy and Christianity are actually incompatible. Machiavelli understood Savonarola's defeat with great penetration, and undertook a completely opposite approach for the salvation of Italy. Inasmuch as God was doing nothing for Italy, Machiavelli invoked a politics without God: as heaven was deaf, he summoned hell.

In turn, Jacob Burckhardt (*Die Cultur der Renaissance in Italien* [*The Civilization of the Renaissance in Italy*], trans. S.G.C. Middlemore [1878; repr., Kitchener: Batoche Books, 2001], 334) reinforces the image of an Italy torn between a proposal for religious and moral reform inspired by medieval ideals, and the lucid but too cold diagnosis of Machiavelli. Burckhardt explains that Savonarola had reunited patriotism and religious regeneration in his preaching. His cure for Italy's moral corruption, however, was a theocracy where men prostrate themselves before God and live only for the soul's salvation. Machiavelli also knew that Italy's problem was a particular type of moral corruption, but he did not realize that its cause was the individualism that had propelled Italy out of the virtuous circle of morality and religion.

36. Quinet, *La Révolution*. 11: 748, 334.

CHAPTER 12: THE NEW ALLIANCE

1. See, above all, Terenzio Mamiani, *Dell'avvenire dell'Italia* (1838), *Documenti pratici intorno alla rigenerazione morale e intellettuale degli italiani*, and *Sul Papato: Lettera ortodossa a Domenico Berti* (1851); quoted from Guido Verucci, *Italia laica: Prima e dopo l'unità* (Rome: Laterza, 1981), 6–7.

2. Verucci, *Italia laica*, 7–8. On Durando, see the corresponding entry edited by Paola Casana Testore in the *Dizionario Biografico degli Italiani* (Rome: Istituto della Enciclopedia Italiana, 1993), 42:97–101.

3. Ibid., 10–12.

4. Raffaello Lambruschini, *Dell'autorità e della libertà. Pensieri di un solitario*, ed. Angiolo Gambaro (Florence: La Nuova Italia, 1948), 313.

5. Ibid., 325, 326.

6. Ibid., 326, 332, 343n1.

7. Ibid. 76. In 1867, Lambruschini (ibid., 349–50) repeats that political liberty needs religion: "The more liberty one demands for the peoples, the more one should provide that they be religious. External restraints can be loosened only when an internal restraint governs passions. True liberty is the removal of the hindrances to following the right precepts of conscience. Morality is inseparable from liberty. Separate them, and you will have the material observance of the duties in the manner of the passive obedience of a slave, on the one hand; license, on the other."

8. Ibid., 152.

9. Angiolo Gambaro, *Riforma religiosa nel carteggio inedito di Raffaello Lambruschini* (Turin: G. B. Paravia, 1926), 1:cxlii.

10. Ibid., 2:102–3, 105–6, 106–107.

11. Compare Stelio Marchese, *La riforma mancata: Le idee religiose di Bettino Ricasoli* (Milan: Giuffrè, 1961), 33.

12. Ibid., 34, 37.

13. Ibid., 40, 43.

14. Ibid., 115–19.

15. Stefano Jacini, *Un riformatore toscano dell'epoca del Risorgimento: Il conte Piero Guicciardini (1808–1886)* (Florence: Sansoni, 1940), 49–70.

16. Ibid., 193–95, 211–12.

17. Ibid., 320, 321–23.

18. Compare Verucci, *Italia laica*, 13–14.

19. Ibid., 15–16.

20. Ibid., 18.

21. Ibid., 19–20.

22. Ibid., 21.

23. Ibid., 35–36.

24. Ibid., 86–87.

25. Ibid., 95–96.

26. Ibid., 110–11.

27. Enrico Fano, *Della carità preventiva e dell'ordinamento delle società di mutuo soccorso in Italia* (Milan: Giuseppe Civelli, 1868), 108, 120.

28. Carlo Lozzi, *Dell'ozio in Italia*, 2 vols. (Turin, UTET, 1870–71). I am quoting Verucci, *Italia laica*, 121.

29. Verucci, *Italia laica*, 123.

30. Ibid., 125.

CHAPTER 13: LITERATURE AND HYMNS OF THE RELIGION OF LIBERTY

1. Alessandro Manzoni, "Il Cinque Maggio 1821" and "La Pentecoste," in *Tutte le poesie, 1812– 1872*, ed. Gilberto Lonardi (Venice: Marsilio, 1997), 109–18.

2. Alessandro Manzoni, *I promessi sposi* (1840; repr., Milan: Arnoldo Mondadori Editore, 2002), 104.

3. Ibid., 104.

4. Ibid., 180–81.

5. Ibid., 181.

6. Ibid., 399, 408.

7. Ibid., 491.

8. Niccolò Tommaseo, *Dell'Italia* (Turin: Unione Tipografico-Editrice Torinese, 1920), 1:25–26.

9. Ibid., 1:185–87.

10. Giacomo Leopardi, "Zibaldone di pensieri," in *Tutte le opere*, ed. Walter Binni and Enrico Ghidetti (Florence: Sansoni, 1969), 2:262, 762.

11. Ibid., 2:857.

12. Ibid., 2:1069, 1056. It is worth noting that in *La crestomazia italiana*, Leopardi selects the page of the *Istorie fiorentine* in which Machiavelli describes Lorenzo il Magnifico as "a man loved in the highest degree by fortune and by God," and also the page from *Vita di Castruccio Castracani* in which the following saying is attributed to a captain from Lucca: "God loves strong men, which can be seen by how He always punishes the powerless by means of the powerful"; Giacomo Leopardi, *La crestomazia italiana*, ed. Angelo Ottolini (Milan: Hoepli, 1926), 219, 221.

13. Leopardi, "Zibaldone di pensieri," 2:149.

14. Ibid., 2:108.

15. Ibid., 2:151.

16. Ibid., 2:150.

17. Ibid., 2:155.

18. Ippolito Nievo, *Confessioni di un italiano*, preface by Emilio Cecchi (Turin: Einaudi, 1964), 260–61.

19. Ibid., 281–84.

20. Ibid., 285.

21. Ibid., 285–86.

22. Ibid., 292–93.

23. Ibid., 427.

24. Ibid., 425–26.

25. Ibid., 428.

26. Ibid., 403.

27. Ibid., 683.

28. Ibid., 686–87.

29. Massimo Mila (*Verdi*, ed. Piero Gelli [Milan: Rizzoli, 2000], 194–95), who, one century after *Nabucco*, found in the religion of liberty the strength to endure fascist imprisonment, wrote:

> Equipped like very few others with those antennas through which artists foresee the future, Verdi was bringing to the scene a new Italian, the Italian of Masaccio in the frescoes of Tributo, instead of the Italian of Botticelli or of Ghirlandaio; it was, that is, the troublesome Italian of Dante and Machiavelli, instead of the agreeable loafers of Boccaccio's *Decameron*: it was that sort of unbending Italian, stiff as a rock, who is rarely seen, but exists, and comes out when he is needed, in critical moments: Francesco Ferrucci, the Piave, the Resistenza. Well, one of those moments was then about to strike on the clock-face of history, and Verdi seemed to know it. Indeed, he knew it, not so much because he was privy to the secret matters of politics, but because of his obscure artistic insight. When the public was not yet aware of this, he already knew that after hearing *Va' pensiero sull'ali dorate* the Milanese would have much more appreciated the solemn allocution of a prophet, understood—in the manner of Rossini's *Mosè in Egitto*—as a shepherd of peoples.

30. Ibid., 191.

31. Ibid., 194.

32. *Nabucco* (music of Giuseppe Verdi), ed. Eduardo Rescigno (Milan, Ricordi, 1987).

33. Ibid., 101.

CHAPTER 14: APOSTLES AND MARTYRS

1. Silvio Pellico, "Le mie prigioni con le addizioni di Maroncelli," in *Opere scelte di Silvio Pellico*, ed. Baudry Parigi (Rome: Libreria Europea, 1837), ii.

2. Ibid., 9.

3. Ibid., 13–14, 23–24, 121, 184.

4. Luigi Settembrini, *Ricordanze della mia vita*, ed. Adolfo Omodeo (Bari: Laterza, 1934), 1:15–16, 62, 64, 84.

5. Ibid., 1:231–33.

6. Ibid., 1:239.

7. Luigi Martini, *Il Confortatorio di Mantova negli anni 1851-'52-'53 -'55*, intro. and notes Albany Rezzaghi, ed. Accademia Virgiliana (Mantua: CITEM, 1952), 1:277–78; published by the city of Mantua on the centennial of the Belfiore martyrs.

8. Ibid., 1:285.

9. Ibid., 2:73.

10. Ibid., 2:95, 111–13.

11. Ibid., 2:165, 185; emphasis in original.

CHAPTER 15: MASTERS

1. Vincenzo Gioberti, *Prolegomeni del primato morale e civile degli italiani*, ed. Enrico Castelli (Milan: Fratelli Bocca Editori, 1938), 225.

2. Ibid., 227; emphasis in original.

3. Ibid., 228–29.

4. Giuseppe Mazzini, "Ai giovani: Ricordi," in *Scritti politici*, ed. Terenzio Grandi and Augusto Comba (Turin, UTET, 1972), 587. See also Roland Sarti, *Mazzini: A Life for the Religion of Politics* (Boulder, CO: Westport Press, 1997).

5. Giuseppe Mazzini, "Alleanza repubblicana," in *Scritti politici*, ed. Terenzio Grandi and Augusto Comba (Turin: UTET, 1972), 1007.

6. See Carlo Cantimori, *Saggio sull'idealismo di Giuseppe Mazzini* (Faenza: Casa Tipografica Editrice G. Montanari, 1904).

7. Giuseppe Mazzini, "I Sistemi e la Democrazia," in *Scritti editi e inediti di Giuseppe Mazzini* (Milan: Daelli Editore, 1864), 7:326–27. In a letter to Francesco Bertioli in January 1833, Mazzini (*Scritti editi ed inediti di Giuseppe Mazzini* [Galeati: Imola, 1909], 5:216) writes:

> I am not a Christian in the sense of believing in the divinity of Christ and like things: I admit of no other revelation than that of the Genius; I believe that religion is an outcome, and an expression, of Society, just like literature, law, politics, etc. [I believe that] religion [is] subject to Progress just like all other things—and in this sense Christianity is the first religion expressing our civilization, i.e., a religion of the modern world as opposed to the ancient—as Christianity in my view has elaborated the Dogma of Equality. And in this sense I am a Christian. Yet I also believe that Christianity has only preached Equality before God, and one's own *individual* improvement, whereas we are now approaching the age in which Equality must be preached before men, and the improvement must be *social*—and in this sense I am not a Christian. However, as everything occurs progressively, we—a society still under the empire of Catholicism—cannot jump with one leap beyond Christianity and preach the pure Deism which is my religion.

8. Giuseppe Mazzini, "Dal papa al concilio," in *Scritti editi e inediti di Giuseppe Mazzini* (Milan: Daelli Editore, 1864), 7:234–35.

9. Giuseppe Mazzini, "Condizione e avvenire dell'Europa," in *Scritti editi e inediti di Giuseppe Mazzini* (Rome, 1891), 8:186. Like Mazzini, other patriots worked for moral and religious reform during the Risorgimento—among them, refugees in Malta and London. From 1847 to 1860, thanks to Salvatore Ferretti, the paper *Eco di Savonarola* was published in London with the explicit objective of backing a religious reform in Italy that would draw its inspiration not from Luther, "from whom endless disgrace has always been brought to Italy," but

rather from the teachings of the friar of Ferrara. A similar program animated the pages of *Il Cattolico Cristiano*, which was published in Malta from 1848 to 1850. As the paper's founder, Luigi De Sanctis, formerly a theologian, stressed, religious reform was necessary for Italy to be able to find her liberty again, and generate new and better moral habits:

> Italy needs a religious reform.... Let the evangelical light appear, and Italy shall be one, shall be free, shall be happy; there cannot be unity, liberty, or happiness unless the principle of brotherhood and love is firmly established; and this principle cannot be firmly established if not through the Gospel.... Let us destroy the papal institutions, which are tyrannical institutions; and inasmuch as the popes have suppressed the Gospel in order to tyrannize, and on its ruins have based their code of oppression, let us overturn this code, and let us rebuild the Gospel from its ruins! This is the only way to free Italy forever.

See Augusto Armand Hugon, "Correnti evangeliche tra gli italiani in esilio 1840–1860," in *Atti del XXXIII Congresso di Storia del Risorgimento Italiano* (Messina, September 1–4, 1954) (Rome: Istituto per la storia del Risorgimento italiano, 1958), 29–36.

10. Giuseppe Mazzini, "A Francesco Crispi (1864)," in *Scritti politici*, ed. Terenzio Grandi and Augusto Comba (Turin, UTET, 1972), 969–70.

11. Francesco Ruffini, a professor at the University of Torino and a senator of the Kingdom of Italy, heavily emphasizes this letter in his book *Ultimi studi sul conte di Cavour*, edited by Adolfo Omodeo and published posthumously in 1936. The book has a nice photo of the author in all his gravity and serenity. Ruffini died on March 29, 1934, "in a bed of the Mauriziano, with only his relatives and a few faithful students around him," remarks Paolo Borgna (*Un paese migliore: Vita di Alessandro Galante Garrone* [Bari: Laterza, 2006], 137–38). On Ruffini, see also Norberto Bobbio, *La mia Italia* (Florence: Passigli, 2000), 19–37.

12. Ruffini, *Ultimi studi*, 19–24.

13. Rosario Romeo, *Cavour e il suo tempo (1810–1842)* (Bari: Laterza, 1969), 301.

14. Ibid., 579–80.

15. Ibid., 307.

16. Ibid., 308–9.

17. Ibid., 311.

18. Ruffini, *Ultimi studi*, 87.

19. Federico Chabod, *Storia della politica estera italiana dal 1870 al 1896* (Bari: Laterza, 1971), 1:229.

20. Marco Minghetti, "Stato e Chiesa," in *Scritti politici*, ed. Raffaella Gherardi (Rome: Presidenza del Consiglio dei Ministri, 1986), 596–97.

21. Alfonso Scirocco, *Garibaldi: Battaglie, amori, ideali di un cittadino del mondo* (Rome: Laterza 2000), 360.

22. Scirocco, *Garibaldi*, 361; see also Franco Molinari, "La religiosità di Garibaldi," in *Garibaldi generale della libertà*, ed. Aldo A. Mola (Rome, 1984), 581–85.

CHAPTER 16: REGRETS AND THE QUEST FOR NEW FAITHS

1. Guido Verucci, *Italia laica: Prima e dopo l'unità* (Rome: Laterza, 1981), 270.

2. Ibid., 271.

3. Ibid., 275.

4. Ibid., 311.

5. Federico Chabod, *Storia della politica estera italiana dal 1870 al 1896* (Bari: Laterza, 1971), 232–33.

6. Francesco De Sanctis, *Storia della letteratura italiana*, ed. Niccolò Gallo and Natalino Sapegno (Turin: Einaudi, 1966), 1:185–86 (Par. 15:130–31).

7. Ibid., 1:233–34 (Purg. 1:71–72).

8. Ibid., 1:319–20.

9. Ibid., 1:328–29.

10. Ibid., 1:369–70.

11. Ibid., 1:443–44.

12. Ibid., 1:486.

13. The last three quotations are from Francesco De Sanctis, *Storia della letteratura italiana*, ed. Niccolò Gallo and Natalino Sapegno (Turin: Einaudi, 1966), 2:568–70.

14. Ibid., 1:568–70.

15. Ibid., 1:603.

16. Ibid., 1:612.

17. Ibid., 1:669–71.

18. Francesco De Sanctis, *La scuola cattolico-liberale e il romanticismo a Napoli*, ed. Carlo Muscetta and Giorgio Candeloro (Turin: Einaudi, 1953), 204.

19. Ibid., 8.

20. Ibid., 220.

21. Ibid., 204.

22. Ibid., 231–32.

23. Ibid., 239–41.

24. Ibid., 242.

25. Ibid., 244.

26. Ibid., 248–49.

27. Edmondo De Amicis, "Cuore," in *Opere scelte*, ed. Folco Portinari and Giusi Baldissone (Milan: Mondadori, 1996), 191–92. Italian scholars have repeatedly ridiculed this work, and in light of this, it is worth citing a page from Piero Calamandrei's *Diario 1939–1945*, ed. Giorgio Agosti [Florence: La Nuova Italia, 1982], 111–12), dated February 9, 1943. A friend of his, Renzo Simi, whom Calamandrei portrays as "perhaps the single Fascist I knew who was in good faith, honest, and intelligent," describes what his students had written two years earlier in a paper titled "Il nostro prossimo" (Our neighbor):

> I have taught my students to frankly say what they think. Well, the result was papers of a dreadful sincerity: "our neighbor is useful only for our own advantage"; "life is a struggle of egoisms in which each must strive to overcome his neighbor, and to be strong by triumphing over the weak":

"altruism and humanity are just trite rhetorical words"; "I will be a physician," one wrote, "not because I like to cure other people's suffering, but because I will make more money in contrast to other professions." A terrible aridity, and, what makes it even worse, it is the aridity of the weakling and the coward. In fact, it is not a manly will to fight: it rather is a cynical impulse of cowards who put on an air of fierceness just because they hope that they will have to do with people who are even more cowardly than they are.

It would have been much better, Calamandrei notes, to continue to teach De Amicis's "Cuore" instead of deriding it.

28. Antonio Fogazzaro, *Piccolo mondo antico* (Milan: Mondadori, 1970), 69–71.

29. Ibid., 152.

30. Ibid., 66–67.

31. Ibid., 127.

32. Ibid., 260, 261.

33. Ibid., 313, 328–31.

34. Luigi Russo, *Carducci senza retorica* (Bari: Laterza, 1957), 346–48.

35. Ibid., 66–67; emphasis in original.

36. Ibid., 68.

37. Ibid., 69.

38. Ibid., 214.

39. Ibid., 220.

40. Ibid., 202.

41. Chabod, *Storia della politica estera italiana*, 1:286.

42. Ibid., 286–87; emphasis in original.

43. Alfredo Oriani, *Fino a Dogali*, 2nd ed. (Bologna: Cappelli, 1927), 143–44.

44. Filippo Turati, *Uomini della politica e della cultura*, ed. Alessandro Schiavi, (Bari: Laterza, 1949), 23.

45. Chabod, *Storia della politica estera italiana*, 1:264–65.

46. Roberto Ardigò, *La morale dei positivisti*, ed. Giorgio Giannini (Milan: Marzorati, 1973), 99–100.

47. Ibid., 102.

48. For an example of anti-Christian socialism, see the leaflet *La religione cristiana svelata al popolo* (Rome: Mongini, 1906), which defines Christianity as "the disgrace of our times" (3, 19).

49. Leonida Bissolati, "La religione e noi," *Critica Sociale*, March 30, 1891, reprinted in Leonida Bissolati, *Scritti giovanili*, ed. Arcangelo Ghisleri and Alessandro Groppali (Milan: Treves, 1921), 215–24.

50. Ibid.

51. Gaetano Arfè, *Storia del socialismo italiano (1892–1926)* (Turin, 1965), 20; Giovanni Zibordi, *Saggio sulla storia del movimento operaio in Italia: Camillo Prampolini e i lavoratori reggiani* (Bari: Laterza, 1930), 70–75.

52. Enrico Decleva, "Anticlericalismo e lotta politica nell'Italia giolittiana: I: L'esempio della Francia' e i partiti popolari (1901–1904)," in *Nuova Rivista Storica*, 52 (1968): 302.

53. Carlo Monticelli, *Socialismo popolare*, 4th ed. (Florence: Nerbini, 1902), 89.

54. Francesco Paoloni, *Una visita di Gesú: Come qualmente Gesú per festeggiare il Natale scende fra gli uomini e scopre le magagne del mondo; e quel che ne segue* (Rome: Mongini, 1905), 29.

55. Giuseppe Rensi, "La fase socialista dell'arte tolstoiana," *Critica Sociale'* 10 (1900): 124–72; cited in Gabriele Turi, "Aspetti dell'ideologia del Psi (1890–1910)," *Studi Storici* 21 (1980): 86.

56. Decleva, "Anticlericalismo e lotta politica nell'Italia giolittiana," 331.

57. Ibid., 334.

58. Ibid., 337–38.

59. Zibordi, *Saggio sulla storia del movimento operaio in Italia*, 7.

60. Ibid., 71.

61. Ibid., 73.

62. Ibid., 75.

Chapter 17: Two Clashing Religions

1. Marla Stone, *The Patron State: Culture and Politics in Fascist Italy* (Princeton, NJ: Princeton University Press, 1998).

2. Emilio Gentile, *Il culto del littorio: La sacralizzazione della politica nell'Italia Fascista* (Rome: Laterza, 1993).

3. Piero Zama, *Fascismo e religione* (Milan: Imperia, 1923), 12–13.

4. Giovanni Gentile, "Caratteri religiosi della presente lotta politica," in *Politica e cultura*, ed. Hervé A. Cavallera (Florence: Casa Editrice le Lettere, 1990), 1:136–38.

5. Ibid., 1:140–41.

6. Compare Gentile, *Il culto del littorio*, 117.

7. Carlo Scorza, "Odiare i nemici," in *Gioventù Fascista*, April 12, 1931, 1–3.

8. K. E. Suckert (Curzio Malaparte), *L'Europa vivente: Teoria storica del sindacalismo nazionale*, preface Ardengo Soffici (Florence: La Voce, 1923); cited in Giorgio Spini, *Italia di Mussolini e protestanti*, preface Carlo Azeglio Ciampi (Turin: Claudiana, 2007), 151.

9. Suckert, *L'Europa vivente*, 153.

10. Giovanni Gentile, "L'Idea Nazionale," *La Tribuna*, November 22, 1931.

11. See Emilio Gentile, *Le religioni della politica: Fra democrazie e totalitarismi* (Rome: Laterza, 2001).

12. Piero Gobetti, "Risorgimento senza eroi," in *Scritti storici, letterari e filosofici*, ed. Paolo Spriano (Turin: Einaudi, 1969), 23.

13. Ibid., 40–43.

14. Ibid., 73–75.

15. Ibid., 75–76.

16. Norberto Bobbio, *Italia civile: Ritratti e testimonianze* (Florence: Passigli Editori, 1986), 141–42, 177–78.

17. Ibid., 127, 129, 132, 128. Bobbio has rightly noted that Gobetti elaborated on the concept of the religion of liberty ten years before Croce; compare

Norberto Bobbio, "Ritratto di Piero Gobetti," in *Italia fedele: Il mondo di Gobetti* (Florence: Passigli, 1986), 29.

18. Piero Gobetti, "Elogio della ghigliottina," *La Rivoluzione Liberale* 1, no. 34 (November 1922), in *Opere complete di Piero Gobetti*, vol. 1, *Scritti politici*, ed. Paolo Spriano (Turin: Einaudi, Torino 1969), 431–34.

19. Piero Gobetti, "Il nostro protestantismo," *La Rivoluzione liberale* 4, no. 20 (May 17, 1925); also in the Protestant review *Conscientia* as "Le democrazie del lavoro e la civiltà della Riforma," December 22, 1923, in *Opere complete di Piero Gobetti*, vol. 1, *Scritti politici*, ed. Paolo Spriano (Turin: Einaudi, 1969), 824, 825–26.

20. Piero Gobetti, *La rivoluzione liberale: Saggio sulla lotta politica in Italia*, in *Opere complete di Piero Gobetti*, vol. 1, *Scritti politici*, ed. Paolo Spriano (Turin: Einaudi, 1969), 923–94.

21. Alberto Cianca, letter sent from Cannes, published in *Il Mondo*, April 13, 1926, in Eva Amendola Kühn, *Vita con Giovanni Amendola* (Florence: Parenti Editore, 1960), 615. See Giorgio Spini, "Filosofia e religiosità in Giovanni Amendola," in *Giovanni Amendola tra etica e politica: Atti del convegno di studio Montecatini terme 25–26–27 ottobre 1996* (Pistoia: Editrice C.R.T., 1999), 67–84; Alfredo Capone, "Moderatismo e democrazia nel pensiero di Giovanni Amendola," in *Giovanni Amendola nel cinquantenario della morte 1926–1976* (Rome: Fondazione Luigi Einaudi, 1976), 93–144.

22. Kühn, *Vita con Giovanni Amendola*, 250–51.

23. Giovanni Amendola, "Il libro non letto," in *Giovanni Amendola. Etica e biografia* (Milan: Ricciardi, 1953), 143.

24. Ibid., 147–48.

25. Ibid., 144.

26. Kühn, *Vita con Giovanni Amendola*, 347.

CHAPTER 18: IN THE NAME OF CHRIST

1. Giovanni Minzoni, cited in Nicola Palumbi, *Don Giovanni Minzoni: Educatore e martire* (San Paolo: Cinisello Balsamo, 2003), 24.

2. Ibid., 21–22.

3. Lorenzo Bedeschi, *Don Minzoni: Il prete ucciso dai Fascisti* (Milan: Bompiani, 1973), 94.

4. Nicola Palumbi, *Don Giovanni Minzoni*, 75–76.

5. Ibid., 82–83.

6. Igino Giordani, *Rivolta cattolica* (1925; repr., Rome: Città Nuova, 1997), 20.

7. Ibid., 49–50, 57–58, 61.

8. Ibid., 66.

9. Ibid., 77–78.

10. Ibid., 80.

11. Ibid., 94, 100, 112, 120, 145–55.

12. Luigi Sturzo, *Italia e Fascismo* (Bologna: Zanichelli, 1965), 258. See Emilio Gentile, *Le religioni della politica: Fra democrazie e totalitarismi* (Rome: Laterza, 2001), 147–53.

13. Luigi Sturzo, "Idolatria collettiva," *El Matì*, December 19, 1933, in Luigi Sturzo, *Miscellanea londinese* (Bologna: Zanichelli, 1967), 2:286.

14. Luigi Sturzo, "Il problema della libertà e la crisi italiana" (1925), in *Scritti politici di Luigi Sturzo*, ed. Mario G. Rossi (Milan: Feltrinelli, 1982), 319–20.

15. Giuseppe Donati, "Il nostro programma politico-sociale," in *Giuseppe Donati cattolico antiFascista*, ed. Nicola Angiulli and Giacomo de Antonellis (Milan: Cooperativa Editrice Donati, 1971), 139–40.

16. Giuseppe Donati, "Cittadini e credenti," *Il Popolo*, June 23, 1923, in *Giuseppe Donati cattolico antiFascista*, ed. Nicola Angiulli and Giacomo de Antonellis (Milan: Cooperativa Editrice Donati, 1971), 152.

17. Giuseppe Donati, "Cattolicesimo e 'gentilismo,'" *Il Popolo*, April 23, 1925, in *Giuseppe Donati cattolico antiFascista*, ed. Nicola Angiulli and Giacomo de Antonellis (Milan: Cooperativa Editrice Donati, 1971), 171.

18. Giuseppe Donati, "Per vincere il Fascismo," *Il Corriere degli Italiani*, April 26, 1926, in *Giuseppe Donati cattolico antiFascista*, ed. Nicola Angiulli and Giacomo de Antonellis (Milan: Cooperativa Editrice Donati, 1971), 177.

19. Francesco Luigi Ferrari, "Ai parroci d'Italia: Prima lettera," in *Scritti dell'esilio*, ed. Maria Cristina Giuntella (Rome: Edizioni di Storia e Letteratura, 1991), 1:338–39.

20. Ibid., 1:344, 345.

21. Aldo Capitini, "Premessa a un libro del '36," in *Dalla Resistenza alla desistenza: L'Italia del "Ponte" (1945–1947)*, ed. Mario Isnenghi (Rome: Laterza, 2007), 158–59, 160.

22. Ibid., 161–62. On the opposition to fascism in the name of the Christian faith, see the important contributions collected in Gianfranco Bianchi, ed., *Cristiani per la libertà: Dalla Resistenza alla Costituzione* (Milan: Vita e pensiero, 1987).

23. Ibid., 162–64.

24. Ibid.

25. Barbara Allason, *La vita di Silvio Pellico* (Milan: Mondadori, 1933). I use the word "dutifully" because the publication date mentions both the year in relation to Christ's birth and the year according to the fascist calendar.

26. Ibid., 65, 66.

27. Ibid., 110, 111.

28. Barbara Allason, *Memorie di un antifascista (1919–1940)* (Rome: Edizioni U, 1946), 70, 88, 112.

29. Ibid., 167–68, 169.

30. Ibid., 185, 205, 287–88.

31. Giorgio La Pira, *Principî* 18 (January–February 1940), supplement to the first issue of *Vita Cristiana*, 1, 3–4.

32. Ibid., 13, 18–19.

33. Giorgio Spini, *Italia di Mussolini e protestanti*, preface Carlo Azeglio Ciampi (Turin: Claudiana, 2007), 145–46.

34. Arturo Carlo Jemolo, *Chiesa e Stato in Italia negli ultimi cento anni* (Turin: Einaudi, 1971), 451. See also Arturo Carlo Jemolo, *Per la pace religiosa d'Italia*, ed. Giovanni Spadolini (1944; repr., Florence: Le Monnier, 1985). See also the corresponding entry by F. Margiotta Broglio in *Dizionario Biografico degli Italiani* (Rome: Istituto della Enciclopedia Italiana, 2004), 62:196–201.

35. Jemolo, *Chiesa e Stato in Italia negli ultimi cento anni*, 452.

36. Ibid., 454.

37. Ibid., 457.

38. Ibid., 464.

CHAPTER 19: INNER LIBERTY

1. Cited in Norberto Bobbio, *Italia civile: Ritratti e testimonianze* (Florence: Passigli Editori, 1986), 97.

2. Piero Martinetti, "Lettere di Piero Martinetti," *Il Ponte* 7 (1951): 343.

3. Piero Martinetti, *La libertà* (Milan: Libreria Editrice Lombarda, 1928), 7, 400–402.

4. Ibid., 491–92.

5. Piero Martinetti, *Gesù Cristo e il cristianesimo* (Milan: Il Saggiatore, 1964), 503, 518–25.

6. Piero Marinetti, *Breviario spirituale* (Milan: ISIS, 1923), 170.

7. In his touching preface to the edition of 1946, a few months after the death of his friend Omodeo, Croce himself invites people to read *L'età del Risorgimento italiano* (*The age of the Italian Risorgimento*) (Messina: Edizioni Scientifiche Italiane, 1946), a work inspired by the religion of liberty:

His [Omodeo's] main vocation was for the concrete drama of history, for which he possessed the necessary qualities to a most notable degree: firsthand research and the capacity to vivify the sources with a sensitive and reconstructive spirit; the elevation above particular and thus unilateral tendencies of persons and parties, in order to investigate the trend of events...; the clear light of a religious faith, the religion of liberty; the affection that gave warmth to his style, and the conceptual rigor that gave it robustness. In his lengthy and solid studies on religious and mainly on Christian history, he possessed the means to enter into the spirit of certain facts and certain historical figures that would otherwise remain obscure. (xii)

Pugliese Caratelli, in his beautiful introduction to the reprint of the work edited by the Istituto Italiano per gli Studi Filosofici, characterizes Croce and Omodeo as "two devoted worshippers of the 'religion of liberty.' "

8. Adolfo Omodeo, "Risorgimento senza eroi," *Leonardo* (1926), reprinted in Adolfo Omodeo, *Difesa del Risorgimento* (Turin: Einaudi, 1951), 439–46.

9. Ibid., 444–45.

10. Adolfo Omodeo, *Lettere 1910–1946* (Turin: Einaudi, 1963), 460.

11. Ibid., 10.

12. Ibid., 11–12.

13. Ibid., 72.

14. Ibid., 89–90. A letter dated July 2, 1917 is revealing (ibid., 206):

I realize that I am becoming a bit, how can I say, Voltairean-sarcastic in my relationships with the good Lord—without too much malignity, though. As I read priestly writings and papers every day, I am starting to lose my patience with and tolerance for the clericals and their mummification of the spirit. But it is a less trivial and vulgar anticlericalism than the current one; it is more satanic. I would like to stay close to my adversaries and shake them more within, sowing and provoking crises by overturning their paper-pulp altars: a more satanic work, typical of a heretic rather than just a Masonic and anticlerical hack reporter. Perhaps this is because I appreciated and valued Christianity more than others. You see what happens when one gets in touch with priests!

15. Ibid., 16.

16. Omodeo, *L'età del Risorgimento*, xviii.

17. Ibid., 300.

18. Ibid., 300, 304.

19. Ibid., 304. This religious understanding of the Italian problem, for Omodeo, was at once the highest merit and the gravest limitation of Mazzini's project—a merit, because it stirred up energies; and a limitation, because, in a non-religious country, the project was doomed to fail. Contrary to Spain and Greece, indeed, there wasn't any accord between religious and national sentiments in Italy; rather, there was an antithesis: the religious sentiment, controlled by the church, was to a large extent far from or hostile to the national cause. Ibid., 307.

20. Ibid., 308.

21. Ibid., 319–20.

22. Adolfo Omodeo, "La religione del Manzoni," *Nuova Italia* (1931) and *La Critica* (1931), reprinted in Adolfo Omodeo, *Figure e passioni del Risorgimento* (Milan: Mondadori, 1945), 53. See also Francesco Ruffini, *La vita religiosa di Alessandro Manzoni*, 2 vols. (Bari: Laterza, 1931).

23. Adolfo Omodeo, *Paolo di Tarso apostolo delle genti* (Messina: Principato, 1922), 38, 172.

24. Adolfo Omodeo, *Religione e civiltà: Dalla grecia antica ai tempi nostri*, ed. Benedetto Croce (Bari: Laterza, 1948), 229–30. Printed for the first time in 1924, *Religione e civiltà* should have imparted, according to Croce, "a severe religious education" to Italian youths. But schools could not use this work because of the rise of fascism, along with the alliance between the Vatican and fascism. In this book, Omodeo shows how, over the centuries, humankind passed from religions in which the religious man and the citizen overlapped, and the former was limited by the latter, to the universal religion that affirmed itself in Christianity, "which is the yeast of the modern age and our age too, and will not perish nor waver until civilization itself—which today is threatened by the return of 'state religions,' which are materialistic, even when they assert that they oppose materialism—will perish and waver" (ibid., vii).

25. Compare Adolfo Omodeo, *Giovanni Calvino e la riforma in Ginevra: Opera postuma*, ed. Benedetto Croce (Bari: Laterza, 1947), 75

26. Ibid., 77.

27. Ibid., 5–6.

28. Adolfo Omodeo, *Studi sull'età della restaurazione*, preface Alessandro Galante Garrone (Turin: Einaudi, 1970), 4–5.

29. Ibid., 5–6.

30. Ibid., 175; Benjamin Constant, *De la religion considérée dans sa source, ses formes et ses développements*, ed. Pierre Deguise (Lausanne: Bibliothèque romande, 1971), 1:xvii–xviii.

31. Omodeo, *Studi sull'età della restaurazione*, 177, 177–78, 182.

32. Omodeo, *L'età del Risorgimento*, xvii.

33. Adolfo Omodeo, *Momenti della vita di guerra (Dai Diari e dalle Lettere dei Caduti)* (Bari: Laterza, 1934), 9.

34. Ibid., 50, 51.

35. Ibid., 128–29.

36. Luigi Russo, *Machiavelli*, 3rd ed. (Bari: Laterza, 1949). The dedication, dated 1945, reads: "I dedicate this book to the memory of my friends Nello Rosselli and Leone Ginzburg, my very affectionate fellows in literary work and political faith, in the moment in which their tragic sacrifice begins to appear, illuminated by the light of liberty and peace."

37. Ibid., 8.

38. Ibid.

39. Ibid., x–xi.

40. Francesco Ruffini, *La vita religiosa di Alessandro Manzoni* (Bari: Laterza, 1931), 2:463.

41. Ibid., 2:465n2.

CHAPTER 20: THE RELIGION OF LIBERTY

1. "Protesta contro il manifesto degli intellettuali fascisti," *Il Giornale d'Italia*, May 1, 1925; on the topic of religion in Croce, see Antonio Di Mauro, *Il problema religioso nel pensiero di Benedetto Croce* (Milan: Franco Angeli, 2000); Michele Maggi, *La filosofia di Benedetto Croce* (Naples: Bibliopolis, 1998), especially chapters 5–6; Roberto Pertici, "Benedetto Croce," *Nuova informazione bibliografica* 3 (July–September 2004): 453–502; Alessandro Savorelli, "La religione di Croce," in *La riscoperta del "sacro" tra le due guerre mondiali*, ed. Sandro Barbera, Cristiano Grottanelli, and Alessandro Savorelli (Florence: Le Lettere, 2005), 33–46.

2. Benedetto Croce, *Storia della età barocca in Italia: Pensiero poesia e letteratura vita morale* (1929; repr., Bari: Laterza, 1957), 7.

3. Ibid., 10.

4. Ibid., 17–18.

5. Ibid., 498.

6. In a letter of May 30, 1925, Croce (*Epistolario*, vol. 1, *Scelta di lettere curata dall'autore 1914–1935* [Naples: Istituto Italiano per gli Studi Storici, 1967], 116) writes to Georg Hermann Stippinger,

But it is better that I don't tell you about my thought and work, which I will continue to undertake in Italy, within the limits that present conditions impose and according to the duty of a good Italian, who is concerned about the best future of his fatherland and the world, of which the fatherland is a part. I will rather tell you that we need all the prudence and patience we can summon. In Italy an extreme nationalism is now celebrating its triumph, and it is a nationalism with which it is difficult to reason. Nationalism is not a movement congenial to the Italian spirit. Unfortunately, however, it is now rampant all over the world, even in Germany. So long as we are under its influence, those who possess a human conscience, or at least a European conscience, have the duty to criticize and oppose all that without hoping to attain immediate success. But I am profoundly convinced that the future does not belong to nationalism. You, too, as a good German, try not to exacerbate the souls with German nationalism. Only by rising to a higher moral and social sphere can one truly triumph over the adversaries. The Italian Risorgimento defeated the Austrians, but its motto was, in the words of the poet, *"Ripassin l'Alpi e tornerem fratelli"* (If they cross the Alps and return to their country, we will be friends again). Today's nationalism is not that old and sound patriotism with a human and Christian background; it is an extreme literary decadence. And you Germans must remember, or learn—if you don't know it—that it is a bad gift that has come to us through Germany itself—through [Friedrich Wilhelm] Nietzsche, adopted and adapted by [Gabriele] D'Annunzio and [Enrico] Corradini, and now resounding on Mussolini's lips. Before that, there was no trace of such a sentiment in Italy.

7. Benedetto Croce, "La religiosità come armonia e aristocrazia," in *Etica e politica* (1931; repr., Bari: Laterza, 1981), 166–67; this text is part of the *Frammenti di etica*, published in 1922.

8. Benedetto Croce, "L'individuo, la grazia e la provvidenza," in *Etica e politica* (1931; repr., Bari: Laterza, 1981), 93.

9. Ibid., 167–68.

10. Benedetto Croce, "Contrasti d'ideali politici dopo il 1870," in *Etica e politica* (1931; repr., Bari: Laterza, 1981), 251.

11. Benedetto Croce, *Storia d'Italia dal 1871 al 1915* (1928; Bari: Laterza, 1977), 1. In his *Taccuini*, Croce remarks: "I've finished the reading of these notes [for the *Storia d'Italia*] for the first part, and deeply thought about the structure of the work. The links of this history with the current situation have led me to painfully reflect on the present and future. It pains me to write the history I have set out to write as a duty to be fulfilled for my fellow countrymen. But this work opens wounds that I could perhaps avoid, if I could engage my mind with other studies, less close to present politics."

12. Ibid., 69, 139.

13. Ibid., 254.

14. Ibid., 238–39.

15. Ibid., 257.

16. Benedetto Croce, *Etica e politica* (1931; repr., Bari: Laterza, 1981), 285.

17. Ibid., 286.

18. As Croce (ibid., 287–88; see also *Storia del Regno di Napoli* [Bari: Laterza, 1925], 168–69) observes,

The perpetual struggle between "state" and "church," which is fought in history, and the impossibility of eliminating one of the two terms, is reflected in the specification of the vocations, and in the attitudes that attach to all the forms and ways of human activity. Therefore, in terms of the time that we are now considering, besides the men of action, politicians, warriors, tycoons, and also shady dealers, intriguers, people of no scruples, and those ready to do favors—that is, besides all the various mundane people who range from the highest to the lowest, from dominators to servants, from the aristocracy to the scum—we find the men of the church, who assist the weak, scold and condemn and anathematize the oppressors, and remind the souls of eternity and God, and mitigate the ferocious contrasts and turn them to the good, adore and pray and announce and prepare the ways of the Lord. "Men of the church" one has to understand simply as "the church," in an ideal sense. In the modern and secular society, these men are represented by lovers of truth, educators of themselves and others, guardians of ideals, and those who, like the priests of religions, undertake the care of souls.

19. Benedetto Croce, *Pagine sulla guerra*, 2nd ed. (Bari: Laterza, 1928), 6.

20. Benedetto Croce, "Contro le sopravvivenze del materialismo storico," (1928) in *Conversazioni critiche*, 5th ed. (Bari: Laterza, 1951), 215.

21. Benedetto Croce, "Dal carteggio di Benedetto Croce: Scritti non pubblicati, appunti, minute di lettere," in *Storia, filosofia e letteratura: Studi in onore di Gennaro Sasso*, ed. Marta Herling and Mario Reale (Naples: Bibliopolis, 1999), 15.

22. Letter from Benedetto Croce to Clemente Maglietta Napoli, November 30, 1930, in *Storia, filosofia e letteratura: Studi in onore di Gennaro Sasso*, ed. Marta Herling and Mario Reale (Naples: Bibliopolis, 1999), 164.

23. Benedetto Croce, *Ultimi saggi*, 2nd ed. (Bari: Laterza, 1948), 255, 258.

24. Benedetto Croce, *Storia d'Europa nel secolo XIX* (Bari: Laterza, 1932), 24, and Benedetto Croce, *History of Europe in the Nineteenth Century*, trans. Henry Furst (New York: Harcourt, Brace and Company, 1933), 19.

25. Ibid.

26. Croce, *Storia d'Europa*, 25–26, and *History of Europe*, 20–21.

27. Croce, *Storia d'Europa*, 31–32, 36, and *History of Europe*, 26–27, 31.

28. Croce, *Storia d'Europa*, 356, and *History of Europe*, 358–59.

29. Croce, *Storia d'Europa*, 358, and *History of Europe*, 360.

30. Benedetto Croce, "Il Beneficio di Cristo," *La Critica* 38 (1940), reprinted in Benedetto Croce, *Poeti e scrittori del pieno e tardo Rinascimento* (Bari: Laterza, 1945), 1:211–28.

31. Ibid., 1:219.

32. Benedetto Croce, "Perché non possiamo non dirci 'cristiani,'" in *Discorsi di varia filosofia* (Bari: Laterza, 1945), 1:13.

33. Ibid., 1:19–21.

34. Ibid., 1:23.

35. Luigi Einaudi, "Major et sanior pars," *Idea* (January 1945), in Luigi Einaudi, *Il buongoverno*, preface Eugenio Scalfari (Rome: Laterza, 2004), 93–94.

36. Norberto Bobbio, "Benedetto Croce e il liberalismo," *Rivista di Filosofia* 46 (1955): 281–86, in Norberto Bobbio, *Politica e cultura*, intro. and ed. Franco Sbarberi (Turin: Einaudi, 2005).

Chapter 21: A Religion That Instills Hope

1. Benedetto Croce, *Lettere 1930–36*, preface Ernesto Paolozzi, intro. Emanuele Cutinelli Rèndina (Naples: Flavio Pagano Editore, 1991).

2. Thomas Mann, "Appello alla ragione," in *Scritti storici e politici* (Milan: Arnoldo Mondadori Editore, 1957), 259–63.

3. Ibid., 7–8.

4. Johan Huizinga, *La crisi della civiltà*, intro. Delio Cantimori, trans. Barbara Allason (Turin: Einaudi, 1966), xxix–xxx.

5. Johan Huizinga, *In the Shadow of Tomorrow* (New York: W. W. Norton Company, 1936), 234.

6. Ibid., 235.

7. Henri-Louis Bergson, "Les deux sources de la morale et de la religion," in *Œuvres*, ed. André Robinet, intro. Henri Gouhier (Paris, PUF, 1959), 1214–15.

8. Julien Benda, *Discours à la nation européenne*, 3rd ed. (Paris: Gallimard, 1933), 76. In *Trahison des clercs*, published in 1927, Benda denounces the mystical character of national passions and the religious features of plebean patriotism. Both Charles Maurras and Victor Hugo speak of the "déesse France" (ibid., 118), and equally heavy is Johann Gottlieb Fichte's "réalisme divinisé," which deifies a terrestrial reality as the nation. Citing Mussolini, Benda remarks that "the state, fatherland, and class are treated as divinities, indeed as the only gods, so that political passions have become at once more realistic and more religious than in the past: neither [Duc de] Richelieu nor [Otto Eduard Leopold von] Bismarck ever attributed religious qualities to exclusively temporal realities" (ibid., 129). The ancient city was put under divine protection, but did not at all believe that it was, in and of itself, divine and eternal. The ancients thought that the duration of their institutions was temporary, always depending on the favor of the gods. "Only the moderns have transformed their city into a tower that challenges heaven" (ibid., 142).

9. Ibid., 103.

10. Ibid., 195, 196.

11. Henry Furst, "Croce's View of 18th Century Europe," *New York Times Book Review*, October 18, 1931. See also "Croce's Liberalism," *Times Literary Supplement*, June 16, 1932:

> It is a fine, at times an eloquent and passionate avowal of Croce's faith in liberalism as a religion, "the one ideal that has the strength and elasticity once possessed by Catholicism and a flexibility which this could never have." It is of its very essence that it cannot reject or condemn absolutely the views of those who differ from it honestly, allowing complete freedom to all opinions which do not seek the overthrow of liberal order. Liberty is, indeed, the fundamental problem of human society, in which alone this flourishes and bears fruit, the only reason for the life of man on earth, and without it life would not be worth living. It is a problem which can never be solved by violence.

12. "Il 'fenomeno' antifilosofico e antireligioso di Benedetto Croce," *La Civiltà Cattolica* 83 (April 1932): 213. See also *L'Osservatore Romano*, March 25, 1932: "The position of Catholicism and liberty, in the criticism and raison d'être of this 'Storia d'Europa,' is arbitrary and false, and the initial misunderstanding inevitably

follows throughout all the historical illustrations. The 'history of liberty in the nineteenth century' must definitely be rewritten. Better: it has not been written yet."

13. "Il 'fenomeno' antifilosofico e antireligioso di Benedetto Croce," 214.

14. "Filosofia e 'religione della libertà' di Benedetto Croce," *La Civiltà Cattolica* 83 (April 1932): 525–26.

15. Giovanni Papini, "Il Croce e la Croce," *Nuova Antologia* 67 (1932): 3–21.

16. Ibid., 7, 14, 21.

17. See Guido Verucci, *Idealisti all'indice: Croce, Gentile e la condanna del Sant'Uffizio* (Rome: Laterza, 2006), especially chapter 4: "The Holy Office: the condemnation of *Storia d'Europa nel secolo decimonono* (1932) by Benedetto Croce and the examination of the whole work by Croce" (ibid., 140–65).

18. Ibid., 147.

19. See the column "Note e notizie," *Giornale Critico della Filosofia Italiana* 13 (1932): 78–79.

20. *La Stirpe*, April 1932, 150.

21. "L'Odissea della libertà," *Gerarchia* 12 (1932): 405–13.

22. "Chiamalo sepolto!…," *Libro e moschetto*, March 5, 1932.

23. Cited in Norberto Bobbio, *Politica e cultura*, intro. and ed. Franco Sbarberi (Turin: Einaudi, 2005), 286.

24. *Luigi Russo—Benedetto Croce, Carteggio 1912–1948* (Pisa: Edizioni della Normale, 2006), 1:243.

25. Ernesto Rossi, *"Nove anni sono molti": Lettere dal carcere 1930–1939*, ed. Mimmo Franzinelli (Turin: Bollati Boringhieri, Torino, 2001), 109, 111, 535.

26. Paper presented at the conference "La crisi italiana del 1943 e gli inizi della Resistenza (The Italian crisis of 1943 and the beginning of the Resistenza)" Milan, December 5, 1954; published in "Il Movimento di Liberazione in Italia," August 1955, in *Scritti*, ed. Enzo Collotti, Giorgio Rochat, Gabriella Solaro Pelazza, and Paolo Speziale (Milan: Feltrinelli, 1976).

27. Drawn from Paolo Borgna, *Un Paese migliore: Vita di Alessandro Galante Garrone* (Rome: Laterza, 2006), 95.

28. Norberto Bobbio, *De senectute e altri scritti autobiografici* (Turin: Einaudi, 1996), 128, 131.

29. Norberto Bobbio, "Benedetto Croce e il liberalismo," in *Politica e cultura*, intro. and ed. Franco Sbarberi (Turin: Einaudi, 2005), 202.

CHAPTER 22: THE RELIGION OF DUTY

1. Gaetano Salvemini, "Per la candidatura Donati," in Gaetano Salvemini, *Stato e Chiesa in Italia*, ed. Elio Conti, in *Opere di Gaetano Salvemini*, vol. 2, *Scritti di Storia moderna e contemporanea* (Milan: Feltrinelli, 1969), 368.

2. Letter from Gaetano Salvemini to Giovanni Modugno, cited in Alessandro Galante Garrone, *I miei maggiori* (Milan: Garzanti, 1984), 126–27.

3. Gaetano Salvemini, "Stato e Chiesa in Italia," in *Opere di Gaetano Salvemini*, vol. 2, *Scritti di Storia moderna e contemporanea* (Milan: Feltrinelli, 1969), 436.

4. Gaetano Salvemini, "Cattolicismo e democrazia," in *Opere di Gaetano Salvemini*, vol. 2, *Scritti di storia moderna e contemporanea* (Milan: Feltrinelli, 1969), 381.

5. Amelia Pincherle Rosselli, *Memorie*, ed. Maria Calloni (Bologna: Il Mulino, 2001), 52–53, 47–48.

6. Ibid., 69.

7. Ibid., 131.

8. Cited in Zeffiro Ciuffoletti, ed., *I Rosselli: Epistolario familiare 1914–1937* (Milan: Mondadori, 1997), 43–44.

9. Ibid.

10. Nello Rosselli, "Ebraismo e italianità," in *Nello Rosselli uno storico sotto il fascismo: Lettere e scritti vari (1924–1937)*, ed. Zeffiro Ciuffoletti (Florence: La nuova Italia, 1979), 5, 3; emphasis in original.

11. Cited in Ciuffoletti, *I Rosselli*, 159, 408, 418.

12. Ibid., 425–26. Those men who lived according to the religion of duty deserve, in Carlo's view, the deepest respect. He writes about this on the occasion of Turati's death in 1932: "Notwithstanding the diversity of one's particular appraisals, Turati's activity always deserves an infinite admiration, if only for the respect and love that Turati brought in all his work. For that religious sense of duty, that extraordinary conscientiousness that one finds in every act of his life—a conscientiousness that induced him at times to let himself be too much absorbed by secondary tasks and therefore forget his role as a leader"; compare to Carlo Rosselli, "Filippo Turati e il socialismo italiano," *QGL* 3 (June 1932); 9–42.

13. Cited in Ciuffoletti, *I Rosselli*, 418, 412.

14. Ibid., 418–19.

15. Ibid., 420, 427.

16. Ibid., 331.

17. Ibid., 332.

18. Carlo Rosselli, *Socialismo liberale*, ed. John Rosselli, intro. and critical essays Norberto Bobbio (Turin: Einaudi, Torino, 1997), 111; emphasis in original.

19. Cited in Giovanni Grasso, ed., *Luigi Sturzo e i Rosselli tra Londra, Parigi e New York* (Soveria Mannelli: Rubbettino, 2003), 51–52.

20. Ibid., 74n116.

21. Carlo Rosselli, "Polemica sulla Chiesa," *GL*, September 13, 1935, in Carlo Rosselli, *Scritti dall'esilio*, ed. Costanzo Casucci (Turin: Einaudi, 1988), 1:211–13.

22. Ibid., 213.

23. Rosselli, *Socialismo liberale*, 111.

24. Antonio Gramsci, *Quaderni del carcere*, ed. Valentino Gerratana (Turin: Einaudi, 1975), 2:1218, 1298; critical edition by the Istituto Gramsci.

25. Antonio Gramsci, *Lettere dal carcere* (Turin: Einaudi, 1947), 132, 192.

26. Ibid., 106.

27. Antonio Gramsci, *Note sul Machiavelli sulla politica e sullo Stato moderno* (Turin: Einaudi, 1949), 3–4, 8.

CHAPTER 23: As If God Existed

1. Ernesto Rossi, *Elogio della galera: Lettere 1930/1943* (Bari: Laterza, 1968), 150.

2. Elide Rossi, "Quaderni del Ponte," in *Lettere ad Ernesto* (Florence: La Nuova Italia, 1958), 28, 29, 30.

3. Ibid., 45.

4. Rossi, *Elogio della galera*, 150.

5. Ibid., 247.

6. Ernesto Rossi, *"Nove anni sono molti": Lettere dal carcere 1930–1939*, ed. Mimmo Franzinelli (Turin: Bollati Boringhieri, 2001), 118–19, 726–27.

7. Ibid., 525.

8. Ibid., 716–17.

9. Rossi, *Elogio della galera*, 151, 398, 398–99.

10. Ibid., 399, 400.

11. Ibid., 62–63.

12. He writes on June 14, 1935:

For your delight, I will tell you that I had the opportunity to read many absolutely edifying books here (had they been equally interesting!), like *Ben Hur* and *Quo vadis?* and that while reading your letter, in certain passages, it seemed to me that I had not changed my reading, and that I was still reading the apostle Peter's sermons in the catacombs. Finally, Grandma, you should know that on Monday the chaplain came to visit me. He is a sturdy and nice young man, who encouraged me with very tactful and great warmheartedness, and who will come back to see me every Monday. Do not worry then, dear Grandmother, for, as you can see, the Lord's hand is on me. Probably he understood that although I prefer to go to the cinema rather than to church, and although I like women more than pulpits and confessionals, nevertheless I am not a bad guy, after all, and I try not to hurt anybody. (ibid., 27)

13. Ibid., 77.

14. Ibid., 106, 103–4, 524–25.

15. Ibid., 359.

16. Ibid., 556–58.

17. Ibid., 112, 185–86.

18. Ibid., 591.

19. Ibid., 611–12.

20. Ibid., 619–20.

CHAPTER 24: ONLY A GOD CAN EXPEL A GOD

1. Alessandro Galante Garrone, *I miei maggiori* (Milan: Garzanti, 1984), 203.

2. Ibid., 203, 204.

3. Ibid., 223.

4. Piero Calamandrei, *Diario 1939–1945*, ed. Giorgio Agosti, trans. Alessandro Galante Garrone (1939–1941; repr., Florence: La Nuova Italia, 1982), 1:211.

5. Ibid., 233.

6. Piero Calamandrei, "Scritti e inediti celliniani," in *Opere politiche e letterarie di Piero Calamandrei*, ed. Carlo Cordé (Florence: La Nuova Italia Editrice, 1971), 4:97–98.

7. Calamandrei, *Diario*, 2:249, 251.

8. Ibid., 2:151.

9. Ibid., 2:22, 80.

10. Ibid., 2:141, 158–59.

11. Both quotations are from Piero Calamandrei, *Diario 1939–1945*, ed. Giorgio Agosti (Florence: La Nuova Italia 1982), 1:162.

12. Ibid., 2:162–63.

13. Ibid., 2:167, 185.

14. Ibid., 2:292–93.

15. Ibid., 2:316.

16. Ibid., 2:147, 168, 154–55.

17. Ibid., 2:365–66.

18. Giorgio La Pira, "Commemorazione di Piero Calamandrei," in *Giorgio La Pira Sindaco: Scritti discorsi e lettere*, ed. Ugo De Siervo, Gianni Giovannoni, and Giorgio Giovannoni (Florence: Cultura nuova editrice, 1988), 2:243, 345.

CHAPTER 25: LEAVING LIFE

1. Bianca Ceva, *1930: Retroscena di un dramma* (Milan: Casa Editrice Ceschina, 1955), 60.

2. Ibid., 114.

3. Ibid.

4. Lauro de Bosis, *Icaro* (Milan: Edizioni Alpes, 1930), 25–26, 55, 55–56, 73, 120–21.

5. Lauro De Bosis, *Storia della mia morte: il volo antifascista su Roma*, ed. Alessandro Cortese De Bosis (Rome: Mancosu, 1995), 79.

6. Lorenze Tibaldo, *Quando suonò la campana: Willy Jervis (1901–1944)* (Turin: Claudiana, 2005), 14–15.

7. Ibid., 30.

8. Ibid., 39.

9. Ibid., 43.

10. Ibid., 135.

11. Ibid., 43–44.

12. Ibid., 51; originally in "Il cristiano e lo Stato," *Gioventù cristiana* 5–6 [1936], 142. See also Giorgio Spini, *Italia di Mussolini e protestanti*, preface Carlo Azeglio Ciampi (Turin: Claudiana, 2007), 211–30.

13. Tibaldo, *Quando suonò la campana*, 54, 55.

14. Ibid., 39–40. The messages that Lucilla, his wife, passed on to Jervis in prison are inspired by the same faith: "May God bless you and preserve you; be brave, I pray that God may unite us soon; I hope that God will help you, and grant you the courage and strength to endure this trial, as he does with me; this trial is very long, but with God's help I am sure that you will be able to endure it; this trial, which we endure together and separately, with the certainty of God's help, in which we trust, will fortify even more our already-firm love; my dear, I pray that God may help you and give you the strength to endure this long trial."

CHAPTER 26: TWILIGHT

1. Raffaele Pettazzoni, *Italia religiosa* (Bari: Laterza, 1952), 73.

2. Ibid., 74–75.

3. Piero Calamandrei, *Passato e avvenire della Resistenza* (Milan: Grafica Milano, 1954), reprinted in Norberto Bobbio, ed., *Scriti e discorsi politici*, vol. 1, *Storia di dodici anni* (Florence: La Nuova Italia, 1966), 49–52.

4. The full Ralph Waldo Emerson remark is: "The contest between the Future and the Past is one between Divinity entering, and Divinity departing. You are welcome to try your experiments, and, if you can, to displace the actual order by that ideal republic you announce, for nothing but God will expel God" (*The Collected Works of Ralph Waldo Emerson* [Cambridge, MA: Belknap Press of Harvard University Press, 1971], 1:188).

5. See Norberto Bobbio, "Benedetto Croce e il liberalismo," in *Politica e cultura*, intro. and ed. Franco Sbarberi (Turin: Einaudi, 2005), 226.

6. Guido Calogero, *Filosofia del dialogo* (1962; repr., Milan: Edizioni di Comunità, 1969), 267.

INDEX

values of, 190–95, 199, 216, 277–78, 317n14; virtue and, 1, 33–36, 145–46; war and, 197–99

Cicero, Marcus Tullius, xii, 18–19, 26–28, 33–34, 37

Cicone, Michelangelo, 99

"Cinque maggio" (Manzoni), 143

Cipriano, Fra, 74

Cisalpine Republic, 90, 95

citizenship, 7; Aristotle on, 3; Calamandrei and, 265; Christianity and, 3, 191, 198, 289n8, 300n48, 318n24; common good and, 2 (*see also* common good); Constituent Assembly and, 280; Declaration of Rights of Man and Citizenship and, 228; Puritans and, 228; religion of duty and, 247; religion of liberty and, 89–90, 94–101, 106, 109–11, 118, 122–23, 130–33, 139, 142, 144, 155–60, 166, 177, 179, 182–83, 222; republican religion and, 15–27, 32–42, 47, 55, 58, 71, 77–86; sacred law and, 37–42; as virtue, 3–4

city republics, xi, 1

Civiltà Cattolica journal, 122, 229

civil religion: images of, 21–28; morals and, 25; religion of liberty and, 92, 95, 115, 125, 151, 154, 183; republican religion and, 21–28, 73, 78, 83, 89

civis genuensis, 84

civitas Dei, 3

Clement VII, 178

Clizia (Machiavelli), 64

club–religion, 191

Commedia (Dante), 46

Comment les dogmes finissent (Jouffroy), 107–8

common good, 1–2, 5; charity and, 25 (*see also* charity); religion of liberty and, 96, 146; republican religion and, 23–26, 29, 32–36, 40–44, 58, 60, 70, 84–85, 287n11, 287n15; Romans and, 41

communes, 15, 20, 22–23, 28, 78

Commune Senarum Civitas Virginis (CSCV), 22

communion, 3, 119, 160, 211, 232, 249, 267

communism, 9, 125, 197–98, 222, 248, 275, 279

Communist International, 215

Confederazione Generale del Lavoro, 251

confession: Catholicism and, 62, 64, 75, 123, 159, 180, 254, 258, 296n26, 325n12; death and, 62, 75; Machiavelli and, 64

Confessioni di un italiano (Nievo), 131–36

Confortatorio dei martiri di Belfiore (Martini), 168

Conforti, Francesco, 97–98

Congress of Peace, Geneva, 152

conscience: Calamandrei and, 265, 267; Catholicism and, 249; Christianity and, 11, 48, 58, 73, 75, 84, 97, 99, 118, 122, 129, 155–56, 182, 184, 186–87, 193, 195–96, 246; Constituent Assembly and, 280–81; Croce and, 219–20, 223–24; emancipation and, 276; fascism and, 8, 186, 276; God and, 276, 280–82; hope and, 226, 229; hypocrisy and, 249–50, 253, 257–58; inner liberty and, 200–2, 205, 208–12; liberation of, 8; Machiavelli and, 58–59; morals and, 8, 99, 282; nationalism and, 205, 319n6; reason and, 154; religion of duty and, 238–44, 246, 248; religion of liberty and, 109, 117, 136, 139, 150–51, 154–55, 158, 162, 164, 167, 215–25, 307n7, 319n6; Risorgimento and, 8

Constant, de Rebecque, Benjamin-Henri, xix–xx, 104–7, 115, 148–49, 209–10

Constituent Assembly, 9, 276–81

consuls, 15, 25, 28, 42, 55, 65, 67

Contemporaneo, Il (newspaper), 121

contextualism, 9–10

Contrat Social, Du (Rousseau), 89

Convito, Il (journal), 269

Convivio (Dante), 25, 46

corpus mysticum, 29

cose fiorentine, Le (Guicciardini), 72

Council Hall, 26

Council of Ministers, 281

Council of Trent, 30, 85, 159

Counter-Reformation, 6–7, Croce and, 216–17; fascism and, 178–79; religion of liberty and, 98, 124, 151, 153, 159, 178–79, 216; republican religion and, 86

Crescenzio, 22

crisi della civiltà, La (Huizinga), 227–28

Crisis of the Early Italian Renaissance, The (Baron), 3

Croce, Benedetto, xi, xviii, 10, 320n11; Amendola and, 185; antifascism and, xvii, 214–16, 219, 225, 230–35, 248; Calamandrei and, 260; Catholic censorship of, 230–31; conscience and,